The Nova Scotia Bicycle Book

Gary Conrod

**Atlantic Canada
Cycling Festival**

**HALIFAX
NOVA SCOTIA**

Atlantic Canada Cycling
P.O. Box 1555
Station M.
Halifax, Nova Scotia
Canada B3J 2Y3

Information enclosed should be viewed as a general planning tool. Caution and good judgement are crucial. Adequate cycling skills and knowledge of vehicular traffic laws are required before operating a bicycle on public roadways.

Safety cannot be guaranteed by following the enclosed routes and no legal liability is assumed for injury or damage which may occur. Routes described are regular highways used by motorized traffic with no special provisions for bicycling. They are suggested as more suitable than others for bicycle travel. Companies and events listed are for information purposes only. They are not, by their inclusion, endorsed or recommended.

Canadian Cataloguing in Publication Data

Conrod, Gary 1957-
   The Nova Scotia Bicycle Book

   Bibliography:p.
   Includes index.
   ISBN 0-9697458-0-X

1. Bicycle touring - Nova Scotia - Guide books
2. Nova Scotia - Description and travel - Guide books
3. Outdoor recreation - Nova Scotia - Guide books
I.Title.

Printed in Canada

Atlantic Canada Cycling and its logo are registered trademarks of Atlantic Canada Cycling Festival

Book sketches by Peter Roberts and Tom Ward

"Out on the Mira" used by permission of Allister MacGillivray

Picture Credits: 41 Nova Scotia Department of Tourism. 45 Nova Scotia Department of Tourism. 53 Nova Scotia Department of Tourism. 61 Nova Scotia Information Services. 113 Haifax Visitors and Convention Bureau. 117 Haifax Visitors and Convention Bureau. 135 Alex Barnes. 155 West Hants Tourism Commission. 159 Jennifer Porter. 181 Nova Scotia Department of Agriculture. 203 Nova Scotia Department of Tourism. 209 Eleanor Blue; Orangedale Train Station Association. 225 Donna MacDonald; Inverness County Tourism Association. 265 Marg Petolas

To Ron Thomas and Kathy Cody... thanks for the obsession

Acknowledgements

This project has been through many stages of revision. It reflects the assistance of those who cared enough to offer their time and creativity.

Special thanks to:
Christin Kyle
Michael McInnis
Jennifer Porter

R aspberry bushes become parking lots...a rough gravel road gets paved ...a new bakery springs up. Not a single day goes by that not bring a change ...a bus company unexpectedly changes its baggage policy ...an old general store becomes a video arcade ...a large number of seals suddenly adopt a beach. Nova Scotia won't keep still. It is a constant job to gather current information. The goal of total accuracy will never be achieved. You must expect changes, at times even a disappointment. Your experiences and contributions are vital for keeping this guide in top condition. If you have suggestions, corrections, or just want to share your discoveries drop us a line. Any contribution you can offer is greatly appreciated, and will be given on-road investigation.

Atlantic Canada Cycling Festival

Atlantic Canada Cycling
Station M.
Halifax, Nova Scotia
Canada B3J 2Y3

Contents

Introduction

Tours

Appendices

Foreword

Yachts bob gently at their moorings on Bras d'or Lake, a land-locked sea in Cape Breton. The morning sun rises above the placid water's surface and the shore's steep green hills. This is a very different scene from Yarmouth, where our first tours begin.

Every turn you make seems to bring a change. You can explore fishing villages, climb coastal mountains, circle an inland sea, journey into dense forests, or meander through valleys of small farms and orchards. The cycling roads of Nova Scotia invite you onward, never letting you get your fill. You quickly come to the conclusion that this place was intended to be explored by bicycle. In fact, Nova Scotia is one of the most popular and highly rated cycling destinations in the world. Unique in both appearance and climate, it clings to the Canadian mainland by only the narrowest strip of land. Surrounded by water, no one factor has shaped it as has the sea. The ocean has been the key to Nova Scotia's economy for centuries. Its dramatic coastline contains harbours, inlets, beaches, bays, capes, marshes, dunes, basins, passages, channels, two guts, and one neck.

You are never more than 56 kilometers (35 miles) from the coast. Varying terrain offers moderate level touring in most areas of the province. Some steeper climbs, such as those found on the ridges of the Annapolis Valley and in Cape Breton, challenge even the strongest of cyclists. A few hardy Nova Scotians can be found touring immediately after the snow fades in late April. They keep going until discouraged by the cold winds of November. For most, however, mid-May through late September is the time frame of bicycle vacations.

We will begin as did the first European explorers, on our South-West coast. Here you will look for traces of the Vikings and ride through the town which lead the world in "*The Age of Sail*". On the romantic French Shore you will meet the Acadians, a people whose native tongue has survived for 400 years. You will learn of a world master mariner, uncover strange tasting delicacies and discover the best place in North America to watch for whales.

The Annapolis Valley is a dense maze of country lanes. There are countless hidden corners, pioneer churches, tiny farms, and fragrant orchards. This is one of Canada's finest cycling regions. You will be guided through the best back roads, and find out what lies up and over its ridges in "*the land of Evangeline*"

The best known face of Nova Scotia is without a doubt along the Atlantic Ocean. Known as the "*South Shore*", the coast is lined with lighthouses, fishing boats, and piers piled high with lobster traps. Postcard villages, filled with colourful houses and alive with the sound of seabirds dot the Atlantic's many harbours. You'll visit the popular ones, but also those with all the charm, but none of the tourists.

The lesser-known regions of Nova Scotia make for some of its best cycling. The Central and Northern sections of the mainland are lined with quiet roads and filled with natural beauty. You will have the opportunity to watch the world's highest tides approach the shore. Inspect the red soil cliffs in search of fossils, precious stones, and the bones of dinosaurs. You will have the opportunity to descend into the world's deepest coal mine. Or climb the cliffs at Cape D'or to watch the turbulent meeting of the Minas Basin and the Bay of Fundy. Swim in the warmest waters north of the Carolinas. Rest by the waterwheel of an attractive old flour mill, discover a coast of now forgotten ship-building towns, and learn of a tiny peninsula where one man ruled like a king.

You can only bike so far eastward on the North American continent. The "*Eastern Shore*" is a coastal road of deep forests, quiet coves, abundant wildlife, and places of solitude. The final rides will take you throughout the spectacular island of Cape Breton. Eight tours, all quite special will very quickly prove to you why it is considered one of the world's prime cycling destinations. The tours follow its rugged ocean shoreline, around a pleasant highland lake, and an atmospheric inland sea. The last tour heads up into the highlands, where you will reach the very top of Nova Scotia.

Nova Scotia is far from heavily populated. Along the road, however, you will by no means go hungry. You will be offered tasty treats - lobster, scallops, pure maple syrup, juicy apples, fresh cider, and wild blueberries. Cycle touring is more than just getting quickly from start to finish. We'll be encouraged to stop and relax, on weathered old fishing wharves, in the breeze of hilltop look-offs, and on the steps of of small general stores.

There's a lot to see and do in Nova Scotia. You will be informed of museums, attractions, major cycling events. You will also be let in on lots of trivia and oddities along the way. Best of all, in Nova Scotia it is all on a personal, unhurried scale. You've found the best way to discover "Canada's Ocean Playground", by bicycle.

Ride the Work of a Lifetime

Updating would go on forever. In terms of crunching words on paper, however, my book was finally completed. I got up from my desk, all the paraphernalia of its creation scattered in front of me- pens, paper, computer, sketches, piles of maps, tape recordings.

I pulled out my Cannondale and went for a ride. I cycled out that early Spring day to East Dover, a little fishing village near Peggy's Cove. Fishing boats rolled softly in the water. The sun was bright, and slowly melting pieces of snow still lingered among the shore's spruce trees. Birds chirped and children could faintly be heard in the distance, but there were no other sounds. I went out onto the wharf. The planks creaked and groaned. I leaned by bike against a pile of lobster traps and dangled my feet over the edge of the pier. One hundred thousand kilometers had been a lot of cycling. In the quiet, I began to think of all the places I had been, and those the people I had met.

I went back, to the hidden corners off the busy highways, those places where changes arrive a bit more slowly. I thought of home cooked meals from strangers, of hospitable farmers and fishing families who shared with me tales of their hard life and tragedies. I remembered spring mornings, waking in my tent to discover frozen waterbottles. I recalled moving through fog so thick as to be unable to see the pavement; of cooking a late night meal during sunset overlooking the Bay of Fundy; of the early morning puttering of fishing boats heading out to sea; of heatwaves; of rainstorms; and sudden encounters with moose, fox, deer, and eagles. I recalled the sweet scent of Annapolis Valley apple blossoms and the taste of wild blueberries; the eerie feeling of a deserted farmhouse and the excitement of arriving at the scene of a village celebration.

The memories seemed endless. When I looked out to sea again, it was getting dark. The spring warmth was fading quickly as I pedalled out of the village and back to the city. I realized I had discovered not the Nova Scotia of history books or tourist guides, but of real places filled with real people. I had found a Nova Scotia unknown to most travelers, only to those, like we cyclists, who take the time to find it.

Introduction

A number of years ago I was among contributors for a new European cycle-touring book. After happily recalling my routes and experiences, a few months passed and the book was released. Eagerly looking inside, I was shocked. I discovered my routes were not only included, but were being presented as the suggested itinerary for two of the featured countries!

I felt honoured. However, my tour had not been a planned one. I rode in the valleys when I was tired. I went into the hills when I felt energetic. I entered towns when I was hungry. This meandering path was published as "the suggested route" for anyone interested in visiting those nations. Hundreds of local cyclists were on the roads. Local cycling clubs were plentiful. And yet, there it was, a hard covered volume by a large international publisher announcing this book as "the authoritative volume". The sad thing is that people are still buying that book and no doubt are wandering along the same random roads I took years ago.

I became suspicious of all touring guides. I began to ask myself "Is this the result of exploring the whole area, piecing together the best parts for the finest routes? Or is this simply where someone went through on a vacation? One tour book on Nova Scotia has been constructed from a one month visit to the region, another from escorted rides with a bicycle club. At least two others have been from outright planning from the seat of an automobile.

Every road in Nova Scotia has been evaluated. Most have been covered many times, in both directions in all seasons. Feedback has been observed from participants during 16 years of tour leading and from several thousand touring inquiries. No anecdotal information has been included. Every suggestion has been investigated personally.

The entire 100,000 of cycling field work has been covered without ever owning an automobile. Thus so, Nova Scotia's transportation network has been thoroughly tested. Every train station, bus depot, airport, and ferry terminal has been used. Almost all conceivable regulations, policies, staff attitudes and bicycle transportation obstacle has been encountered.

I want to supply you with as much touring information as possible. This book, therefore, will not be a detailed dissertation of bicycle selection, repair, or fitness training. Entire books continue to be produced on these subjects, as well as from magazines, bike shops, and clubs. When you travel It is good to see special attractions and big events. However, cars and bikes do dot mix, traffic around big events can easily ruin your cycling. This volume is not intended as competition for general tourism guides.

If this writer were to see one wish concerning this work come true, it would be for you to use this book, but not simply become a tourist. My intention is not to offer yet another "turn right', "turn left" cookbook type bicycle guide! I have attempted to turn what is essentially a dry exercise of listing directions, into an enjoyable experience.

Loops and Through Routes

There are two distinct groups of cyclists this volume is attempting to please. One group travel with their automobile or motor home, taking day rides from fixed locations. These riders want to do a loop, preferrably with different roads out and back. The other group are cycling unsupported. They are travelling from "A" to "B". They want tours which will link up with one another to create a through route. Therefore, there will be both circle tours, as well as one-way trips.

Tour Selection

It would be politically best, in this tourism sensitive province, to have a ride or two in each area. Every local business, tourism bureau, and recreation agency would be pleased and supportive. Tours however, have been chosen solely on their own merit. Good cycling is dependant on natural beauty and road layout. This project has not been subject to any influence to please any local Chamber of Commerce to please, or any hotel to fill.

We will keep our explorations away from challenged urban neighborhoods, industrial zones, and suburban sprawl. Are you getting a distorted view of Nova Scotia? Perhaps. This is, however a bicycle touring book and the routes presented have been found to be the preferred ones to see. Sociologists and "post-industrialists" will have to read between the lines and root around.

Even though there are 39 tours, there are no "duds". There is no need for "padding" to come up with a collection. Nova Scotia happens to have a large number of good cycling areas. If a tour was not considered worthwhile, it would not in any way be included.

It is important to share with you why each tour is listed. Attempts will be made to explain what makes each route worth your visit.

History and Heritage

In this day of television saturation, fast-food, and the "information highway"- when you can take an air-conditioned bus ride across Africa, it is becoming harder and harder to tell one place from another. History helps fuel your imagination. It brings you back to when the world was a bigger place, when each place along the way lived a little differently. Knowing what went on before you arrive provides a greater appreciation of what you see. Echoes of Gaelic Highlanders, memories of the tall ships, isolated islands and outports- these all wait to live again, if you open your mind to the hints along the way. The love Nova Scotians have for the continuation of their traditions is not just because tourists demand them. They themselves are addicted. It has been remarked by Nova Scotian social critic Paul Davison that "There are more pipers at the store entrances of Nova Scotia today than ever walked the highlands of Scotland." This is, of course, an exaggeration, but it does serve to remind us what can happen when commerce plays on heritage. Along with the "must see" and "must do", the special touches of Nova Scotia are still alive along the road less travelled.

Nova Scotia is far more than simply a second Scotland. The kilts, the highlands, the bagpipes, the woolens, the Gaelic language, the list goes on of the icons related to Scottish culture. Because its imagery is seen as the most marketable, it is played out on top of a surprisingly diverse ethnic palette (a kilted bagpiper welcomes ferry arrivals to Yarmouth, a town which happens to actually be the centre of Nova Scotia's French Acadians). Along the way it will be pointed out communities settled by the English, Germans, Swiss, Welsh, Newfoundlanders, escaped Black slaves, New Englanders, as well as the Mic Mac aboriginal people.

How to Use This Guide

ours are designated only as a suggestion. They may be adjusted. Cover them in your preferred time span. Take more time to cover the distance, leaving more days over the same distance will make any tour easier. Your only concern will be in scheduling accommodations.

The small population, rural nature, and appeal of the province to outsiders results in most users of this guide being "from away". For Nova Scotians, at times there will be the stating of the obvious.

In some instances you will be covering routes in the opposite direction than that listed. Don't feel hindered by going against the stream. Reversing "left" and "right" will enable you to follow along. Also feel free to do part of a loop. Often short-cuts bring long or moderate sized routes to a shorter option. Read to see if an option for an easier ride exists before passing up a tour.

Side Trips: Additional side trips, ranging from a two minute ride, to a full day's cycling will be mentioned as merited. These allow customizing your interests and riding level to the size of the tour. A small ride can be extended to a longer outing with a diversion or two.

Cues: Atlantic Canada is infamous for its poorly marked backroads. There is an assumption that if you are on these roads you are from the area. There is also an irritating custom of road signs giving a general direction, toward major communities. Many roads in the region will have the same same general signage, not allowing you to actually note where you are. Prepare yourself for getting lost, and enjoy the experience!

It is important to read descriptions carefully. Churches are used frequently as landmarks, as unlike other structures, they seldom change. Read two or three cues ahead, as without warning, an area of several turns may come up and you could stray off the route.

Be Prepared: Read the tour desription over before heading out. If there appears to be few stores, stock up beforehand. This advice goes further when considering bank machines, drug stores, and other services.

When making accommodation reservations, say what time you expect to get there. Cyclists usually arrive later than car tourists do. Your hosts may panic, thinking you will not be showing up.

Special Attractions: Remember, hours and days of operation change, particularly with small museums and any volunteer dependant activity. Check ahead before making a special visit to a museum or indoor point of interest. Shoulder season requires stricter verification, as many operations close down, some even before they have printed they will.

Your Standards: Until you have established how your guage of terrain matches with that of this book, it is suggested that you be conservative with your daily distance. Nova Scotia tends to be rolling in nature, more so than many other places. In the hilly parts of the province remember you will cover less ground than on flat terrain.

Symbols Used in this Book

Food Codes

(G) Grocery Store
(C) Convenience Store
(R) Restaurant

Distance Cues

121.5 (74.0) Metric Distance (Milage Distance)

Touring Regions

To make your touring selections and the use of this guide easy, Nova Scotia has been divided into 8 distinct regions. Each has its own mixture of natural features, economy, history, traffic patterns, even different cultures and languages. If you are just learning about Nova Scotia, the first part of each section will give you a basic idea of what makes that region special.

Bicycle Touring Regions

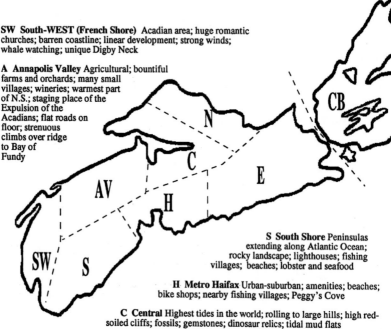

SW South-WEST (French Shore) Acadian area; huge romantic churches; barren coastline; linear development; strong winds; whale watching; unique Digby Neck

A Annapolis Valley Agricultural; bountiful farms and orchards; many small villages; wineries; warmest part of N.S.; staging place of the Expulsion of the Acadians; flat roads on floor; strenuous climbs over ridge to Bay of Fundy

S South Shore Peninsulas extending along Atlantic Ocean; rocky landscape; lighthouses; fishing villages; beaches; lobster and seafood

H Metro Haifax Urban-suburban; amenities; beaches; bike shops; nearby fishing villages; Peggy's Cove

C Central Highest tides in the world; rolling to large hills; high red-soiled cliffs; fossils; gemstones; dinosaur relics; tidal mud flats

N Northern Warmest salt water north of Carolina; sandy coast; most days of sunshine; least hilly coastline; rolling interior; blueberry plains; maple sugar camps

E Eastern Forests; wildlife; low population; quiet ocean coast roads; aquaculture

CB Cape Breton Small coastal mountains; inland sea; cooler temperature; sheep farming; eagle colonies; Scottish heritage; Fortress Louisbourg; the Cabot Trail

The Nova Scotia Bicycle Book

Bicycle Tours

South-West

I f you are among the large percentage of cyclists travelling to Nova Scotia who arrive by ferry at Yarmouth, this is the first area you will see. If so, your initiation may offer a challenge. The most predictable tailwinds in Nova Scotia await you in this far corner of the province. Most often forcefully strong, it will be your friend or enemy as you travel the scenic routes of this largely French speaking region. From the south-west, it pushes up the barren coast. The interior, better protected by forests, offers shelter.

The government of Nova Scotia bundles this region with the Annapolis Valley on its **Evangeline Trail** (Trunk highway #1). These are however, two very different areas. The hot and humid roads of the valley floor have little in common with these misty coastal roads through Acadian lobster ports.

Norse explorers are considered to have visited and even settled in the region around 900-1000 A.D. Traces of foundations, stone inscriptions, and journals point to Nova Scotia as a landing place on their travels.

Beginning centuries ago, Western Europeans visited the coast on fishing expeditions, and a fur-trading post was set up in 1627. Acadians, returning from their exile, found the coast to be one of the few areas not occupied during their absence by New Englanders.

Like the South Shore, the people of this area gained wealth from appetites for alcohol during the years of American Prohibition.

Fishing is by far the major livelihood of the region. Secondary industries are lumbering, farming, sheep raising, fur farming, and whale watching.

French areas lie in both directions outside of Yarmouth. Business is conducted with strangers in English, unless you first initiate conversation in French. If you know any French, even only a few words learned in high school, don't be afraid to try. Acadians are a very proud people, and will be delighted that you have shown respect for them.

Rappie Pie is a unique dish of the area. This acquired taste includes de-starched potatoes with layers of meat (purists say it should be eaten with molasses).

Digby Neck is a region all its own. The peninsula and islands are the remnants of an ancient, and now submerged mountain chain. Not a French speaking area as the others, it shares the wealth of the Bay of Fundy on one side, and St. Mary's Bay on the other.

One of the foggiest places in North America, mid-summer here is the only time when you may not be constantly shrouded with atmospheric mist, and cool ocean air.

Throughout western Nova Scotia, lupines grow wild along the roadsides. Tall, with many blossoms, they stand in brilliant purple, pink, and occasionally white, making the old homes they grace even more photogenic.

tic Canada
ng Festival

Whitewings, widow's walks, and wild lupins

Tour 1   Yarmouth

Tour at a glance

Chebogue

START/ FINISH	Yarmouth
DISTANCE	55 km (34 mi.) Short tour 21 km (13 mi.)
DIRECTION	Counter-Clockwise
TERRAIN	Flat to slightly rolling
CLIMATE	Often foggy and damp
TRAFFIC	Low to Moderate
REST STOPS	Ellenwood Park
FOOD	Yarmouth (R)(G)(C); Arcadia (C); Tusket (C)
REPAIRS	Yarmouth
TOURISM	Yarmouth
HOSPITAL	Yarmouth
POLICE	Yarmouth

Forchu

START/ FINISH	Yarmouth
DISTANCE	25 km (15 mi.)
TERRAIN	Flat
CLIMATE	Often foggy and damp
NOTES	Area of lighthouse dangerous during storms
TRAFFIC	Low
REST SPOTS	Forchu lighthouse
FOOD	Yarmouth (R)(G)(C)
REPAIRS	Yarmouth
TOURISM	Yarmouth
POLICE	Yarmouth
HOSPITAL	Yarmouth
AMBULANCE	Yarmouth

New arrivals off the ferry will find this a good tour to acquaint themselves with Nova Scotia. If you would like a day to get your legs back, are waiting to return home, or are just passing through, here are two rides which can fit in with your time exploring the Yarmouth area.

Both can be started directly from the dock where passengers arrive from Maine. A tour through **Chebogue** has two options, one a short run around Chebogue Point, the other an extension running inland. Its route runs counter-clockwise for shore views. A campsite about 3/4 along, puts you on track to head along the French Shore (upper side) of the province toward the Annapolis Valley.

The point towards Chebogue is barren. If conditions are rough in Yarmouth, expect a lot worse as you move toward the point. Its "V" shape should pay you back as much wind as you must face.

During early summer, lupines flourish in this part of Nova Scotia in colourful pink, white, and purple. Look for them in protected roadside areas. They were first introduced to at Chebogue Point, by a woman famous for her flowers. Phoebe Robbins, although completely blind, drew visitors from all around to her magnificent gardens. Her lupines have since spread throughout the entire western end of the province.

Forchu's huge lighthouse is the first thing mariners see, the warning from its horn the first thing they hear. It has for many generations guided ships into Yarmouth Harbour with beacons seen from far out

Nova Scotia's golden age of sail

During the age of what is known as the "*Golden Age of Sail*", Nova Scotia reached prominence which it has never seen since. Almost one third of all the world's ships were registered in Nova Scotia.

Yarmouth, of all the busy boat-building towns in the province, led the way. By 1870, it had close to 300 ships-for its size, more shipping than any port in the world! Picture in this town, 26 busy wharves. Ships were being built everywhere along the shore, and even inland on lakes.

Houses lining Yarmouth's streets are large, testimony of prosperous ship owners and crew. Seamen arrived home, fresh with the latest styles and ideas for their homes. Would you like to live in the house at number 10 Parade Street ?

Be sure to pick up information for a tour through the town's old streets. They generally follow Parade, Collins, Clements, William, and Forest streets. Many of the older homes have a feature known as a "*widow's walk*". These rooftop porticos were designed as "look-

for sign of their return. Very difficult to maintain, you will notice buildings with flat sections on top, which used to rest these wee attics. Perhaps the finest is one with coloured glass, near the corners of Clements and Cliff Streets.

Many waited in these look-offs in vain- there have been 100 ships sailing out of Yarmouth that have never been heard from again.

Of these many tragedies, some oddities:

On the morning of December 31, 1881, the steamer "*Moravian*" scuttled off the coast. It's cargo: 701,241 pounds of cheese. No doubt every child of that time developed a hatred for dairy products. It is recalled that every pantry on the coast was stocked to the brim with cheddar.

For a few hundred years, Yarmouth was Nova Scotia's main point of entry. After the Age of Sail, Yarmouth settled into its role as the terminus point for passenger ships from The United States.

to sea. The second tour goes here, weaving through fishing areas to the cape. This recommended part-day trip is 25 km (15 mi.) round-trip from downtown Yarmouth.

A very big part of the "*Age of Sail*", there are over 50 marked historic sites in the county. Today Yarmouth has settled into its role of terminus of two ferry systems connecting the state of Maine.

A little known fact is that Yarmouth is a major supplier of ambulances throughout the world. They are specially customized for use in places as diverse as Scandinavia, the Phillipines, Morroco, and Turkey. When you watch your evening news, you may see some of these, as they are sent to many places of dire need, such as hot spots like Northern Ireland and Iraq.

Two special museums

Yarmouth County Museum- This award-winning and recommended museum displays exhibits and records of the area, including a huge collection of ship portraits, models, period rooms, costumes, and pioneer artifacts. Operated by Yarmouth County Historical Society; (small admission); 22 Collins St., downtown Yarmouth; 742-5539

Firefighters Museum- This unique museum displays almost every type of fire engine ever used in the province as well as a floor of national exhibits. Interesting items can be found in gift shop. Part of the Nova Scotia Museum system; (small admission) 451 Main St., downtown Yarmouth; 742-5525

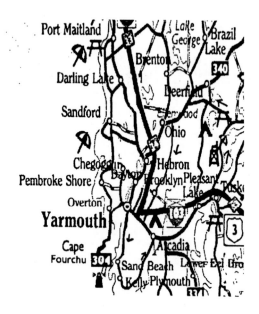

Tour 1 A Chebogue

START at Ferry Terminal. Head right on Main St. (#1) along Yarmouth Harbour. Chebogue Point is the mariner's first sighting of land. Along this barren and quiet road, you may see the huge passenger ferries steaming into port. You may be the only moving shoreline object; don't be surprised to find a few dozen people on deck waving to you!

Bunker Island, on your right, was the site of the original homesteads and war-time fortress, built to guard the harbour from American raiders. Great views can be had here of the harbour and town of Yarmouth. Watch on your left for the 1768 home of Congregationalist clergyman Jonathan Scott. This weathered building features a peaked "*widow's walk*", where mariner's wives would watch out to sea for their return.

The next road to the right takes you to **Sunday Point**, a birdwatching area.

8.8 (5.5) **SIDE TRIP:** To your right is a road to **Chebogue Point**, and views of Chebogue Harbour's many islands. It is roughly 4 km (2.4 mi.) past old pasture lands to the point. This is a good area to spot willets. Known locally as "*whitewings*", these huge sea birds can be seen resting on shoreline rocks between here to Wedgeport.

In December, 1735 the brigantine "*Baltimore*" was found in Chebogue Harbour. The huge ship was covered with blood. A lone woman, the only person found on board, claimed a party of Indians had boarded and killed all the crew. Later it was learned the real story. The ship had left Ireland, bound for Maryland, U.S.A. filled with 60 convicts. They were the ones who had killed the crew, and then fought amongst themselves until only 9 survived, as well as the captain's widow. After heading into Chebogue for directions, the remaining convicts were ambushed by the Indians, who then boarded the ship, and were driven off by the woman, with the captain's pistols. Considered bad luck, the ship after seven years was brought out to sea and burned.

In March 1771, a privateer ship from Boston came into the harbour to escape British vessels. The people of the area cared for the 140 crew, until the British were gone to allow safe passage back to Boston.

SIDE TRIP- Town Point Cemetery: Turn right at Chebogue United Church. A short road runs to the shore. This was the landing site of the first New England settlers to the region. There is an old cemetery here. For over one hundred and thirty years it has been visited, photographed and written about. Several interesting monuments can be found here, including memorials to sea captains. On a knoll overlooking the Chebogue River, you will find a life-size marble figure of a young woman clutching a scythe. "*Ruth the Gleaner*" is a romantic tribute to a young woman from her husband. Halifax doctor Frederick Webster met the young Scottish woman during studies in Glasgow. It was love at first sight. However, she died suddenly, not long after her arrival in Canada. The grief stricken doctor searched the province for her resting place. At last, he brought her remains to Yarmouth for internment at the Town Point cemetery. Not long afterward he commissioned a white marble memorial, still considered one of the best pieces of hand-carved art in Canada. Why the doctor envisioned her in a field of wheat, no one can say, but his tribute will continue to be admired for years to come.

Arcadia is named for a large ship built in 1817. Near the village centre is a hill with a light-green house on it. A little-known fact is that Paul Revere, the U.S. patriot is believed to have earned his trade in freemasonry in this building.

15.8 (9.8) **RIGHT** onto #3 at Arcadia

SHORT-CUT: To your left, a small piece of Trunk #3 will connect you back to Yarmouth, making a

7

21 km (12.8 mi.) loop.

25.2 (15.6) **LEFT** (toward Lake Vaughan, Deerfield, and Ellenwood Park) just before the bridge into Tusket The village was once a booming shipping and trading centre, as its large houses might suggest. From Tusket you can pedal out to Surette Island, one of the scenic Tusket Islands.

Forests now begin to thicken, as you move away from the coast. When the Loyalists arrived after the American revolution, they found wild cattle and old cultivated lands near Tusket Falls. Ancient cellars have been declared to be authentic Norse foundations. They are believed to be those of Lief Erickson's *"Great House"*, written of in his diaries.

Carry on, crossing over a small canal built to channel water to a generating station. Another suspected Norse habitation, "Harlsefni's Settlement" is at the northern end of Lake Vaughan. This is the probable site of the first battle involving Caucasians in the New World around 1015 A.D.

33.3 (20.7) **LEFT** At Raynardton toward South Deerfield. A small cottage colony sits along Ellenwood Lake

39.7 (24.6) To the left is Ellenwood Lake Provincial Park. It has camping and a supervised beach. A 2 km (1.2 mi.) woods trail is in the park. Roads to your right will connect you with #340 and Tour SW-2.

41.4 (25.7) **LEFT** at car dealer (Hardscratch Rd.). You now head back into Yarmouth via back roads. Upcoming on your left is Chebogue Meadows Walking Trail 4.5 km (2.8 mi.) of trail through wildlife habitat. You can pick-up a brochure on the trail in Yarmouth at the Department of Natural resources, 10 Starrs Rd. (highway #3).

48.4 (30.0) **CROSS** intersection. Continue, passing where #103 begins.

52.3 (32.5) **CROSS** #3 (Shopping centres to the right) Pass Yarmouth Airport (becomes Haley Rd.)

53.4 (33.2) **RIGHT** Forest St.

55.3 (34.4) **END** Ferry Terminal

Proof of the Vikings?

he **Runic Stone** weighs about 400 pounds and has a flat section across the top containing 13 clearly-cut characters believed to be Norse runes. The inscription has been translated to read *"Leif to Erik raises this monument"*.

Recognition of the stone as proof positive that Leif Erickson visited these shores almost 500 years before Columbus holds momentous possibilities.

From Icelandic sagas, it is considered reasonably certain that Leif, son of Eric the Red, sailed south along the Atlantic Coast from Greenland in the year 1001 or 1002 and returned the following spring. It may, therefore, be reasonable to suppose that during the winter of 1002 or 1003 Leif cut, this inscription to his father whom he had tried to persuade to make the voyage with him.

According to the sagas preserved in Ireland and the Vatican Library, Leif l in about 1001, sailed from Greenland describing in detail the number of days sailed and the nature and appearance of the coasts he travelled. His description of one area is consistent with south-western Nova Scotia, presumably Tusket Bay with its islands and leading up to the Tusket River. Four other Norse expeditions are said to have been made to these shores by other pioneers, the last one in 1007. America's leading Norse authority declared cellars found in the region to be of ancient Norse masonry construction.

Tour 1 B Forchu

START	Yarmouth Ferry Terminal
0.2 (0.1)	**LEFT** on Main St. (#3)
2.1 (1.3)	**LEFT** Vancouver St. at the **Milton Horse Fountain.** It was a common sight at this major intersection to see horses and their owners refreshing themselves. Plodding ox-teams would also satisfy their thirst from the same place, and it was common to see a horse drinking inches away from a yoked ox, both animals eye to eye and watching each other carefully.
2.8 (1.7)	**LEFT** Grove Rd. (#304) at Hospital. A Nova Scotian breed of dog is from this area. **Nova Scotia Duck Tolling Retrievers,** small, reddish coloured dogs with white markings, are growing in popularity with hunters for their abilities, and as a pet for their good nature. Raised locally at **Harbour Light Kennels** in Overton, they are interestingly, the only dog bred completely in **Canada.** (Lief Erickson Drive/ Grove Rd. 1.3 Km (.8 mi.) from the Yarmouth Hospital.)
	Just before your next turn are remains of one of the last constructed dykes. **Salt Pond Dyke,** built in 1799, enclosed marshland and reclaimed it from the sea.
7.4 (4.9)	**LEFT** Yarmouth Bar Rd.
	"The Churn" can be reached on your right. It gets its name from the vigorous wave actions there. In strong wind the water "churns" a funnel into the air.
	Another bend takes you around False Harbour. This name results from so many ships mistaking it as the entrance of Yarmouth, and breaking up on its rocks.
	John's Cove has Stanwoods Beach, a small sandy area with dunes. The fascinating **Runic Stone** was found here. Transcriptions tell of a **Viking** voyage from the year 1007! An attractive fishing village lies at a connecting causeway which connects the cape with the mainland. From here a wooded trail may be followed along the ridge above the highway to the lighthouse (this can not be biked.)
12.3 (7.6)	**Cape Forchu** The lighthouse is one of the most powerful on earth, reaching as far as 50 km (30 mi.) out to sea! The rocks here have long attracted visitors. Note: The areas near the lighthouse can be dangerous during storms due to huge waves! The famous explorer **Poutrincourt** nearly lost his life in a fall from the cliffs.
	RETURN via the same route in.
19.7 (12.2)	**RIGHT** Grove Road
21.8 (13.6)	**RIGHT** Vancouver Street
22.5 (14.0)	**RIGHT** Main Street (#1)
24.7 (15.4)	**END** Yarmouth Ferry Terminal

Accommodation

Best Western Mermaid Motel 545 Main St., Yarmouth, N.S., B5A 1J6 (902) 742-7821

Capri Motel 577 Main St., Yarmouth, NS B5A 1J6, (902) 742-7168

Clementine's Bed and Breakfast Evelyn and Ron Gray, 21 Clements St., Yarmouth, NS B5A 2B9, (902) 742-0079

Journey's End Motel 96 Starrs Rd., Yarmouth, N.S., B5A 2T5, (902) 742-1110

Lakelawn Motel Cheryl MacAvoy. 641 Main St., Yarmouth, NS B5A 1K2, (902) 742-3588; Off-season (902) 742-8427

Mid-Town Motel Rosalie and Victor Indig. 13 Parade Street, Yarmouth, NS B5A 3A5, (902) 742-5333 Downtown, In area of old houses

Murray Manor Guest House Bed and Breakfast Lori and James Colbeck. 17 Forest St., Yarmouth, NS B5A 3L1, (902) 742-9625 Across from ferry dock

Rodd Colony Harbour Inn 6 Forest St., Yarmouth, N.S., B5A 3K7

Rodd Grand Hotel 417 Main St., Yarmouth, N.S., (902) 742-2446

Victorian Vogue Bed and Breakfast Dawn-Marie Skjelmose. 109 Brunswick St., Yarmouth, N.S., B5A 2H2 (902) 742-6398

Camping

Lake Breeze Campground Del and Pearl Kuehner, P.O. Box 1990, R.R. #1, Yarmouth, NS, B5A 4A5 (902) 649-2332. 14.5 Km (9 mi.) east of Yarmouth. showers, trail.

Loomer's Campers' Haven F. W. Loomer. R.R. #4, Yarmouth, NS B5A 4A8 (902) 742-4848. Open & wooded campground on lake. On Route #3, 4 km (2.5 mi.) east of Yarmouth. Washrooms, free showers, camp store, hiking trail, boat and canoe rental, lake swimming, deep-sea fishing and whale watching arranged.

Ellenwood Lake Provincial Park Province of Nova Scotia. Deerfield NS (902) 761-2400. Forest campground on lake. Route. 340, 19.3 km (12 mi.) northeast of Yarmouth, 1.6 km (1 mile) from Deerfield. Washrooms, pay showers, swimming. No reservations.

Atlantic Canada
Cycling Festival

Tailwinds, romantic churches, and the decendants of Acadia

Tour 2

French Shore

Tour at a glance

START	Yarmouth (Ferry Terminal)
FINISH	Digby
OTHER STARTING POINTS	Digby
DISTANCE	117 km (73 mi.)
DIRECTION	South-West - North-East
TERRAIN	Gently rolling
CLIMATE	Very strong winds; little protection from elements
NOTES	Traditional Rappie pie available along route
TRAFFIC	Moderate to Busy
REST SPOTS	Sandford drawbridge; Smuggler's Cove Park; Meteghan
FOOD	Frequent stores and take-outs
REPAIRS	Yarmouth; Digby
TOURISM	Yarmouth (Ferry Terminal) 742-5033
	Meteghan (Smuggler's Cove) 645-2389
	Digby
HOSPITAL	Yarmouth; Digby
AMBULANCE	Yarmouth; Digby
POLICE	Yarmouth; Meteghan; Digby

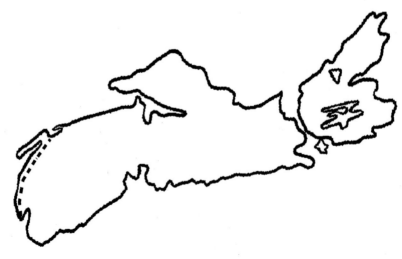

t the Digby County line, north of Yarmouth, French-
speaking fishing villages begin lining the shore of St.
Mary's Bay. Referred to as "*the longest main street in
the world*", one continuous habitation runs all the way to
ymouth. The shore closely follows the beauty of the Bay of
dy and several magnificent old churches. In season, colourful
nes line the roadside. The tall plants of white, pink, and
ple, offer little protection, on your way along this barren,
dswept landscape. The most predictable tailwind in the
vince should be behind you. Usually strong, often ferocious,
winds from the south-west will be your friend or enemy as
edge along the water.

en the Acadians returned from their tragic expulsion, they
nd their old homes in the annapolis Valley occupied, by
comers brought in from other lands. Many resettled along
the windswept coast, now referred to as the French Shore.
ge, romantic, churches have been constructed overlooking the
. Towering structures, they are remarkable in their scale
pared to the small villages which constructed them. Lasting
aments to faith and hard work, some seat several times the
sh's population.

dians celebrate their heritage during Festival de Clare, held
second week of July. They welcome you as a visitor, to join
However, the pleasure of cycling the busier highway at this
e must be left to personal judgement. If arriving in July,
ire at the Yarmouth or Digby Tourist bureaus before
lizing your plans.

ernate Route/Loop Option: A return loop can be cycled
veen Yarmouth and Weymouth on the hilly but attractive
ck road" (#340). Old homesteads and a number of fur farms
the road. A smaller run is to turn inland at Church Point.

or some perverse reason the wind is against you, remember
: the interior is forested, and you will do better against the
d. As mentioned, the shore is one continous community. If
find yourself in the mood to be alone, then you might also
sider the "back road".

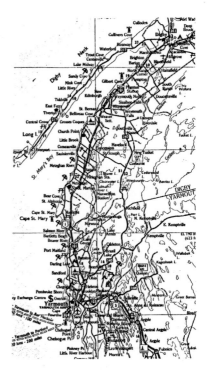

START	Yarmouth Ferry Terminal- head north on Main St. (#3). See Tour 1A for details on leaving town.
2.1 (1.3)	LEFT Vancouver Street
2.8 (1.7)	LEFT Grove Rd. (#304)
4.8 (3.0)	RIGHT Shore Road. About 1 km (.6 mi.) along to the left is Pembroke Beach
12.0 (7.4)	LEFT toward **Sandford**, home to North America's **smallest working drawbridge**. A picnic area is set up along the shore, providing views of the shore cliffs of High Head. The first of several wooden drawbridges was erected at Sandford during the First World War over the entrance to the "*boat hole*", a sheltered basin where fishing vessels find protection from heavy seas. Spanning a section of water about 6 m (20 ft.) wide, the village's most recent bridge, built in 1984, retains the honour.
	Stay left along the shore, passing the turn to Darling Lake. You will soon again see the rocks of High Head. Views from the fields along the route here are rewarding. At **Port Maitland** there is a provincial park, with a sand and stone saltwater beach.
24.4 (15.2)	LEFT #1. Soon begins the largest Acadian region in Nova Scotia! A long, unbroken settlement, it stretches along the shore 60 m (200 ft.) wide, and 80 km (50 mi.) long! Largely French speaking, business will be conducted in English, unless you initiate conversation in French. Directly at the county line, a road goes left to the shore. Here is Bartletts Beach. A track-like road runs from the shore to further up at Salmon River.
	Cape St. Mary's is accessible from a road to the left near Mavillette. In the village is a breakwater, overlooked by a

13

lighthouse. **Mavilette Beach Provincial Park** has camping close to a long sandy beach. Marshes behind the sand dunes make for good bird-watching. On the way in is a motel and restaurant, which serves rappie pie. A rugged trail runs from near the end of the cape, going across the barrens to Bear Cove 8 km (5 mi.) away. It passes coves and small caves that were used to hide liquor during prohibition.

Continuing on route, highway #1 again reaches the bay. To the left is **Smugglers Cove Provincial Park**. A steep path leads down to one of the small caverns, used during prohibition to hide illegal liquor bound for the United States.

Meteghan is a good spot to take a break. It is the largest community between Yarmouth and Weymouth. You will find food, and if needed, refuge from the wind. The community has a large and varied fishing fleet, and is the biggest wooden boat building centre in the Atlantic Provinces. **La Vielle Maison** is a local museum preserving Acadian life along the bay (small admission fee). In the village cemetery lies the grave of the mysterious man known as **Jerome** (see Tour 3).

SIDE TRIP: 1 km (.6 mi.) north of Meteghan River Bridge to the right a road (Placide Comeau) takes you to **St. Benoni Waterfall.** Proceed beyond the high school, look for the St. Benoni sign (next right) and follow the paved road to the steel bridge. Upstream is a spectacular waterfall, which makes for a pleasant spot for a break.

Saulnierville has the region's largest fish plant. Processed here are the region's famous scallops. **Comeauville** is also known for its food. *Pate a la Rapure-* known to English speakers as **Rappie Pie**, became introduced commercially here.

St. Mary's Church will soon be seen far in the distance. Built from 1903-1905, this is the **largest wooden church in North America**. Seating over 1000 people, it is a romantic structure, both inside and out. Ceilings 19.3 m (63 ft.) high were quite a feat to construct out of wood. The winds on the shore have proved to be so strong, that ballast has been put in the spire to keep it from swaying to a dangerous extent. The church is often open for visiting. There is no charge, but upkeep donations are appreciated. Nova Scotia's only French college, **Universite Sainte-Anne** sits next door, preserving Acadian culture. A pleasant walk around the back takes you down Chemin de Phare to the shore lighthouse. Here, you will find additional good photo spots of the church.

An almost bizarre sight to see here is **St. Bernard Church**, which dominates the landscape for a long distance. This immense granite cathedral is a monument to the skills and ideals of the inhabitants of this tiny village. Built entirely by the local parishioners, it took them 32 years to complete. The entire population of a large portion of the county could fit inside (it seats 1000 people). It is open to the public. Visitors may support the upkeep of this huge structure by purchasing local handicrafts.

Cross over the Sissiboo ("large river" in Mic Mac) River into **Weymouth** (accommodations, and food supplies). The area was founded by **James Moody**, a Delaware farmer, who did not support the American Revolution because it was settled by violence. The rural Black community of **Weymouth Falls** was settled following the war. Loyalists, they were later joined by merchant seamen from the West Indies, who jumped ship. Too far inland to support even meagre crops, they suffered for many years, a subsistence life. **Sam Longford** is perhaps its most famous son. A member of the Boxing Hall of Fame, he was considered one of the best ever in the heavy-weight category.

MERGE with the #101 at Weymouth North. From here the route primarily serves the function of conneting the shore with Digby. Traffic is not too bad, and you have a shoulder. Gilbert Cove has a restored lighthouse often open for visiting. **Savary Picnic Park** at Plympton is situated along a fine beach with birch trees and tidal pool.

114.8 (71.4)   LEFT Route #303 Exit 26 at Digby

116.9 (72.6)   END at Digby Tourist Bureau

Accommodation (Yarmouth area see Tour 1; Digby area see Tour 3)

Duck Pond Inn and Space Barn Museum Harry and Tina Taylor. R.R. 1, Box 2495, Beaver River, NS B5A 4A5 (902) 649-2249. Operated by space scientist. Adjoining museum features presentations on space research.
Cape View Motel Victor Deveau. Box 9, Salmon River, NS B0W 2Y0 (9020 645-2258. Near beach at Mavillette.
Anchor Inn Marie and Hans deMan. 8755 route 1, Box 19, Meteghan Centre, NS B0W 2K0 (902) 645-3390
Bluefin Motel Sandra Deveau. Box 4, Meteghan, NS B0W 2J0 (9020 645-2251
Tea and Lace Inn Pam Smith. P.O. Box 96, Meteghan, NS B0W 2L0 (902) 769-3450
Bayshore Bed and Breakfast Ted and Connie Murphy. Box 176, Saulnierville, NS B0W 2Z0 (902) 769-3671
L'Auberge En Campagne Bed and Breakfast Paul LeBlanc. R.R. #1, P.O. Box 213, Church Point, NS B0W 1M0, (902) 769-2856
Chez Benoit Stuart Bed and Breakfast Benoit Stuart. P.O. Box 23, Church Point, NS B0W 1M0, (902) 769-2715
Gilbert's Cove Farm Bed and Breakfast Hope and John Spencer. R.R. #3, Weymouth, NS B0W 3T0, (902) 837-4505
Goodwin Motel Pat and Arnold Comeau. P.O. Box 15, Weymouth, NS B0W 2R0, (902) 837-5120 (902) 769-3160 (902) 769-2868
Westway Inn Gordon and Evelyn Burnham. Plympton, NS B0W 2R0 (902) 245-5071
Barton House Bed and Breakfast Laurette Deschenes. Box 33, R.R. 1, Barton, NS B0W 1H0 (902) 245-6695
Bay Motel John and Doreen Morehouse. R.R. 2, Brighton, NS B0V 1A0 (902) 245-4713
Brookvale Bed and Breakfast Barry and Gladys Jennings, R.R. 2, Brighton, NS B0V 1A0 (902) 245-2957

Camping

Lake Breeze Campground Del and Pearl Keuhner. Box 1990, R.R. 1, Yarmouth, NS B5A 4A5 (902) 649-2332. 14.5 km (9 mi.) from Yarmouth
Ellenwood Lake Provincial Park Province of Nova Scotia. North-east of Yarmouth off #340. No reservations; no showers
Belle Baie Park Rita Stuart. Church Point, NS B0W 1M0. Open and wooded campground on ocean.

Atlantic Canada
Cycling Festival

*Ferry-hopping into a
haven for whales*

Tour 3   Digby Neck/Bear River

Tour at a glance

START/ FINISH	Digby
DISTANCE	118 Km (73 mi.)
DIRECTION	Same route return
TERRAIN	Moderate- hills up from ferry docks
CLIMATE	Expect fog and moist air
	Strong sea winds
NOTES	Recommend overnight trip
	2 ferry crossings each way
	Recommend advance accommodation reservation
TRAFFIC	Low
REST STOPS	Lake Midway; Sandy Cove
FOOD	Digby (R)(G)(C); Sandy Cove (C); Westport (C)
REPAIRS	Digby, Kingston (off-route)
TOURISM	Digby Ferry 245-2201; Digby 245-5714;
	Tiverton 839-2853
HOSPITAL	Digby
AMBULANCE	Digby
POLICE	Digby (R.C.M.P.)

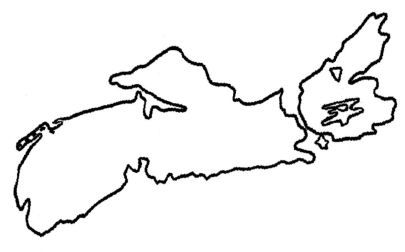

For anyone who looks over a map of Nova Scotia, it is easy to become intrigued by this long arm reaching into the Bay of Fundy. It perks the imagination, and many are curious what it is like. You don't go to Digby Neck on your way to somewhere else. This is a special tour off the beaten track. You must make it your destination, because there is nowhere else beyond.

No- Digby Neck is not Nova Scotia's Key West! It is not highly developed, nor does it have a large population. The island is a quiet place, a refuge for birds, and with whales offshore. The remains of an ancient mountain chain, there are unique land formations. The peninsula is often protected from the strong winds by trees. Short side roads take you to secluded spots on both the Bay of Fundy, and the smaller St. Mary's Bay. Two ferry rides are featured on this interesting tour bringing you to the beauty of Brier Island. This is recommended as at least a two day tour, and reservations should be acquired for indoor stays well in advance before you head out.

We begin in Digby itself. The area was settled by Loyalist refugees. Their numbers included many Black Loyalists who settled in nearby communities. Some Acadians move in to the area from along the French Shore. Servicing traffic from the St. John, New Brunswick ferry, and one of the world's largest scallop fleets make up most of its economy. Admiral Digby Museum, near the tourist bureau has models, old maps, and brochures of walking tours through town. On the walking tour is Trinity Anglican Church, built by fishermen, which on the inside looks like an inverted hull.

At the north end of town, on the way to the ferry is Digby Pines. One of the original chain of romantic Canadian Pacific Hotels, remaining almost identical from its past. Trails lead off providing magnificent views over Annapolis Basin.

Fresh scallops, Acadian rappie pie, and "*Digby Chicks*", (a local recipe of smoked herring) are available in town. The scallop fleet wharf makes a good stop. The dock is huge, with ladders for the fishermen to climb down to their boats at low tide. It makes for great photography.

SIDE TRIP: Consider taking a mini-cruise to St. John, New Brunswick and back, spending a day in the Bay of Fundy.

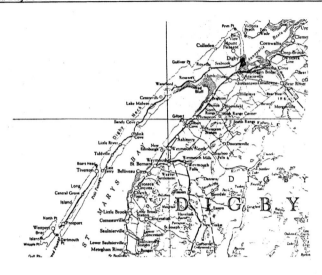

START   Digby Tourist Bureau on Water Street.

0.7 (0.4)   **LEFT** Carleton St.

1.6 (1.0)   **LEFT** Victoria St. (#303)

SIDE TRIP- **Prim Point Lighthouse:** Toward where the ferry leaves for New Brunswick, this light overlooks the Bay of Fundy. The scallop draggers are busy below, at times followed behind by whales, seals, porpoises, and gulls. The huge passenger ferry steams through narrow Digby Gut on several daily trips from New Brunswick. If it is a clear day you may be able to see all the way across. From downtown Digby follow Water Street and the signs to the Saint John Ferry and provincial information bureau, both on Shore Road. The next street up the hill is the Lighthouse Road.

1.8 (1.1)   **RIGHT** #217 (Prince William St.). Head out along Digby Neck. **Gulliver's Cove** many believe is where Gulliver the pirate had his base of operations and somewhere has buried his treasure.

Lake Midway has picnic facilities by its pond, and in adjoining woods. **Sandy Cove** is a scenic small village, with a circular harbour. A back harbour is close by, on the other side of the neck. Both have beaches, (visit the Fundy side) although the water may a bit bracing.

Life is strange, and Digby Neck has known its share of the mysterious. In 1864, a fisherman was walking along the beach. He came across a man dressed in fresh white linen on a large rock. Both of his legs had recently been amputated at the knee. He sat holding a can of biscuits and a jar of water. He gave the impression that he also could not speak.

Some guessed that he was an injured lumberjack from New Brunswick, dumped off to no longer be a burden. Others surmised that he had been cast away from a ship, even perhaps part of a mutiny. He was taken to Meteghan, in the hopes that he would respond to French. Stories and rumours of his origin were rampant, over time further obscuring his origin. Some claimed he must be able to speak, as they had heard him mumble something in his sleep. Others reported seeing visitors speaking to him in an unknown language. **Jerome**, as he became known, was cared for by the local residents for the next 58 years. He was laid to rest in Meteghan, his story still remains a mystery.

18

To your left is Little River Cove, with a fish plant and light. **Whale Cove** is the next access to the bay, on your right.

33.5 (20.8)   **East Ferry.** The mainland ends and your next objective is crossing the neck's two islands. Long periods of stormy weather have an effect on the normal life of the islands. Heating oil, gasoline, milk and other staple commodities are trucked to the ferry and cross the passage only under favourable conditions. So much depends on the ferry today that when it is not in operation the results are immediately felt on the two islands and their fifteen hundred population. The *Joshua Slocum* will take you across **Petit Passage** to **Long Island**. **Caution:** Take care on the ferry ramps- water and exaust from waiting cars can make them slippery (it takes a long time for medical care to reach the islands)!

Tiverton is named after the town in southern England. The visitor information centre has a period garden and a small museum devoted to the islands and the ferries. Operated by the Islands Historical Society; Free (upkeep donations appreciated) (902) 839-2853

Upon arrival, a short run to your right can take you out to the light at **Boars Head**, which looks out at Petit Passage.

At **Central Grove Provincial Park**, half-way across the island, you will find picnic sites. An attractive 1 km (0.6 mi.) trail to the Fundy shore.

51.0 (31.7)   **Ferry to Brier Island** (on the hour every hour). Operations across this turbulent passage began her many years ago here by a boy of only fourteen years of age. Byron Blackford designed a scow to move people and vehicles across Petite Passage. He accepted a wide variety of passengers and freight. Once he even carried a live bear. The beast grew restless and it was feared it might jump overboard or even capsize the boat. The captain saved the day by singing in the beast's ear.

51.5 (32.0)   **Brier Island:** You are well into the Bay of Fundy. 7 Km (4 mi.) long and 2.5 km (1.5 mi.) wide, Brier is a sister isle of **Grand Manan**. Until recent years most trade went on between the islands, and with Maine. A short 25 nautical mile boat trip between them, reaching Manan by bike would take you an entire week! (It is accessed by ferry from Black's Harbour, New Brunswick).

Brier lies surrounded by some of the most dangerous waters on earth. In 1846 for example, out of 25 ships sailing down the bay, only 9 survived. Wind and fog are frequent. Gales have been known to knock down cyclist's tents and if not occupied, send them rushing away. If you plan to camp, consider a protected area.

Off this island came a master mariner. **Joshua Slocum**, trained on these rocks, went on to become the **first person to sail alone around the world!** His voyage took 3 1/2 years. And hear this America's Cup followers, he did it without any money! Such a skilled and resourceful sailor was he, that when he found himself shipwrecked on a desolate beach in South America, he got to work and built himself another ship with mere hand tools. A book written by him in 1900 is even today popular with adventurers, and is still in print.

Slocum's practice of taking numbers of unattached young women for cruises on his ship drew the wrath of the island. Insolated in the mores of the Victorian age, where "disorderly walking" was censured, and table legs were covered, think of the talk when single women went out in the boat of a man whose wife was left behind in a Boston boarding house.

Franklin D. Roosevelt considered Brier a favourite during his explorations through Nova Scotia as a young man. He returned to the island in later years to much fanfare, as President of the **United States.**

Westport is the "capitol" of Brier Island (pop. 353). Huge old homes have protected its residents from the elements since the days of isolation from the mainland. The Oddfellows Hall at Westport was built about 1909 from lumber salvaged from a shipwreck.

Brier is an island for lovers of nature. A stopping point on long bird migrations, this is one of the major bird study areas on the continent. Bird watchers have noted more than 150 species that frequent the island. Large numbers of hawks visit in September. It is an important link in a chain of island sanctuaries ringing the Gulf of Maine and lower Bay of Fundy. By being exposed to the open sea, Brier Island offers excellent nesting opportunities for coastal and open ocean species as well as the harbour porpoise and white-beaked and white-sided dolphin. To the north of the village is a road leading to a lighthouse. This is a bird banding station, operated by Acadia University. From the lighthouse you can see the treacherous

19

waters between the islands. Sunsets are spectacular from here.

On land, coyotes have recently reached the island (without the use of the ferry). The southeast third of the island, consists of forests, fields, marshes, bogs and a pond, surrounded by more than 10 km (6 miles) of ocean coastline. Purchased by the Natural Conservancy of Canada, plants found nowhere else in the country are protected here. These include mountain avens, an alpine species ordinarily occurring only in the New Hampshire mountains; arctic birch, and the curly grass fern, which is rare elsewhere in Nova Scotia.

From the lower part of the village, where the back street ends by the church, a road running inland crosses the island to the west side at Lighthouse Cove.

Eastward the pavement goes to the Joshua Slocum Monument. Just before that, to the right, across from the breakwater, a small dirt road heads inland. A recommended walk here will take you to a place called the Ridge of Rocks (Green Head). It is a spectacular spine of unusual formations (basalt columns). Volcanic in nature, they are similar to the Giant's causeway in Ireland. **WARNING**: Please use extreme caution near the rocks! Also take care with the area's tides.

Return to Digby by the same road in.

52.0 (32.3)	**Ferry** to Freeport, Long Island (on the half-hour, every hour)
69.5 (43.1)	**Ferry** to East Ferry (once an hour on the hour)
116.4 (72.3)	**RIGHT** Victoria St. (#303)
116.5 (72.4)	**LEFT** Sidney St.
117.4 (72.9)	**RIGHT** Water St.
117.6 (73.0)	**END**

Watching whales

O n the entire east coast of North America, there is no place better to watch whales than in Nova Scotia. All summer long you can meet "in person" these magnificent mammals. Two regions are optimum areas. The Bay of Fundy's waters are rich in plankton, which attracts large numbers of fish, which in turn attract the whales. The most numerous is the Pilot Whale. Larger whales, such as the well-known Humpback Whale play in these waters. There are also Finback, Minke and the endangered North Atlantic Right Whale. Dolphins and porpoises, and seals can be also seen up close.

Pilot Whales also live in the Gulf of St. Lawrence, off the Cabot Trail in northern Cape Breton.

Whale-watching tours offer you the good chances to view them up close from July to late September. They are most abundant in August and September.

Whale and Seabird Cruises Westport, N.S. B0V 1H0 (902) 839-2995.

Ocean Explorations P.O. Box 719, Tiverton, N.S. B0V 1G0 (902) 839-2417

Pirate's Cove Whale Cruises Tiverton, N.S. B0V 1G0 (902) 839-2242

Bear River

Spruce and cherry trees adorn steeply rising hills around what was once a busy shipbuilding centre. **Bear River**, known as "*Little Switzerland*" is a very pleasant village of 900 souls on the river of the same name. Distinctive verandahs of century-old houses rise up the steep hills. A good photographic opportunity is overlooking the village and it's stores standing on stilts over the river.

The village has seen an infusion of artisans in recent years, mixing with the long time residents. A restaurant and bake shop are also in the village. Ask for directions to the "*swimming hole*". At the small Bear River Indian Reserve, (in the woods not far to the back of the village) Mic Mac crafts can be seen in production and purchased. The Indians moved to the area in the 1800's from along the French Shore.

From Acaciaville (Exit 25 or 26 on the #101) you get a great view of Bear River. On the way, the view behind you overlooks the Annapolis Basin. The dirt road from South Range and Weymouth is even wilder. It turns to pavement just before an incredibly steep downhill (the author once broke a hub while braking on it). The road bypassing highway #1 through Clementsvale comes into the village, but the view is obscured by trees. Deep Brook (Exit 23) is a more gradual descent, with splendid views of the river. The road in from Smith's Cove (Exit 24 on the #101) is the village's only easy cycling access, providing a flat route along the river.

From Bear River, a back road runs along a parallel road. A winding downhill run emerges at Clementsport, with many old buildings. Another road runs in a more diagonal direction to Annapolis Royal from the end of the Bear River road. This inland route is hilly, but is recommended as you will avoid traffic on route #1, which hosts a military base (Cornwallis), and theme park at Upper Clements.

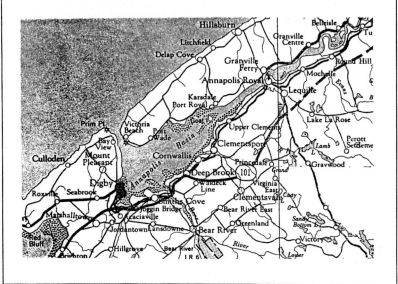

21

Accommodation

Digby
Admiral's Landing Bed and Breakfast Theresa and Robert Marshall. 115 Montague Row, P.O. Box 459, Digby, NS B0V 1A0, (902) 245-2247

Kingfisher Motel Warwick St. P.O. Box 280, Digby, NS B0V 1A0, (902) 245-4747

Siesta Motel Helen and Bob Eisener. 81 Montague Row, P.O. Box 250, Digby, NS B0V 1A0, (902) 245-2568

Thistle Down Inn 98 Montague Row, P.O. Box 508, Digby, NS B0V 1A0, (902) 245-4490

Westway House Bed and Breakfast 6 Carleton St., Digby, NS B0V 1A0, (902) 245-5071

Digby Neck
Olde Village Inn Dixie and Bob Van. Sandy Cove NS B0V 1E0 834-2202

The Brier House Claire Leng. Westport, NS B0V 1H0, (902) 839-2879

Brier Island Lodge Ray and Virginia Tudor. P.O. Box 1197, Westport, NS B0V 1H0, (902) 839-2300

Sandy Cove Bed and Breakfast Joyce and Louis Morin. 6363 Route 217, Sandy Cove NS B0V 1E0 834-2286

Westport Inn Roland and Nancy Swift. P.O. Box 1226, Westport, NS B0V 1H0, (902) 839-2675

Wingberry House Mrs. Shirley Pelletier, Sandy Cove, NS B0V 1E0 834-2516

Bear River
House on the Hill Bed and Breakfast C. Gene Samson. R.R. #1, Bear River, NS B0S 1B0 467-3933.

Inn Bear River Bed and Breakfast Doug Dockrill and Nancy Onysko. P.O. Box 142, Bear River NS 467-3809

Lovett Lodge Inn Bed and Breakfast Adrian Potter. Main Street, P.O. Box 119, Bear River NS B0S 1B0. 467-3917

Camping

Digby (Smith's Cove)
Fundy Spray Trailer Park and Campground Laird and Carol Banks. P.O. Box 74, Digby, NS B0V 1A0. Showers, heated pool. 245-4884; 245-4963

Smith's Cove Tent and Trailer Park Diane and Reg Walker. R.R. #1, Smiths Cove, NS B0S 1S0 showers, heated pool 245-4814

Digby Neck
Moby Dick Campground Lee and Mary Buckman, R.R. #1, Tiverton, N.S., B0V 1C0 (902) 839-2290; off season (514) 692-1842. Located 5 km (3 mi.) west of Tiverton at Central Grove; showers

Digby
House on the Hill Tenting Experience C. Gene Samson . R.R. #1, Bear River, NS B0S 1B0 467-3933. "Walk-in " sites, showers

Annapolis Valley

You no doubt have in your mind a destination you most want to see, possibly Cape Breton, perhaps the South Shore. If you will take the time, however, and permit yourself to be shown around, you too may develop a love affair with this region. While initial trips through the **Annapolis Valley** may be to another destination, many soon find themselves planning future visits to explore its many green and pastoral back roads. Most regions of Nova Scotia are linear. You see most of what is possible to see on your first trip through. The Annapolis Valley, however, invites you to explore so many first-class bicycle touring roads, that it could keep you busy for an entire summer! (One member of the Velo Halifax Bicycle Club has been frequently touring the valley for twenty years- he says he is still finding new backroads!)

There is no section of Canada so rich in romance and brutality. Religion, literature, language, agriculture, industry- the future of North American civilization was decided by the tragedies and triumphs throughout this magnificent valley. For centuries, this historic region's deep soil has been among the most productive on the continent. It is here where Canada's first European settlements took root, where bloody battles raged, and where one of its most shameful events took place. Today it offers you Nova Scotia's most carefree bicycle touring.

With orchards, strawberry fields and farms, Kings County alone contains 1/3 of the total value of all Nova Scotia's produce. Farms are family sized and their activities vary greatly; from cattle to corn; from pears to plums. The valley even produces tobacco and grapes! Dairy products, poultry, and honey operations also supply a large portion of the province's food demand.

This is the warmest part of Nova Scotia. Both mountain ridges, while not extremely high, manage keep warm air contained in the valley. Here lie the region's famous apple orchards, in late May a riot of pink and white blossoms. Autumn is perfect here, as trees with multi-coloured leaves cover the valley. Harvest time in October still offers exceptional cycling - falling leaves,

wagons filled with pumpkins and plenty of places to get warm.

Most people in the valley today trace their ancestors back to several immigrations of New Englanders. Known as the Planters, they developed, or in the case of the property of the Acadians after their tragic expulsion, took over, well maintained farms. French names recall those who escaped deportation, now scattered throughout the valley. Descendants of Black Loyalists live in the market towns and a couple of villages. Two tiny Mic Mac Indian Reserves lie hidden outside Cambridge and Horton.

The Evangeline Trail, the tourism route designated several decades ago, runs along the valley floor. This road is an endless string of pretty villages and towns. However, for cycling, the traffic between them is irksome, and in a few places unbearable. The farms and orchards between the communities are being converted to commercial activity and new housing. Highway # 1 is NOT a recommended route for cycling in more than small doses. Since the Evangeline Trail was selected, better routes for cycling have been paved. You do not have to miss the trail's restaurants, shops and cosy accommodations. They can still be accessed by way of the many intersecting cross-roads.

Most of your biking will be in the valley itself. Its floor is as flat as Nova Scotia gets. With a high road density, unlike most of the province, here choices for you abound. You may become lost; but only temporarily. For your bearings, there will be the North Mountain to one side, and South Mountain to the other. The four-lane highway #101 cuts through the middle, so you should be able to tell what side of the valley you are on, and if you are moving east or west.

Most valley traffic hums along on highways #1 and #101, oblivious to the scenic roads around them. Dozens of country roads, all reasonably spaced apart run along its floor. It is not difficult to get away from cars. Here you can cycle for hours and not worry about where you're headed. Small communities lie every few kilometres. This is a comfort not found in other regions of Nova Scotia. Here you will not go thirsty, hungry, or have to carry several pounds of supplies with you. Intersections allow you to turn back on parallel roads at your convenience.

Some of the valley's roads are called "streets". Don't worry, it does not mean this is a huge urban area. Its just a reminder of the overenthusiasm of the original settlers.

While ocean air is elusive in the valley itself, cool ocean breezes are only an hour's ride away. One of the most appreciated areas this writer has sent cyclists to, and have led tours in is up and over North Mountain. ("Mountains" here are in context only, the valley ridges would hardly seem a hill in the Rockies). The inclines getting you up are tough, but short climbs, a few of them more challenging than others. Once you are on top, you quickly crest the ridge and start heading down, to the shores of the famous Bay of Fundy.

A far different environment from the valley floor lies in hiding on the other side. Delap Cove, Port Lorne, Harbourville, Morden, Halls Harbour, Baxter's Harbour, Scots Bay- these and other coastal villages are connected by roller coaster shore roads. A few hide, alone at the end of dead-ends. They each sit in solitude, visited daily by the world's highest tides. Exploring this shore can be an entire vacation just in itself.

Those who are planning a circle tour from Yarmouth (or Halifax) will be looking at passing through a third region. The South Mountain Ridge is the sister range of North Mountain. The climbs up get more difficult as you move eastward from Annapolis Royal. Past Berwick they become challenging.

Four different roads connect the Annapolis Valley and the South Shore. They are routes #8, #10, #12, and an unnumbered road between Aylesford and Mahone Bay. Route #8 does not have much more in the way of scenic beauty than do the others. This road, however, is being promoted as the "Kejimkujik Scenic Trail". This can only be deducted as a scheme to enhance the various enterprises on the periphery of Kejimkujik National Park. Now that the signs are up, it will be even less "scenic" to bikers, as additional cars, busses, and campers will be added to the traffic! Route 10 is the quietest of the three trunk roads, with number 12, the busiest. The unnumbered route between Aylesford and Mahone Bay is reccomended. It is virtually unpopulated, with christmas tree farms. There are several big hills near the South Shore side. Directions are not well signposted, but you will need to make few turns.

Side roads connect these through routes to allow various combinations. None of the routes are so busy as to discourage cycling. There is such a low population inland, however, that police coverage of the roads is limited. Expect to encounter occasional speeders.

Tour 4, Annapolis Valley Tour will take you through the entire region. From Annapolis Royal it suggests the shore road, as well an interior road, before running along the valley floor, terminating in Wolfville.

Tours 5, and 6 are both loop tours. Both make for relaxed 2 day outings, but can for experienced bikers be covered in one day. Dozens of combinations are possible. You can start on either end or start in the middle. From a central base, such as Bridgetown, or Berwick, each end of the tours can be explored over two days, creating two "mini-loops".

Tour 7, 8, 9, 10, and 11 all radiate out of the Wolfville/ Kentville area. They are all day tours, with Tour 9, to Blomidon suggested if possible over 2 days.

ntic Canada
ing Festival

The mountain and the valley

Tour 4   Annapolis Valley

Tour at a glance

START	Annapolis Royal
FINISH	Wolfville
OTHER STARTING POINTS	Bridgetown; Middleton; Kingston; Berwick; Kentville; Wolfville
DISTANCE	141 km (88 mi.)
DIRECTION	West-East
TERRAIN	Hilly then flat
	"Low Road Option": Rolling then flat Warm and humid
CLIMATE	Cool and misty on "High Road Option" along Bay of Fundy
TRAFFIC	Low to Moderate
REST STOPS	Hampton wharf; Port George; Silver Lake; Prescott House
FOOD	Annapolis Royal (R)(G)(C); Port George (C); Melvern Square (C); Somerset (C); Grafton (C); Woodville (C); Centreville(C); Canning (R)(G((C); Port Wiliams (C)
REPAIRS	Kingston (off-route; Wolfville
TOURISM	Annapolis Royal; Wolfville
HOSPITAL	Annapolis Royal; Middleton; Kentville (off-route)
AMBULANCE	Annapolis Royal; Middleton; Kentville (off-route); Wolfville
POLICE	Annapolis Royal; Bridgetown; Middleton; Kingston (R.C.M.P.); Wolfville

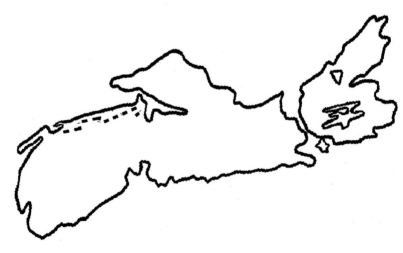

ycling the Annapolis Valley could keep you busy for an entire summer! Presented for you here is a selected through route, to bring you across the region. It samples a few of the prime touring areas. your time is limited, perhaps this through-route could be pplemented with one of several good day tours out of olfville.

ur 5 follows the western half of the tour. On the eastern le, refer to **Tour 8** for deatils on the Starr's Point area, and ur **10** for Wolfville information. Small communities lie ery few kilometres. except for the stretch along the shore. u have a comfort not found in other regions of Nova otia. In most places of the province, stores and sheltered pping places are limited. Here you have many villages, th their general stores. In addition, highway #1 is not far f-route, which is a continuous stretch of communities. me of the valley's roads are called "streets". Don't worry, does not mean this is a huge urban area. Its just a reminder the overenthusiasm of the original settlers.

There are two options, a "high road", and a "low road". The first option is a far different environment from the valley. Here villages are connected by roller coaster shore roads. A few hide, alone at the end of dead-ends. They each sit in solitude, visited daily by the world's highest tides.

"LOW ROAD OPTION: This will take you on a much flatter route and rejoin the "high road"option at Pleasant Street, just north of Kingston. Begin by turning right out of Fort Anne onto George Street. Cross Highway #1 at the lights. Go a short distance past the Historic gardens, and turn LEFT onto route #201. Follow #201al the way to Nictaux. Turn LEFT on the road before, or on, route #10. Go through Middleton. Cross the Main Street and head over route #101. Turn RIGHT on Spa Springs Road, and follow it all the way to its end. Turn RIGHT, and Pleasant street is your next LEFT.

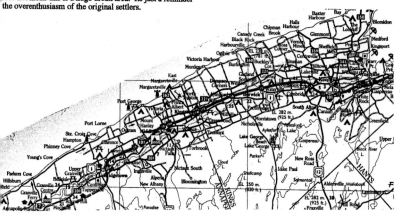

START   Begin at **Fort Anne** in Annapolis Royal. **Refer to Tour 5 for route details**. Head left on George Street along the water. You are now on the oldest town street in the country! Numerous museums and interesting buildings line the road,

0.9 (0.5)   LEFT St. Anthony (at hardware store).

1.3 (0.8)   LEFT #1 (at Fire Station). Cross Annapolis Basin. **Annapolis Royal Tidal Power Plant** demonstrates the generation of energy from the immense Fundy tides. Tourism information also available (free 532-5454).

4.1 (2.5)   LEFT Parker's/ Delap Cove Road (at Irving station). You soon arrive at the famous Bay of Fundy. Even in the warmest parts of the summer, just up and over the ridge of the valley, the shores of the bay can be cool with mist or fog.

10.3 (6.4)   RIGHT (at Olco station at Parker's Cove). You now follow the shore road along the bay. A much more protected coast than the Atlantic, along the cliffs are pools, which lie full between visiting tides, providing varieties of coastal habitats. Continue along the shore. **Hampton's** wharf offers a pleasant spot to relax on the wharf and watch the boats come and go (a sign announces it as Hampton Beach, but there isn't much of a swimming area).

27

36.8 (22.9)	**LEFT** go down hill to Port Lorne. Turn at village and climb steep hill to ridge.
42.8 (26.6)	**LEFT** at top of hill. Follow pavement.
44.6 (27.7)	**LEFT** at old Mount Hanley Schoolhouse
57.3 (35.6)	**LEFT** #362 downhill into Margaretville, a pretty village on the bay, with a large general store
61.6 (38.3)	**RIGHT** Go up hill onto ridge. You can also go through the village and then go up at East Margaretville. Come down hill into valley. Pass #221 on your left, and Spa Road on your right. Pass store, and look for Pleasant Street.
69.7 (43.3)	**LEFT** Pleasant Street. **Junction of "low road" option.** Accessible from the upcoming roads on your right are Kingston and **Greenwood.** In Kingston is Andy's Bike shop. In Greenwood is a mall, fast food outlets, and Tim Horton's coffee shop.
78.3 (48.7)	**LEFT** small jog in road
78.7 (48.9)	**RIGHT**
94.9 (59.0)	**LEFT** road merges onto wider section of road coming from Berwick.
98.5 (61.2)	**LEFT** at Grafton
99.2 (61.7)	**RIGHT** #221. You are now in the heart of apple and pear country.
102.6 (63.8)	**LEFT** Bligh at Boates U-Pick, church, and gas station.
103.5 (64.3)	**RIGHT** Woodville Road (first paved road)
107.2 (66.6)	**LEFT** #221. Silver Lake Park is an attractive swimming pond and grassy field for a break ,
	SHORT-CUT: Lakewood Road to the right will go directly toward Kentville. It goes through an old tobacco producing region. Turn right at the flashing light on #359 toward town.
114.0 (70.8)	**LEFT** #221 Centreville. Route makes small jog
114.2 (71.0)	**RIGHT** #221 after short jog
115.4 (71.7)	**LEFT** Eaton Branch
116.4 (72.4)	**RIGHT** Baines Road. **Atlanta** was named in the mid-1800's as the name of a new train depot. Follow through to Sheffield Mills. The road will twist and turn.
120.0 (74.6)	**RIGHT** Sheffield Mills Road. At this point, there is a confusing layout of roads. Signposting is limited. Do not be surprised if you become temporarily lost. This is a nesting area for some Bald Eagles.
121.1 (75.3)	**LEFT** #221. Follow on road through Canning. There is a grocery store and restaurant in village.
125.5 (78.0)	**RIGHT** Canning Aboiteau
126.7 (78.7)	**LEFT** Saxon Street.
128.9 (80.1)	**RIGHT** #341. To the left is the ghost port of **Picket's Wharf**, and excellent views of **Blomidon Mountain.**
130.6 (81.2)	**LEFT** Wellington Dyke. You now follow in reverse direction **Tour 8** around Starr's Point. **Refer to it for route details.**
133.0 (82.7)	**LEFT** Church Street
133.6 (83.10)	**LEFT** at Old Town Schoolhouse. The road then turns a bend. **Prescott House** approaches on your right.
135.7 (84.4)	**LEFT** #358 at Port Williams
137.5 (85.50)	**LEFT** #1 at Irving station
140.6 (87.4)	**LEFT** Centre Street
140.7 (87.5)	**RIGHT** Front Street
140.8 (87.5)	**END**

Accommodation/ Camping
(see Tour 5 for Annapolis Royal, Bridgetown, Middleton, Kingston, Western Valley listings)
(see Tour 6 for Kingston, Aylesford, Berwick, Central Valley listings)
(see Tour 10 for Kentville, Wolfville, Eastern Valley)

Atlantic Canada
Cycling Festival

Over the mountain to a secluded, misty shore

our 5   West Valley

Tour at a glance

START/ FINISH	Annapolis Royal
OTHER STARTING POINTS	Bridgetown; Valleyview Provincial Park; Middleton; Kingston
DISTANCE	128 km (80 mi.) Several short-cut options
DIRECTION	Clockwise
TERRAIN	Hilly to Very Hilly
CLIMATE	Warm and humid in valley; cool and often foggy on bay
NOTES	Very flexible tour- many short cuts and extensions
TRAFFIC	Low on shore; Moderate in valley
REST STOPS	Hampton wharf; Port George
FOOD	Annapolis Royal (R)(G)(C); Bridgetown (R)(G)(C)
REPAIRS	Kingston (off-route)
TOURISM	Annapolis Royal 532-5454
HOSPITAL	Annapolis Royal 532-5769 Middleton
AMBULANCE	Annapolis Royal; Middleton
POLICE	Annapolis Royal; Bridgetown; Middleton

The exact spot where the battle for North America unfolded is where you begin this tour of the western half of the Annapolis valley. Religion, literature, language, agriculture, industry- the future of North American civilization was guided from the events which unfolded here. The town of Annaplois Royal lies at the end of the Annapolis Basin, overlooked by the forests of both the North and South Mountain ridges. It is here that the Annapolis Valley begins.

This ride attempts to offer you the advantage of prevelant south-west winds along the Fundy shore, guiding your return in the more protected valley. If the wind is not from the S.W., consider a reverse dieection to better enjoy the shoreline views. *Note:* remember that wind does not pick-up intil midmorning.

Being a long, narrow loop, you can easily make a ride to suit tiding style. Note the several cross - roads. Staying at Annapolis Royal, Bridgetown, or Valleyview Provincial Park, Middleton, or Kingston, you can do half the loop. Staying at midpoint, you can set up a base, to cycle the route on two smaller day loops.

The tour will start at Fort Anne Historic Park in Annapolis Royal. Canada's oldest National Historic Site, this is the fourth fort to stand here. It is said that the region, with this citadel as its key, has changed hands more times than any other place in North America! Displays and furnishings through its 30 rooms tell of the beginnings of this country, and its many battles bloody battles (free admission 532-2397). Note: If you have a car with you, check with the tourist bureau about parking. Spaces in town are limited.

You begin on the Fundy shore, after one of the easiest climbs of all along the North Mountain ridge. North Mountain is not by most standards actually a "mountain". Here it must be considered in context only, the valley ridges would hardly seem a hill in the Rockies). Cool ocean breezes of the shore are in contrast of that in the valley. only an hour's ride away. While it can be hot and humid in the valley, on the shore, at Hampton or Port George you may need a jacket! A far different environment from the valley floor lies in hiding on the other side. The villages sit in solitude, visited daily by the world's highest tides.

Some of the valley's roads are called "streets". do not be fearful that this is an urban area. Its just a reminder of the overenthusiasm of the original settlers.

A beauty that awed the first explorers

Events here long ago shaped the destiny of North America. Countless battles raged for control of the continent between the English and the French. Canada's oldest European settlement and the first permanent one north of the Gulf of Mexico, saw the introduction of Christianity. The first court of law in Canada was held here. It also saw the continent's first social club, the first play, as well as the introduction of apple trees, dandelions, and rats.

The **Port Royal** settlement had a peaceful start. By 1613, however, conflicting French and English claims to the territory around the Bay of Fundy sparked the warfare that was to be a part of colonial life in North America for the next 150 years. Both the English and French had designated it as their colonial capital.

The small garrison town continued to grow, despite the colonial military battles. Attacked by pirates, and frequently looted by backwoods opportunists, the area was a violent place. The fort was captured by the British and recovered by the French **five** times before its final capture by a British colonial force in 1710.

Port Royal was renamed **Annapolis Royal** in honour of **Queen Anne**, the British monarch. It was also here that the stage was set to become one of the three major bases of operations for the **Expulsion** of the French speaking Acadians. In its third century, after the conflicts it became a placid Victorian town and seaport. Almost 400 years of history have left a lasting impression. The town has preserved its appearance, and has kept control over new develoments.

START   Begin at **Fort Anne** in **Annapolis Royal**. Head left on George Street. Follow along the waterfront. You are now on the oldest town street in the country! The **Farmer's Hotel** is the oldest building in English Canada. Numerous museums and interesting buildings line the streets, demanding inspection after your tour.

0.9 (0.5)   **LEFT** St. Anthony (at hardware store).

1.3 (0.8)   **LEFT** #1 (at Fire Station). Cross Annapolis Basin. **Annapolis Royal Tidal Power Plant** demonstrates the generation of energy from the immense Fundy tides. Tourism information available (free 532-5454).

Road curves to right

SIDE TRIP: Port Royal- "The Beginings of Canada": To the left, is a quiet road along the north shore of Annapolis Basin. It leads to **Port Royal Habitation**. This National Historic Site, about 10.5 km (6.5 mi.) out is where **Samuel de Champlain** established the first European settlement north of Florida. Here stands an exact reconstruction. Mic Mac natives became the first North Americans to recieve a European style education. The **Order of Good Cheer**, North America's first social club, started within its walls, and invites you to become a member (free admission 532-2898).

At the very start of this road is **North Hills Museum** (part of the Nova Scotia Museum Complex- no charge). This 18th century home displays an outstanding collection of Georgian furnishings, ceramics, glass, and silver. On the way to the habitation, you will pass the historic village of **Granville Ferry**. Once connected with Annapolis Royal by a ferry, many old Victorian houses line the road. You are now on a road which was once part of the original "pony express" route. Messages would be relayed from ocean steamers arriving at Halifax by horse along this road. At Victoria Beach they would be sent to New Brunswick and points further on. Finally, you reach the end of the road. You can see why the area's tidal power project was built. Here, where the North Mountain halts abruptly, Digby Gut, a narrow passage exists before starting again, as Digby Neck. At tide times you can see just how much water flows in and out of this bay. Passenger ferries regularly go through here on several daily trips from Saint John, NewBrunswick. Digby, and the ferry dock, seem so close from here, but actually, they represent almost an entire day's bike ride.

32

4.1 (2.5)   **LEFT** Parker's/ Delap Cove (at Irving station). You soon arrive at the famous Bay of Fundy. Even in the most sunny and warmest parts of the summer, just up and over the ridge of the valley, the shores of the bay can be cool with mist or fog.

10.3 (6.4)   **RIGHT** (at Olco station at Parker's Cove). You now follow the shore road along the bay. A much more protected coast than the Atlantic, along the cliffs are pools, which lie full between visiting tides, providing varieties of coastal habitats.

SIDE TRIP- Delap's Cove: Going westward, a roller coaster road runs to Delap Cove. This once was a thoroughfare in the early 1800's for freed slaves from the United States. These pioneers faced a brutal existance here on the shore. Enduring the hardships of Fundy's exposed conditions, stone walls and foundations remain here as a testament to their hard work and spirit. Groomed trails wander along the coast. 12.1 km (7.4 mi.) long, one features Bohaker brook, which plunges 15 metres (48 ft.) into Bohaker Cove. One trail offers glances over the bay, where draggers of Digby's world famous scallop fleet may be at work.

SIDE TRIP- Hampton Wharf: A sign announces it as Hampton Beach, but there isn't much of a swimming area). Pleasant spot to relax on the wharf and watch the boats come and go.

SIDE TRIP/ SHORT-CUT- Valleyview Provincial Park/ Bridgetown: On the way up the ridge, and before Valleyview Provincial Park is a "magnetic hill". You may feel that you have gone up an incline, without pedalling. The illusion is given from the land's terrain, that you are going uphill, when actually you are going down. The look-off from here takes in a panorama of the meandering Annapolis River, deep valley, and patchwork of verdant fields far in the distance.

36.8 (22.9)   **LEFT** go down hill to Port Lorne. Turn at village and climb steep hill to ridge.

42.8 (26.6)   **LEFT** at top of hill. Follow pavement.

44.6 (27.7)   **LEFT** at old Mount Hanley Schoolhouse

57.3 (35.6)   **LEFT** #362 downhill into Margaretville, a pretty village on the bay, with a large general store

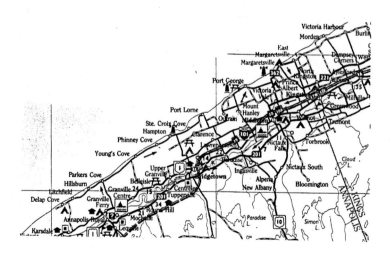

33

Taking the cure

The native Mic Mac believed strongly in the healing powers of mineral springs. They would journey to the Annapolis Valley to drink the water, and bathe in mud saturated with it, to cure skin ailments. In 1817, the owner of the land on which mineral springs were located at Spa Springs began to promote its healing virtues. Over time, more and more visitors arrived to *"take the cure"*. From all over Eastern Canada and New England they came, including those willing to pay big money to delay the ravages of time.

After a number of years, a new and greatly enlarged Spa Springs Hotel was built. Sporting Victorian architecture, the large resort could house 200 guests. They paid $8 to $12 each per week- a great deal of money in 1880- to drink and bathe in its healing waters. The surrounding outdoor gardens would feature lawn games, such as croquet, quoits, and tennis, played with all the airs of a British estate. On the grounds at any time could be seen those of fortune and influence. Samuel Cunard, the founder of Cunard Steamship Lines, Joseph Howe, a very influential early Nova Scotian politician, beer baron Alexander Keith, clergymen, New England manufacturers, among others, were to be seen arriving at the spa.

It was the first big health craze, and Nova Scotians were in on it in a big way. Then, like today, money was to be made in serving human yearnings for health, beauty, and eternal youth. Even more visitors began streaming to the spa. The most famous of whom was most certainly Prince George of Wales (later to become King George V), who is said to have visited in disguise.

The endorsements stretched belief. Amongst the royalty and well-heeled, a horse was registered for a stay at the spa. About to be destroyed, it could no longer support itself with its poor legs. It is reported that after drinking pails of the spring water, and having a treatment of mud, it grew strong. It not only went on to live a long life- but to win horse races. An old war veteran with a cork leg was said to have bathed there. The claim was made that flesh grew over the cork until no one could tell the difference between the artificial leg and the real one. And so the stories went.

In 1889, the Spa Springs Hotel burned. The springs soon returned to nature, beneath the ground. Today, it seems as if nothing had ever happened, not a sign can be seen, except the hidden spring waters occaisionally bubbling to the surface.

61.6 (38.3)   RIGHT Go up hill onto ridge (you can also carry on through the village and then go up).

Come down hill into valley. Pass #221 on your left.

69.3 (43.1)   RIGHT Spa Springs/ Clarence Road (just before road). **Connection point with Tour 6**

SIDETRIP- Kingston/ Greenwood: Going straight ahead instead of turning will take you into Kingston. It has services, such as Andy's Bike shop, a grocery store, a fruit stand, and a restaurant. Across the river is Greenwood. It is a major base of the Canadian Air Force. There are fast food outlets and a Tim Horton's coffee shop. Near the river is a pleasant break spot.

77.1 (47.9)   LEFT #362. Head into Middleton. The town has services including stores and restaurant.

80.3 (49.9)   RIGHT #1

80.4 (50.0)   LEFT #10 at Needs store.

Cross bridge and go straight at yellow flashing light.

82.8 (51.5)   RIGHT #201. Expect rolling hills, as the road toys with climbing South Mountain. Since the building of the tidal power project at Annapolis Royal, the river has not been the same. Once the water was a muddy brown, churned up daily by the incoming tide. The banks are now turning green with foilage.

Bridgetown will approach just off to the right. Located at the head of navigation on the Annapolis River, it may seem strange among the farms and orchards, but this was a shipbuilding centre during the "*Age of Sail*". The homes around this small town attest to its prosperous past. There are stores and restaurant in town. Jubilee Park along the bank makes a good rest spot.

At Centerlea, **Bloody Creek National Historic Site** marks where British forces were ambushed by the French and Mic Mac natives. Britain and France were engaged in a struggle for control of the North American continent. A team of English soldiers from Annapolis Royal were on a search for missing compatriots. As the soldiers reached and began to cross the creek, a group of Acadians and their Indian allies, who had hidden themselves in the undergrowth, opened a deadly fire. Taken by surprise, the troops, new arrivals just conscripted from Ireland, went down quickly. Twenty -four of them were killed instantly. The British, with their bright red coats, and regimented style were easily spotted and susceptible to surprise attack. After initial castrastophe, they batteled back bravely, storming the Acadians, and forcing them to flee into the woods. Incidents like this went on continously for one and a half centuries. It illustrates for you the bitterness, the violence, and the bloodshed which comprise the early chapters of Nova Scotia's history.

Tupperville, as the name may suggest, is derived in honour of early Prime Minister **Charles Tupper**. **Tupperville School Museum** is occasionally open, depicting a one-room schoolhouse of the early 1870's. It is operated by members of the local historic society, who have supplied the old desks, books, and momentos. Occasional treats are offered for sale, and a home-made ice cream party is held in late July (free admission; upkeep donations appreciated).

126.4 (78.6)   RIGHT #8 Lequille is the site of the first water-powered mill in North America, built by **Poutrincourt**, the French explorer in 1607, A recently built structure has been decorated to resemble the original mill. It has hand-split cedar shingle roof and the sides are faced with old brick of a type made during the 1600's (off-route, 1.5 km to the left).

Head into Annapolis Royal. Along the road in are immense Victorian homes. Some are now part of the village's large selection of bed and breakfasts. Note to your left the grounds of the **Annapolis Royal Historic Gardens**. An immense amount of effort goes into maintaining this series of theme gardens.

127.8 (79.5)   CROSS highway #1

128.0 (79.6)   END Fort Anne, Annapolis Royal

Accommodation

Bread and Roses Inn Richard and Monica Cobb. 82 Victoria St., Box 177, Annapolis Royal, NS B0S 1A0 (902) 532-5727 No smoking
Garrison House Inn Patrick Redgrave. 350 St. George St. Box 108, Annapolis Royal, NS B0S 1A0. Registered historic property.
The Poplars Bed and Breakfast Syd and Iris Williams. 124 Victoria St., Box 277, Annapolis Royal, NS B0S 1A0 (902) 532-7936. No smoking.
The Queen Anne Inn Leslie Langille. 494 Upper St. George St., Annapolis Royal, NS B0S 1A0 (902) 532-7850. Registered historic property; no smoking.
St. George House Bed and Breakfast Donna and Michael Susnick. 548 Upper St. George St., Box 34, Annapolis Royal, NS B0S 1A0 (902) 532-5286; (902) 425-5656. No smoking. Registered historic property.
The Turret Bed and Breakfast Barb and George Dunlop. 372 St. George St., Annapolis Royal, NS B0S 1A0. Registered historic property
Mount Hanley Austria Inn Erwin and Maria Schnetzer. Mount Hanley Rd., RR 1, Middleton, NS B0S 1P0 (902) 825-3744. On downhill to Port George
Best Western Aurora Inn 831 Main St., Kingston, NS B0P 1R0 9902) 765-3306
Sweet Dreams Bed and Breakfast Barbara and Arthur Leduc. Box 1928, Greenwood, NS B0P 1N0 (902) 847-1822. In Greenwood, near Kingston
Morse Century Farm Bed and Breakfast Dick and Barbara Morse. Box 220, Middleton, NS B0S 1P0 (902) 825-4600. Near Middleton.
Fundy Spray Motel 443 Main Street, Box 609, Middleton, NS B0S 1P0 (902) 825-3424
Mid-Valley Motel 121 Main St., P.O. Box 1312, Middleton, NS B0S 1P0, (902) 825-3433
Orchard Queen Motel 431 Main Street, Box 249, Middleton, NS B0S 1P0 (902) 825-4801
Victorian Inn Bed and Breakfast P.O. Box 1665, 145 Commercial St., Middleton, NS B0S 1P0, (902) 825-6424
White's Motel and Cottages George White. RR 1, Wilmot, NS, B0P 1W0 (902) 825-4380.
Alberta's Place Bed and Breakfast Alberta Dumas. 670 Main St. West, RR1, Lawrencetown, NS B0S 1M0. (902) 584-7222
Bridgetown Motor Inn 83 Granville St. East, Box 453, Bridgetown, NS B0S 1C0 (902) 665-4403
Carlton Motel and Cabins Lynda Barkhouse. RR3, 4101 Hwy 201, Bridgetown, NS B0S 1C0 (902) 665-4716. On route #201
Cherryhill Bed and Breakfast RR#4, Bridgetown, NS B0S 1C0 (902) 665-4572. 1 km (0.6 mi.) from town.
Chesley House Bed and Breakfast 304 Granville St. Bridgetown, NS B0S 1C0 (902) 665-2904. No smoking
Gingham Dog Bed and Breakfast Mavis Thwaites. 325 Granville St. East, Bridgetown, NS B0S 1C0 (902) 665-2786
Newcombe Brook Farm Bed and Breakfast Ted and Louise Sanderson, RR 1, Box 1170, Granville Ferry, NS B0S 1K0 (902) 665-2988. Located 400 metres (0.3 mi.) west of Bridgetown on route #1.
Best View Acres Bed and Breakfast Ester and Alan Spurr. Box 28, Annapolis Royal, NS B0S 1A0 (902) 532-5307; At Round Hill, between Bridgetown and Annapolis Royal on route #201.

Camping

Dunromin Campsite Joe and Dora Yeoman, P.O. Box 5, Granville Ferry, NS B0S 1K0 532-2808; 532-5181; close to Annapolis Royal.
Fundy Trail Campground Alton and Twila Calnek, P.O. Box 95, Port Williams, NS B0P 1T0 532-7711; 542-3295. Located off-route at Delaps Cove, along Fundy shore. Very good hiking trails close by.
Valleyview Park Province of Nova Scotia. Open and wooded sites on North Mountain ridge, 5 km (3 mi.) from Bridgetown. No reservations; no showers; spectacular view from park over the valley.
Fundy View Campground Don and Sandra Casey. R.R. #1, Middleton, NS, B0S 1P0. At Port George on Fundy shore; showers; grocery items
Orchard Queen Motel and Campground 431 Main St., P.O. Box 249, Middleton, NS B0S 1P0, (902) 825-4801; showers; close to town
Sunnyvale Estate Campground P.O. Box 2039, East Dartmouth, NS B2W 3X8 825-4533; 435-0307. On ridge, not far from Margaretsville
Bayview Farm and Campground John and Sandra Chute. R.R. 1, Margaretsville, NS B0S 1N0 (902) 765-3461
White's Tent and Trailer Park George White. R.R. #1, Wilmot, NS B0P 1W0. Showers; laundromat. Located just east of Middleton. on highway #1.
Holiday Haven Camping Park Gwen Hudgins. R.R. #1, Kingston, NS B0P 1R0, Showers; laundromat; trail

lantic Canada
cling Festival

Back roads and blossoms-
heart of the valley

Tour 6   East Valley

Tour at a glance

START/ FINISH	Kentville
OTHER STARTING POINTS	Kingston; Berwick
DISTANCE	104 km (65 mi.) Many short cut options
DIRECTION	Clockwise
TERRAIN	Flat as Nova Scotia gets
CLIMATE	Expect warm/ hot temperatures with humidity
NOTES	Expect farm dogs
	Exercise caution passing tractors on back roads
TRAFFIC	Low to Moderate
REST STOPS	Silver Lake
FOOD	Kentville (R)(G)(C); Somerset (C); Grafton (C)
REPAIRS	Wolfville (off-route); Kingston (off-route)
TOURISM	Bridgetown 665-4585
HOSPITAL	Kentville
AMBULANCE	Kentville
POLICE	Kentville: Kingston/ Greenwood (off-route)

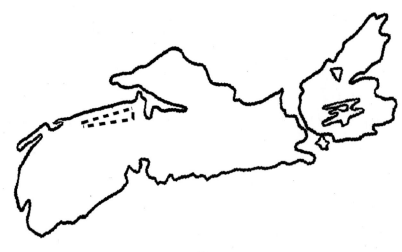

O n this pleasant rolling tour you will pass through orchards and fertile farmland on the floor of the Annapolis Valley. You begin by following a meandering and quiet tarmac road. After a very ort turn brings you back on route #221, past prosperous ple orchards and views up the valley. Since there are so any short-cuts using side roads, you can cross over at merous points, tailoring the route to your taste.

'e will go clockwise. This route will go westward into e valley along the cosy and protected Brooklyn Road to inimize headwinds. Return will be on the more open 221 to take advantage of them.

ur tour begins in Kentville. To connect from Wolfville, rst go to Port Williams, then turn left and go along elcher Street to Oakdene Street, and into Kentville. It is st as easy to start the loop at Kingston. Berwick is at id point. You can from here, do the entire loop, but also) it in two halves, or just one section. This enables this ur to be tasted by most cyclists.

Most people along the way trace their ancestors back to several immigrations of New Englanders, known as the Planters. Small communities lie every few kilometres. These offer comforts not found in other regions of Nova Scotia. Villages and general stores follow the route, and not far away on highway #1. For this reason, this is perhaps the best very early/ late season ride in the province. Some of the valley's roads are called "streets". Don't worry, it does not mean this is a huge urban area. Its just a reminder of the over-enthusiasm of the original settlers.

This is the warmest part of Nova Scotia. Both mountain ridges, while not extremely high, still manage keep warm air contained in the valley. Here lie the region's famous apple orchards, in late May a riot of pink and white blossoms.

Autumn is perfect here, as trees with multi-coloured leaves cover the valley. Harvest time in October still offers exceptional cycling - falling leaves, wagons filled with pumpkins and plenty of places to get warm.

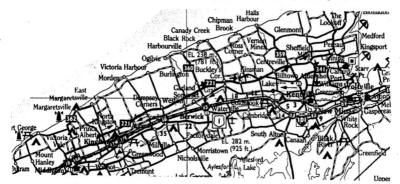

START	At the corner of Main Street (#1) and Cornwallis Street in Kentville (an eclectic castle-like building which was once a hotel, is on the corner). Start by heading up Cornwallis Street. Cross over Cornwallis River. Extending along the river is a 400 metre (0.3 mi.) path, the remains of a road Acadians once used to haul hay from their dykes.
0.5 (0.3)	LEFT Brooklyn Road at Shell station, and tire store just after bridge. A connection from Wolfville meets here. Go straight, at times this road will try to throw you off, with turns to larger roads leading off it. A waterfowl area is just to your left as you leave town. Further on, note the tank crossing areas and their impressions on the sandy soil as you pass Aldershot Military Reserve. Small red fox are often sighted in this area of the valley.

Grafton makes a good rest stop at the store.

Note: The following turn in the route is often missed, watch for it after Grafton!

| 20.9 (13.0) | RIGHT at Shaw Road |
| 37.1 (23.1) | LEFT small jog in road |

39

SIDE TRIP- Kingston/ Greenwood: To the left, by way of Bishop Mountain or Marshall Roads, there is only about a 2 km (1.2 mi.) stretch into Kingston. You will find there a few stores, a grocery, fruit stand, restaurant, and bicycle shop. Nearby Greenwood, a primary base of the Canadian Air Force, you will find a number of fast food outlets and a coffee shop.

37.3 (23.2)   **RIGHT**

43.9 (27.3)   **RIGHT** Margaretville Road. **Connection point with Tour 5.** This marks the turning point of the loop. A store is on the left. Go part way up hill. You will turn before it gets steep.

45.8 (28.5)   **RIGHT #221.** Following the base of North Mountain, you will now go along a series of small rolling hills.

75.8 (47.1)   **LEFT** Bligh Road at gas station church, and Boates U-Pick.. Watch for fresh honey for sale. Bees thrive on the thousands of fruit trees in the area demanding pollen. You can also taste the freshest possible sweet apple cider.

76.7 (47.7)   **RIGHT** Woodville Road (first paved road)

80.4 (50.0)   **LEFT #221.** Morton's General store ia on your left. A good rest spot is coming up, **Silver Lake Park** offers a small swimming area and grassy field for lunch

       SHORT-CUT: Lakewood Road to the right will go directly toward Kentville. It goes through an old tobacco producing region. Turn right at the flashing light on #359 toward town.

87.2 (54.2)   **LEFT #221** Centreville

87.4 (54.3)   **RIGHT #221** after short jog

88.6 (55.1)   **LEFT** Eaton Branch

89.6 (55.7)   **RIGHT** Baines Road. **Atlanta** was named in the mid- 1800's as the name of a new train depot. Follow through to Sheffield Mills. The road will twist and turn.

93.2 (57.9)   **RIGHT** Sheffield Mills Road. At this point, there is a confusing layout of roads. Signposting is limited. Do not be surprised if you become temporarily lost. This area has some Bald Eagles. They are most plentiful in late autumn, when many arrive from Cape Breton for winter nesting.

94.2 (58.6)   **RIGHT #221**

95.3 (59.3)   **LEFT** Middle Dyke Road. Continue across Saxon Street.

97.6 (60.7)   **LEFT #341** at church for very short jog.

97.7 (60.8)   **RIGHT** Middle Dyke Road. You now cross a marshland around the Canard River.

       CROSS the intersection at Chipman's Corner. To your left on the corner is a very old Loyalist cemetery. Among those buried here is **Abraham Gesner** (1797- 1864). The discoverer of **kerosene oil,** he dramatically changed 19th century society. More important to us as cyclists, however, is the fact he also helped develop **asphalt paving!** He was a major player in creating the black ribbons that today criss-cross our globe! Thank him as you ride by.

101.8 (63.3)   **RIGHT** Mee Road. Turn left here if heading for Wolfville.

102.9 (64.0)   **RIGHT** Belcher Street. Belcher turns to Oakdene.

103.8 (64.5)   **LEFT** Cornwallis Street. Cross bridge

103.9 (64.6)   **RIGHT** Aberdeen Street. Kentville has one-way streets. follow around the block.

104.1 (64.7)   **LEFT** Main Street

104.4 (64.9)   **END**

Accommodation (see Tour 10 for Kentville/ Wolfville area)

Berwick Inn Bruce and Anne Drummond. 160 Commercial Street, Berwick, NS B0P 1E0 538-8532. Short distance off-route from Somerset.
Rice's Motel 183 Commercial Street, P.O. Box 201, Berwick, NS B0P 1E0 538-3156. Short distance off-route from Somerset.
Sweet Dreams Bed and Breakfast Barbara and Arthur Leduc. P.O. Box 1928, Greenwood, NS B0P 1N0. Off route in Auburn.
Best Western Aurora Inn Maureen Banyard. 831 Main Street, P.O. Box 609, Kingston NS B0P 1R0 765-8228. On highway #1.

Camping

Holiday Haven Gwen Hudgins. R.R. 1, Kingston, NS, B0P 1R0, 765-2830; showers; pool; laudromat
Klahanie Kamping Robert and Alice Montgomery. 1144 Victoria Road, P.O. Box 190, Aylesford, NS, B0P 1C0 847-9316; 847-9411
The Plantation Campground W.H. Scrymgeour. 6316 yukon St., Halifax, NS B3L 1G1; 538-8888; off-season 423-5105; showers; laundromat

Atlantic Canada
Cycling Festival

Orchards to ocean

Tour 7   Hall's Harbour

Tour at a glance

START/ FINISH	Wolfville
OTHER STARTING POINT	Kentville
DISTANCE	65 km (40 mi.)
DIRECTION	Counter- clockwise
TERRAIN	Two large climbs on ridge
CLIMATE	Hot and humid in valley; cool ocean air, often damp and foggy in Hall's Harbour
NOTES	Bring jacket or sweater- the air at Hall's Harbour is cool
TRAFFIC	Moderate
REST STOP	Hall's Harbour
FOOD	Wolfville (R)(G)(C); Hall's Harbour (C); Centreville(C)
REPAIRS	Wolfville
TOURISM	Wolfville 542-7000
HOSPITAL	Wolfville; Kentville (off-route)
AMBULANCE	Wolfville; Kentville (off-route)
POLICE	Wolfville; Kentville (off-route)

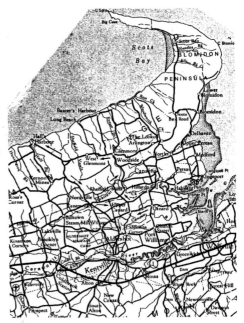

V isit one of the prettiest villages in Nova Scotia! Halls Harbour is an important lobster port. It is visited twice daily by the Bay of Fundy's huge tides, which leave the boats ~gh and dry. Your route will follow pleasant ~untry roads on your way to the bay. Cosy ~rmhouses lie surrounded by cultivated fields, and ~uit-laden orchards. On top of the ridge before your ~scent you will pass mostly woods.

~ou will face two big hills. Both involve negotiating ~e North Mountain. There is only one store after ~rt Wiliams, one in Hall's Harbour itself, so backup ~acks are recommended (both could be closed).

~ increase the length of the ride consider adding a ~sit to Baxter's Harbour. A waterfall there flows ~rectly into the bay, an attractive yet unvisited spot.

~ connect this tour from Kentville, go eastward on ~elcher Street to Port Williams and there meet our ~ute.

START	Begin on Front Street (just below Main). A health food store sits just across the street. You will be heading south-west. Just before your first turn is a swifts nest.
0.2 (0.1)	**LEFT** Elm St.
0.3 (0.2)	**RIGHT** Main St. (#1 -traffic next 3 km). A popular fruit stand is to your left as you leave town.
3.4 (2.1)	**RIGHT** #358 at Irving Station. CAUTION: dangerous train tracks
5.3 (3.3)	**LEFT** Belcher St. at Port Williams. The village was once a busy port, loading valley fruit and other produce, before the era of super-highways. Today it is a major poultry centre.
6.8 (4.2)	**RIGHT** Sutton
	Merge with #358
	Cross Saxon Street and #221. This region, around **Sheffield Mills**, is a nesting site for Bald Eagles. These magnificent birds of prey arrive from Cape Breton in Autumn.
₄8.8 (11.7)	**RIGHT** Bains (at end of road)

43

20.3 (12.6)   LEFT Gospel Woods

Keep left and head for the ridge. In comparison, the climb is one of the easiest of those along the North Mountain. Some cyclists may still expect to walk up.

24.0 (14.9)   LEFT Glenmont at top of ridge

SIDE TRIP: Baxter Harbour is a quiet village with a waterfall flowing into the bay. The turn is 1 km ahead to the right.

28.8 (17.6)   RIGHT #359 Hall's Harbour Road. Descend down to the Bay of Fundy. In only minutes you will experience a change from the warm micro-climate of the valley's ridge, to the often bracing sea air of the bay. **CAUTION:** Be aware of the sharp turn at the bottom of the hill into the village!

34.2 (17.9)   Lunch at Hall's Harbour. Twice attacked by pirates in the 1800's, a third raid saw the villagers victorious, seizing a chest of gold. Being "blood money" the villagers refused to use it, instead burying it on the shore. The exact spot has over the generations been forgotten, the treasure never recovered.

The local lobster pound welcomes visitors daily. You can inspect their holding pens. The store also at times has *dulse* for sale. Some say dulse, a type of dried seaweed from the bay, is an aquired taste. **Note:** If exploring along the coast, take extreme care concerning the bay's tides. The people at the store will know the current times.

After your break, continue on the other side of the harbour. The road back up North Mountain, after an initial shock will be gradual.

39.9 (24.3)   LEFT Brow Road (at end of road)

42.1 (25.7)   RIGHT #359. **CAUTION:** Steep downhill! One of the fastest descents in the province will take you into Centreville. The only turn coming down is a gradual bend to the right. Check your brakes, baggage, and racks. Please exercise care.

DETOUR: Thorpe Road is a dirt lane to your right at the bottom of the hill (just where you will probably be moving too fast to want to stop). If you take this road for a few kilometers you will pass the vineyards of Grand Pre Wines. Pleasant farms and orhards lead you towards Woodville and Kinsman's Corner. If you have a Mountain bike and want a perverse challenge, try going up the road to the right 7.1 km (4.4 mi) in! Look for the small garage with a "cow" weathervane.

46.6 (28.9)   LEFT #221 at Centreville

48.8 (28.9)   RIGHT Gibson Woods. Gibson Woods Road becomes #341 at UpperDyke Village.

53.2 (33.0)   LEFT Church Street.

Cross the next intersection (Chipman's Corner). A very old pioneer Loyalist cemetary is at the corner.

55.1 (34.2)   RIGHT Tiny Parish

56.6 (25.2)   LEFT Belcher Street

60.3 (37.5)   RIGHT #358 at Port Williams. Just after crossing the bridge, look to your left. You can see the earthen dykes built by the Acadians, to reclaim the marsh. You can go all the way to Wolfville on this, although it is a bit too rough to ride on road bikes.

62.1 (38.5)   LEFT #1 at Irving station (Main St. -traffic next 3 Km)

65.2 (40.5)   LEFT Centre St.

65.3 (40.6)   RIGHT Front St.

65.4 (40.7)   END

Accommodations (see Tour 10)

lantic Canada
ycling Festival

*Tree-shaded lanes and old graceful
houses- wandering through apple country*

Tour 8   Starr's Point

Tour at a glance

START/ FINISH	Wolfville
OTHER STARTING POINT	Kentville
DISTANCE	42 km (25 mi.) (short cuts-available)
DIRECTION	Counter-Clockwise
TERRAIN	Flat- Slightly rolling
CLIMATE	Warm temperatures with sea breezes
TRAFFIC	Low to Moderate
REST STOPS	Prescott House; Canning; Canard Picnic Park
FOOD	Wolfville (R)(G)(C); Canning (R)(G)(C)
REPAIRS	Wolfville
TOURISM	Wolfville 542-7000
HOSPITAL	Wolfville; Kentville (off-route)
AMBULANCE	Wolfville; Kentville (off-route)
POLICE	Wolfville; Kentville (off-route)

This very enjoyable tour cycles through very old farms and ports of the past. It passes graceful old farmhouses and scented orchards. Tall old trees line the winding road along the shore of Minas Basin. At times they offer canopies of foilage, shade from the valley sun.

Consider this tour for a leisurely outing. Watch for birds, take pictures, and stop for plenty of breaks. It includes a visit to the graceful grounds and period rooms of Prescott house. A large Georgian era estate, you can relax amid its gardens, rare shrubs, and tall trees. Each area of Nova Scotia has its own distinct background- Scottish in Cape Breton, Germanic in Lunenburg, and others Acadian. The area of this attractive ride owes its heritage to the North-East United States. Visitors from New England should find it interesting to learn the background. Most people are direct descendants of a group known as the New England Planters. The English as we know well, forced out the Acadians in the famous expulsion. They did so as they were afraid the French population would not at some point remain neutral, and

disrupt their control of North America, through contrrol of Nova Scotia. Immediately upon their evacuation, New Englanders (as well as others) were offered the vacated farm lands. It was like a gold rush , as thes prime sites required zero clearing of land. Like most of the early arrivals, they were of various religious sects, many frowned upon in Europe. They brought with them these beliefs to the Annapolis Valley.

Some of the valley's roads are called "streets". Don't worry, it does not mean this is a huge urban area. Its just a reminder of the overenthusiasm of the original settlers.

Our tour begins in downtown Wolfville. To connect from Kentville, go eastward on Belcher St., which connects onto this route.

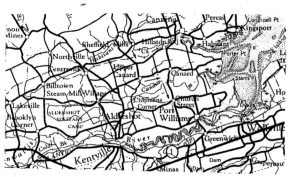

START Begin on Front Street. (just below Main St.) A health food store sits just across the street. You will be heading south-west. Just before your first turn is a swifts nest

0.2 (0.1) **LEFT** Elm St.

0.3 (0.2) **RIGHT** Main St. (#1 -traffic next 3 km). A popular fruit stand is to your left as you leave town.

3.4 (2.1) **RIGHT** #358 at Irving Station. **CAUTION:** dangerous train tracks

5.2 (3.2) **RIGHT** Starrs Point Rd. (High St. by church- towards Prescott House). These lowlands are home to a great variety of birds, including at certain times of the year, hawks and eagles.

7.7 (4.8) **LEFT** Starrs Point Road. A monument to the New England Planters is to the right.

Prescott House soon emerges amid tall trees on your left. **Charles Prescott** introduced the popular Gravenstein apple among others from here. Antiques fill the building (free admission 542-3984).

Stay on pavement at sharp turn.

47

10.3 (6.4)   **RIGHT** at T-intersection by Old Town Plot Schoolhouse. You turn corner and are on Church St.

10.9 (6.8)   **RIGHT** Wellington Dyke

13.3 (8.2)   **RIGHT** (at yellow house after short hill)

15.0 (9.3)   **LEFT** Saxon Street (first left turn). Ahead of where you turn the road dead-ends. This is the ghost port of Pickett's Wharf. From here are splendid views of Blomidon Mountain. The focal point from all directions, this small, but dramatic peak rises up out of the Bay of Fundy with sharp red soil cliffs.

17.2 (10.6)   **RIGHT** Canning Aboiteau. Built in 1812 to extend the dykes built by the Acadians, this dyke has a gate, known as an aboiteau, which opens to allow fresh water to drain out at low tide, while preventing incoming high tides to go in.

18.4 (11.4)   **LEFT** #221

SIDE TRIP- Kingsport: Just beyond where you turn is the once busy port of Kingsport. At one time, when most cargos went by ship, most of the Annapolis Valley's apples shipped through the port. Kingsport Beach offers at high tide a small swimming area.

Canning is the largest community on this route. Originally it was known as Apple Tree Landing. Ships and trains once pulled in and out to load valley fruit and produce. Trucking and changing preserving techniques dealt a blow to the village. Today it is a cosy tree-lined place, demanding you to stop and take a rest. Take advantage of the grocery store, restaurant and tea house during your visit.

They say that Canning was "made" by the potato. One year a potato disease ruined the entire New England crop. The famine sent the price of the vegetable sky high, and the renowned growers of the valley cashed in. Canning became a boom town. Ships stood ten deep at the wharves to load their potatoes, with ox-carts jamming the roadways as the farmers brought the potatoes in.

Canning was also visited by disaster. One summer evening a fire broke out in the village. Quickly spreading through the dry wooden structures, the only escape from the flames lay on the river. Hundreds of villagers poured down to the water, carrying children and household goods. Only the day before a new ship was launched, yet to be named. When the fire raced through the village the new vessel became crammed with people and goods, floating on the river away from the flames. Soon after the disaster they named the vessel. Suitably, it was christened *"The Escape."*

Carry on westward on #221 past Sheffield St. and Irving station

25.3 (15.7)   **LEFT** Turn with #221 at Sheffield Mills. This region, is a winter nesting area for the Bald Eagle. These birds arrive from Cape Breton in autumn.

26.3 (16.3)   **LEFT** Middle Dyke Rd.

CROSS Saxon St.

28.7 (17.8)   **LEFT** #341 at large church.

31.6 (19.6)   **RIGHT** at #358 is a shaded picnic park is at the corner

Continue on #358. Pass through Port Williams. Just after crossing the bridge, look to your left. You can see the earthen dykes built by the Acadians, to reclaim the marsh. You can go all the way to Wolfville on this, although it is a bit too rough to ride on road bikes.

38.7 (24.0)   **LEFT** #1 at Irving station (Main St. -traffic next 3 Km)

41.8 (25.9)   **LEFT** Centre St.

41.9 (26.0)   **RIGHT** Front St.

42.0 (26.1)   **END**

Accommodation / Camping (See Tour 10)

A seacoast mountain of natural beauty and Mic Mac legend

Tour 9   Blomidon

Tour at a glance

START/ FINISH	Wolfville
OTHER STARTING POINT	Kentville
DISTANCE	71 km (44 mi.)
DIRECTION	Counter-Clockwise
TERRAIN	Very hilly
CLIMATE	Expect warm temperatures with humidity
TRAFFIC	Moderate
REST STOPS	Prescott House; Look-Off; Canning; Canard Picnic Park
FOOD	Wolfville (R)(G)(C); Port Williams (C); Look-Off (R-summer only); Canning (G)(R)(C)
REPAIRS	Wolfville
TOURISM	Wolfville 542-7000
HOSPITAL	Wolfville; Kentville (off-route)
AMBULANCE	Wolfville; Kentville (off-route)
POLICE	Wolfville; Kentville (off-route)

Blomidon dominates the landscape. Dramatically rising out of the Bay of Fundy, it stands as the focal point from all directions. From within the Annapolis Valley, from along the coast of the Noel Shore, and fron across the Bay of Fundy along the Cobequid Hills- all look up to this small, but very beautiful mountain.

Two days will give you time to fully explore this wonderful corner. Bring a book and a lunch and stay here on the mountain top as long as you can. Wise visitors will arrange an overnight stay at the campground, so that they can watch the spectacular sunrise from this lofty vantage point.

You will be following Tour 8 until reaching Kingsport. It has further details on the first area of the tour.

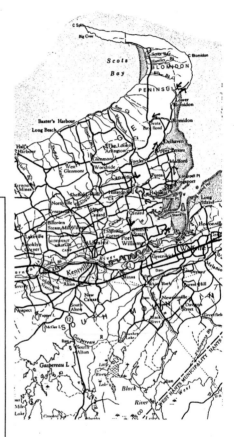

The legend of Glooscap

The first inhabitants of Nova Scotia, the Mic Mac, believed that this region was home to Glooscap, the legendary man-god. From atop Blomidon Mountain he held court. Looking down, he controlled the mighty Fundy tides, the highest in the world. Peaking several stories high they fall so much as to leave freighters and fishing boats stranded on the mud.

Along the shores of Minas Basin, he, and his animal friends lived in almost perfect harmony. Across the bay, near Advocate Harbour- he made his herb garden in the fertile soil and there set out feasts for his "children". The animals were his friends, but one or two became insolent and mischievous. When Beaver taunted his people, Glooscap's voice rose with the wind and he cast five huge clumps of mud at him. Islands rose from the sea, which today you can see from from the Cobequid shore near Economy and Five from Islands Provincial Park.

It was said that Glooscap scattered glowing jewels-jasper, agate, onyx, and amethyst along the shores for his grandmother. Rock-hounds from all over the world, amateurs and professionals alike, gather each year for the annual Rockhound Roundup to appreciate his gifts.

51

START	Front Street in wolfville (just below Main Street)
0.2 (0.1)	**LEFT** Elm St.
0.3 (0.2)	**RIGHT** Main St. (#1 -traffic next 3 km). A popular fruit stand is to your left as you leave town.
3.4 (2.1)	**RIGHT** #358 at Irving Station. Go into Port Williams.
5.2 (3.2)	**RIGHT** Starrs Point Rd. (High St. By church- towards Prescott House).
7.7 (4.8)	**LEFT** Starrs Point Rd. (Monument to the new England Planters is to the right).
10.3 (6.4)	**RIGHT** at T-intersection by Old Town Plot Schoolhouse. This is Church Street.
10.9 (6.8)	**RIGHT** Wellington Dyke
13.3 (8.2)	**RIGHT** (at yellow house after short hill)
15.0 (9.3)	**LEFT** Saxon Street (first left turn).
17.2 (10.6)	**RIGHT** Canning Aboiteau.
18.4 (11.4)	**RIGHT** #221 Go to very end of road in Kingsport. An old port, Kingsport was once a busy commercial centre. A four-masted barque of 2061 tons was built here in 1890, making it one of the largest wooden ships ever built.
22.7 (14.0)	**LEFT** short street in behind the beach
23.0 (14.3)	**LEFT**
23.2 (14.4)	**RIGHT** Medford Road
26.7 (16.5)	**LEFT** North Medford
28.0 (17.4)	**RIGHT** Jackson Barkhouse Road (you can ride on the dyke at the bottom of the hill).
28.9 (17.9)	**RIGHT** Blomidon Road. Along the rolling section approaching the hill are chicken and turkey farms. Continue along rolling hills to road's end. Enter **Blomidon Provincial Park** and go up hill. The hill is steep, and quite a challenge. If you would rather walk, you will reach the top reasonably quickly. Pass through the park gates and continue to the very end. The top of **Blomidon Mountain** rewards you with a stunning view of several counties. (If camping, try to get up early and go to the look-off for the morning sunrise over the bay). Interesting rocks are occasionally found here, a reminder of the region's past volcanic origin. Semi-precious gemstones amethysts and agates, can be discovered. There is a 9.6 km (6.0 mi.) trail system in the park, through the mountain top, with several scenic views over the bay (too rough for average mountain biking). Be certain of the tide times before heading out on it, or you could become stranded for hours. Another walking path follows along the shore.
38.8 (24.1)	**RETURN** down hill. CAUTION: Steep downhill with pedestrians at bottom
45.7 (28.4)	**RIGHT** Steward Mountain Rd. (dirt). Slated for paving (as it has been for years now), This dirt road is in good shape and will take you up on the ridge again. *Note:* Many cyclists opt to not carry on with the tour here, since they must face another hill, and do not want to leave the beauty of coast. It is recommended however, that you persevere and make the trip up. The climb is not that bad, especially considering what you will be rewarded with.
48.7 (30.20	**LEFT** #358 pavement resumes. You are now back on top of the ridge. You will know when you arrive at **Look-Off**. This famous photo spot takes in a sweeping panorama of the eastern Annapolis Valley. Spring sees the entire region an expanse of pink and white apple blossoms. In summer, you will view a productive patchwork of farms, and in autumn a spectacular view of the multi-coloured leaves. A small canteen is often open.
53.2 (33.0)	**LEFT** #358 (go down hill). Exercise Caution!
58.4 (36.3)	**RIGHT** #221 Main St. (at monument). Huge trees line the main street, demanding you to stop and take a rest. A grocery store is in the village.
59.1 (36.7)	**LEFT** #358 Sheffield Street (just past Irving station). Continue on #358 across Saxon Street. Cross #341 (small picnic park is at corner). Cross Church St.. Pass through Port Williams and cross the bridge. To your left are earthen dykes built by the Acadians, to reclaim the marsh. You can go all the way to Wolfville on this, although it is a bit too rough for road bikes.
68.1 (42.3)	**LEFT** #1 (Main St.-traffic next 3 Km)
71.2 (44.2)	**LEFT**
71.3 (44.3)	**RIGHT** Front St.
71.4 (44.4)	**END**

Accommodation / Camping (see Tour 10)

antic Canada
cling festival

Echoes of the Acadians in the land of Evangeline

Tour 10 Wolfville/Grand Pre

Tour at a glance

START/ FINISH	Wolfville
OTHER STARTING POINT	Grand Pre
DISTANCE	32 km (20 mi.)
DIRECTION	Counter-Clockwise
TERRAIN	Hilly
CLIMATE	Expect warm temperatures
TRAFFIC	Low
REST STOPS	Black Rock; Grand Pre
FOOD	Wolfville (R)(G)(C); Gaspereau (C); Melanson (C); Grand Pre (R)
REPAIRS	Wolfville
TOURISM	Wolfville 542-7000
HOSPITAL	Wolfville; Kentville (off-route)
AMBULANCE	Wolfville; Kentville (off-route)
POLICE	Wolfville; New Minas (R.C.M.P.); Kentville (off-route)

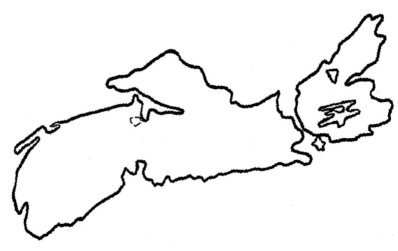

54

So much to see and do, for so little cycling! This is the land of **Evangeline**, celebrated in Longfellow's famous romantic poem. This tour's route winds its way through the pretty Gaspereau Valley. It leads by way of back roads, to Grand Pre National Historic Park. Here was executed the fateful orders to carry out the **Expulsion** of the Acadians. You may visit the chapel, which stands on the site where the notice was read, sending these settlers away from their homeland for refusing to swear allegiance to England.

The Gaspereau Valley is old Acadia. There is very little unsightly development here, just old farms, orchards, and trees. It is actually a "valley within a valley", just over the **Wolfville Ridge**, which separates it from the Annapolis Valley. The ridge is a climb, but by no means a mountain. About 150 metres (450 ft.) high, going up is broken into a couple of sections. If desired, they can he walked quite quickly and easily.

From Grand Pre Park the route will take a slightly different way of returning to Wolfville. It is possible to ride along the centuries old dyke, which heads directly into town. It is a dirt surface. and of course will not he in great condition if it has recently rained. If you desire to go directly back to Wolfville from Grand Pre, a short stretch on Main Street (#1) will take you in.

Welcome to Mud Creek

A peaceful, scholarly atmosphere greets you as you enter the town of Wolfville. An enchanting place of huge wooden homes, and tall stately trees, the small town provides a comfortable base to explore the eastern Annapolis Valley. The pace of the town is made for cyclists. The elm trees, along with the small shops create a "home away from home" feel. Its tiny downtown is largely free of commercial sleaze. Malls and fast-food strips are nowhere to be seen (they are out of town, down the road in New Minas).

It began as a little place named **Mud Creek**. In 1893 it became only the second incorporated town in Canada. But it happened without being christened as Mud Creek. It appears a judge's daughter became too embarrassed to tell others where she came from, and thus began a search for a more stately name.

Internationally famous artist **Alex Colville** has some of his high-realism work on display at the **Beveridge Arts Centre's** gallery at Acadia University. Also on display is the distinct maritime work of **Francis daSilva**. A native to Portugal, he spent most of his life painting in Hantsport, where he arrived as a stowaway.

Untrained as an artist, he painted in his own style, for the owner of the town's shipyards. **Acadia Unversity Art Gallery** is at the corner of Main Street and Highland Avenue (free 542-2201 ext. 373). The university also has a large pool which, at times, is open to the public. Dorms are available during the summer. Coming with a stay is a wide variety of recreational options, including the pool and gym.

On Front Street you will see a lone chimney. The purpose of this structure is as a swifts nest. Saved from a demolished warehouse, it was relocated to act as an attraction, in addition to saving their nest. A Wolfville phenomena occurs each evening, just before dark. At that time, hundreds of the birds appear. Whithin just a few seconds, they form a funnel and quickly flow inside for the night. Some town officials are now worried, however, that the swifts are losing interest in the chimney. Now that it has become a sanitized attraction some birds have already moved on, to other old warehouses.

55

START   Begin on Front Street (just below Main street). A health food store sits just across the road. You will be heading south-west. Just before your first turn is the swifts nest.

0.2 (0.1)   **LEFT** Elm Street

0.3 (0.2)   **RIGHT #1** (Main Street). Your next turn is by the church just ahead of you.

0.4 (0.3)   **LEFT** Highland Street. Go up the hill. You have had no time at all to warm up, but here is the biggest climb of your tour. To your right as you ride (or walk) is Acadia University.

Go under highway overpass. The road then turns to the right at the top of **Wolfville Ridge**. To your left at the turn is **Stiles Park**, for years the party spot for Acadia students. This first rest spot overlooks the **Gaspereau Valley**. Looking down, you will see where you will be in an hour or more. As you continue along the ridge, you are presented with views to the right as well, across the Annapolis Valley to the North Mountain.

NOTE: Stay on Ridge! When the road turns quickly downward, do not go down. Many cyclists fail to notice the road continuing on the other side and instinctively take the downhill, ending up in New Minas.

The road now zig-zags up the final section of WolfvilleRidge to take you to White Rock. A continuous view looks out over the eastern section of the Annapolis Valley. The road then descends its other side.

8.3 (5.1)   **LEFT** White Rock Rd. at flashing light.

SIDE TRIP- White Rock: If you keep going straight at the light there is a small lake. Just at the edge of the lake is a pathway. It leads a short way (there is a short set of steps) to a lovely lunch spot at an old water powerhouse. A dirt road leads from here uphill for 1 km, and then right for 2.4 km to Lumsden Pond and dam, where a swimming area has been set up. You could from there take Davison street (paved) 2.3 km more ahead, which will take you down Gaspereau Mountain into the Gaspereau Valley.

16.4 (10.2)   **RIGHT** Small jog in road at Melanson (named after the founder of Grand Pre). Opposite Melanson, at Simpson's Bridge is an old **Planter's** cemetery. The site also served as a **Mic Mac** encampment for an estimated one thousand years.

16.5 (10.3)   **LEFT** Toward Avonport

18.1 (11.2)   **LEFT** Grand Pre Road (just past Wallbrook Mountain Road). After going under the freeway, you will discover **Covenanter Church**. This simple but beautiful structure sitting in the shade was built by the New England Planters soon after their arrival. In excellent state of preservation, the door is sometimes open to allow visits. You may often meet bird watchers in the old Planter burying ground.

20.4 (12.7)   **CROSS Highway #1.** You will see directions to Grand Pre. Just to your left on Route 1, is Grand Pre Wines, Nova Scotia's first major winery. Visitors can visit the greenhouse, presshouse, and main cellar. Mitchell Hill Road, which soon crosses your path, is a pleasant Tree shaded lane which passes some Planter era homes. Grand Pre's most famous son is **Robert Laird Borden**, who grew up and taught at a school here. He went on from here to become Prime Minister. Eastward, where the road curves toward #1, a road left descends to Horton Landing. This was the landing place in 1760 for the New England Planters. Six boats of Connecticut families with all their possessions, including livestock, were transported here courtesy of the Nova Scotia government. They desired the Acadian lands filled as soon as possible. The first newcomers were quickly followed by thousands of more New Englanders.

21.4 (13.3)   **Grand Pre**, after Peggy's Cove, is Nova Scotia's most well known village. Here lies **Grand Pre National Historic Park** (free of charge).

Leaving the park you have two choices. You can head back along the way you came in, turning right just before #1 and go Mitchell Hill Rd., which connects you to the highway. You also have the option of continuing on this route, which will prove to be a little different. It will include a stretch of 200 year old earthen dykes. It is negotiable, even for road bikes, and side roads are available if you want a break. You should find it a rewarding ride or even walk. Don't expect to set any speed records. Since it is soft earth, it could be wet after a day of rain.

Begin by heading to the back of the park. You will see a sign, announcing that the next area you will pass through will be **below sea level!** 3,013 acres sit behind 8,675 m. (28,455) ft. of dyke. If you have an altimeter type speedometer, now is the time to test its accuracy!

24.1 (15.0)   **LEFT**

SIDE TRIP to the right by the church is a short road to Evangeline Beach, a small rest area with shallow flats.

Road turns to dirt

26.0 (16.1)   **LEFT** Onto dyke at shoreline. It is just before the road ends.

30.7 (18.7)   **End of dyke.** Dismount and cross rail track. Walk around car barrier. Before you leave this area, however, take a look around. See the water (mud, if it is low tide)? You would normally pass by. Take a walk around the **smallest harbour in the world!** This is, in fact, actually nor a river, but a tidal estuary, connected with the Bay of Fundy, and the Atlantic Ocean. Boats (those that could somehow turn around) can sail in! Another town, said to be in France disputes the claim (how do you measure such things)? In any event, this is one port which will never see much ocean liner trade.

30.9 (18.8)   **RIGHT** Main Street. Just to your right is an ice cream shop. Valley Stove and Cycle Bike Shop is just around the corner.

31.6 (19.2)   **RIGHT** Gaspereau Extension

31.7 (19.3)   **LEFT** Front Street

32.0 (19.5)   **END**

Grand Pre- 'Great Meadow'

The tiny chapel at Grand Pre marks perhaps the most tragic event in all Canadian history. It was here at the "great meadow" that the order was given to commence the **Expulsion of the Acadians**. The small church, built by the descendants themselves, has become a symbol of the preservation of their culture. Many make special trips to visit this important site. Often to be seen at the site are Americans of French-Canadian descent.

The British, upon gaining control of Nova Scotia grew increasingly uneasy. They were concerned over the presence of the prescence of the large number of French speaking Acadians. They were peaceful people, and almost non-political, wishing to be left to their farms. However, they were friends with the native Mic Mac, who made live difficult for the British, as they wantedto control their land, not share it. The Acadians also would not agree to swearing alliegience of loyalty to the crown. Therefore, in the summer and fall of 1755, New England soldiers were sent to clear out the villages. This was done with much brutality, with families separated, and their farms destroyed.

The chapel and grounds are now preserved and run by Parks Canada. The grounds, with the tall willows and elms, and the garden-like setting makes for a good rest spot, regardless of the historic importance. A photographer's delight, the grounds are quite lavish. However, it is a little ironic that in the interests of presenting a Nova Scotia attraction, that the grounds now appear more like a British garden than a place with the modest and functional preferences of the Acadians.

To the east of the park is an iron cross. This historic marker, just off where the train track ran through (on private property), is the exact spot where the Acadians were packed like animals onto ships and expelled. Since that time, the dykes they were in the process of building have completed draining the land. At this cross, where there are today fields in all directions, was once the shoreline, where the large number of ships were docked!

From here they were dispersed at random, to England, France, and along the Atlantic coast. A large number were sent as far south as Louisiana, where they became known an "Cajuns". Many returned to Acadia, including one group of 800, who walked through the woods all the way from Massachusetts. They arrived to find their lands occupied, mostly by New Englanders. Many settled along what is today known as the French Shore, between Yarmouth and Digby.

A well-crafted statue of **Evangeline**- the tragic heroine of poet **Henry Longfellow** graces the grounds. Her face depicts two sides, one in her happy days during the time of Acadia, the other after the deportation, as she awaits those separated from her.

Accommodation

Wolfville
Birchcliff Bed and Breakfast Leah Patterson, Box 736, 84 Main St., Wolfville, N.S., B0P 1X0, (902) 542-3391
Blomidon Inn Donna and Jim Laceby, Box 839, 127 Main St., Wolfville, N.S., B0P 1X0, (902) 542-2291. Restored 1877 sea captain's mansion.
Old Orchard Inn Box 1090, Wolfville, N.S., B0P 1X0, (902) 542-5751. Tennis courts, saunas, trails for off-road biking or walks.
Roselawn Lodging The Townsends. 32 Main St., Comp A5, Site 6, R.R. 1, Wolfville, N.S., B0P 1X0, (902) 542-3420
Tattingstone Inn Betsey Harwood. 434 Main St., Wolfville, N.S., B0P 1X0, (902) 542-7696. Steam room, pool, tennis, music room
Victoria's Historic Inn and Motel Urbain and Carol Cryan. 416 Main St., Box 308, Wolfville, N.S., B0P 1X0, (902) 542-5744. Registered historic property.

Kentville/ New Minas
Allen's Motel Jessie and Art Coakley. 384 Park St., Kentville, N.S., B4N 1M9, (902) 678-2683
Auberge Wandlyn Inn R.R.1, Coldbrook, N.S., B0P 1K0, (902) 678-8311. West of Kentville
Greensboro Inn Grant Forbes. 9016 Commercial St., New Minas, N.S., B4N 3E2, (902) 681-3201
Sleep Inn Judy Saunders. Box 1090, Wolfville, N.S., B0P 1X0, (902) 681-5000
White Spot Motel W.J. Milligan, Jr., 9060 Commercial St., New Minas, N.S., B4N 3E2, (902) 681-3244
Sun Valley Motel Jeanette and Lester MacKeen. 905 Park St., Kentville, N.S., B4N 3V7, (902) 678-7368
Wildrose Inn Bed and Breakfast Janet andLester Mackeen, 905 Park St., Kentville, N.S., B4N 3V7, (902) 678-8466. Shed for bicycles.

Port Williams
Country Squire Bed and Breakfast J. Earl and Rose Doyle. 990 Main St., Port Williams, N.S., B0P 1T0, (902) 542-9125
Old Rectory Bed and Breakfast Ron/ Carol Buckley. R.R. 1, Port Williams, N.S., B0P 1T0, (902) 542-1815. 3 km north of village
The Planters (Barracks) Country Inn Allen and Jennie Sheito. Starrs Point Road, R.R.1, Port Williams, N.S., B0P 1T0, (902) 542-7879. Oldest building in Nova Scotia (1778) used as a country inn. Mountain bikes available for guests.

Grand Pre
Grand Pre 's Evangeline Motel Marjorie Stirling. Grand Pre, N.S., B0P 1M0, (902) 542-2703
Inn the Vineyard Bed and Breakfast John Halbrook and Cathy Jordan. Box 66, Grand Pre, N.S., B0P 1M0, (902) 542-9954
The Presshouse Inn Bed and Breakfast Glenda Allen. Box 18, Wolfville, N.S., B0P 1M0, (902) 542-1470

Canning
The Farmhouse Inn Bed and Breakfast Carolyn and Ken Clark. Box 38, Canning, N.S., B0P 1H0, (902) 582-7900
Valley View Bed and Breakfast Mrs. Renate Glodde. R.R. 3, Canning, N.S., B0P 1H0, (902) 587-7711. Located near Sheffield Mills.

University Dorm

Acadia University Wolfville, N.S. Dormatory accommodation. Cafeteria, showers, recreation facilities.

Campgrounds

Sherwood Forest Camping Park Hills and Kaye Shaw. Coldbrook, N.S., B0P 1K0, (902) 679-6632
Palmeter's Trailer Park 655 Park St., Kentville, N.S., B4N 3V7, (902) 678-7333
South Mountain Park The Dansart Family. Box 474, Kentville, N.S., B4N 3X3, (902) 678-0152
Highbury Gardens Tent and Trailer Park Marvin Barfoot. R.R. 3, Kentville, N.S., B4N 4K1, (902) 678-8011
Long's Camping Grounds Waldo Long. R.R. 2, Wolfville, N.S., B0P 1X0, (902) 542-5148. Past White Rock at Sunken Lake.
Blomidon Provincial Park Province of Nova Scotia. (902) 582-7319Large group reservations only; showers; hiking trails. Located on top of Blomidon Mountain, incredible views
Look-off Family Camping Park Bill and Pauline Parker. R.R. 3, Canning, N.S., B0P 1H0, (902) 582-3373. Located at Look-off. spectacular setting.

A challenging ride over a
dramatically changing landscape

Tour 11   Kings County

Tour at a glance

START/ FINISH	Wolfville
OTHER STARTING POINT	Kentville
DISTANCE	116 km (72 mi.)
DIRECTION	Counter-Clockwise
TERRAIN	Very hilly
CLIMATE	Expect warm/ hot temperatures with humidity
	Air change and temperature drop at Hall's Harbour
TRAFFIC	Moderate
REST STOPS	Prescott House; Look-Off: Hall's Harbour; Silver's Lake; Coldbrook
FOOD	Wolfville (R)(G)(C); Port Williams (C); Look-Off (R-summer only); Hall's Harbour (C); Centreville (C); Coldbrook (R)(G)(C); South Alton (C); Gasperau (C)
REPAIRS	Wolfville
TOURISM	Wolfville 542-7000
HOSPITAL	Wolfville; Kentville (off-route)
AMBULANCE	Wolfville; Kentville (off-route)
POLICE	Wolfville; Kentville (off-route)

T his is perhaps the finest day ride in the province. The reason is simple- VARIETY. The Cabot Trail is spectacular, but you don't have as dramatic a constantly changing back drop, and by no means the solitude of this route. If you want a first-class, full day of cycling, you can not do any better in all Nova Scotia!

Note: This is a long tour, which covers routes covered in detail on Tours 7, 8, 9, and 10. Read the descriptions on these to provide further background on the sections you will be covering on this tour.

This ride comprises a "Greatest Hits" tour of highlights from the tours of the eastern Annapolis Valley. Parts of Tours 7, 8, 9, and 10 have been put together to form one incredible ride.

It must be mentioned straight away that this outing will be **challenging** to many casual cyclists. Shortcuts are possible at many spots, offering direct routes back to Wolfville, or Kentville. If you do not like hills, or want to enjoy a leisurely ride, tours 7, and 8 have been specially designed. On a hot day this could be a work-out. There will be several big uphills. You will also have one of the fastest downhills on the Nova Scotia mainland into Centreville, and a long gradual downhill into the Gaspereau Valley. Sea breezes, which come in at Halls Harbour will be much appreciated.

Please do not get an impression that this is merely a series of hills. This has been designed for you to sample one of the finest cycling regions of the country. A dozen first-rate areas will be available for rest breaks. Halls Harbour is about half-way, and will, as mentioned, on a warm day be the most refreshing spot on your route.

Our tour begins in downtown Wolfville. To connect from Kentville, go eastward on Belcher St., which connects directly onto this route.

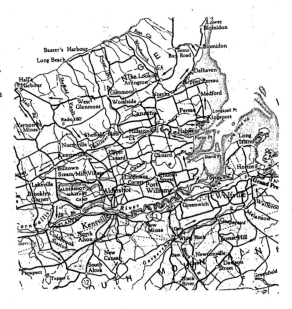

START	Tour begins by the parking lot in downtown Wolfville (just below Main St.). Head south-west.	
0.2 (0.1)	LEFT Elm St.	
0.3 (0.2)	RIGHT Main St. (#1 -traffic next 3 km). A popular fruit stand is to your left as you leave town.	
3.4 (2.1)	RIGHT #358 at Irving Station.	
5.2 (3.2)	RIGHT Starrs Point Rd. (High Street. By church- towards Prescott House)	
7.7 (4.8)	LEFT Starrs Point Rd. (Monument to the New England Planters is to the Right)	
10.3 (6.4)	RIGHT at T-intersection by Old Town Plot Schoolhouse. You turn the corner and are on Church St.	
10.9 (6.8)	RIGHT Wellington Dyke	
13.3 (8.2)	RIGHT (at yellow house after short hill)	
15.0 (9.3)	LEFT Saxon Street (first left turn)	

15.0 (9.3)   LEFT Saxon Street (first left turn)

17.2 (10.6)   RIGHT Canning Aboiteau

18.4 (11.4)   RIGHT #221. Go to very end of road in Kingsport to beach (there is a chance you may arrive at low tide).

22.7 (14.0)   LEFT Short street in behind the beach

23.0 (14.3)   LEFT

23.2 (14.4)   RIGHT Medford Road

26.7 (16.5)   LEFT North Medford (dirt Road)

28.0 (17.4)   RIGHT Jackson Barkhouse (dirt road). At the bottom of the hill you can ride across the dyke, parallel to the road.

28.9 (18.5)   RIGHT Blomidon Rd.

31.9 (20.4)   LEFT Steward Mountain Rd. (dirt)

35.4 (22.0)   LEFT #358 pavement resumes on top of the ridge. Look Off is the name of a small village, a famous photo spot of the sweeping panorama of the eastern Annapolis Valley.

            NOTE: STAY ON RIDGE! Many cyclists turn left here and go down the hill, even though the road continues straight. Keep up on the ridge until #359.

50.4 (31.3)   RIGHT #359 Halls Harbour Rd. Descend down to the Bay of Fundy. Be aware of the sharp turn at the bottom!

55.8 (34.7)   Halls Harbour. Continue on other side of harbour. After an initial shock, the road back up North Mountain will be gradual.

61.5 (38.2)   LEFT Brow Rd.

63.7 (39.6)   RIGHT #359. CAUTION: Steep downhill- one of the fastest in the province! Exercise caution!

68.1 (42.3)   RIGHT #221 at Centreville. Upcoming is a break site at Silver Lake. Continue on #221

75.1 (46.7)   LEFT Woodville Rd. Just past Morton's General Store

78.1 (48.5)   LEFT Brooklyn Rd.

80.1 (49.7)   RIGHT Lovette

83.0 (51.6)   RIGHT #1 (traffic next 0.3 Km)

83.3 (51.8)   LEFT English Mountain Rd. To your right is Coldbrook, the only commercial area you will pass all day. It includes a picnic park, a fish hatchery, and a certain chicken franchise. You are about to go up one of the toughest hills in the province. Like most mainland Nova Scotia hills, if you get off and walk, you are only looking at a few minutes. The view from this one is incredible, overlooking the entire eastern valley, so take your time. Once on top head along and cross route #12.

95.6 (59.4)   RIGHT (at church)

96.0 (60.2)   LEFT Go down into Gaspereau Valley. Go straight through flashing light at White Rock

            SIDE TRIP: This has been a vigourous tour for even the accomplished cyclist. You are almost home now, so relax at the river. However ... look to your right. See the road going up this hill from the gas station? Gaspereau Mountain is argued among cyclists to be perhaps after Blomidon, our hardest hill outside of the Cabot Trail- are you up for it?

            Continuing on tour, follow along the Gaspereau River

95.7 (59.5)   RIGHT Small jog in road at Melanson

95.8 (59.6)   LEFT Toward Avonport

97.4 (60.6)   LEFT Grand Pre Rd. (just past Wallbrook Mountain Rd.). To your left after crossing Ridge Rd., and going under the freeway is Covenanter Church.

109.8 (68.3) LEFT #1. Grand Pre Wines will be soon to your right. You will see directions to continue across road toward Grand Pre.

            SIDE TRIP- Grand Pre National Historic Park lies just down the road if you cross #1

115.9 (72.0) RIGHT Gaspereau Ext.

116.0 (72.1) LEFT Front St.

116.1 (72.2) END

Accommodation / Camping (see Tour 10)

South Shore

What do you think of when you hear the words "Nova Scotia"? Do you picture fishing boats, lighthouses, deserted beaches, and piers piled high with lobster traps? This is the South Shore, the best known part of the province. Fishing has for centuries been a rugged way of life and the seafaring tradition is still strong here. The boats are no longer powered by wind and canvas, but the struggle with the sea continues. Despite modern advances, more boats still go out to sea than return in "Canada's Ocean Playground".

This is an area of stories. Tales are told of pirate ships, rum-runners, and ship wrecks. They come from the jagged rocky coastline and misty harbours. Barren headlands here have yet to recover from great glaciers of the last Ice Age. Granite boulders, deposited by their retreat, stand as silent reminders along the shores. Thirty lighthouses from Yarmouth to Halifax protect mariners from the rocks and guide them safely home. Long sandy beaches line the shores, visited by the bracing Atlantic waters.

This area grew rich off smuggling liquor during American Prohibition. Rum-runners, based on the shore, roamed the North Atlantic Seaboard. Many large homes are a lasting reward from the profits of satisfying our southern neighbour's thirst.

A major Mic Mac (Indian) area was inhabited deep inland. Isolated settlements also emerged along the shore. They travelled the coast by canoe, quick travel when their only other option was wooded pathways.

Nova Scotia was never quite the same after the American Revolution. The cry "America- love it or Nova Scotia" rang out through the United States, and British Loyalists hastily fled.

Numbering in the thousands, the outcasts, including many Blacks, swamped the small towns and villages of Nova Scotia and New Brunswick. The exodus included the largest single migration of English people in history, (10,000) departing New York City in 1783.

They arrived to towns such as Shelburne and Liverpool. Both have a fascinting history to share, including the tales of privateers (legalized pirates).

Germans and Swiss originally settled the eastern section of the shore, in Lunenburg County. Invited to Nova Scotia by the British to fill their new colony with Protestants, they arrived to farm, but later inevitably turned to the sea. Mic Mac natives saw the settlers as pawns of the British. Unlike the Acadian French, the new arrivals had no intention of sharing the land. Many battles ensued between these new settlers and the natives. German is no longer heard along the shore, however you will detect a distinct accent. In fact, on some of the peninsulas you may feel at times you need an interpreter!

There are strawberry patches, a few cows and some farming but, for the most part- as you will see from the piles of lobster traps- people depend on the sea for their livelihood.

When roads were laid down so long ago, cycle touring was not a concern. Protection of horse and carriage travellers from the ravages of the ocean were. When you look over a map, roads appear to follow the coast. That they do, but you will often find yourself just far enough inland, protected by design, to often be out of reach of the water. You will hear the ocean, and you will even smell the salty air, but you will often find yourself going frustrating distances between stretches of access.

Hills are encountered seemingly at random. Seldom will you find any flat stretches. Queens County is known for its extensive "drumlin" fields, in its northern section they are the main feature of the landscape. Low rounded hills, it is felt that they were created by movements of glaciers during the past Ice Age.

To best enjoy the South Shore by bicycle some exploration will be required. Select at least one or two peninsulas and cycle out onto them to see the real Nova Scotia. Yes, you must backtrack. You will however, discover roads with small amounts of traffic, and places that rarely see visiting cycle tourists.

There is little of interest inland, away from the water, until you are east of the old Loyalist town of Liverpool. Here the interior begins to open up. For a marine dominated region, lumbering does not immediately come to mind. However, from the Atlantic Ocean to the farms of the Annapolis Valley, dense woods fill most of the interior. In fact, Queens County was once named "The Forestry Capital of Canada". This is quite a title, when you consider it includes reign over all of Canada's forest resources: Quebec, Northern Ontario, British Columbia, and our north. There are even lumberjack competitions. Scattered farms, pioneer churches, and undisturbed lakes randomly appear on the interior's roads, offering alternatives to the shore route. In the "loop" of routes #8, 3, and 340, are dense forests and marshes. This region provides a habitat for a healthy number of deer, moose, and even bears.

You may see oxen on some of the family farms. This is a famous region for the traditional competition of "Ox pulls". The plodding beasts of burden were used on many Nova Scotian farms since they could negotiate the rocky soil better than horses. Once a symbol of a farmer's ability to plough the fields, working with oxen continues to be a revered Nova Scotian tradition at county fairs. In these competitions, pairs under coaxing from their owners, pull loads as heavy as 6,350 kg (14,000 lbs.)!

Fishing towns appear regularly along the coast. Smaller communities sit between them, with houses of many colours stretching in linear fashion. If at all possible, spend a day in Lunenburg, the fishing town of them all.

Grocery stores are found only in the larger centres, of which only appear evey 50 -70 kilometres (30-45 miles). There are convenience stores, but do not expect to find your favourite health foods.

Residents of this region have a major challenge ahead of them, to overcome having among the highest smoking, as well as obesity rates in all Canada. This generality can be told by the reaction to bicyclists. There are still so few active cyclists, that people automatically assume that if adults go by riding bicycles, they must be "from away". In fact, when the Velo Halifax Bicycle Club goes tours along the shore, it is not uncommon for locals along the road to ask "What state are you from"?

66

Atlantic Canada
Cycling Festival

Canada's ocean playground

Tour 12   Lighthouse Route

Tour at a glance

START	Yarmouth
FINISH	Halifax
OTHER STARTING POINTS	Liverpool; Lunenburg; Chester; Halifax
DISTANCE	538 km (335 mi.) Many short-cut options
TERRAIN	Rolling Hills
CLIMATE	Often foggy and damp
NOTES	Sections of main highway are necessary
	Peninsulas needed to be cycled for best route
	Expect cool air and fog
TRAFFIC	Low to Busy
FOOD	Yarmouth (R)(G)(C); Tusket (C); Pubnico (R)(C);
	Barrington Passage (R)(G)(C); Port Clyde (C); Ingomar (C);
	Shelburne (R)(G)(C); Sable River (C); Liverpool (R)(G)(C);
	Vogler's Cove (C); Crescent Beach (C); La Have (C);
	Lunenburg (R)(G)(C); Mahone Bay (R)(G)(C); Western Shore (R)(C);
	Chester (R)(G)(C); Hubbards (R)(G)(C); Black Point (C); Tantallon (C);
	Peggy's Cove (R); White's Lake (C); Halifax (R)(G)(C)
REPAIRS	Yarmouth ; Lunenburg; Halifax
TOURISM	Yarmouth; Shelburne; Lunenburg; Mahone Bay; Chester; Halifax
HOSPITAL	Yarmouth; Shelburne; Liverpool; Bridgewater (off-route); Lunenburg
AMBULANCE	Yarmouth; Shelburne; Liverpool; Bridgewater (off-route); Lunenburg
POLICE	Yarmouth; Barrington; Shelburne; Liverpool; Lunenburg; Mahone Bay;
	Chester; Hubbards; Halifax

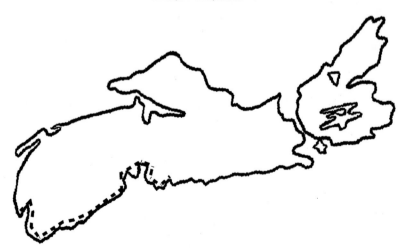

The best known part of Nova Scotia is not the hills of Cape Breton, not the orchards of the Annapolis Valley, not the streets of Halifax. The seacoast, and mainly that of the South Shore, is where most post cards are sent depicting Nova Scotia. It is also the source of the largest amount of its immense wealth of traditional story and song.

Fishing has been the major industry of Nova Scotia for centuries. Despite severe environmental damage to the fish stocks, the seafaring tradition is still a large provider of livelihood. The love-hate relationship with the sea continues. In some communities, however, the bond has for now been put on hold. As the result of modern technology, overfishing has added to the damage caused by the polluting of the seas, to force the closure of scattered fish plants along the shore. When you enter such a community so fatefully chosen, you can immediately sense it, for fishing is not just a job, it is a very way of life.

The arrival of Loyalists, those who supported England, and displaced after American victory of independence, established at that time the 4th largest city in North America- Shelburne, Nova Scotia. However, due to unfair trading taxes, the flourishing city collapsed by 1800. Today it is today a beautiful town, noted for its colonial restorations and Loyalist heritage.

From 1760 until the War of 1812, privateers called the South Shore home. These legalized pirates roamed the North Atlantic, plundering American vessels. A diary of Simon Perkins chronicles life in this era at Perkins House Museum in Liverpool. It is considered a landmark colonial document, unique in North America.

In the east, the tour passes through Lunenburg County, site of several suggested tours. Settled by German-speaking Swiss, you will encounter a distinct accent. The route then passes beaches, and a pleasant route around Aspotogan Peninsula. Before heading into Halifax you visit magnificent Peggy's Cove, Nova Scotia's most popular village.

Originally the plan was to present a shorter, high quality day tour, representative of the shore. The demand of cyclists, however, is to have a tour running along the entire coast, as so many are doing long from the ferries. This tour therefore will go the entire distance from Yarmouth to Halifax.

It must be mentioned that the best touring spots are concentrated in particular sections. Parts of this tour are included simply to connect them, and not as places presented as "must sees". Between the fishing

harbours are connections across peninsulas. Most quickly rise up from the water and then soon bring you to the next stretch of coast. Several times, however, you must go on long sections through the woods. The major thoroughfare (#103), has at these points been built over the old trunk, so you must put up with the increased noise and traffic. There is, as consolation, an almost two foot paved shoulder.

Taking every loop, in addition to the suggested peninsula dead-ends, is your option. This is of course time-consuming. Not all are included, in deference to those without an entire summer to cycle Nova Scotia. Choosing which loops to include took much consideration, and was painstaking. What perhaps was the major factor in deciding was the distance in places of the roadway from the ocean. This is why, after all, cyclists ride the South Shore. When roads were laid down so long ago, fishermen could not care less that people known as bicycle tourists would one day want to pass by and smell the salt air. What the mariners most wanted was to get away from the sea, if only for their day of rest. They built their houses in from the shore. In addition were the horses and carriages, which were best protected inland. A couple of hundred metres is difficult to discern on a highway map. The loops where you will have the least access to the shore have been minimized.

Remember that this is a heavily touristed area. Select at least one or two peninsulas and cycle out onto them to see the real Nova Scotia. You find on these roads places that rarely have visiting cycle tourists.

Fishing towns appear regularly along the coast. They offer a variety of services. Smaller communities sit between them. Stores are found frequently in the small villages. Expect to find, however, a heavy emphasis on snacks, soft drinks, and lottery tickets.

This is the longest of all the tours. You no doubt will not have to go the full 538 kilometers for your odometer to fall out of sync with this guide. This is an easy region, however, to find your way around. Generally, the Atlantic will be on one side of you, and deep forests to the other. There are few huge hills, but you will find yourself frequently shifting gears. An abandoned railway line allows cycling much of the way between Yarmouth to Liverpool. Conditions vary along the way. Near Liverpool it is maintained as a recreational trail. In other spots it is a bit more in the rough (at a few points you pass where the trains once loaded at fish plants- the aroma is perhaps not that of the pine or spruce trees you might be expecting).

Mirth of a nation

The islands offshore of Tusket are currently bird sanctuaries. They hardly seem like a place that would cause an international incident.

That is exactly what did happen, however, in 1949. The island's owner was an American tuna fisherman. One day, with no advance notice, he and a group of men made an important announcement. They proclaimed that that they were declaring the islands an independent republic!

Outer Baldonia was officially the world's newest nation. First recognition came from the Washington, D.C. telephone company, who created a listing as "Outer Baldonia, Principality of". Soon after that, official mail and cocktail invitations began to drift in. The National Geographic Society and Rand McNally map company inquired as to the country's exact latitude and longitude. A U.S. state department call arrived inquiring about the nation's exports.

Postage stamps were made and even passports created. Tuna boats were inducted into the Outer Baldonia Navy. A 20 by 30 foot stone castle was erected, centrally located in the 3 acre nation.

A Declaration of Independence was drafted. It guaranteed "the right to drink, gamble, swear, lie and be believed, sleep all day, stay up all night, and the freedom from shaving." A national holiday was proclaimed for the day of its tuna tournament, after which citizens of all nations are invited into the castle for "refreshments".

Perhaps sensing tourism gold, the Nova Scotia government added to the sham by sending out a press release, declaring that it was undecided about recognition of the new state. Outer Baldonia recognized Canada's right to exist, and offered full support in the event of any emergency. It was announced, however, that it would not recognize the United States, since the islands were too small to hold all the money and security administration missions that would be sent.

In Germany they took all this seriously. As well, the actions of the tiny new nation invoked anti-imperialist fervour in the Soviet Union. They railed that the republic was being run by "a capitalistic cannibal" whose aim was to enslave the fishermen, as well as corrupt them by "not adhering to the ethical and moral laws that have been established by mankind"

Once currency was produced, and called "tunars", the fact that it all was a joke was finally getting across, and one of the wildest hoaxes in the history of international affairs had been completed.

The fishermen later donated the islands as a bird sanctuary. Today, arctic terns, guillemots, and leach's petrels soar over the republic, while wild sheep rule over its crumbling castle.

START   Begin at Yarmouth Ferry Terminal Tourist Bureau. Head right on Main St. (#1). Follow around Chebogue Point (details on Tour 1).

                SHORT-CUT: Head up Starr St. past malls and the airport to Arcadia.

15.8 (9.8)   **RIGHT #1 at Arcadia**

                SIDE TRIP- Wedgeport This peninsula, settled in the late 1700's by Acadians returning from exile, has a dozen side roads to heritage homes, lobster pounds, and a large Catholic Church. A connecting road will take you out to even quieter peninsulas at Comeau Hill and Pinkneys Point.

                SIDE TRIP-Pubnico: One of the oldest Acadian regions, the Pubnicos were settled in the 1650's. Despite the English signs, this is a French area and perhaps the best place in all Nova Scotia to try a traditional Acadian recipe. Rappie Pie, (best with molasses), can be ordered at the Red Cap Motel, 5.2 km (3.5 mi.) from highway #3. There is an Acadian Museum at West Pubnico.

                SHORT-CUT: Route #103 shaves off a long stretch, but runs directly through the brush and is quite tedious.

                SIDE TRIP- Cape Sable Island: Connected with the mainland in 1949, on a "figure 8" route of the island, you will find fish plants, wharves, and building shops, where the world famous Cape Island boats originate. The island is moderately populated, but you can find quiet sandy rest spots, mainly off roads on the east side. Its tip at The Hawk is the **furtherst south** you can bike in Nova Scotia. Here, you can discover remnants of an ancient forest, preserved for thousands of years, now peeking out of the sand on the beach. The lighthouse, on the small island just beyond, is the second most southerly point in Canada. Cape Sable Island Fishermen's Co-operative Ltd. stores live lobsters until needed for market. It can hold 50,000 of the creatures. A license is not required to try your luck fishing mackerel off the causeway. The **Archelaus Smith Museum** is named for one of the early residents of the area, the museum contains displays and artifacts pertaining to lobster fishing and the shipbuilding industry. It is open daily, 9:30 am to 5:30 pm from the last Sunday in June to the third Sunday in September.

                Route #103 merges with #3 at Barrington.

98.3(61.1)   **RIGHT off #3 along shore onto unnumbered road.**

101.3(63.0)   **DETOUR:** Crossing the road is the old railway bed, which you can take to Shelburne. Doing just sections of it are possible, as it nears the road occasionally.

Sand Hill Provincial Park at Villagedale offers your first rest stop. Watch sea birds along its sand dunes or look for foundations here from a very old Acadian settlement.

112.7 (70.1)   **LEFT** Port La Tour

SIDE TRIP- Baccaro: From the lighthouse you can overlook the village fishing fleet and sandy beach.

SIDE TRIP- Cape Negro: To your right, a road leads a short distance down to a canal which was dug out years ago so fishing vessels could avoid going around the peninsula.

Just as you enter **Port Clyde**, the "railway" comes through and you may again ride the bed if you have an off-road bike (or are an accomplished road biker).

128.23 (79.7)   **RIGHT** Port Clyde. The road now takes you close to the shore around John Point. If you are in need of food, you can pedal up the connecting road to Clyde River at highway #103. The waterway was named by Scottish settlers after the river back home.

Rolling hills begin after Ingomar, providing views of Shelburne Harbour. **Round Bay** has a large crescent beach. **Roseway Beach** is another, accessible from a 2.5 km (1.5 mi.) dirt road. It has large stretches of sand bars at low tide, and bird-watching opportunities.

One **Alexander MacNutt** was a man of great charisma. This Irishman, a captain, but billing himself as "colonel", was an impressive sight, with silver buckles and gold lace coat trim, carrying a sword, said given to him by King George II. He a given gift of persuasion, and used it to obtain huge sums of land. His biggest dream was to create a settlement here in one of the world's finest harbours. He would name his city **New Jerusalem**. After modesty was encouraged upon him, it was changed to **Shelburne**.

He also owned and named the island to your right in the harbour, which he named after himself. Settlers from far and wide purchased lots for sale from his literature depicting **McNutt's Island's** rich farmlands and new homesteads, cleared and ready for habitation. Upon arrival from Europe, they were surprised to not find a structure in sight. Only two people (both relations of MacNutt), were to be found, just starting on the first

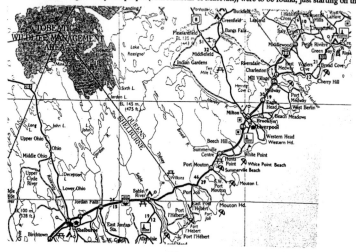

house! Infested with rocks, thick thorns and brush, and occasionally visited by hostile Mic Mac natives, it was far from what they thought they had purchased. Far from Europe, and with Mr. McNutt suddenly hard to find, they set to work to quickly clear the land and build shelter before winter. Thus began a community.

The island was inhabited until only recently. Records report an airlift of many of the island's 23 children when an influenza gripped the island in the 1960's. Even a post office was still operating until just a few years ago. Believed to be a suitable place for Nazi landing, fortifications were erected during World War II (fishing vessels had been torpedoed near here in World War I). Today they lie hidden by the encroaching forest.

Today, the island is vacant. Only an occasional keeper of the lighthouse spends any time there (his light was built in 1788). The island's roads have grown over, and the houses have collapsed, or have been swallowed by the forest. Wild sheep forage in what were once farms. In winter, they survive on scraps of seaweed and exposed grasses. No regular ferries go to the island, but many people go over in fishing boats for picnics and parties.

5.43 (102.8) **RIGHT #3** It will be hard for you by looking at it now, but **Birchtown** was at one time one of the largest Black communities outside of Africa! Named for the man who gave refuge to Blacks who supported the British during the Revolutionary War, the town boomed, along with Shelburne, as shiploads of Loyalists arrived in 1783. Food was scarce and a smallpox epidemic in 1787 added to their misery. Slowly their numbers decreased as promised lands throughout Nova Scotia were granted. Today it is a tiny village.

The Islands Provincial Park lies across the harbour from Shelburne. Once a quarry, its stone was used for buildings, and for cobblestones for the streets of Europe.

72.4 (107.2) **RIGHT** Water Street at Dairy Treat

73.7 (108.0) **RIGHT** onto extension of King Street

73.8 (108.1) **LEFT** Dock Street along Shelburne Harbour. **Shelburne** is today the seat of the county of the same name. At one time it was more prominent, in fact, the fourth-largest place in North America! Its importance came from a large flood of refugees from the United States. The arrivals were those who were loyal to Britain, during the American Revolution. Old buildings along its waterfront chronicle this era,

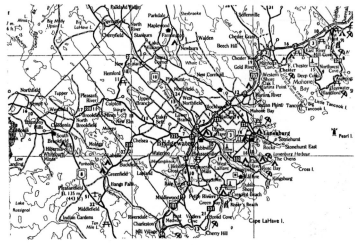

The run for rum

The United States government thought tough penalties would put an end to its citizens increasing demand for alcohol. They did not take into account, however, the ingenuity of those in surounding countries to provide aid for its people's thirst.

Prohibition became law in the United States at 12:01 a.m. on January 17, 1920. Rum-running as a major Nova Scotian industry got underway at about 12:02 a.m. the same day.

One Sunday morning, the *Saucy Arethusa*, a Nova Scotian schooner, sailed to just off the harbour of Atlantic City, New Jersey. Several small craft drifted by the vessel. Within earshot, the skipper mentioned over the rail that he had champagne and brandy aboard. The thirsty Americans bought on the spot and raced ashore to tell their friends. By that evening, hundreds of ships were swarming around the skipper's vessel- and he was $75,000 richer.

Within weeks, fishing for codfish was taking a backseat to doing direct service to mankind. Schooners from ports along the South and French shores gave up their fishing grounds, and joined the bonanza. At sea, in the dark of night, they would load up from mother ships off the coast of the French colony of St. Pierre, (near Newfoundland), and the Caribbean.

Rum-running cargoes were desguised as lobsters, coal, or canned goods. Off the coast of Maine, the skipper unloaded onto high-powered speed boats. The fleet would then wait at Rum Row, the name given to the line of ships anchored in international waters off the United States. At a given signal, they would start off in diferent directions. Boats acted as

decoys, so the U.S. Coast Guard would be lured away as others moved to shore without incident. The schooners could move much faster than the U.S. government ships (one vessel was even equipped with two aeroplane engines).

The stories were fantastic. An underground cavern, on the shores of Halifax Harbour, was found with a capacity of 100,000 gallons. Caves, such as that at Smuggler's Cove on the French Shore, were used as small warehouses. Motherships began firing ashore torpedoes, filled with rum. Ocean liners started to include Rum Row on their itineraries as the Atlantic became filled with floating liquor stores.

One rum-runner from Lunenburg, William McCoy, became a folk-hero of sorts. He was so adept at dodging the U.S. customs in his bullet proof boat, that east coast speak-easies guaranteed his whisky as "the real McCoy".

Profits became enormous. By the mid-1920's, rum-running was clearly becoming a dangerous business. Gun battles and fatalities were common. Organized crime moved in, and some liquor was cut with dangerous substances. Transactions at sea, under the glow of kerosene lamps, turned over counterfeit money or kegs of water. Ships sank under the weight of overloading. Rum Row was pushed further and further out to sea to avoid hijackers and the 26 navy destroyers added to the U.S. Coast Guard.

A few years later the government revoked a most unpopular law, and rum-running became a part of history. Today the large ornate homes along the coast stand as a reminder of a short but prosperous and colourful era.

several being museums. Today, Shelburne bills itself as the **"Lobster Capitol of Canada"**. Its harbour is recognized as being one of the finest in the world. Considering its rating, and its location between the Eastern Seaboard and Europe, it is certainly one of the most underutilized.

74.3 (108.3)   **LEFT** To #3

76.5 (109.7)   **RIGHT** Leave #3 onto road toward Jordan Branch.

78.1 (110.7)   **LEFT** toward #3 at Jordan Falls. A monument stands in tribute to **Donald Mackay**, renown designer of the clipper ships.

83.5 (114.1)   **RIGHT** #3

01.3 (125.2)   **RIGHT** toward Louis Head

                  SHORT CUT #3 toward Sable River

48.3 (135.7)   Merge with #3

22.3 (138.2)   **RIGHT** #103 at Sable River. You now must ride on a long section of the main highway. For a breather, consider going down one of the several desolate peninsulas or the National Park adjunct.

                  SIDE TRIP- Kejimkujik National Park Seaside Adjunct: The adjunct protects one of the last undisturbed tracts of Atlantic coastline in all North America. The trailhead is 5.5 km (3.4 miles) down St. Catherine's Road, off Route # 3 between Port Joli and Port Mouton. The trail stretches 2 km (1.2 miles) to the shore, arriving after about 35 minutes walking time at St. Catherine's River Beach, a sandy stretch almost 1.6 km (1 mile) long. Sections of the beach are closed from late April to late July, to protect key nesting areas of the endangered **Piping Plover**. A second access begins near Willis Lake at Southwest Port Mouton. This trail is 5 km (3 miles) long, ending at another undeveloped beach at Black Point. The park offers no facilities, although overnight camping is permitted in designated areas. Permits are available at the warden's office in Liverpool. Contact: Superintendent, Kejimkujik National Park, Box 36-A, Maitland Bridge, N. S., B0T 1N0 682-2772.

49.6 (155.2)   **RIGHT** #3 at Summerville Centre. At Summerville Beach, the rail bed has been reconditioned for the stretch into Liverpool.

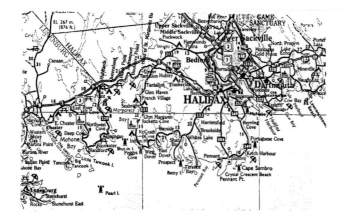

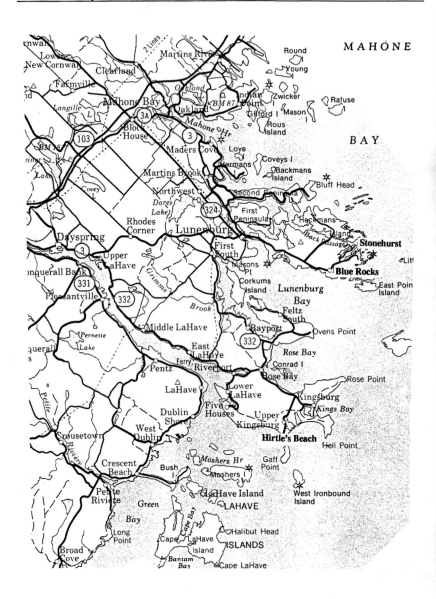

267.1 (166.1)   **Liverpool** is an important stopping point on cycling trips. In terms of cycling, it is a long way to Shelburne, Bridgewater, and Kejumkujik National Park. It therefore is an essential resting place and supply stop. A cairn at **Fort Point** commemorates the first landing of deMonts and Champlain in 1604. There is another monument which praises the work of the **"Liverpool Privateers"**. They were in essence legalized pirates, though it must be said that many went far beyond their mandate. Government charter permitted them to attack any vessel of an enemy country. **Simon Perkins'** diary is an important artifact of that time. His notes tell of Liverpool's illicit trade with the United States. The wild times of the town are recounted on entries concerning the antics of shore visits of the privateers and the Royal Navy's recruitment gangs.

         A short ride away is the loop around Western Head. You'll discover a lighthouse/weather station and a lookout area where you can view the broad Atlantic in one of its various moods. Liverpool is the home of famed country musician **Hank Snow**.

271.5 (168.8)   **RIGHT** Stay right after the bridge in Brooklyn along the shore towards a picnic spot and refuge for piping plovers at the beach at Beach Meadows. Between Brooklyn and Mahone Bay is perhaps the best cycling area on the South Shore. Big old captain's homes overlook the Atlantic, which you will often be directly next to.

         SIDE TRIP-Port Medway was once a much larger community - a far cry from the village you may see today. In 1870, there were 2,100 persons living here. There were several shipyards and much trade was done with the West Indies and other countries. In 1869 alone, one hundred and fifty-nine vessels sailed with cargo from the port.

286.2 (166.7)   **CROSS** #103. Turn at Mill Village and head back toward highway. The large white ball you may see through the trees is an Earth Satellite Station, open to visitors.

290.3 (180.5)   **CROSS** #103. Highway #331 begins. At Vogler's Cove, you join Tour 13. Refer to it for detailed notes.

324.2 (201.6)   **FERRY** to East LaHave

324.2 (201.6)   **RIGHT** #332

339.2 (210.9)   **RIGHT** Corkum's Beach Road

345.9 (215.1)   **RIGHT** Falkland Street. in Lunenburg. Refer to Tours 15, and 16 for details, including next leg to Mahone Bay.

345.7 (215.0)   **LEFT** Dufferin Street. Name changes name to Maple.

347.5 (216.1)   **CROSS** #332 onto #3

348.5 (216.7)   **RIGHT** (at first picnic park sign)

349.5 (217.3)   **LEFT** (away from picnic park)

351.7 (218.7)   **RIGHT** Sunnybrook (at old mill). Straight ahead through next intersection.

356.7 (221.8)   **RIGHT** #3 Main Street, Mahone Bay

360.0 (223.8)   **RIGHT** #3 Edgewater Street (by Petro Canada)

361.0 (224.5)   **RIGHT** Indian Point Road (just after bridge).

366.8 (228.1)   **LEFT** Inland by bridge

369.8 (229.9)   **RIGHT** #3. A moderate amount of traffic is on this section, with hills between Western Shore and East Chester. Just up the hill from Chester Basin is Corkum's Bucket Factory. Once the manufacturer of countless buckets and tubs used in the fishing industry, the output is now turned somewhat to manufacturing wooden ornamental containers.

         SIDE TRIP-Chester: Founded largely by New Englanders, including descendants of the Mayflower,

Chester has a decidedly New England feel. For many years popular with Americans, Chester is in some ways comparable to what Cape Cod is considered to have been like 50 years ago. One of Canada's finest "summer towns", Chester is in no way typical of the average Nova Scotian settlement. Grand properties run from in the shore, with large lawns. Small islands also hide huge summer homes. Yachts are everywhere, and there is much playing of tennis and golf.

SIDE TRIP- Tancook Island: For generations this island has been famous for its cabbage and sauerkraut. Its name is believed to have come from the Mic Mac who called it "*Uktankook*"- great rock facing the sea. It is a life that breeds a fierce independence but gradually the younger people are leaving to work on the mainland. They marry and settle down, perhaps going home for a visits a year. In the early thirties the population on Big Tancook was about 850, it is less than 300 today. Most are retired, or involved in the fisheries - still the mainstay of the island's economy. Scores of brightly-coloured boats tie up at the wharf.

It was considered at first as cheap farm sites, fences not being needed. The farmers soon turned to the sea. Their homes still stand in away from the shore. Tancook is 5 km (3 mi.) long, and 1.5 km (1mi.) wide. Little Tancook, its sister, is 1.5 km (1 mi.) long and 1 km (0.6 mi.) wide. Home to just a few families, pathways run across the smaller island, but there are no roads. The islands are world known for their excellent sauerkraut, cabbage, and production of summer savory. The island has a dirt road running along one side. It also has walking trails where you may be able to get a mountain bike through. There are very few automobiles on the island (two or three cars, however, seem to drive back and forth all day). Big Tancook has a Bed and Breakfast, and a store. Inquire with passengers on your trip over for advice if you plan to camp on the island.

Passenger ferry service operates from Chester to Big and Little Tancook Islands. The trip over is enjoyable, giving you a view of the bay, its islands, and if lucky, sea birds and animals. The voyage is about an hour long and allows passengers to soak up sunshine on the top deck or in the enclosed cabin below. The vessel is equipped to carry passengers only, with a portion of deck space set aside for crates of provisions, and the Tancook mail. A limited number of bicycles are able to be put on board.

98.8 (247.9)   RIGHT #329 East River Road (see Tour 17). Follow around the Aspotogan Peninsula. This adds a fair amount of distance, but is reccomended (see tour 17).

49.2 (279.3)   RIGHT #3 at Hubbards. Three very good sand beaches run between Hubbards and Tantallon. Note: Expect at times high traffic levels from here to Halifax. If possible avoid weekends.

71.6 (293.2)   RIGHT #333 at Tantallon (see Tour 18).

SHORT-CUT: Highway #3 cuts off a lot of kilometers. It is, however, a mostly bland route through growing suburbs. The Peggy's Cove route is reccomended.

SIDE TRIP- Peggy's Cove, Nova Scotia's most famous attraction

34.3 (332.2)   RIGHT #3

38.4 (334.7)   End Halifax(Armdale) Rotary.

commodation

Tour 1 for Yarmouth area listings; Tour 15 for Lunenburg/ Bridgewater area listings; Tour 20 for Halifax listings)

ghan Lake Bed and Breakfast George and Dale Duncanson. R.R. 1, Tusket, NS, B0W 3M0 (902) 648-3122
z Marie Bed and Breakfast Marie d'Entremont. Box 66, West Pubnico, N.S., B0W 2S0, (902) 762-2107
aronnie A.L. d'Eon. Box 40, Middle West Pubnico, N.S., B0W 2M0, (902) 762-3388. Off-route on Pubnico Peninsula
Cap Motel Carol d'Entremont. Middle West Pubnico, N.S., B0W 2M0, (902) 762-2112. Off-route on Pubnico Peninsula
sie's Bed and Breakfast Sherry Shears. R.R. 1, Woods Harbour, N.S., B0W 2E0, (902) 723-2496
oria Hotel and Motel Jacqueline Hewitt. Box 502, Barrington Passage, NS B0W 1G0, (902) 637-2945
e Island Bed and Breakfast Sheila Evans. Box 9, Clark's Harbour, N.S., B0W 1P0 (902) 745-1356. Off-route on Cape Sable Island
thouse Walk Bed and Breakfast P.O. Box 10, R.R. 3, Barrington, NS B0W 2S0, (902) 637-3409. No children under 10
Laren Inn Bed and Breakfast Mrs. Eva Haeghaert. Port Clyde, Shelburne, NS B0W 2S0
Bear's Den Elizabeth Atkinson. P.O. Box 883, Shelburne, NS B0W 2S0, (902) 875-3234. Shed for storing bicycles
e Cod Colony Motel Douglas and Pat Stewart. 234 Water St., Box 34, Shelburne, N.S., (902) 875-3411
Cooper's Inn 36 Dock St., P.O. Box 959, Shelburne, NS B0T 1W0, (902) 875-4656. Registered historic property on waterfront

DeRoest Bed and Breakfast R.R. 2, Shelburne, NS B0T 1W0, (902) 875-4370
Harbour House Bed and Breakfast Mary Dyous. 187 Water St., Box 929, Shelburne, N.S., B0T 1W0 (902) 875-2074
Loyalist Inn P.O. Box 245, Shelburne, NS B0T 1W0, (902) 875-2343
MacKenzie's Motel and Cottages Lawrence and Patricia West. 260 Water St., Box 255, Shelburne, N.S., B0T 1W0 (902) 875-2842
The Mill Stones Country Inn Julie and Gary Jeschke. 2 Falls Lane, Box 758, Shelburne, N.S., B0T 1W0 (902) 875-3958
Ox Bow Village Motel Stephen and Mark Strange. Box 459, Shelburne, NS B0T 1W0, (902) 875-3000. 5km (3 mi.) east of town.
Toddle Inn Tony Caruso. Box 837, Shelburne, NS B0T 1W0, (902) 875-3229.
Wildwood Motel Minto St., P.O. Box 837, Shelburne, NS B0T 1W0, (902) 875-2964
Locke's Island Bed and Breakfast Linda Balish. North Street, Box 238, Lockeport, N.S., B0T 1L0 (902) 656-3222. Off-route in Lockeport.
Seaside Cottages Thelma and Mark Snow. Box 348, Lockeport, N.S., B0T 1L0 (902) 656-2089 Fax only. Off-route in Lockeport.
Pillar and Post Bed and Breakfast June Williams. Sable River, N.S., B0T 1V0, (902) 656-2695
Stonehaven Motel Anna Mackenzie. Port Mouton, N.S., B0T 1T0, (902) 683-2020
Sea View Bed and Breakfast John and Judy Adams. Box 32, Central Port Mouton, N.S., B0T 1T0, (902) 683-2217
Hunts Point Beach Cottages Willem Noback. Box 131, Hunts Point, N.S., B0T 1G0, (902) 683-2491
Ocean View Cottages Jim and Paula Jenner. Box 177, Hunts Point, N.S., B0T 1G0, (902) 683-2012; 434-9060
Summerville Beach Bed and Breakfast June Lohnes, R.R.1, Port Mouton, N.S., B0T 1T0, (902) 683-2874.
Quarterdeck Cabins Frank MacIntosh. Summerville Beach, R.R.1, Port Mouton, N.S., B0T 1T0, (902) 683-2998; 354-3811
White Point Lodge Box 9000, Liverpool, N.S., B0T 1G0, (902) 354-2711. Large resort near Hunts Point
Hopkins House Bed and Breakfast 120 Main St., Liverpool, N.S., B0T 1K0, (902) 354-5484
Lanes Privateer Inn and Bed and Breakfast Ron Lane. Box 509, 33 Bristol Ave., Liverpool, N.S., B0T 1K0, (902) 354-3456
Royal Bed and Breakfast Reg and Carole Thompson. Box 285, Liverpool, N.S., B0T 1K0, (902) 354-5368
Morton House Bed and Breakfast Barbara and Bill Beveridge. 147 Main st., Box 351, Milton, N.S., B0T 1P0, (902) 354-2908
Second Home Bed and Breakfast Sally Kaulback. 380 Main St., Milton, N.S., B0T 1P0, (902) 354-3573. Just north of Liverpool
Motel Transcotia Derinda Sparkes. Box 299, Brooklyn, N.S., B0J 1H0, (902) 354-3494
South Shore Country Inn Avril Betts. Route 331, Broad Cove, N.S., B0J 2H0, (902) 677-2042
Little River Bed and Breakfast Joan Patterson. R.R. 1, Box 2A-4, B0J 2P0, (902) 688-1339
Macleod Cottages Jack and Miriam MacIntosh. Green Bay Beach, Petit Riviere, N.S., B0J 2P0, (902) 688-1339
Oceanus Housekeeping Cottages Emmalee Hopkins. Green Bay Beach, Petit Riviere, N.S., B0J 2P0, (902) 688-2504
Oak Island Inn Western Shore, N.S., B0J 3M0, (902) 627-2600
Isles View Tourist Home Max and Gloria Bowman, R.R. 3, Box 17, Chester Basin, N.S., B0J 1K0, (902) 627-2925
Captain's House Inn Nicki and Jerry Butler. 129 Central St., Chester, N.S., B0J 1J0, (902) 275-3501
Casa Blanca Guest House Margaret Marshall. 463 Duke St., Box 70, Chester, N.S., B0J 1J0, (902) 275-3385
Mecklenburgh Inn Bed and Breakfast Suzi Fraser. 78 Queen St., Box 350, Chester, N.S., B0J 1J0, (902) 275-4638
Stoney Brook Bed and Breakfast Jeanne and Ned Nash. Box 716, Chester, N.S., B0J 1J0, (902) 275-2342
Windjammer Motel Kim and Richard Johnson. Box 240, Chester, N.S., B0J 1J0, (902) 275-3567
East Chester Inn Bed and Breakfast Jess and Ross Davis. R.R. 1, East Chester, N.S., B0J 1J0, (902) 275-3017. 1.5 km (1 mi.) east of Chester
The Cove Bed and Breakfast David and Martha Farrar. Box 16, Big Tancook Island, N.S., B0J 3G0, (902) 228-2054; 228-2562. On Tancook Island. Small store on premises.
Deep Cove Resort R.R. 1, Deep Cove, N.S., B0J 1T0, (902) 228-2400
The Anchorage House Gordon and Judith Morrison. R.R. 2, Hubbards, N.S., B0J 1T0, (902) 857-9402
Dauphinee Inn 167 shore Club Rd., Hubbards, N.S., B0J 1T0, (902) 857-1790
Rosewood Cottages Phyllis Hind. Hubbards Cove, Shore Club Road. Mail: 141 Basinview Drive, Bedford, N.S., B4A 3J9, (902) 835-8514
Grand View Motel Ralph and Marjorie Comeau. Black Point, N.S., B0J 1B0, (902) 857-9776
Bay Breeze Motel Boutiliers Point, N.S., B0J 1G0, (902) 826-2213
Saltwater Shore Bed and Breakfast Elizabeth and Jack Salton. Box 1101, R.R. 1, Tantallon, N.S., B0J 3J0, (902) 823-2579
Clifty Cove Motel Ainsley and Christine Hubley. Box 10, Site 30, R.R. 1, Tantallon, N.S., B0J 3J0, (902) 823-3178
Like-Home Cottages Nora Zinn. Box 1, Site 25, Indian Harbour, N.S., B0J 3J0, (902) 823-3172
Lover's Lane Cottages Roseville and Helen Hubley. Box 1701, R.R. 1, Tantallon, N.S.,B0J 3J0, (902) 823-2670
Peggy's Cove Bed and Breakfast Aubrey O'Leary. Peggy's Cove, N.S., B0J 2N0, (902) 823-2265; (902) 235-2447. Overlooks village
Oceanside Bed and Breakfast Tom and Dorothy Code. Box 105, Armdale, N.S., B3L 4J7, (902) 823-2765. At West Dover, near Peggy's Cove
Prospect Bed and Breakfast Helena Prsala. Box 68, Prospect, N.S., B0J 2V0, (902) 852-4493. Off-route at village of Prospect

Camping

Bayberry Campground R.R. 1, Barrington, NS , B0W 1E0, (902) 637-2181. On route, towards Villagedale, "solar" shower
The Islands Provincial Park (902) 875-4304. Open and wooded campground just west of Shelburne; small beach; no reservations, no showers
Louis Head Beach Campground Marilyn and Herb Foote. Lydgate Post Office, Shelburne Co., NS B0T 1M0 (902) 656-3129; 656-2258
Rood's Head Campground Town of Lockeport. P.O. Box 76, B0T 1L0 (902) 656-3406. Off-route at Lockeport.
Pine Hills Campground Madeline Wills, Sable River, NS B0T 1V0 (902) 656-3400
Rissers Beach Provincial Park (902) 688-2034; (902) 688-2010. Open and wooded sites along ocean. No showers; no reservations
Graves Island Park Province of Nova Scotia. (902) 275-4425. Open and wooded sites along ocean. No showers; no reservations
Hubbards Beach Campground Clyde Harnish. Shore Club Rd., Hubards, NS B0J 1T0 (902) 857-9460. Showers, laundromat, off route #3.
King Neptune Campgound Vincent Richardson. Box 1641, Site 28, R.R.1., Tantallon, NS, B0J 3J0. On ocean at Indian Harbour. showers
Seaside Camping Ground Garfield Drake. Box 9, Site 16, R.R. 1, Tantallon, N.S. B0J 3J0. (902) 823-2732. showers
Wayside Camping Park Douglas George. Box 9, Site 18, R.R. 1, Tantallon , N.S. B0j 3J0 (902) 823-2271; 823-2547. showers; along ocean
Juniper Park Kenneth Doyle. R.R. 3, Box 6, Site 15, Armdale, N.S. B3L 4J3 (902) 876-2814. On route #3 at Hubley; showers

Atlantic Canada
Cycling Festival

*Unsurpassed marine beauty
along a wave-battered shore*

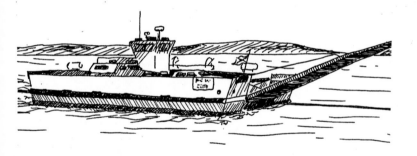

Tour 13   Risser's Beach

Tour at a glance

START/ FINISH	Lunenburg
OTHER STARTING POINTS	Riverport, Bridgewater, Vogler's Cove
DISTANCE	107 km (66 mi.) 70km/ 43 mi. from Riverport)
DIRECTION	Counter-Clockwise
TERRAIN	Rolling hills
CLIMATE	Strong Atlantic Breezes; cross-winds on coast
TRAFFIC	Moderate; high along shore on weekends
REST STOPS	Conrad's Beach; Crescent Beach; Risser's Beach
FOOD	Lunenburg (R)(G)(C); Riverport (C); Pleasantville (C); Vogler's Cove (C); West LaHave (C)(Bakery)
REPAIRS	Lunenburg
TOURISM	Lunenburg
POLICE	Lunenburg
HOSPITAL	Lunenburg; Bridgewater (off-route)
AMBULANCE	Lunenburg; Bridgewater (off-route)

A pple Cove, Cherry Cove, Broad Cove, Vogler's Cove- this tour offers ocean front riding at its finest! Some of the province's best beaches and most pleasant marine atmosphere is to be experienced along this rugged shore.

From Lunenburg, this ride first follows South Cove, off LunenburS Bay. You will have the opportunity to watch for huge Osprey nests as you cross a short inland stretch. A ferry ride will take you to West LaHave. There you will follow the scenic LaHave River to Conquerall Bank, before cutting cross-country, returning along the beautiful beaches and seacoast of the Atlantic.

A short-cut of 6.4 km (4.0 mi.) is possible by going both ways through Indian Path Rd., and not through Riverport.

Connections with this tour are convenient from Bridgewater. The own has accommodations, and more support services than Lunenburg, however, it lacks its unique maritime atmosphere. From town it is about 7.0 km (4.0

mi.) to Pleasantville to connect with our route. The tour's total is then only 84.6 Km (52.5 mi.), and you will still enjoy the best part of the tour.

From Riverport, this tour is much shorter. It comes in at around 70 km (43 mi.).

START	Lunenburg Tourist Bureau Go down Blockhouse Hill
0.2 (0.1)	RIGHT Sawpit Rd
0.3 (0.2)	RIGHT Pelham Rd. Pass through town of Lunenburg
0.8 (0.5)	LEFT Lincoln St.

0.9 (0.6)   LEFT Falkland St. at Lunenburg Common. Keep to left, becomes Tannery Rd. just past the High School and Belroy Motel, then later Mason's Beach/ Corkurn's Beach Rd. As you go up hill by golf course, look behind you for a great view of Lunenburg.

7.9 (4.9)   LEFT onto #332

12.1 (7.5)   RIGHT Indian Path will take you on a quiet, tarmac surface through an osprey nesting area. Look for high poles, erected just for the ospreys. They were put up because the birds were building nests so large on telephone poles that service was hindered.

15.8 (9.8)   RIGHT #332

16.5 (10.2) FERRY to West LaHave: Ferries leave hourly on the 1/2 hour.

16.5 (10.2) RIGHT off ferry onto #331.

SIDE TRIP- LaHave Bakery: Mike and Gail Watson have earned an excellent reputation for this bakery, near the west dock of the ferry. It is recommended for energizing for the ride ahead!

18.2 (11.3) **RIGHT** onto the shore road at Pentz. It takes you off the highway along a small lane.

19.6 (12.2) **RIGHT** onto #331 again.

28.4 (17.6) **LEFT** Conqueral Mills/ Hebb's Cross Rd. You now slowly climb 100m (300 ft.) from the river, and soon come to a rest area at Fancy Lake.

CROSS #103 to Camperdown. A series of rolling hills will continue until you are near the Atlantic.

44.5 (27.6) **LEFT** Middlewood.

CROSS #103 at Exit 16

59.7 (37.1) **LEFT** #331 at Vogler's Cove, named for a Prussian settler (note: last store before beaches). After going up a tiny ridge (Hog Hill) watch for a turn-off to beautiful, quiet Conrad's Beach.

SIDE TRIP- Conrad's Beach (Cherry Beach): Turn right onto dirt road by Cheny Hill Fire Hall to a spectacular ocean spot, known as a great area for shell collecting. NOTE: Turn-off is easy turn to miss!

Magnificent coastline and more beaches continue as you cycle along the Atlantic shore. Several large homes were constructed from beach stones early this century. Studios featuring marine artists begin to appear, inviting you in to see a continuing tradition of painters and crafts people. At Petite Riviere, a road south takes you to Green Bay with a beach, rental cottages and a canteen.

One of the finest stretches of sand in all Nova Scotia is Risser's Beach. Supervised by a lifeguard, the water is cool, but you will see most locals taking it in stride. It makes a pleasant spot to stop, especially during the more quiet weekdays. A boardwalk takes you through a saltwater marsh. Camping and picnic facilities are available. There is an area to lock your bike (do so).

SIDE TRIP- La Have Island: Connected to the mainland by a long sandy causeway, a short visit is well worth a ride over. Crescent Beach runs along its side. Quieter than Risser's, though not kept as clean, it is popular with surfers, clam diggers and partiers.

Fort Saint Marie de Grace Museum and Historic Site is found 0.8 km (0.5 mi.) before the ferry on the right (turn-off is easy to miss). This was the first land reached by French explorer DeMonts in 1604, naming it Cap de la Havre. A fort was constructed and. established as the capital of the colony. By 1634 there stood a settlement of 40 families. An English expedition in 1658 attacked and many were killed. In 1705 a Boston privateer came upriver, burned every dwelling remaining, and destroyed the crops. Fort Point Museum on the site is operated by the Lunenburg County Historical Society. A tiny white sand beach is maintained nearby.

LaHave Bakery is to your right 200 metres before ferry

84.0 (52.2) **FERRY** to East LaHave. It runs across the river once an hour, on the hour.

84.0 (52.2) **RIGHT** #332

86.8 (54.0) **LEFT** onto unmarked road through back of Riverport (just before bridge).

88.3 (54.9) **LEFT** #332 (by church)

99.0 (61.5) **RIGHT** Corkum's Beach Mason's Beach Rd. A fantastic view of the town of Lunenburg is afforded by the hill at the golf course, a great photo opportunity for those with telephotos. Follow back through town back to the tourist bureau.

107.3 (66.7) **END**

Accommodation/ Camping (See Tour 15)

antic Canada
ling Festival

Ox bells and river ferries

Tour 14

LaHave

Tour at a glance

START/ FINISH	Lunenburg
OTHER STARTING POINTS	Bridgewater
DISTANCE	76 km (47 mi.)
DIRECTION	Clockwise
TERRAIN	Flat (Optional extension of tour hilly)
CLIMATE	Pleasant- sea breezes but more protected than coast
NOTES	Plan ride to connect with ferry (hourly)
TRAFFIC	Moderate; busy for short stretch through Bridgewater
REST SPOTS	Bridgewater
FOOD	Lunenburg (R)(G)(C), Riverport (C),
	West Lahave (C)(Bakery); Pleasantville (C);
	Bridgewater (R)(G)(C),
REPAIRS	Lunenburg
TOURISM	Lunenburg, Bridgewater
POLICE	Lunenburg, Bridgewater
HOSPITAL	Lunenburg, Bridgewater
AMBULANCE	Lunenburg, Bridgewater

O n this easy tour, you explore both sides of the LaHave River. Open to the ocean, this scenic waterway has both a fresh as well as a saltwater section. A short-cut of 6.4 km (4.0 mi.) is possible by a return through Indian Path Road.

Several spots will be available to take breaks. A short ferry ride transports you across the LaHave to follow the edge of its western shore.

At Bridgewater, the salt water section of the river is met by fresh water flowing from inland lakes. You can here extend your tour by going further up the river. Crossing over, you can return on the other side.

The town of Bridgewater is directly on this tour. Doing the loop from here to Riverport and back is only 36.2 km (22.5 mi.). It has accommodations, and more support services than Lunenburg, however it lacks its unique maritime atmosphere.

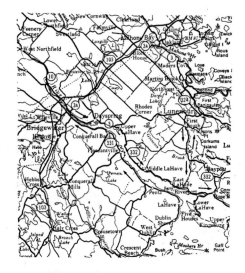

START   **Lunenburg Tourist Bureau** Go down Blockhouse Hill

0.2 (0.1)   **RIGHT** Sawpit Rd

0.3 (0.2)   **RIGHT** Pelham Rd. Pass through town of Lunenburg

0.8 (0.5)   **LEFT** Lincoln St.

0.9 (0.6)   **LEFT** Falkland St. at Lunenburg Common. Keep to left

1.2 (0.7)   **LEFT** Becomes Tannery Rd. just past the High School and Belroy Motel, then later Mason's Beach/ Corkum's Beach Rd. As you go up hill by golf course, behind you is a great view of Lunenburg.

7.9 (4.9)   **LEFT** onto #332

12.1 (7.5)   **RIGHT** Indian Path Rd. will take you on a quiet, tarmac surfaced road past osprey nesting areas.

Look for high poles. Erected for the ospreys, they were building nests so large on telephone poles that service was hindered.

15.8 (9.8)   **RIGHT #332**

16.5 (10.2)   **FERRY** to West LaHave. Ferries leave hourly on the 1/2 hour

16.5 (10.2)   **RIGHT** after ferry onto #331

SIDE TRIP: Just 200 metres to your left from the ferry is **LaHave Bakery.** Mike and Gail Watson have earned an excellent reputation for this bakery, below their hostel. It is recommended for energizing for the ride ahead! **Fort Saint Marie de Grace Museum and Historic Site** is found just a short distance further to the left (see Tour 13).

18.2 (11.3)   **RIGHT** onto the shore road at Pentz. It takes you off the road along a small lane.

19.6 (12.2)   **RIGHT** onto #331. Pleasantville marina usually has a large number of yachts active in the river.

Bridgewater is the commercial centre of the South Shore, you will pass through its pleasant downtown. The town is known as the shipping point for thousands of **Christmas trees.** In addition, Michelin has a large tire operation here. Several food stores and restaurants are available. Highway #331 becomes King St. Continue straight through until reaching the bridge. DesBrisay Museum (left on Jubilee Rd. as entering town) is set in a 25 acre park. Artifacts include Mic Mac native handicrafts featuring porcupine quillwork and an interesting child's cradle.

Bridgewater is home of **South Shore Exhibition,** featuring the famous **International Ox Pull.** Farmers arrive from all over the province with their teams of oxen for this Nova Scotian tradition.

DETOUR- Upper LaHave River: Bridgewater is where the rapids of the fresh-water part of the La Have River meets its ocean, salt-water section. If you would like to extend your tour, there are several crossings further up the river. Continue on King St., which becomes Trunk #10. There is a crossing at Bruhm Rd. to the other side at West Northfield. Further up, you will be looking at short dirt road crossings until reaching New Germany.

33.9 (21.0)   **RIGHT** Old Bridge St. CAUTION: Steel gratings on the bridge can cause bikes to slip. Use caution, or walk on the sidewalk.

34.3 (20.7)   **RIGHT #3** (At Tim Horton's Donuts). Pass the mall and you are quickly out of town.

SIDE TRIP: A rest area and a series of trails groomed for cross-country skiing provide an excellent spot for mountain biking, or walking. The Municipal Activity and Recreation Complex can be reached by turning left at Snyder's Shipyards (near Irving station). Go 0.1 km (0.1 mi.) to the M.A.R.C. entrance. The woods paths are just to the back. If open, the recreation office may have maps available.

40.5 (25.1)   **RIGHT #332.** Herons can frequently be seen feeding along the shore at low tide. Pass LaHave ferry.

55.0 (34.1)   **LEFT** back road through back of Riverport (near bridge into village)

56.5 (35.1)   **LEFT #332** (by church)

67.2 (41.7)   **RIGHT** Corkum's Beach/ Mason's Beach Rd. A great view of the town of Lunenburg may be seen from the hill at the golf course.

73.9 (45.9)   **RIGHT** Falkland St.

74.2 (46.1)   **RIGHT** Lincoln St.

75.3 (46.8)   **LEFT** Blockhouse Hill

75.5 (46.9)   **END**

Accommodation/ Camping (See Tour 15)

Atlantic Canada
Cycling Festival

An easy ride to a postcard village

Tour 15   Lunenburg

Tour at a glance

Blue Rocks

START/ FINISH	Lunenburg
DISTANCE	15 km (10 mi.) or 25 km (15.5 mi.)
TERRAIN	One long gradual hill
CLIMATE	Occasional fog
TRAFFIC	low to Moderate
REST STOPS	Blue Rocks wharf
FOOD	Lunenburg (R)(G)(C)
REPAIRS	Lunenburg
TOURISM	Lunenburg
HOSPITAL	Lunenburg
POLICE	Lunenburg

Hirtle's/ Kingsburg

START/ FINISH	Lunenburg
OTHER STARTING POINTS	Bridgewater
DISTANCE	49 km (30 mi.) (Short-cut available)
TERRAIN	Two hills in each direction
CLIMATE	Occasional fog
TRAFFIC	Moderate
REST SPOTS	Hirtle's or Kingsburg Beach
FOOD	Lunenburg (R)(G)(C); junction of kingsburg road (C); occasional opening of canteen at Hirtle's Beach
REPAIRS	Lunenburg
TOURISM	Lunenburg
POLICE	Lunenburg
HOSPITAL	Lunenburg

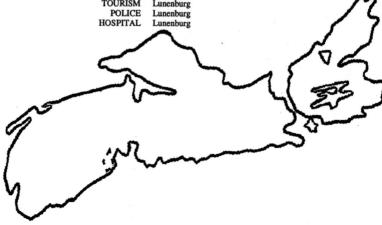

Explore one of the most photographed and painted villages in Nova Scotia. Then, relax and enjoy a day at an ocean beach. Revealed here are two of the many destinations you can reach from Lunenburg, Nova Scotia's "City of the Sea".

With little doubt, it can be said that this area will be a favourite for many using this guide. The fishing village of Blue Rocks has as much scenic beauty as Peggy's Cove-without the crowds. Isolated fishing sheds perch precariously on rocks in small coves, as Cape Islander boats putter in and out of the bay.

Stonehurst East and West are recommended as side trips. They are well worth the 10.6 km (6 mi.) detour. There are several such diversions to extend the ride to make a longer outing.

This is a ride to go slow and enjoy. You can easily spend all day enjoying the view and marine atmosphere. It also makes a great evening ride , from your campsite or Bed and Breakfast.Hirtle's and Kingsburg Beach: Selected for you on this ride are two pleasant sandy beaches, in beautiful surroundings. Water on Nova Scotia's Atlantic shore has a range in temperature-from freezing to bracing. However, the sands are warm and provide a nice spot to relax, read, or simply look out at the sea.

This is another easy ride. The only hills are just starting out of Lunenburg, and the crest just before the beach. There will be from low to moderate traffic. Starting the tour from The Ovens Park or Riverport reduces your cycling considerably, giving you a very pleasant route with few cars- a perfect tour to relax and enjoy the ocean!

Lunenburg is the tour start point of both tours, so prepare there before departure.

Last of the tall schooners

The famous schooner **Bluenose** is from Lunenburg. A fishing vessel of the Grand Banks, it never once lost a major race, and it was challenged often.

The Bluenose became immortalized as a legend among seafaring people. Today her image is to be seen on our ten cent piece.

The Second World War continued the pleasure and pride Nova Scotians took in the Bluenose as it was pressed into cargo service. However, sadly, this proud ship ended its life off the coast of Haiti.

As a salute to the magnificent Lunenburg *"saltbanker"*, an exact replica was launched from the same shipyards, by many of the same craftsmen, on July 23, 1963. Now, more than ever a symbol of Nova Scotia, she travels up and down the Eastern Seaboard as a sailing ambassador.

Tour 15 A Blue Rocks

START   At Lunenburg Tourist Bureau

0.2 (0.1)   **RIGHT** Sawpit Road

0.3 (0.2)   **LEFT** Pelham Road

2.8 (1.7)   **MERGE** with Lunenburg by-pass (Back Harbour Road - Route #322), The fish plant down the road is considered to be the largest in the world.

Watch for the **Lunenburg Bike Barn's** fancy sign coming up on your left. **Alan and Merrill Heubach** have turned an old barn into a two-story bike shop. Al is an experienced mechanic, and well equipped to deal with technical problems. Unlike most bike shop owners, he also personally bikes a lot.

The road generally follows the shoreline. Reaching **Blue Rocks,** you can see its slate rocks sloping down to the sea. Houses, wharves and fish sheds nestle together , and small boats float at anchor in the shelter of yet more rock. This is the setting for many visits by marine artists. You may spot on or two along the shore.

9.8 (3.6)   **RIGHT** *NOTE: EASYTOMISS!* a small road just after passing fishing sheds.

Stay along shore

11.2 (4.5)   **Road ends- Return along shore.** Great lunch spots.

SIDE TRIP- Stonehurst East and West are recommended as a scenic addition, worth the extra 10.0 km (6 miles). Visit both of them. Houses and sheds cling to rocky perches, as your narrow road winds its way around their tiny coves. Go into the centre of Blue Rocks and look for the road going northward. Spectacular beauty lies at every turn along the road to Stonehurst. One road tapers off at a romantic house only accessible by a foot-bridge. Like many fishing villages, both are on the ends of peninsulas, and require retracing your steps to the main road at **Blue Rocks.**

12.6 (5.4)   **LEFT** Blue Rocks/ Lunenburg Road

Continue straight past Lunenburg by-pass Coack Harbour Road, Route #322).

22.0 (13.5)   **RIGHT** Sawpit Road

22.1 (13.6)   **LEFT** Blockhouse Hill

22.2 (13.7)   **END**

Nova Scotia's city of the sea

All who visit **Lunenburg** agree on one thing- they are pleased they made a visit to this historic and interesting sea town. Home of Canada's largest offshore fishing fleet, deep sea trawlers bring in tons of fish every day to this, one of the world's major fishing ports. In terms of architecture, it is one of the most distinctive towns in North America. Bright red and yellow clapboard shops and huge old houses rise upward on a hill, making Lunenburg extremely photogenic. These homes, from those of modest workers, to wealthy ship owners, were all built with pride. The skill which went into making the best ships in the world also went into the building of these Georgian homes. Erected primarily from 1880 to 1890, wealth from the sea allowed improvements, and the houses took on decorative airs, which today emit a peculiar charm. **St. John's** is the second oldest church in Canada. Painted white and trimmed in black, the **Lunenburg Academy** is one of the finest examples of Victorian architecture on the east coast. It stands impressively over the small town.

Today Lunenburg has roughly 3,500 inhabitants. Settlement began in 1753. **German-Swiss** protestants were brought to the area by the governing English, to lessen the influence in the province of its second largest number of settlers, the Acadians.

The **Age of Sail** brought shipbuilding and trade, in addition to the abundant fishing harvests. By the mid 1820's, so many ships were in Lunenburg that it was said you could cross the harbour on their decks!

Built on a long peninsula with both a front and rear harbour, Lunenburg provides images to last a lifetime. Great views are available from the golf course hill, the road leading to it, from the fish plant, and countless angles on the towns hill and waterfront. The tourist bureau, itself a good viewing point, can supply you a route for a walking tour, the best way to appreciate this special town.

The **Fisheries Museum of the Atlantic** was Lunenburg's project in 1967 for Canada's Centennial. It is considered by many the best fishing presentation in the world! The glory of the past, and the hard life of the families depicted in the displays and powerful photo exhibition are sure to stay with you forever. Included are a fish aquarium, theatre, Bluenose momentos, and a working dory shop. A schooner and a trawler along the shore may be boarded (634-4794).

Tour 15 B   Hirtle's/ Kingsburg Beach

START	At Lunenburg Tourist Bureau. Go down Blockhouse Hill
0.2 (0.1)	**RIGHT** Sawpit Road
0.3 (0.2)	**RIGHT** Pelham Road. Pass through town of Lunenburg.
0.8 (0.5)	**LEFT** Lincoln Sreet.
0.9 (0.6)	**LEFT** Falkland Street at Lunenburg Common. Keep to the left.
1.2 (0.7)	**LEFT** Becomes Tannery Road just past the High School and Belroy Motel. It then shortly becomes Mason's Beach, then Corkum's Beach Road. As you go up the hill by the golf course, look behind you to take in the great view of Lunenburg.
7.9 (4.9)	**LEFT** onto #332
12.1 (7.5)	**RIGHT** Indian Path Road will take you on a quiet tarmac surface. Along the way are ospreys. Look for high poles, with their gigantic nests. The poles were specially built for the birds, as their nests are so large that telephone service can be interupted when choose to nested on phone poles.
15.8 (9.8)	**LEFT** #332
18.1 (11.2)	**LEFT** at Riverport. A couple of stores can be found in the village. Short dead-ends lead past marshes, fish plants and old Captain's houses. Right at the house with the cannon takes you to tiny Oxner's Beach.
20.2 (12.4)	**RIGHT** Kingsburg Beach Road. A store sits at the intersection.
24.0 (15.0)	**RIGHT** Hirtle's Beach Road (by Gladee's Canteen sign). Kingsburg Beach is straight aead, just down the hill.
25.6 (15.9)	**Hirtle's Beach** (a canteen is sometimes open here). Being on the Atlantic, the surf can be cool- some may find entering the water requires a short burst of courage.
	Return after break the same way you came in.
27.2 (16.1)	**LEFT** Kingsburg Beach Road
40.4 (25.1)	**RIGHT** Corkum's Beach/ Mason's Beach Road
47.1 (29.4)	**RIGHT** Falkland Street
47.4 (29.4)	**RIGHT** Lincoln Street
48.5 (30.1)	**LEFT** Blockhouse Hill
48.7 (30.3)	**END**

Accommodation

Belroy Motel 39 Knickle Road, R.R. 2, Lunenburg, NS B0J 2C0, (902) 634-8867

Bluenose Lodge Ron and Grace Swan, P.O. Box 399, Lunenburg, NS B0J 2C0, (902) 634-8851. Victorian mansion dated 1865. Located at Falkland Ave. and Dufferin St.

Blue Rocks Bed and Breakfast Merrill and Al Heubach. R.R. #1, Blue Rocks Rd., Lunenburg, NS B0J 2C0, (902) 634-3426. On route to scenic Blue Rocks. A bicycle shop is on the premisis! Limited space, reservations recommended. Lunches prepared for day rides. Lots of touring advice.

Boscowen Inn Lunenburg, NS B0J 2C0, (902) 634-3325. 1888 mansion overlooking harbour.

Compass Rose Inn 15 King St., Lunenburg, NS B0J 2C0, (902) 634-8509. Listed in Where to Eat in Canada

Snug Harbour Bed and Breakfast Nancy Callan. 9 King St., P.O. Box 1390, Lunenburg, NS B0J 2C0, (902) 634-9146. Sundeck overlooking harbour; no smoking.

Bridgewater Motor Inn 35 High St., Bridgewater, NS, B4V 1V8, (902) 543-8171

Fairview Inn 25 Queen St., Bridgewater, NS, B4V 1P1, (902) 543-2233. Gourmet pastries

Tannery Hollow Lodge Theresa Peck-MacLennan. R.R. 1, Petit Riviere, NS B0J 2P0, (902) 688-2186. Hiking trails nearby.

Barrett's Bed and Breakfast 543 Feltzen South, R.R. 1, Riverport, NS B0J 2W0, (902) 766-4655. At end of peninsula at Feltzen South.

Sou' Wester Inn Bed and Breakfast 788 Main St., P.O. Box 146, Mahone Bay, NS B0J 2E0, (902) 624-9296. Victorian shipbuilder's home.

Longacres Bed and Breakfast Ross and Sandy Hayden, 122 Clearland Rd., P.O. Box 93, Mahone Bay, NS B0J 2E0, (902) 624-6336

Bayview Pines Country Inn R.R. 2, Indian Point, NS B0J 2E0, (902) 624-9970. Trails through Christmas tree farm

Three Buoys House Bed and Breakfast Malcolm and Julia Stick. R.R. 2, Mahone Bay, NS B0J 2E0, (902) 624-6375. At Indian Point; full (cyclist's) breakfast; rowboat available

Hostel

LaHave Marine Hostel P.O. Box 92, LaHave, NS B0R 1C0, (902) 688-2908. Directly above the LaHave Bakery. Decorated with photographs and clippings recording days when the building outfitted Grand Bank schooners.

Camping

Lunenburg Board of Trade Campground P.O. Box 1300, Lunenburg, NS B0J 2C0, (902) 634-8100. Open area overlooking harbour, next to tourist bureau; showers available. Open field in town, do not leave gear in your tent.

Haywagon Campground P.O. Box 1300, Lunenburg, NS B0J 2C0, (902) 634-8100. Wooded site on Route 3.. .

Ovens Natural Park P.O. Box 38, Riverport, NS B0J 2W0, (902) 766-4621. Wooded campground with ocean setting. Interesting caverns known as "ovens" along the shore. Cottages available.

Risser's Beach Provincial Park (902) 688-2043/ (902) 688-2010. Wooded sites near beach; no reservations

Bayport Campground Martin's River, NS B0J 2E0, (902) 627-2678. Located to east of Mahone Bay on river; showers.

Shore Boat View Camping Bayport, NS B0J 2X0, (902) 766-4873. between Rose Bay and Lunenburg on #332.

Atlantic Canada
Cycling Festival

Privateers, phantom ships, and pirate treasure

our 16   Mahone Bay

The Nova Scotia Bicycle Book

Tour at a glance

START/ FINISH	Lunenburg
OTHER STARTING POINTS	Mahone Bay
DISTANCE	44 km (27 mi.) / 29 km (18 mi.)
TERRAIN	Rolling hills
CLIMATE	Protected from ocean; mildest conditions of tours in region
TRAFFIC	Low; Moderate through Mahone Bay
REST STOP	Mahone Bay
FOOD	Lunenburg (R)(G)(C), Mahone Bay (R)(G)(C)
REPAIRS	Lunenburg
TOURISM	Lunenburg, Mahone Bay
HOSPITAL	Lunenburg
AMBULANCE	Lunenburg; Mahone Bay
POLICE	Lunenburg (R.C.M.P.), (town); Mahone Bay

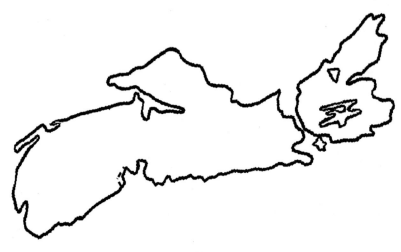

Y ou could live for a day on each of the reported 365 islands of Mahone Bay. Your stay on a few of them would not leave you much room perhaps, but this idea gives you an indication why for centuries this bay has attracted everything from pirates to pleasure craft. The word Mahone comes from the French word mahonne- a low-lying craft used by pirates.

Flat to rolling lanes twist along the shore from the attractive port of Lunenburg into Mahone Bay. The town at the end of the bay, with the same name, has tree lined streets and a pleasant atmosphere, making for a good break on a day of leisurely cycling.

A beautiful stretch continues past fishing boats and old homes to Indian Point, near some of the bay's many islands.

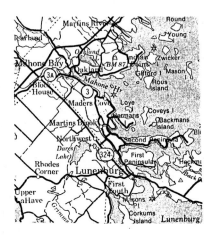

The largest treasure hunt of them all

M any people are convinced that millions of dollars worth of treasure is buried on Oak Island. A mysterious system of underground tunnels and chambers has been found. Wood and artifacts examined by scientists date them to about 1575, the same time pirates sailed up and down the shore.

Our story begins in 1795, when a boy discovered a hollow. Digging began, and went on for several years, with the dream of finding buried treasure. What they were digging in was clearly an old shaft of some kind. What was strange, was that every few meters they struck a wooden barrier, which had to be broken apart and removed before they could continue. After several years and many encountered barriers, they gave up.

Professional miners searched in the early 1800's. They too kept hitting wooden barriers. Finally, at over 30 metres (100 ft.), they struck something. A stone with mysterious coded markings that they could not understand, was excavated. Only lately has it been deciphered as reading *"40 feet below two million pounds are buried"*.

When they removed the platform under the rock, water suddenly filled the pit, killing the miners. The barriers

had actually been hydraulic seals! To bring water into the chamber, somehow rock tunnels, going into the bay, had been built far underground.

For generations since, eager fortune hunters have searched for the treasure (including a young **Franklin D. Roosevelt**). Every few years sees a new owner or project. No one has yet to reach the bottom of the pit.

At this point, to many, the buried treasure is secondary. The real mystery is, how can countless excavation schemes and specialists, millions of dollars of investment, and modern high tech machinery be unable to undo the work of pirates 400 years ago?

One thing is for certain, this mystery will continue for years to come!

The island lies only a few kilometres off Tour S-5, across a short causeway just before the village of Western Shore. At times, Oak Island is open to visitors and audio presentations made available. So much digging has gone on however that the oaks are long gone and much of the island looks more like the moon than a treasure isle. Check with the Mahone Bay Tourist Bureau, just to the east of the 3 churches.

97

START   Lunenburg Tourist Bureau Go west on Blockhouse Hill on Kempt Rd.

0.2 (0.2)   **LEFT** Lawrence St.

0.5 (0.3)   **RIGHT** Cornwallis St.

0.6 (0.4)   **LEFT** Kissing Bridge Rd.

1.0 (0.6)   **LEFT #332** Lunenburg Back Harbour Rd.

2.0 (1.2)   **RIGHT #3**

3.0 (1.8)   **RIGHT** (at first picnic park sign)

Side Trip- Second Peninsula: To your right is a good cycle ride to the tip of this attractive peninsula. It has a 46 acre picnic park with beach. It is a good place to spot an osprey.

4.0 (2.5)   **LEFT** (away from picnic park)

6.2 (3.8)   **RIGHT** Sunnybrook (at old mill). Straight through next intersection.

11.2 (7.0)   **RIGHT #3** Main St. The peaceful image of the three majestic spires at the head of the bay has for over 1 1/2 centuries helped create **Mahone Bay's** special atmosphere. This attractive, cosy little town demands browsing, filled with antique shops, restaurants, and Victorian era homes. The houses here are more ornate than the simpler style found elsewhere in Atlantic Canada, its one time prominent social and economic position. Stay and explore the town, or continue on, for a scenic ride to Indian Point and Martin's River. Mahone Bay was an area of much clandestine marine activity. In June 27, 1813, *The Young Teazer*, an American privateer (pirate ship) entered the bay, intent on taking the town's winter supplies. A British vessel quickly entered the cove, and cornered the U.S. ship. On board with the Americans was a British deserter. Realizing that escape was impossible, and that he would hang when captured, the deserter dropped a torch into the ship's powder magazine. According to legend (and to some town residents), the burning ship appears every year on the anniversary of the explosion.

14.5 (9.0)   **RIGHT #3** Edgewater St. (by monument and Petro Canada). Pass churches and tourist bureau.

15.5 (9.6)   **RIGHT** Indian Point Rd. (just after the bridge). Turn around to see one of the most photographed scenes in Nova Scotia. This view of Mahone Bay is a popular selection for calendars and postcards (a point not lost when they built of the huge gas station). **Indian Point** is an attractive fishing village, supplying mussels and oysters. It is named after an ancient burying ground of the Mic Mac. Watch for herons along the shore.

21.3 (13.0)   **LEFT** Inland from bridge takes you through wooded stretch to #3. Indian Point Road continues a bit further along the shore. Note the "Union" church, a rarity in Nova Scotia, one chapel shared by several faiths.

24.3 (14.8)   **LEFT #3** (becomes Edgewater St.)

Side Trip- Martin's Point/ Oak Island: Going right a short distance after connecting with highway #3, brings you to a very strange collection of *"Folk Art"*. Primitive, and times in a way macabre and pagan figures stand in a yard along the roadside. These bizarre creatures are constructed from garbage, much of it washed up along the shore. Recycling at its weirdest, this is far from a sanitized tourist operation. Further on is home of Oak Island, and the **Largest Treasure Hunt of All Time**.

29.5 (18.3)   **LEFT #3** Main Street at monument and Petro Canada station in Mahone Bay

32.7 (20.3)   **LEFT** Mader's Cove- Cross next intersection (small roads)

37.7 (23.4)   **LEFT** (at old mill). Stay along shore- **Ignore Lunenburg signs!** Take road through Prince's Inlet

41.0 (25.5)   **LEFT #3**

42.0 (26.0)   **LEFT #332** towards Blue Rocks (Don't make first right)

43.0 (26.7)   **RIGHT** Kissing Bridge Rd. (at bottom of hill) Go up toward large white school (Lunenburg Academy), and return to the Lunenburg Tourist Bureau.

44.0 (27.4)   **END**

Accommodation / Camping (See Tour 15)

Metro Halifax

Parks, beaches and active fishing villages lie within short distances from the amenities of Nova Scotia's capital. The outlying regions along the coast are some of the rockiest in the province - Peggy's Cove, Terence Bay and Prospect, sit among giant granite boulders and barren ground.

Built as an English garrison, today most people claim a solid British background. Its door on the ocean, many universities, and easy-going pace has enticed a wide range of other arrivals. Halifax's port in fact, is where most Canadians can trace their arrival to this country.

The largest majority-Black communities in Canada lie on the city's fringes, in the Preston and Hammonds Plains area.

The Halifax Metropolitan area has over 300,000 people, making it the largest urban centre of Canada's 4 Atlantic Provinces. Almost 1/2 of all Nova Scotians live within 100 km (60 mi.) of the city. The area does not seem to belong, centred among such quiet and outstanding cycling regions.

Everything is relative, and the area's population may seem of modest proportions to some. However, its traffic patterns deserve some amount of respect from every cyclist.

For years people have been drifting into the area from declining fishing villages and factory towns. It must be understood that during this time the city has expanded outward, without the addition of many new roads. Linear development has spread along Nova Scotia's typical narrow two lane highways. Within 50 km (30 mi.) of the city in all directions, there are at certain times, periods of busy traffic. If judgement is used, however, you can enjoy cycling in the Halifax "Metro" area.

A meandering peninsula of beaches and bays

Tour 17   **Aspotogan**

Tour at a glance

START/ FINISH	Hubbards
OTHER STARTING POINT	Chester
DISTANCE	51 km (31 mi.)
DIRECTION	Counter-Clockwise
TERRAIN	Hilly
CLIMATE	Expect changing wind conditions
	Occasional fog on coast
TRAFFIC	Moderate
REST STOPS	Bayswater Beach; Northwest Cove
FOOD	Hubbards (R)(G)(C), East Chester (C), Deep Cove (C)
REPAIRS	Halifax (off-route)
TOURISM	Halifax 424-4247; Hubards (seasonal)
HOSPITAL	Halifax (off-route)
AMBULANCE	Halifax (off-route)
POLICE	Hubbards (R.C.M.P.); Chester (R.C.M.P.) (off-route)

This loop is one of the finest cycling routes in Nova Scotia! Despite being near the city, you will find this to be both a quiet and scenic outing. Coastline for all but a short stretch, the road dips in and out of fishing villages and past beaches. The route is hilly, but well worth your effort.

You will encounter only a moderate number of cars. There certainly will be far fewer, in comparison with its sister peninsula across St. Margarets Bay, through Peggy's Cove. The loop is in a counter-clockwise manner to best enjoy the shore. Expect changing wind conditions, as you circle the peninsula. Thick "pea soup' fog often rolls in at its point.

Those living here may tell you they are "South Shore" people. You will see many of them still fishing the sea, and may detect traces of the distinct South Shore accent. However, this scenic loop is now being considered commuting range of Halifax, and long-time residents are finding transplanted neighbours.

Hubbards, your starting point, is cottage country. If someone from Halifax tells you he or she has a weekend place, chances are it is in, or close to Hubbards. The only community of note on this loop, it has also been known as a tuna and swordfish centre.

An optional tour starting place is from one of the several Bed and Breakfasts in the quaint yachting town of Chester. From here you can cycle Route 1 for a short stretch, and turn onto the tour at #329 at the store at East Chester. Expect a few hills until you reach the tour starting point.

If cycled return from Halifax, it is just about a "century", 100 miles (161 km). After much deliberation, this ride has been included in the "Metro Halifax" section. The octopus arms of suburbia are now closing in on this pretty area. Make the trip and enjoy it now, it may not be the same in a few years.

START	**Hubbards Shopping Centre** Depart to the right, out of the lot to the south-west, to do the cross-peninsula stretch first. This section of Trunk #3 almost touches the newer #103, so traffic is diverted away. Simms Settlement Park is about half-way across, and has a wooded rest area. A long downhill to East Chester provides your first glimpse of **Mahone Bay.**
10.1 (6.3)	**LEFT** **#329** at store at the corner (small Irving gas station and store). Shortly after passing the only major industry of the day, a hardboard plant, you arrive at the shore of Mahone Bay. From here, the coast wanders along rolling hills, passing through a few small old settlements.

In the middle of the peninsula **Aspotogan Mountain** stands roughly 245 m (800 feet) high. It provides a view looking out across Mahone Bay and its over **three hundred islands.** You can find a footpath that climbs it on the left, 250 m (0.2 mi.) before the shore at Deep Cove.

Side Trip At the Upper Blanford junction, turn right if you are interested in a short scenic ride past fishing wharves, boats and some attractive homes.

You are now at the point of one of the North Atlantic's famous **whaling stations.** Closed in only recent memory, there are few reminders of its one-time existence. There are no museums or historic plaques. History has recessed far faster than the short time passed should allow. Nova Scotia currently has a love affair with the whale. Increasing numbers of people are travelling to the province with the hope of getting close enough to see them. Perhaps this is what makes it difficult to acknowledge the bloody harvests of our recent past.

Blandford was originally settled by a group of Irish immigrants around 1750. Soon afterward English arrived in the area, and in 1809 a group of German- Swiss immigrants purchased large tracts of land. Originally fishermen, many of the area's people have left the sea in favour of more commercial jobs in Halifax and Dartmouth.

Aspotogan (pronounced As-po-to-gun) comes from the Mic Mac language and means *"where they block the passageways for seals".* It is another picturesque village, at the turning point on the peninsula. You next begin to edge **St. Margaret's Bay.** Plan a rest stop for Bayswater Beach. This stretch of pure white sand is seldom overcrowded.

Bluefin Tuna often frequent St. Margaret's Bay. The big fish arrive on what is known locally as the *Strawberry Run,* about the same time the wild berries appear. Tuna like mackerel, and since St. Margaret's Bay is a major spawning grounds, they are drawn to the area. Their numbers are unpredictable and their habitat depends upon the fish stocks. If this resource is properly cared for, large amounts of revenue could come to the area, especially from Japan, where tuna is a delicacy.

Northwest Cove is the peninsula's most painted and photographed village, posed around a sharp downhill bend in the road.

Shortly after passing **Fox Point** and its large lobster pound, take either road at the forks into Hubbards.

50.4 (31.3)	**LEFT #3**
50.8 (31.6)	**RIGHT** to Hubbards Shopping Centre
51.0 (31.7)	**END**

Accommodation (See Tour 20 for Halifax listings)

Deep Cove Resort and Marina R.R. 1, Hubbards, N.S., B0J 1T0, (902) 228-2200
The Anchorage House and Cabins Gordon and Judy Morrison, R.R. 2,
Hubbards, N.S., B0J 1T0, (902) 857- 9402
Dauphinee Country Inn 167 Shore Rd., Hubbards, N.S., B0J 1T0, (902) 857-1790 Victorian mansion on Hubbards Cove.
Casa Blanca Guest House and Cabins 463 Duke St., P.O. Box 70, Chester , N.S., B0J 1J0, (902) 275-3385
Stoney Brook Bed and Breakfast General Delivery, Chester, N.S., B0J 1J0, (902) 275-2342
Windjammer Motel P.O. Box 240, Chester, N.S., B0J 1J0, (902) 275-3567
East Chester Inn Bed and Breakfast R.R. 1, East Chester, N.S., B0J 1J0, (902) 275-3017

Camping

Hubbards Beach Campground Clyde Harnish, Shore Club Rd., Hubbards, N.S., B0J 1T0, (902) 857-9460 Pay showers
Graves Island Provincial Park (902) 275-9917 Attractive camping park on small island east of Chester; no showers, no reservations

A famous fishing village-
a photographer's dream

Tour 18   Peggy's Cove

Tour at a glance

START/ FINISH	Halifax (Armdale Rotary)
OTHER STARTING POINT	Tantallon
DISTANCE	91 km (57 mi.)
DIRECTION	Counter-Clockwise
TERRAIN	Rolling
CLIMATE	Sea breezes; Frequent cool air and frequent fog; Rain is usually cold
NOTES	Save money on film/ sundries - purchase before heading out
TRAFFIC	Moderate/ Busy Avoid weekends
REST STOPS	Peggy's Cove, East Dover
FOOD	Frequent stores, restaurants, and take-outs
REPAIRS	Halifax
TOURISM	Halifax 424-4247
HOSPITAL	Halifax
AMBULANCE	Halifax
POLICE	Halifax

The best known attraction in Nova Scotia, Peggy's Cove has captured the hearts of visitors for decades. A photographer's and artist's delight, immense rocks stand scattered randomly along the coast. Retreating glaciers during the last ice age removed most of the area's soil. The resulting 415 million year old "devonian" granite barrens will surround you around the edge of the peninsula.

For decades the village has been a haven for painters and crafts people. Where artists lead, tourists soon follow. Nothing threatens the life and character of a community as does the emergence of it as a tourist centre. Loved to death by hordes of guests, there are at times, as many tour busses as fishing sheds. One can easily imagine the expansion of fishing at Peggy's Cove being discouraged, due to the smell being offensive to the "visitors".

This beautiful area is the type of small scale place many feel meant best experienced in solitude. There are times to visit which will ensure you enjoy the village in the way it deserves. As an operator of a slow moving vehicle, this means adjusting your itinerary to best enjoy the cove and your ride there.

Campgrounds and inns are close by. Staying in the area enables you to visit before or after the mid-day crush. You can find refuge at any time, however, simply by taking a short walk away from the lighthouse along the giant granite rocks.

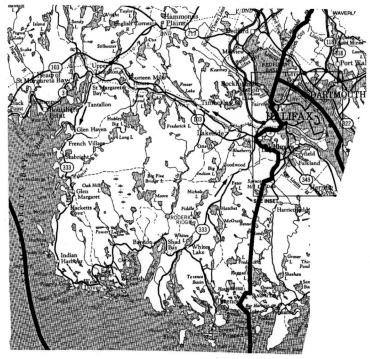

107

Make the best of your trip to Peggy's Cove

If you adjust your plans to the reality of Peggy's Cove's popularity, you should greatly enjoy this tour! The following is not intended to detract you from going, rather to insure that you have the most rewarding experience possible:

* **What to See:** The section of this tour to see is between **Tantallon** and **White's Lake.** The rest, mainly consisting of of new housing strung out along the road, you can easily do without. If you can find a way to cycle only the coast, you will not miss one metre of the tour's scenery.

* **Out and Back:** In addition to doing the full loop, You can go to Peggy's Cove from either Tantallon or Halifax and return. Of the two, from Tantallon is preferred. If going direct from Halifax, without doing the loop, follow the 1st left turn going to Peggy's Cove, when the listed route tour goes across the peninsula. From Tantallon, a good spot to start from is the health food store, at the intersection of highway #213

* **Traffic:** Keep in mind weekday commuting times. It is busy from White's Lake toward Halifax, and on the other side from Glen Haven along the #3 at rush hours. Most traffic will be going the other way from you, however there is little room for any vehicles behind you to go by, as the oncoming lane is busy. If you can, head out before 7:30 a.m. or wait until 9.

Not much truck traffic follows this route. Your main concern here are tour busses, and pleasure drivers. The Motorcoach Association reports Peggy's Cove as their third most visited site in Canada. Most of the 3000 tour busses visiting Nova Scotia each summer at some point pull into the village.

There is one point here to remember: These motorcoach tours are on schedules. Peggy's Cove is often the highlight of their day. Most arrive late in the morning or early afternoon, to time their visit for lunch.

* **Avoid the crowds:** If you want peace and quiet, get up and bike early to time your arrival before noon, or late in the day.

Weekends should be avoided, as at this time the local population joins the tourist traffic. Unlike the bus drivers, who are professionals (and have 40 witnesses), a handful of weekend drivers feel they can include you as part their entertainment.

Shoulder seasons are preferred over the peak months (July and August).

Sunrises and sun-sets are perfect backdrops. These are the times when the coast is at its most beautiful and majestic (the absolute best time is during a storm, but biking there is hardly fun).

Staying at a Bed and Breakfast or campground not far away allows you, as a cyclist, to be on hand for the optimum times. Visit without the crowds and having to leave Halifax very early or late.

* **Prepare:** Avoid the "tourist trap" syndrome. It is a good idea for you to buy film, sun block, and such items in town before starting off.

* **Sister Villages:** There is one good thing about the love affair people have with Peggy's Cove. It takes the pressure off other fishing villages. Places such as Blue Rocks, Stonehurst, Halls Harbour, Little Dover (near Canso) and many others, continue to operate as real fishing villages, offering just as much atmosphere. East and West Dover are two more, on this tour, sitting unvisited just off the road.

108

START   The tour begins at the Armdale Rotary. This is a traffic circle by the Hyland Theatre at the end of Quinpool Road, and down Chebucto Road from mall parking lots at The Bay, Sears, and Eatons.

If the traffic circle is busy, you may choose to walk to your exit. You want the one going up hill behind the church at "2 O'clock". Cycle up St. Margaret's Bay Road (#3 toward the South Shore). The first kilometre/ mile of your tour is the hardest of the day!

NOTE: At the top of the hill (2.5 km/ 1.5 mi.) **DO NOT** go left where it says Peggy's Cove! This is where you return! Keep going under the #103 overpass toward Vantage Point Plaza and the industrial park. Stay on this road, curving right just after the CJCH Radio technical building.

Highway number #3 is becoming a suburban strip, with only a two lane roadway. However, as you move out, the build-up will calm down.

15.7 (9.7)   Go over highway #103

At Lewis Lake, to your right a few kilometres before you reach the intersection of highway #333, there are picnic facilities, and a pier on the lake.

At the intersection of highway #213, and within sight of your turn-off for route #333, is a small plaza with a health food store.

24.4 (17.2)   **LEFT #333.** This is where you join or leave the tour if connecting with the South Shore. Soon you arrive along the shore of St. Margaret's Bay. You will be protected from the wind, as you pass a series of islands and forested peninsulas. As you turn around the coast however, barren land resembling moonscape greets you. Among the rocky crevices (and maybe attempting to cross in front of you), are large numbers of porcupines. Two fine restaurants are in Indian Harbour just as you near Peggy's Cove. This is also the primary zone for campgrounds and Bed and Breakfasts.

49.6 (30.8)   **RIGHT** Peggy's Cove Rd. Turn in on the road past the weathered sheds and trim houses of the village toward the lighthouse.

Peggy's Cove: The most visited village in Atlantic Canada has been set aside as a designated preservation area. This picturesque setting is justly famous for its marine beauty. The lighthouse, during summer months, is home to a post office. This is the only post office/ lighthouse in North America, and when you mail a letter from Peggy's Cove, a unique lighthouse imprint is placed over the official Canadian stamp.

There is a restaurant in the village where business is brisk. Be prepared: they have not been afraid to say "no service" to wet or cold cyclists wishing to warm up with coffee or soup, to make way for the next tour bus.

Most visitors do not stray far, so with a short walk, you can have a piece of the shore for yourself. Remember to exercise caution among the rocks!

Return on same road out of the village.

51.2 (31.8)   **RIGHT** onto #333

Until West Dover, this area is protected from development. To your right are pathways leading to quiet and attractive coves. Here, among the granite rocks it is easy to become disoriented and lost. The rocks are also smooth, quite slippery in wet weather. If you explore off the road please take care!

DETOUR- East Dover: An attractive and real fishing village, out of the limelight of its famous sister down the coast. From the highway, a winding road past large rocks takes you to the village wharf.

109

Weeping Widows Island in Shad Bay got its name from a reputed connection with **Captain Kidd.** It is said he selected the island you will curve around in the bay to store some of his treasure. Pits were dug on it by 43 men Kidd had rescued from various pirate ships. The holes completed, he killed the men who had dug them and interred them along with the treasure. He then sailed away, creating 43 weeping widows! It has since been renamed "Cochran's Island", but the legend remains.

SIDE TRIPS- Prospect and Terence Bay, despite their closeness to Halifax, have retained a great deal of their charm. Surrounded by the same type of bleak granite rocks as Peggy's Cove, both also make good day tours from Halifax.

On April 1, 1873, the *S. S. Atlantic,* a passenger ship propelled both by power and sail, was on its way on the popular run from Liverpool, England to New York. Calling on Halifax for fresh coal supplies, it left port in a storm. Soon after, it met with tragedy off the perilous coast.

A fisherman spotted through the gale hundreds of people flailing in the raging Atlantic waters. Racing into the village, he gave his tragic news. To his bewilderment he was met with laughter! With the many tricks and tales a fishing village would hear on April Fools Day, who would believe such a story of disaster?

Of all the families on board, only one child managed to fight his way ashore. Death came to 562 of the 976 sailing during this, the first major passenger liner disaster. A monument in Prospect's graveyard is dedicated to the victims of perhaps the greatest loss of live at sea until the time of an even larger disaster (also near Nova Scotia) ...*the S.S. Titanic.*

Continuing on your route, your remaining stretch back through Hatchet Lake and Goodwood takes you past linear housing and scattered lots of trees, a small "payment" for your tour along the ocean.

87.1 (54.1)   RIGHT #3

Once again you pass Halifax's old watershed before returning to the traffic circle. The ride down can be at times be quite hair-raising, as there are cars turning out into the roadway. Take it very easy, and if you are uncomfortable, don't even try to negotiate the rotary. Walk the final stretch, unless you know what lanes you need.

91.2 (57.2)   END

A *one-man tribute to the the sea*

A small park as you enter Peggy's Cove commemorates **William deGarthe** and his monument to the Canadian inshore fishery. Hand carved from a 30.4 M (100 foot) granite outcropping in his yard, the sculpture took several years to complete. Mr. deGarthe arrived from finland in 1926. From his arrival, he was constantly busy on his noted marine art. His final work before he passed away was an ambitious 10 year project to carve in stone a tribute to the sea. It depicts 32 fishermen and their families (some of whom still live in the village). A guardian angel, with outspread wings stands over them. Also included is his rendering of *"Peggy of the Cove"*, said to have been a lone survivor of a nearby shipwreck, and of whom the village was named.

Lobster- Prized Catch of the Sea

Nova Scotia lobsters, a highly prized delicacy, are in high demand around the world. At one time however, lobsters were considered a poor person's food and the practise of eating them was frowned on. The first settlers collected Nova Scotia lobsters along the beaches after a storm and used them for fertilizer.

Our first residents, the Mic Mac Indians, had long ago developed a taste for this large crustacean. Today it is the base of a huge industry. Nova Scotia lobsters are especially popular in France and Japan (the French like them for Christmas dinner, a huge convoy of aircraft is needed to meet the demand).

Live lobsters are dark green- almost black. When they are cooked, they gain their better known bright red colour. Lobster eggs, attached to the females' tail, hatch in the summer, sometime between June and September. An incredible 50,000 of them are hatched at one time. However, the odds are against them. After their hatching, they float to the ocean surface. After a month, unless eaten, (which is a 98 out of a 100 chance), they sink to the bottom again. If a lobster survives this floatation period, it has a good chance of survival.

After six to eight years, the legal catching size of one pound is reached. At this time it faces more bad odds, only five chances in a hundred it will get through the fishing season. Lobsters are "trapped" in wood-slat and mesh traps (called "pots"). Contrary to popular belief, the traps are not then placed on car roofs. That comes later, first they are dropped to the ocean floor. The trap is constructed with a mesh funnel through which the lobster can enter to get the bait, but can not get back out. Herring, mackerel or other small fish are used for bait.

Always a tug of war between supply and demand, prices fluctuate wildly. Seasons for fishing are complex, with zones throughout the Maritime Provinces opening at different times. The traps are marked in the water by brightly painted floats. Each fisherman has his own distinctive colour for easy identification.

Lobster fishing at times can be a very lucrative livelihood. In fact licenses are hard to come by. Unlike many professions, where old equipment is thrown away as an expense, used lobster traps make an excellent souvenir. They are sold at the road side to tourists, who bring them home. In a profitable irony, the more aged and battered they are, the more people want them!

Opening of lobster season in a way resembles a gold rush. The fishermen are up at four a.m. and are soon down on the wharves, baiting their traps. After a social drink to toast each other, they engage in a mad rush for the open sea. There, in a frenzy, they battle to lay their traps in what where they feel will be the best places. This first day panic often brings tragic news to families waiting back on the shore.

111

Accommodation (See Tour 20 for Halifax listings)

Clifty Cove Motel Ainsley and Chistine Hubley. P.O. Box 10, Site 30, R.R. 1, Tantallon, NS B0J 3J0, (902) 823-3178. 2.5 km (1.5 mi.) from Peggy's Cove.

Like-Home Cottages Box 1, Site 25, Indian Harbour, R.R. 1, Tantallon, NS B0J 3J0, (902) 823-3178

Lover's Lane Cottages Box 4, Site 31, R.R. 1, Tantallon, NS B0J 3J0, (902) 823-2670

Peggy's Cove Bed and Breakfast Audrey O'Leary, Peggy's Cove, NS B0J 2N0, (902) 823-2265. In village (near the church). reservations recommended.

Oceanside Inn Bed and Breakfast Box 105, Armdale, NS B3L 4J7, (902) 823-2765. 5 km (3 mi.) east of Peggy's Cove

Camping

King Neptune Campground Box 19, Site 28, R.R. 1, Tantallon, NS B0J 3J0, (902) 823-2582. 3 km (2 mi.) west of Peggy's Cove

Wayside Camping Park Box 9, Site 18, R.R. 1, Tantallon, NS B0J 3J0 (902) 823-2271. 8 km (5 mi.) west of Peggy's Cove

Seaside Camping Grounds Box 9, Site 16, R.R. 1, Tantallon, NS B0J 3J0, (902) 823-2732. 11.2 km (7.0 mi) west of Peggy's Cove

antic Canada
ling Festival

Great cycling in the shadows of Nova Scotia's capital

Tour 19

Sambro

Tour at a glance

START/ FINISH	Halifax
DISTANCE	64 km (40 mi.)
TERRAIN	Hilly'
CLIMATE	Ocean breezes; few degrees cooler than Halifax
TRAFFIC	Moderate
REST STOPS	York Redoubt; Chebucto Head; Crystal Crescent Beach
FOOD	Halifax (R)(G)(C); Herring Cove (C); Sambro (R)(C)
REPAIRS	Halifax
TOURISM	Halifax 424-4247
HOSPITAL	Halifax
AMBULANCE	Halifax
POLICE	Halifax (R.C.M.P.) 426-1323

This scenic coastal journey to a sandy beach provides a brief excursion into Halifax County's historic and military past. Along the approaches of Halifax Harbour are a multitude of vessels ...tug boats, container ships, oil tankers, military destroyers and supply ships, the coast guard, occasional cruise liners, fishing boats, and countless pleasure craft.

Crystal Crescent Beach awaits you, just past the fishing village of Sambro. Diversions are available along the way turning this, if desired, into an all-day excursion.

As you can note from a map, going in a loop is possible. However, the interior is a bit drab, with a long linear stretch of new housing and truck related industry. This ride will return the same way, along the shore. The change in direction on your return provides completely different views.

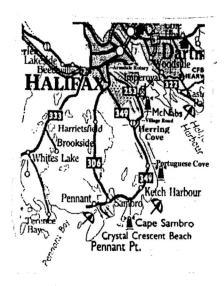

START	At the Armdale Rotary traffic circle, at the end of Quinpool Road. You want the rotary exit going up hill at "10 o'clock" (#349 toward Sryfield, Herring Cove, and Sambro). Your next turn will be a left, a short way up the hill. At times tricky, move into your lane from a distance behind, as traffic backs up.
0.7 (0.4)	**LEFT** Purcell's Cove Road (#253). Just past the large Greek church, a short shoreline stretch passes the attractive marina of the Armdale Yacht Club. In the cove sits **Melville Island**. The original buildings still stand where French and American prisoners were taken from the Napoleonic Wars until the 20th century.

DETOUR- "The Dingle"- You next head up a large hill. Near the top is the entrance to **Fleming Park**. *"The Dingle"* as it is popularly known (a name for a type of property in Scotland), was donated to Halifax in 1908. Its donor was native son **Sir Sandford Fleming**, as his monument to parliamentary institutions. Mr. Fleming, known as builder of the Intercolonial and Canadian Pacific Railways and the inventor of Standard Time, received donations from across the British Empire for its construction. A tall stone tower commemorates the first representational government in the Commonwealth (outside of Britain itself). If it is open, you can climb to the top of its stone stairwell for a view out over the Northwest Arm's exclusive homes and yachts. Its entrance is flanked by a magnificent pair of bronze lions. Donated by the British Parliament, they are a match to those at Trafalgar Square in London. They don't seem to mind having their pictures taken with visitors. There is a small swimming area and walking trails weave through the woods. An exit around the back of the tower offers a short-cut (but a very steep one) back to the tour.

115

Continuing on tour, the following wooded section hides large expensive properties. Next to the Sarguay Club is the **Royal Nova Scotia Yacht Squadron.** Terminus of the reknown **Marblehead to Halifax Yacht Race**, it is the oldest **sailing club in North America**. It is, as well, one of the few yacht clubs in the world granted permission to use the word *"royal"* in its title.

After edging **Purcell's Cove**, you climb up yet again. At the top of this hill stands **York Redoubt**. To add an element of overkill to England's major defence centre in the New World, additional forts to the **Halifax Citadel** were put up in the 1700's on the harbour islands and along both shores. Many of them have been replaced with modern fortresses of economics, such as an oil refinery on the Dartmouth side. York Redoubt has survived. Put into service again during World War II, the fort served as a submarine surveillance centre. It guarded against German vessels, mainly submarines, which regularly crept into Nova Scotian waters (even landing in some places it is claimed). The fort is now open during summer months. A tunnel-like walkway through its walls takes you out to a path, which leads you down to the harbour.

Leaving the fort, if you see a structure on fire during your next downhill, don't panic, the military fire-fighter training centre may be in session. As the road makes its next turn there is a scenic pull-off. A popular viewing point of Halifax Harbour. If your bike is secure, you can walk along the shore to the point. **Herring Cove** is the closest fishing village to the city. At its point is a monument to a 13 year old boy, who single-handedly saved two people clinging to wreckage during a storm.

11.6 (7.2)   **LEFT** Village Road, to the side of Floyd's Store (where the main road turns to go up hill).

12.7 (7.8)   **LEFT #349.** You now stay on this road all the way to Sambro. **Portugese Cove** offers views across the mouth of the harbour. There is almost always some form of ship traffic spotted from here.

SIDE TRIP-Chebucto Head: Just past the fire station on the left is a road with two diversions. Going off it to the right is the village, around a small cove. A trail leads to lookout bunkers used during the Second World War. Taking the left fork brings you to the lighthouse and command centre of **Halifax Harbour Traffic Control**. From this position all ships entering and leaving the harbour are guided through a series of points along its approaches. Atop the cliff is a recommended spot for you to sit and watch the sea and its ships.

Sandy Cove Road leads to a view of **Sambro Island Lighthouse.** Considered to be the **oldest still in use** in North America, it was erected way back in 1759, from proceeds collected from a government lottery!

RIGHT turn at T-intersection. To the left is the village of **Sambro**. An inscription carved into a cairn briefly records the history of the Sambro Island Lighthouse. From here it can only barely be seen. You may see its light occasionally poking over the trees of the nearby peninsula ("at 10 o'clock as looking out at sea).

Stay along the shore. Pass the intersection with #306 (Halifax via Harrietsfield). Continue past the ball field.

29.8 (18.6)   **LEFT** at radio receiver station.

30.8 (19.1)   **RIGHT** dirt road (if you miss it you will dead-end at the huge Teleglobe Canada Satellite Station). **Crystal Crescent Beach** is the turn-around point of the tour. In addition to its excellent sandy beach, you can go toward the right over a trail in the woods, which goes all the way to Pennant Point. Along the way you may find World War II lookouts (if going for a walk, lock your bike).

RETURN following the same route. Heading back, you see the coast in a different direction, with other vantage points

51.1 (31.7)   **RIGHT** Village Road, Herring Cove

52.2 (32.5)   **RIGHT** onto #253 by Floyd's Store. Following back along the shore, Halifax rises up before you, as you glide down into Purcell's Cove. The **Sailor's Memorial** can be seen at the tip of **Point Pleasant Park**. The large red and white cranes of the city's two container piers can be seen in the distance towering above the trees.

63.1 (39.2)   **RIGHT** #349 Herring Cove Road at traffic light. Your final leg returns you to the traffic rotary. If you find the traffic busy, you can simply walk across.

63.8 (39.7)   **END** Armdale Rotary

Accommdation (See Tour 20)

Atlantic Canada
Cycling Festival

The Atlantic for a doorstep,
Canada for a backyard

Tour 20   Halifax

Tour at a glance

START/ FINISH	Halifax
DISTANCE	14 km (9 mi.)
TERRAIN	Hilly
CLIMATE	Frequent fog
TRAFFIC	Moderate to High
	Suggestectime for tour: Between 9 Am and 3:30 pm; or after 6 pm
NOTES	Designed to be covered at slow speed
REST STOPS	Expect some walking- sharing a few sections with pedestrians
FOOD	Halifax (R)(G)(C)
REPAIRS	Halifax
TOURISM	Halifax (Provincial) Historic Properties 424-4247; (City) 421-8736
HOSPITAL	Halifax
AMBULANCE	Halifax
POLICE	Halifax

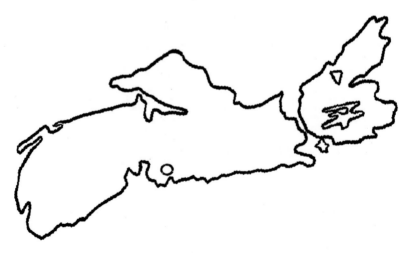

"Free boat fare, free housing, free food for a year, and forgiveness of all debt"

This unusual offer appeared in a London newspaper in 1749. Incentives needed to be large to lure anyone from England to the dense forests of Nova Scotia. Two thousand, four-hundred (2,400) people were inticed by the offer (mostly those in debt or on the wrong side of the law). Soon 13 ships set sail, and weeks later they arrived at a wide, wooded harbour. Starting work immediately, building what would become the British stronghold of the New World.

The Mic Mac (native "Indians') were the first tenants along its shores. Their land taken, they had reasons for making life difficult for the colonists. New settlers from Germany, before being moving on to their newly granted land near Lunenburg, were given the task of building tall wooden walls around the town for protection.

The city continued, through boom eras, and those of stagnation. It has always played an important role as the country's major east coast port. Most Canadians can trace their roots to the waves of immigrants who arrived in the new world through Halifax's docks. During both World Wars, huge Allied convoys assembled in its harbour, as had rescue missions for the ill-fated cruise ship, the S.S. Titanic.

Halifax is still a military town, but it also a large shipping port. At almost any time, you can see some form of activity on the water, from cruise ships to submarines; passenger ferries to single person kayaks.

Halifax stays young with 7 colleges and many other training centres, attracting thousands for studies. It also serves as Atlantic Provinces base for regional offices of business and government. Known mostly as a "paperwork" town, it is low in heavy industry. Filled with many trees- it is estimated per person, it has more than any other North American city.

Today Halifax, including environs has 300,000 people, making it Atlantic Canada's primary centre. The city consists of a peninsula, with the harbour in front, and a fiord-like arm of the sea known as the North West Arm in back. The harbour is the world's second largest (after Sydney, Australia). Across it lies Dartmouth,

Halifax's twin city. Suburbs connect the two cities around the large end of the harbour (Bedford Basin).

Small in area, with compact streets and fresh ocean air, Haligonians (inhabitants of Halifax) enjoy a green and walkable city. A historic section lies along its waterfront, mixed with newer buildings. Victorian and Georgian era houses fan out creating a fascinating contrast in architectural styles.

People have suggested that exploring cities is best done on foot. Others prefer getting the feel for an area by bike, then walk the parts they take an interest in later. Here for you is a shorter version of a tour I helped lay-out for the Velo Halifax Bicycle Club almost 20 years ago. Later, it was used in altered form for the publication "Bicycle Tours of Nova Scotia". Over the years, I have noticed that most cyclists on the tour enjoy the south-end of the city, preferring to explore the other parts of the city on additional explorations.

This is intended as a slow tour. An old city, its many interesting sites sit close to each other. Short sections of your route will be on paths and harbour boardwalks. Since they are shared with pedestrians, you should prepare to walk your bike for these brief, but interesting sections.

If you have a car- yes, parking will be a problem. Leave it where you are staying, or use a downtown parking garage (don't forget the low clearances- take bikes off before going in).

Note: After carefree cycling in the rural parts of Nova Scotia, many cyclists arrive into Halifax with their guard down. The city has a low crime rate for its size (very low if compared with some cities further south). However, chances are you have only one bike on hand, and losing it can make or break your trip. It is common knowledge in the capital of this tourism sensitive province, that visiting cyclists are about. Lock your bike (with a good lock) and take removable accessories with you. In addition, do not stay at a Bed and Breakfast or Inn that asks you to leave your bike outside, in a yard or on a porch!

119

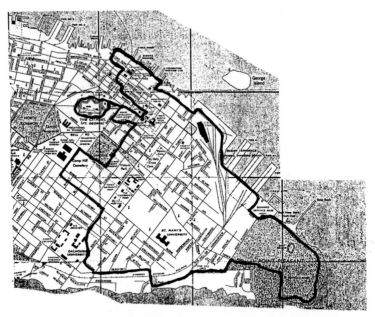

START   Halifax War Memorial, on the Grand Parade Ground, City Hall. Tourism Halifax is located on the other side of City Hall, at its entrance at the corner of Barrington and Duke.

Begin by going up the short path to Argyle Street past **St. Paul's Church.** The oldest building in Halifax, St. Paul's is Canada's first English, and Protestant Church (1749). It once served as the cathedral for as far inland as present day Chicago, Illinois.

Inspect the upper windows outside along Argyle Street. A well known Halifax piece of trivia, and reported in **Ripley's Believe it or Not,** concerns the famous **Halifax Explosion.** The disaster, perhaps the largest man-made explosion until **Hiroshima,** caused incredible devastation to the city. St. Paul's remained standing. Upon inspection of the building, one damaged window had produced a silhouette- **the exact profile of the church minister!** It has been preserved, with replacement glass laid over it.

Go southward along Argyle St.

0.3 (0.2)   **RIGHT** Blowers at end of Argyle

0.4 (0.2)   **LEFT** Grafton St. This arear has become a late-night snack trap, primarily intended to snare the city's thousands of college students.

0.5 (0.3)   **RIGHT** Spring Garden Road. Gathering on the library lawn is a Halifax tradition. You should find at any time a multitude of food vendors, musicians, executives and eccentrics. On your left as you turn are a number of points of interest. **St. Mary's Basilica** is the primary Catholic Church for the province. It features an impressive interior, and one of the tallest granite spires in the world. **Maritime Centre** is the large office building at the foot of the street. It is mentioned here as it has glass window elevators, which offer you excellent views on both sides, of Halifax, Dartmouth, and the harbour.

Government House is the large sandstone building with the canopy. It is the residence of Nova Scotia's **Lieutenant-Governor** (representative of the Queen of Great Britain). The influential guests of its many galas and receptions are no doubt unaware that they are actually entering through the back door! The original front door now opens into the garden. The building also stands as the **oldest consecutively occupied executive mansion in North America**, due to the burning of the White House. *NOTE:* by total coincidence, the person responsible is interned across the street!

The Old Burying Grounds (1754) is the site of the only **Crimean War** memorial in North America. The only cemetery in Canada that is a historic site, many important figures from history are buried here (maps and information on the gravestones are available from St. Paul's Church). Among those buried is **General Robert Ross**, who commanded troops that captured **Washington** and burned the **White House** in 1814 (the Americans caught up with him in Baltimore, sending him back to Canada in a rum barrel)!

0.6 (0.4)   **RIGHT** Brunswick St.

0.8 (0.5)   **LEFT** Sackville St.

0.9 (0.6)   **RIGHT** Through Citadel Hill gate.

CIRCLE HILL- Descend and exit same entrance you came in. This circle provides a view out over the harbour, and will give you a feel for the city. Halifax's kite lovers enjoy this attractive setting, as they take advantage of the hilltop winds. **Citadel Hill is Canada's most visited historic site.** The **Town Clock** is a symbol of Halifax. Built for a military town by a leader with an obsession for punctuality, it has kept Haligonians on time for 200 years (be on the hill for the daily firing of the noon day gun). Some of the features of the Citadel include the vaulted rooms, the dry moat, the ramparts, and as you will see, magnificent views in all directions. A concise and enjoyable history of Nova Scotia is shown through a recommended film presentation. Halifax Citadel's **Army Museum** has a superb collection of 18th, 19th and 20th century artifacts. British and Nova Scotian militaria include uniforms, medals, weapons and firearms. A cosy museum, you meander through its rooms in the fortress walls (admission fee 422-5979)

2.4 (1.5)   **RIGHT** Sackville St. (same entrance you came in)

2.6 (1.6)   **LEFT** Queen St. As you turn you will see at the corner Bollard House, built in 1838, and considered the narrowest house in Halifax (note the 1920's gas station just ahead of your turn).

2.8 (1.8)   **RIGHT** Spring Garden Rd. This is downtown Halifax's main shopping area, migrated in recent years from Barrington St. You are now in the city's major area. Be aware of the traffic here- busy intersections, pedestrians, bicyclists, and skateboarders.

The **Public Gardens**, coming up on your right, is considered the **finest Victorian garden in North America**. A floral showplace, the gardens are a throwback to a more graceful time. Welcoming you at the entrance is a magnificent ornamental gate imported from Glasgow, Scotland. Inside are flower beds, arranged in French-Formal and English Romantic styles. Several swans grace its pond.

Bikes must be left outside. The gardens has an iron fence, fine for locking bikes to, and visible from park walkways. One hundred years ago bikes were allowed in. This was a popular group photograph spot for the highwheelers of early Halifax cycling clubs.

3.5 (2.2)   **RIGHT** Summer Street

3.8 (2.4)   **LEFT** Jubilee. Just as you make the turn, the **Nova Scotia Museum** stands across the street. The main building of the entire provincial system, it follows Nova Scotia's human and natural history. It has a relaxing quiet mood about it, perfect for a rainy day (424-7353 admission fee in summer) Go around the building, and look up- is the giant frog out?

Another **Ripley's Believe It or Not** is coming up. This time you can file it under one of their

121

"*technicality*" claims. "*The only traffic light in a graveyard*" was a feature for one of their columns. As you can see at the corner of Robie Street, Ripley never *actually* lies.

Cross Robie Street (4 lane street)

4.6 (2.9)   **LEFT** Edward Street, continue a few blocks.

5.2 (3.2)   **RIGHT** University Ave. **Dalhousie University** encompasses the buildings which now surround you. With an enrolment of 10,000, including part-time students, its faculties of law and medicine are world renowned.

5.5 (3.5)   **LEFT** At the very end of University Avenue you will see a short sidewalk to your left. This connects to another campus road. It passes an athletic track, and curves left, onto South St.

5.9 (3.7)   **RIGHT** South St. **Dalplex**, a huge fitness centre, is part of the college, across from where you turn onto South Street. Guest passes are available. *Note:* the bike racks here are renown for problems. A suggestion is to walk back later.

6.0 (3.6)   **LEFT** Dalhousie St. (or at stop sign at Oxford St.).

6.2 (3.7)   **LEFT** Beaufort Ave. Roads to your right lead to the North-West Arm, and grand waterfront homes. Go to end of Beaufort

6.9 (4.3)   **RIGHT** at lane at end of Beaufort. Cross bridge. Below you is a major engineering work. Trains pass to downtown Halifax through this long cut-away through solid rock, the result of a massive effort years ago. Go downhill on the small lane. *NOTE:* You are now on a public access right. From near the bottom of the hill, a very short walk crossing through a wooded section takes you to more pavement on the other side.

Pass through the gates onto Franklin St. Go along Franklyn. On your right is the **Atlantic School of Theology.**

7.8 (4.8)   **LEFT** Point Pleasant Drive

8.0 (5.0)   **RIGHT** Tower Rd. (parking lot).

Point Pleasant Park comprises of 75 ha (186 acres) of forest at the very southern tip of Halifax's peninsula. Here you will discover 40 km (25 mi.) of nature trails. Ruins of old forts and munitions towers are revealed throughout the woods. A trip along the shore will offer you great views of the harbour, and McNab's Island. Bicycles are allowed in the park. On weekends however, they must be walked. Head in on the main path. Heather grows wild throughout the park- one of the few such areas outside of Scotland. (How did it get there? It is thought from seeds shaken out of the mattresses of British sailors many years ago).

8.6 (5.3)   **RIGHT** at the sign for Martello Tower. This fort made so great an impression back in England, that large numbers of them appeared along the British coast (also defence against French invasion). Once standing all around the harbour, today, only the one in Point Pleasant Park remains intact. Luckily, it is the first one, built in 1796-98. With stone walls 2.4 m (8 ft.) thick, the tower could, in very close quarters house 200 soldiers. Guns were set up on the parapet, and since at that time the trees were been cleared, there was a view from here of the harbour. On these grounds, Haligonians settled many disputes with duels! Continue past the tower and down the hill to the shore.

9.0 (5.5)   **LEFT** at the bottom. Scenic views look out from the end of the city's peninsula. Here stands Canada's **Naval Memorial**, and a plaque to honour the founding of the world famous **Cunard** Shipping Line by Haligonian Sam **Cunard**.

Black Rock Beach does its best to lure swimmers into Halifax Harbour. If you think the water is a bit bracing, come back on New Year's Day, when there is a "*Polar Bear*" swim! Leaving the park, you will pass a canteen. For years, this area has been a nightly meeting place. Like a time-warp from the 1950's, there is much posing around cars, revving of engines, and parading of motorcycles. Cyclists are looked upon like visitors from another planet at this nightly celebration of noise.

The looming cranes you see are part of Halifax's container terminals. Military tanks, exotic animals, double decker busses...you never know what you might see!

DETOUR- ALTERNATE ROUTE: You now have a choice. Along the shore, the route will go through the Port of Halifax. You could, however, also from here continue up the hill and make your first right. Young Avenue, is a street of many large old homes and many feel *the* place to live in the city. Turn right on Inglis, go to the bottom at Barrington. Go right a few metres, to the train tracks, and then look for a short passageway under the tracks, bringing you back on route.

11.2 (7.0)   RIGHT at the port gates. This is a rarity. Very few cities permit access of its citizens to its port facilities. Halifax is one of them. You will see here ships from all over the world, trading for Canadian products. A large portion of our country's immense grain crop is shipped from the gargantuan structure to your left. CAUTION: Be careful of train tracks, at a couple of points they run along in a sharp diagonal line. The buildings you soon pass on your right are sheds from which most Canadians can trace their roots! Wave after wave of immigrants passed through the docks of Halifax, answering the call of opportunity to settle one of the largest countries on earth. Sadly, like so much of Canadian history, these extremely important buildings sit neglected and unrecognized. It was at one time an extremely busy place. Ocean steamers, including those of native son Samuel Cunard were pulling into port, customs offices brimming were with immigrants, and gleaming stainless steel rail cars of Canadian National awaited to take the newcomers across the country. It was a place of great emotion, that of leaving home, perhaps forever, and the optimism of starting a new life, in a new country. It was also the scene of great confusion, arrivals from the much smaller nations of Europe exited the customs buildings, expecting short journeys to their new homes (many was the telegram sent to Winnepeg or Vancouver asking friends or relatives to "please meet me at the station in Halifax").

12.9 (8.0)   RIGHT (Lower) Water Street. On your left after a small downhill is The Brewery, an award winning historical restoration. Converted from Canada's oldest brewing plant, it serves a variety of uses, including a lively farmer's market held every Friday and Saturday morning. George's Island looms close to shore. On it is weather recording information. Another part of the region's fortification system can also be detected. An old Halifax legend tells of a tunnel, which connects the island with the fort on Citadel Hill. Work crews occasionally unearth under the pavement, old brick culverts, which people immediately rush to see if possibly could be the fabled tunnel.

As you can tell, the harbour shore here is currently used as a parking lot. The cars are resting on however, some of the most expensive real estate in Canada.

Note: Watch for the next turn!

13.3 (8.1)   RIGHT Salter St. Go down the short lane toward the harbour.

13.4 (8.2)   LEFT Here, along the walkway you will visit Halifax's hard-working team of tug boats. These sturdy vessels get to guide everything from glamorous ocean liners to damaged fishing boats.

Continue, following along the meandering waterfront pathway. If during peak summer, you may need to walk the following section. Two sculptures grace the small plaza. "The Sailor" is a tribute to all who have served in our forces. *The Wave* stands nearby (the rocks were later placed around it to remove its irresistible appeal from skateboarders).

Pass directly behind the Marine Museum of the Atlantic. This is a major part of the Nova Scotia Museum system. It documents the maritime history of Atlantic Canada. Exhibits feature the Navy, the Golden Age of Sail, the Age of Steam, shipwrecks and lifesaving, a small boat display, and the restored ship chandlery of William Robertson and Son. Docked at its wharves is the C.S.S. Acadia, Canada's first hydrographic vessel. The H.M.C.S. Sackville, the last of Canada's World War II

Corvettes, was restored after a tremendous effort mounted by veterans, it is now a floating memorial to the courage of all who served in Canada's navy and merchant marine (424-7490; 424-7491).

Continue along the harbour, you will see (but more likely first detect the fragrance of a local landmark- the Halifax fish market.

Dartmouth Ferry: the oldest saltwater ferry system in North America began in 1752, when boats shuttled from timber and whaling stations set up in Dartmouth. This same ferry service still operates today, with high-tech, multi-directional propelled boats. They are so progressive that bicycles have always been allowed, and racks are installed on each boat! This is a great way to see the city!

Pass the terminal, along the harbour for a visit to the oldest part of the city. **Historic Properties** encompasses several blocks of North America's oldest surviving waterfront buildings. These magnificent stone warehouses and shops once composed Halifax's old downtown. There is always a lot of activity here. The province's primary tourist bureau can assist you with information for your travels. **Pair of Trindles** is an interesting shop featuring a wealth of Atlantic Canadian books.

Go up the lane between Historic Properties and the Sheraton Hotel. Bluenose II often docks here in summer.

13.9 (8.4)   **CROSS** Lower Water Street by using the cross-walk from the Sheraton Hotel across to the historic Morse's Tea Building. Go around to the front.

14.1 (8.6)   **LEFT** Hollis Street. To your right you pass another section of refurbished old buildings. Built at the same time, their Italianate designs are unique in North America. Their fronts around the block on Granville street, have been enclosed in a small plaza, in summer a lively place. Being near an art college it is filled with bikes, some of them at times a bit eccentric. The Nova Scotia **College of Art and Design** rambles above the shops throughout the block. The first art college in Canada, it was founded by **Anna Leonowens** (of "The King and I Fame") in 1857.

14.4 (8.8)   **RIGHT** George Street. The **Nova Scotia Art Gallery** lies on your left. **Province House** is across the street. The house to Nova Scotia's government, it is Canada's first legislature and Britain's first colonial parliament. Called "A gem of Georgian architecture" by **Charles Dickens**, tours are available when it is not in session.

CROSS Granville St. To your left two blocks down, you will find a book lovers paradise. The Book Room, (Canada's oldest-1839), and a great rambling one, stuffed to the ceilings with old collectibles (Doull's). (Note: it's a one-way street, from here you must walk).

CROSS Barrington St.

14.9 (9.1)   **END** Grand Parade

Exploring Metro: suggested rides

Central and Northern Halifax

Most old buildings and tourist sites seem to be in the city's south end (from downtown to Point Pleasant Park). Throughout the city, however, are many interesting neighbourhoods. Streets of wooden houses, bakeries, art galleries, soul music record stores, pawn shops, and inexpensive restaurants ...a collage of both vitality and decay.

A memorial park at Fort Needham overlooks the section most devastated by the **Halifax Explosion**. (Note the replacement houses along Novalea Drive, built with thick blocks, in fear of a repeat blast). A modern bell tower stands in memory of the disaster. A tablet on a cut-stone monument commemorates **Captain James Cook** (1728-79), famed British naval officer and Pacific Ocean explorer. Cook lived in Halifax from 1758-62 during the campaigns against the French. While in the city, he compiled navigational charts of the St. Lawrence waterways, as well as supervised the construction of the city's naval dockyard.

Fairview Cemetery's mass grave testifies to the many unidentified victims. They lie at rest not far from those of another tragedy ...the sinking of the *S.S. Titanic*.

Dartmouth: City of Lakes

Halifax's sister city has its own downtown, old houses and points of interest. The Dartmouth waterfront has walkways walks that lead from the ferry Terminal, providing excellent views of the harbour islands, the two bridges, and Halifax. The city, of about 80,000, has 23 lakes, many with swimming spots. Some of its earliest structures were erected by the New England Quakers, who set up a whaling company. Historic Quaker Whalers' House, 57 Ochterloney Street (admission free) is associated with their arrival. A Quaker burial ground is nearby.

Newer outlying sections of the city are reached only by way of a few large arteries. The city grown without planning for cyclists.

Out of Halifax; Suggested Day Trips

York Redoubt/ The Dingle (Tour 19), a ride out just as far as the fort makes for a great short ride.

Prospect (See Tour 18)

Terence Bay (See Tour 18)

Highway #318 (Waverley Road) makes a good mid-afternoon or evening run. It follows a pleasant chain of lakes, once used for the ill-fated Shubenacadie Canal.

Cowbay A nice loop, if you visit off-peak commuting hours. The Halifax-Woodside ferry can be used to take you over.

The Halifax Explosion

On December 6, 1917, a collision in Halifax Harbour created the most powerful non-nuclear explosion ever.

At 8:40 am, two ships, the S.S. Imo, a Belgian relief ship, and the Mont Blanc, a cargo ship filled with 2,500 tons of explosives, approached each other off a berth known as Pier 8. For some unknown reason, the ships, under clear skies, collided.

An explosion followed, beyond any past earthly experience. A mushroom cloud rose high over the city, raining debris for miles, and destroying forever the heavy industries and ornate Victorian residential areas of North End Halifax. Areas of the city were completely levelled by the blast, creating a loss from which Haligonians would take nearly quarter of a century to recover.

Most panes of glass were broken, smashing windows as far as the town of Truro - 100 km (60 mi.) away. The huge ship's anchor was sent flying 3 km (2 mi.) away. 1,600 sailors, factory workers, and school children on their way to classes met immediate death that bitterly cold morning, hundreds more during the following days. Approximately 8,000 others were injured and over 20,000 left homeless following the greatest man-made explosion until Hiroshima.

Being an important military town during World War I, citizens feared the blast was an enemy attack. They fled for their lives, many sheltered within the walls of the Citadel. The navy were brought on shore, and the servicemen desperately joined those digging to save citizens trapped in the rubble. To add to the suffering, a severe winter storm howled all that night and the following day.

Despite the shortages and hardships caused by the war, relief efforts were quickly put into action from around the world. The greatest assistance came from the people of Boston, Massachusetts. Each year Halifax expresses its gratitude by erecting one of the largest Christmas trees in the province in Boston's Prudential Square.

The reason for the Imo steaming into the Mont Blanc? We may never know, due to the deaths of many of those involved during the explosion - was it error or an enemy plot?

126

Accommodation This can only be a random sample of the large selection of area lodging. Emphasis has been placed on accommodation most accessible to bicyclists, away from major highways or close to the city. Halifax and Dartmouth have been include together. Obtain a copy of the Nova Scotia Department of Tourism Guide for further listings. (*Note:* City accommodation prices tend to be higher than in the country- inquire on rates before making reservations).

Airport Area
Airport Hotel Halifax P.O. Box 250, Enfield , NS B0N 1N0 (902) 873-3000; fax 873-3000. 1km from airport. Complimentary shuttle from terminal. Bicycle boxes will be held for patrons during their trip.

Inn on the Lake Ron and Sue Nelson. P.O. Box 29, Waverly, NS B0N 2S0; (902) 861-3480. Complimentary shuttle from terminal.

Halifax/ Dartmouth Area
Boutiliers Bed and Breakfast Anne Mettam. 5 Boutiliers Grove, Dartmouth, N.S., B2X 2V9, (902)435-4094

Brightwood Bed and Breakfast Lyla Macmichael. 60 Slayter Street, Dartmouth, N.S., B3A 2A3, (902) 469-2109

Caroline's Bed and Breakfast Caroline McCully. 134 Victoria Rd., Dartmouth, N.S., B3A 1V6, (902) 469-4665

Cambridge Suites Hotel Paul Stackhouse. 1583 Brunswick St., Halifax, N.S., B3J 3P5, (902) 420-0555

Chateau Halifax Victor Ferreira. 1990 Barrington St., Halifax, N.S., B3J 1P2, (902) 425-6700

Chebucto Inn J. Georgantas. 6151 Lady Hammond Road, Halifax, N.S., B3K 2R9, (902) 453-4330

Citadel Inn G. Fred Repp. 1960 Brunswick St., Halifax, N.S., B3J 2G7, (902) 422-1391

Delta Barrington Peter Semadeni. 1875 Barrington St., Halifax, N.S., B3J 3L6, (902) 429-7410

Fresh Start Bed and Breakfast Innis and Sheila MacDonald. 2720 Gottingen St., Halifax, N.S., B3K 3C7, (902) 453-6616

Halifax Hilton 1181 Hollis St., Halifax, N.S., B3H 2P6, (902) 423-7231

Haliburton House Inn Richard Stinson. 5184 Morris st., Halifax, N.S., B3J 1B3, (902) 420-0658

Harbourlights Bed and Breakfast Verena and Tracey Croft. 66 Shore Rd., Dartmouth, NS B3A 1A3, (902) 469-1253. Continental breakfast 7-9am.

Hilton Hall Bed and Breakfast Dennis Zwicker. 1263 South Park St., Box 324, Station M., Halifax, N.s., B3J 2N7, (902) 423-1961

Holiday Inn Dartmouth 99 Wyse Road., Dartmouth, N.S., B3A 1L9, (902) 463-1100

Holiday Inn Halifax Centre 1980 Robie St., Halifax, N.S., B3H 3G5, (902) 423-1161

Keddy's Halifax Hotel 20 St. Margaret's Bay Road, Halifax, N.S., B3N 1J4, (902) 477-5611

King Edward Inn 2400 Agicola St., Halifax, N.S., B3K 4B9, (902) 422-3266

Lord Nelson Hotel 1515 South Park St., Box 700, Halifax, N.S., B3J 2T3, (902) 423-6331

Marie's Bed and Breakfast Marie Wilson. 3440 Windsor St., Halifax, N.S., B3K 5G4, (902) 453-4987

Prince George Hotel 1725 Market St., Halifax, N.S., B3J 3N9, (902) 425-6048

Queen Street Inn Alfred J. Saulnier. 1266 Queen St., Halifax, NS B3J 2H4, (902) 422-9828

Running Lights Inn Bed and Breakfast Ian Ripley and Tracey Cameron. 2060 Oxford St., Halifax, N.S., B3J 2N7, (902) 423-9873

Sheraton Halifax 1919 Upper Water St., Halifax, N.S., B3J 3J5, (902) 421-1700

Sterns Mansion Inn Bed and Breakfast Bill and Holly de Molitor. 17 Tulip St., Dartmouth, NS B3A 2S5, (902) 465-7414, Fax (902) 469-4412. Restored century home with antique bedroom furnishings. 2 rooms with jacuzzi spa. 4-course breakfast. Evening tea and sweets. No smoking

Tartan Motel Ken Murray. Box 14, Armdale, N.S., B3L 4J1, (902) 876-2301. By lake on route 3 outside of city.

Valhalla Bed and Breakfast Ted and Maureen Larsen. 1632 Oxford St., Halifax, NS B3H 2Z4, (902) 423-8492. 3 rooms, 1 shared full bath/shower. Continental breakfast 7-9am. No smoking.

Virginia Kinfolks Bed and Breakfast Lucy and Dick Russell. 1722 Robie Street, Halifax, N.S., B3H 3E8, (902) 423-6687

Waken 'n Eggs Bed and Breakfast Mary Lou and Al Keith. 2114 Windsor St., Halifax, NS B3K 5B4, (902) 422-4737. 3 rooms, private or shared bath. Full breakfast.

Waverley Inn A.J. Leventhal. 1266 Barrington St., Halifax, N.S., B3J 1Y5, (902) 423-9346

Camping

Laurie Park Province of Nova Scotia. Located on route #2, 28 km (17 mi.) from Dartmouth. No reservations, no showers

Shubie Park City of Dartmouth. P.O. Box 817, Dartmouth, NS B2Y 3Z3, (902) 464-2334/ (902) 464-2121 Open campground near lake. Jaybee Dr., on Route #318., 3.2 km (2 miles) from Mic Mac Parclo (traffic circle). Free showers, washrooms, laundromat, supervised swimming, fishing, easy trails for mountain bikes, tennis court.

Colonial Camping Don and Pat Huntley. Upper Sackville, N.S., B4C 3B1, (902) 865-4342. Located on highway #1, west of Bedford and Sackville. Showers, laundromat

Woodhaven Park Bernie Buchanan. Site 80, Comp. 32, R.R., 32, Bedford, N.S., B4A 2W9, (902) 835-2271. On route #213 at Hammonds Plains. Showers, laundromat.

*Grassy sand dunes where
swimmers and sea-birds throng*

Tour 21   Lawrencetown

Tour at a glance

START/ FINISH	Cole Harbour
OTHER STARTING POINTS	Dartmouth, Halifax
DISTANCE	68 km (42 mi.)
DIRECTION	Counter-Clockwise
TERRAIN	Hilly
CLIMATE	Sea breezes; rain is cold
TRAFFIC	Moderate
REST STOPS	Lawrencetown Beach; Porter's Lake Park
FOOD	Cole Harbour (R)(G)(C), Seaforth (C), Porter's Lake (G)(C)
REPAIRS	Dartmouth (off-route)
TOURISM	Halifax 424-4247
HOSPITAL	Dartmouth (off-route)
AMBULANCE	Dartmouth (off-route)
POLICE	Cole Harbour R.C.M.P.

Beaches...lakes...coastal marshes...fishing villages...there is much of interest to explore, just outside the city. Here is a route encompassing the coastline from outside Dartmouth, Halifax's sister city, through Lawrencetown to Chezzetcook, and return. NOTE: This ride is not recommended for weekends.

This ride can be used in connection with Tour 29, along the Eastern Shore (Marine Drive). The ride will not start in the city itself, but closer to its edge, avoiding most of the suburban sprawl. It begins in Cole Harbour. "*Wonpaak*" was the name given it by the Mic Mac (Indians). It means "*still water*".

There is an abandoned railway on this tour for those who might want to putter about on mountain bikes. It runs from just before Lawrencetown Beach towards Chezzetcook. (You cannot follow the trail directly from the ride start due to a railway bridge being removed). Plans are in the works to turn it into a recreation path.

Connecting from Halifax/Dartmouth: Take the ferry from the foot of George St. (near Historic Properties and Sheraton Hotel) to Dartmouth. If there is no ferry running, you must walk the MacDonald Bridge on the sidewalk. (It is the first bridge from downtown). Once across the bridge, turn right just off it, at the Holiday Inn, and continue down the hill. Just past the library (Alderney Gate - big pink building) at the bottom is where you turn onto Portland Street at the ferry terminal. From the ferry, at the foot of Portland St. Go up Portland Street through Dartmouth's downtown. You will go uphill, passing Penhorn Mall, across the large Circumferential Highway (#111), and go down again past more commercial establishments. You will then climb Breakheart Hill (named for the poor horses who used to have to climb it). The name will change to Cole Harbour Rd., also known as #207. Watch for the Tim Horton's on your left, in a plaza parking lot, at the corner of Forest Hills Parkway.

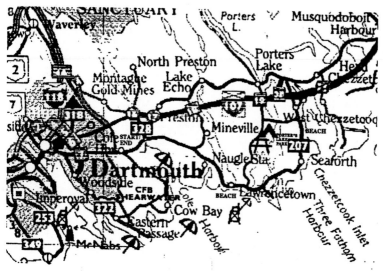

START   Tim Horton's at Cole Harbour Plaza. Go left on Cole Harbour Road (#7) (down hill past Dairy Queen). Bissett Road approaches to your right. It is said that along this road lived one **George Harper**, who moved to the United States. He operated a ferry services at a strategic location, later to be know as...**Harper's Ferry**. After a short rise, you will head down a steep hill towards **Cole Harbour**. Although close to the city, the large estuary supports a wide variety of marine wildlife.

The first beach you see is not suitable for swimming, due to dangerous currents. Watch for the abandoned railway bed for off-road biking, crossing the road just before Lawrencetown Beach. Continue on 0.4 km (.3 mi.) to the safer waters of the clearly marked **Lawrencetown Beach Provincial Park**. Lifeguards are on duty, changing facilities are available, and there is a canteen. The beach is always popular, with many swimming the bracing Atlantic waters.

SIDE TRIP - 3 Fathom Harbour: This interesting fishing village lies ahead, on the third paved road to your right after the beach. Once an island, it is now linked to the mainland by a causeway. It has served as an inshore fishing camp for well over a century.

Seaforth, Grand Desert and **West Chezzetcook** are three fishing and farming villages lying on the western side of Chezzetcook Inlet. Thus far avoiding suburban expansion, the inhabitants are descendants from early French Acadian settlers. Along the shore is a large baroque-style church. Watch for Grand Desert Beach after the coast turns northward at Seaforth, down a short road to your right.

33.5 (20.8)   **LEFT #7.** To your right highway #7 continues toward Musquodoboit Harbour and Tour 29. If heading that way, you will find a plaza with a grocery store, restaurant, and other services, just a short way along.

37.2 (23.1)   **LEFT** Porter's Lake Rd. (at convenience store)

    DETOUR: If you go straight ahead on Highway #7, you pass through Preston. Comprised of several communities, mostly in off the road, this is the nation's oldest and largest majority Black area. Until recent Caribbean and U.S. immigration to central Canada, this was the most populous Black region. They are descendant of several groups of arrivals: servants of British Loyalists, arriving after the American Revolution, following theWar of 1812, and freed American slaves from the Chesapeake Bay area in 1816.

The most curious of all was a short lived **Jamaican** community. Mountain people, former slaves of the Spanish, they were sent by the new rulers of the island, the British, to make control of the island easier. Known as the "*Maroons*", they took on the task of building much of the Halifax Citadel. This contribution is only now being recognized. These rebellious mountain people did not fare well in Canada. Upon planting their fields in Preston, complaints arose that their bananas and cocoa would not grow like at home. They also reported few wild hogs to hunt among the maples and spruce. They intensely disliked the winter, and their lack of freedom to live as they desired. When the emerging African nation of **Sierra Leone** took an interest in attracting these tough mountain people, most departed.

The **Black Cultural Centre For Nova Scotia** houses a library, auditorium and exhibit rooms, dedicated to the preservation of the interesting history and culture of Blacks in Nova Scotia, dating back to the 1600's. Themes include community life, religion, military service and migration. Genealogical records may be of help tracing back ancestors. All are welcome (admission is free 434-6223).

Continuing on tour, **Porter's Lake Park** is on your left. A picnic area is near the lake, and is protected from the wind.

50.4 (31.1)   **RIGHT #207** at Lawrencetown. Follow the same road back as the first part of your ride. Go up the same large hill you started off coming down.

67.5 (41.9)   **END**

Accommodation (See Tour 20 for Halifax listings)

Rosebank Cottage Jack and Vernie Friis. West Lawrencetown, NS B0J 2S0, (9020 434-8189. Near beach.

Camping

Porter's Lake Provincial Park   (902) 827-2250 No showers, no reservations. wooded campground and picnic grounds.

Central

S olitude rarely descends upon a traveller in an automobile. The radio is left on, the air is filled with continual conversation, and time is passed with minor distractions until reaching the desired destination. Constant, more subtle beauty fades into the background. Only superlatives sink in enough to prod the senses, much less be memorable.

Bicyclists move slowly, and can sense the character of an area. For years, this scenic and varied region has seen visitors zip through to better known places. For cyclists, this has been a blessing, because today they can explore an undeveloped coast- free of tourist hype, and with people who see strangers as visitors and not as sources of income.

This is perhaps the most underrated area in Nova Scotia. It sits squeezed in, between the allure of the marine atmosphere of the South Shore, the pastoral nature of the Annapolis Valley, Cape Breton's highlands and the golden beaches of Prince Edward Island. Transported anywhere else, this region would strongly stand out as a cycling attraction, but here it gets lost in the crowd!

Quite a contrast to the rocky and barren Atlantic shore, the Central area is known for its high red-soiled cliffs, with forests growing right up to the edge. Twice daily the Bay of Fundy pushes the world's highest tides funnelling up the coast. During storms, the waves take bites out of the soft cliffs, eating away the coastline. When the earth breaks off, it reveals semi-precious stones. Near Parrsboro and Joggins other gems are found -fossils and the bones of dinosaurs, millions of years old.

Extensive intertidal pools are created at low tide by the departing waters. Food is exposed for large numbers of sea-birds. This coast provides important waterfowl breeding and migratory areas. In spring and fall you can see flocks of plovers and pipers along the shore. At dusk, the huge swarms display wondrous acrobatics, turning in unison.

The tidal shores follow from the Nova Scotia/ New Brunswick border to Windsor. Preferring to be considered "Gateway to the Annapolis Valley", Windsor is actually a distance away from that famous landmark. ("Gateway to Central Nova Scotia" perhaps does not have the same ring to it).

From Truro, the Northern side of the bay is known as the "Cobequid Shore". The range of hills also known as the Cobequid run along not far inland. At Advocate the range moves along shore, creating some huge rolling hills. Steep on occasion, they are not so big as to make walking them unpractical. As Truro and the end of the basin approaches, the land becomes flat.

Human origins here go back a very long time. Implements of human activity have been uncovered indicating a presence in this part of Nova Scotia at least 10,000 years ago, when the Ice Age was just retreating, and the pyramids of Egypt were still centuries before construction.

Among Europeans, the Acadians first settled the land. They were later expelled by the British, with great brutality. Northern Irish immigrated to this coastline when they were denied religious freedom in Ulster. Further north. Cumberland County was settled by arrivals from Yorkshire. Remaining in the few towns of the region are tiny enclaves of descendants of Black Loyalists and refugees from the War of 1812.

Lumbering and scattered farms make up the base of the economy, in this quiet region. In its northern reaches is part of the world's largest wild blueberry production area. The Truro region serves as a dairy production centre, and transportation base.

Maple sugar camps are thriving, and some welcome visitors. In October the colours of the trees turn brilliant red, orange, and yellow. It is said that this is the area where the red maple leaf was adopted as Canada's national symbol.

133

The gateway to Nova Scotia

Cross the tiny Missaquash River from New Brunswick and you enter Nova Scotia. Here, at the very end of the Bay of Fundy, Nova Scotia and New Brunswick are connected by the Isthmus of Chignecto. This low, flat area is largely covered by marsh and swamp. The strong crosswind at the end of the Bay of Fundy is strong, at times known to rock vehicles as they cross!

Coming from New Brunswick, your first glimpse of Nova Scotia will not be of lobster traps and sand dunes. Like most entry points, traffic circles, gas stations, souvenir shops, and other commercial enterprises will be vying for your attention. There are actually two roads you can us to enter this "almost-island" province. A second entrance runs from Port Elgin, New Brunswick to Tidnish. This is a quieter entry point, with not much more fanfare at the border than a small sign and at times a lone official in a shed counting traffic.

Tantramar Marsh is the largest in North America, at 207 sq. Km (80 sq. miles). When the Acadians arrived here in the 1700's, they preferred to build dykes to reclaim soil, rather than face the task of clearing the forest. Settlers from Yorkshire later maintained the dykes after the Acadians' Expulsion. Referred to as "*the largest hayfield in the world*", this is an extremely important resting and breeding site for waterfowl. Millions of birds pass through on their migrations.

Busy Amherst

Welcoming you to Nova Scotia is the town of Amherst. The geographical centre of the Maritime Provinces, Amherst lies at the junction of two great touring regions. The Sunrise Trail along the Northumberland Strait (Tour 25), and the Minas Basin along the Bay of Fundy (Tour 22). The town's tourist bureau has a long history. Included as a car on Canada's 1982 **Discovery Train**, it also served for many years on passenger runs, and was presented at expositions. For a long time it even served as a bullet-proof car for high-ranking officials.

Large sandstone structures and huge old homes, such as on Victoria Street, take you back to the days when it was known as "*Busy Amherst*". The town boomed during the early 1900's. A Foundry, clothing plants, a woolen mill, and a piano works were among its many factories. Even automobiles were produced here, by the MacKay Motor Company from 1910-1914.

There were more millionaires per capita in Amherst than any place in the nation. Products from here were in demand, and were shipped to rapidly growing Central and Western Canada. Ironically, these growing markets would pull the population centre away, and place Nova Scotia in a less influential position on the edge of the country.

Pugsley's Pharmacy was founded by Sir Charles Tupper, who went on to become Prime Minister. It holds the distinction of being Canada's oldest continuously operated drug store (since 1843)! Few people know that during World War I, Amherst was the location of a prisoner-of-war camp. Leon Trotsky was incarcerated here for a time in 1917.

The great chimneys that poured black smoke over the town are gone. The chugging of trains arriving for goods; the whistles and bells announcing day's end; and the masses of workers. their faces pasted with foundry soot as they left company gates, are gone as well. And with them went much of the prosperity of "Busy Amherst".

Atlantic Canada
Cycling Festival

Fossil cliffs, folk tales,and forgotten villages

Tour 22   Chignecto Bay/Minas Basin

Tour at a glance

START	Amherst
FINISH	Truro
OTHER STARTING POINTS	Parrsboro; Truro
DISTANCE	220 km (136 mi.)
TERRAIN	Rolling; very hilly near Advocate and Economy
CLIMATE	Moderate conditions
NOTES	3 to 5 days suggested for tour
TRAFFIC	Low to Moderate
FOOD	Amherst (R)(G)(C); River Hebert (G)(C); Joggins (R)(C); Advocate (R)(C); Port Greville (C); Parrsboro,(R)(G)(C); Economy (C); Great Village (C); Bass River (C);
REPAIRS	Glenholme (R)(C); Truro (R)(G)(C)
TOURISM	Amherst; Truro;
	New Brunswick border (off-route); Amherst 667-1575; Joggins 251-2825; Parrsboro 254-3266: Economy 647-2920; Truro 893-2922
HOSPITAL	Amherst 667-3361; Parrsboro 254-2540; Truro 893-4255
AMBULANCE	Amherst; Parrsboro; Truro
POLICE	Amherst; Parrsboro; Truro

136

This is one of the most scenic and unpublicized areas of Nova Scotia. You are sure to find this a most unexpected surprise. Wide open spaces, and magnificent scenery lie along the reknown **Bay of Fundy**. Divided into two sections, the tour "restarts" at Parrsboro, to enable convenient conections, and to focus on the distinct natures of each part.

Along the coast between Joggins and Sand River lies one of the world's prime fossil areas. Old shipbuilding communities, created by the mighty *"Age of Sail"*, now sit silent along the pristine shore. Many have been completely forgotten. Abandoned to the forest, in places hardly a soul can be found for miles.

The road is now completely paved. Maps may still show it as gravel. Possibly, it could be too far to cycle the leg between Amherst and Parrsboro in one day. In that case, you must either camp in the rough along the way, or make arrangements at Reid's Century Farm at Advocate. Even then, it may still be a long

Often referred to as the *"miniature Cabot Trail"*, spectacular hill-top views are commonplace between Advocate and Diligent River. There you face switchback turns. One minute you are up on a look-off, then you go on a roller coaster descent or hairpin turn, never losing sight of the bay below. Unlike the Cabot Trail, almost no cars will be on hand as you creep up and race back down these spectacular shoreline vistas.

Easier than "Leg One", more services are available on "Leg Two". Parrsboro can be reached by way of a gentle, but not nearly as interesting route on highway #2, from Amherst or Springhill. Mid-way between Parrsboro and Truro, **Economy Mountain** stands overlooking Minas Basin. Expect the remainder to be slightly rolling landscape. Along the beaches, semiprecious stones are revealed in soil eroded from the cliffs. Acadian dykes still line the marshes, and blueberry fields run up into the hills. It is a region for delicacies- the blueberries, maple syrup, dulse (an edible seaweed), and clams, fresh from the bay.

START Leg One begins in Amherst, at corner of Church and Victoria St. (by Pugsley's Pharmacy). Head west, crossing the train tracks.

Cycle over the #104 (Trans-Canada) towards Nappan. Stay to the left at Boomer Loop. Your first stretch is through the flat area of **Tantramar Marsh**. This, the **largest marsh** in the world, is an important bird migration zone (200 species). It is also a haven for hikers and nature lovers. Good views of its ponds and lakes are available at the **John Lusby Trails**, coming up on your left.

At Amherst Point, the road curves left. Little pieces of this area may be home on your kitchen table. The **Canadian Rock Salt Company** operates a mine here, to your left. A different system is used than at the province's other operation at Pugwash. Here, water is pumped in and salt is brought to the surface in the form of brine. Along the road, watch for good examples of **dykes**, built several hundred years ago by the **Acadians**. Instead of facing the back-breaking task of clearing the forest, they chose instead to claim the tidal lowlands. Their seawalls, of natural materials, still keep back the Bay of Fundy. Notice where the road at times is lower than the water alongside! Their reclaimed marshlands have resulted in the creation of the *"largest hayfield"* in the world.

Cross the **Maccan River**, a tidal tributary. Your next turn is after the railroad track.

10.4 (6.5) **RIGHT in Nappan** onto #302 at cemetery, towards Maccan. Soon you will pass the **Canada Department of Agriculture Experimental Station**. Visitors are welcome at this over one hundred year old farm. You can look in on their current tests on feed and fertilizers, and visit the cattle and sheep. If you can find a non-marshy spot along the shore, you will have a good place to watch the *"tidal bore"*.

300 Million year old souvenirs

I magine creatures who fed in the forests during and even before the dinosaurs. This is one of the world's most important fossil as well as rockhounding regions. Here in petrified mud, strange tracks have been frozen in time. Fossilized plants, trees, reptiles, and even insects of a tropical forest million years old are are to be found near Joggins and Parrsboro.

The lowlands along the Minas Basin are made of soft sandstones and shales. They were formed when the land was flooded by silt from the Cobequid Hills (which at that time were mountains). The forests were preserved intact, the trees covered while still standing. Tides wear away at this sandstone, exposing impressions in the eroding cliffs. What is unique about the fossils here, is that since there is constant erosion by the tides, more are displayed each year. Most visible are the tree stumps of the ancient forest.

In 1985, one of the most significant finds ever was unearthed near Parrsboro. The discovery consisted of more than 100,000 pieces of 200 million-year-old fossils. This made it the largest single collection and the first that old discovered outside of South Africa. Included were **dinosaur footprints**, each the size of a penny, the smallest ever found.

A Rockhound's Paradise: Parrsboro is a rock collector's dream. Visitors should be on the lookout for agate, amethysts, jasper, zeolite, and other rocks. They can be found anywhere, even along the harbour in town. It is said that samples of almost every mineral on earth can be found in the region. An annual 3 day "*Rockhound Roundup*" celebrates everything to do with rocks. During the summer there are several guided tours, and there are museums devoted to this subject.

NOTE: You are not allowed (by law) to disturb anything intact in the cliffs. Some sections are protected, restricted to scientific study. Anything you find along the beach, however, is yours to keep. Take extreme care with the area's tides. Rock falls are frequent, so do not get too close to any overhanging parts.

Fundy Geological Museum 3 Eastern Ave. At tourism bureau in Parrsboro. Collection of fossils, gemstones, maps and exhibits.

Joggins Fossil Centre Don Reid. Mitchell Street, Joggins, NS B0L 1A0, (902) 251-2727 off-season: (902) 251-2618. Museum is based on over 40 years experience with the area's fossils and gemstones. Two hour guided tours show the fossilized trees and plants. Tours dependant on tide times.

Parrsboro Rock Shop Eldon George. 39 Whitehall Road, Parrsboro, NS (902) 354-2981. The world's smallest dinosaur footprints and the largest crocodile footprint are on display as well as rocks, gems, shells, and fossils. Daily tours.

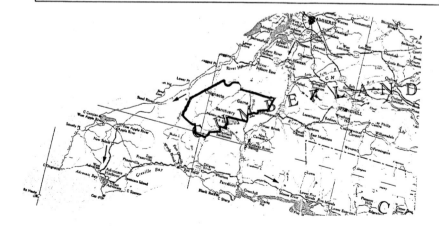

15.4 (9.6)   **RIGHT #242 at garage. Cross over small bridge.** Maccan is just ahead of where you turn. Villagers can help direct you to the prime **tidal bore** viewing areas. The bore here is among the highest in the world. Stay on #242. An abandoned train track bed, lined with years of old coal tailings, crosses the highway (power poles follow it). It allows some off-road exploration for mountain bikers. Just before River Hebert are good examples of the Acadian dykes along both sides of the river.

DETOUR Chignecto Game SAnctuary: A road known as the Boar's Back makes for an interesting ride through this wildlife preserve. From its name, you can guess it is of a rolling nature. Paved, then turning to gravel, it goes along an esker, the result of a melting glacier. The road is like ribbon candy, a real roller coaster. There are no guarantees, but you could spot deer, moose or even a bear as you pedal through.

Once a coal town, now **River Hebert** lies more silent, a commuting and retirement village. A monument stands as a memorial to the miners who lost their lives in mine explosions. The **Heritage Model Centre** features replicas of local historic buildings made to scale by village resident **Reginald Johnson**. He has constructed area homes, the Chignecto Ship Railway, a local church, an old schoolhouse, a creamery, a theatre, a sawmill, and a blacksmith shop. Season mid-June to Labour Day, other times by appointment (small admission).

SIDE TRIP Where "King" Seaman Reigned Accessed from River Hebert, the **Minudie Peninsula**, at one time was a busy and prosperous Acadian area. After their famous expulsion, the land eventually became controlled by one Amos Seaman. He operated a quarry here, from which its natural grindstones were found to be perhaps the best in North America. Becoming very wealthy, he ruled the area like a king. An old one-room schoolhouse tells of this tiny corner's history. Operated by Minudie Tourist Council. Ask locally for current hours. Just before entering Joggins you may notice traces of its old coal mines.

Joggins looks like many old mining towns, with houses scattered randomly about and mining memories in between. It sits directly on top of coal reserves. As you explore, you may come across small, mini-mines, some in people's back yards. Smoothed out by all-terrain vehicles and motorcycles, the mounds and small trails among the tailings make for fun playing around on mountain bikes. Today, Joggins

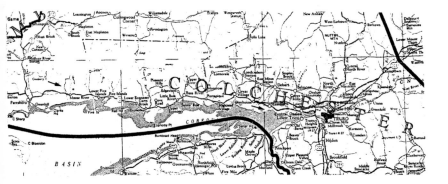

139

is to say the least, quiet. In late fall, it stirs somewhat to life, as hunters use it as a base for their treks off the deeply wooded trails. An exciting hike awaits along the coastline. It gives you an opportunity to gaze at the world-famous Joggins fossil cliffs, which include a stand of ancient trees. Check with the Fossil Centre, or anyone in town for directions. CAUTION: Hikers must be aware of the tides, which could prove deadly to anyone who heads off without first checking arrival times. A small restaurant is located in the village and a store can provide additions to your food supply. Eat well and stock up for your long run to Advocate!

33.8 (21.0) LEFT at Irving Station. Leaving the village, the headwaters of the Bay of Fundy quickly come into view. Staying mainly up on a plateau, you have scenic views across to New Brunswick. The tall hills you notice are part of Fundy National Park. You will now begin a long stretch of isolated road. Through deep forest, you will be in the home of plentiful numbers of deer, porcupines, raccoons, and other wildlife. Overhead are birds of prey, including hawks, and osprey.

Shulie was one of the quickly erected ship-building ports, once with a few hundred people. Other than a couple of cottages, all that remains is an old cemetery, a couple of cottagres, and remnants of several wharves along the river. Sand River Road to the left, takes an unpaved dirt road through wilderness all the way to Ward's Brook.

A House in the Bay

Once the entire coast was lined with busy little shipbuilding towns. Today, almost nothing remains. Entire villages have disappeared off the face of the earth. Between Joggins and Apple River, little trace remains that anything ever existed along this forested shore. But exist it did- and what strange spectacles of folly the shore's pioneers had to behold.

One day in 1919, villagers could be heard yelling out from along the shorelines. Residents ran to see what was the excitement. They were directed to a most strange sight- a house in the bay! It was even more startling to see smoke coming from the chimney, and crowing roosters wandering about a raft the structure was floating on. Everyone wondered- What was this house doing, sailing in the Bay of Fundy?

It appears a Mr. Goldstein of Advocate had closed down his business. His decided to move on to the then busy coal town of Joggins. This of course would mean leaving his house behind, one in which he had lived his entire life and in which his children had grown up. He could not bear to leave it... so he decided to take it with him! Since the only means of transportation was water, he made an agreement with a local tug owner to tow it up the bay, along with his family and hens. Today, this house stands across from the Joggins liquor store.

The Barge

One day, out of nowhere appeared one James Leary of Brooklyn, New York. He approached the villagers of the shore with an incredible plan. He had an idea of launching a giant raft. This barge would be so big that it would carry enough logs to build entire pier systems for New York City, as well as a few ships to dock there!

The residents of the shore went along with the plan. Upon its launch however, the raft broke up, sending logs floating all over the Bay of Fundy. Mr. Leary was not easily deterred. In fact he upped the ante and ordered an even larger one! Residents of the shore now became concerned. So big was this one mammoth cigar-shaped log raft that villagers feared all the region's good trees would be taken!

After six months of labour the gargantuan mass of logs was launched. The Halifax Morning Chronicle reported: "The raft is 598 feet long, 52 feet wide, and 35 feet in diameter, tapering to 10 feet at the ends. It contains 22,000 pieces of timber, averaging 38 feet in length. Its weight is estimated at 11,000 tons. It is therefore the largest structure ever launched." The mammoth barge of 1,375,000 m (4,500,000 ft.) of timber made its impressive entrance into New York harbour on Aug. 18, 1888. Another raft was attempted years later at Port Greville.

Before Apple River another rugged inland route, this one marked Shulie Lake Road, comes out in Port Greville.

At **Apple River**, you will see the first houses and possibly, people since you left Joggins. It is built around wetlands, hemmed in by dykes. A tiny store is located at the gas station.

73.9 (46.0)   **LEFT** just past the church. The small village of **New Salem** announces your arrival into **blueberry** country. Here, and then again later on the Fundy Shore, you will see huge fields of the wild berries. A family bakery is occasionally open in the village.

DETOUR- Eatonville: Going straight from Apple River, the pavement turns to a dirt road, which you can take around the cape to Advocate. **CAUTION: This detour is recommended for accomplished cyclists.** The road quality varies. Newer logging roads can be dis-orienting and it is easy to become confused and lost. At Apple River Bay, its sandy bar exposes wreckage of at least two ships. After a deserted section of the bay, littered with driftwood, the road turns inland. Crossings over rivers were junction points for roads to shipbuilding sites on the shore. Eatonville, once stood about 2 km (1.2 mi.) from where you turn inland. A decaying path along Eatonville Brook once led to the village's port, where in the mid 1800's was a large wharf, mill and shipbuilding facility. Boards, bricks, and girders lie scattered among the encroaching woods. It must have been quite a place, ringed by the harbour's magnificent vertical cliffs rising on both sides. Neither the village, once bustling with several hundred people, nor the harbour is identified on current road maps. No longer accessible by cars, its residents now are skunks and raccoons. Another vacated area, New Yarmouth, can be detected by old apple orchards. Here you rejoin the provincial highway map. A dirt road leads to a fire tower, and one of the most spectacular views in Nova Scotia. CAUTION:- the shoreline can be dangerous to explore alone. It is possible to become trapped in a cove with vertical cliffs, or even Eatonville Harbour itself, by the incoming tide. Know arrival times before walking the shore.

Continuing the tour, you enter the **Cobequid Hills**. Soon you reach the shores of the Bay of Fundy. Isle D'Haute (lofty isle) will appear on the horizon. Ringed by tall cliffs, this dramatic island frequently dense with fog, is home to tales of ghosts, and buried treasure. For the **Mic Mac** (Indians) it was a place of solitude and healing.

The hills now become challenging. Switchback turns begin as the road descends to cross rivers. **Advocate** lies behind a 7 km (4 mi.) sand bar. The beach now laden with driftwood, once hosted much shipbuilding. Many boats would be under construction at once, with up to 100 found working per vessel.

Spencer Beach (at bottom of large downhill), has a canteen and small camp area are along the water. A cairn by the store marks the spot where the famous mystery ship the *"Mary Celeste"* was built in 1861. The story of this vessel has become a classic among the strange tales of the sea. The ship was in Mid-Atlantic, on a voyage from New York to Genoa, Italy. Noting her erratic sailing, another vessel (also Nova Scotian) approached. Boarding, the crew could find no trace of any of the 10 passengers or crew. The table was set, prepared for supper. There had been no storms. The ship did not leak, and there was no evidence of fire or looting by pirates. Only the ship's papers and the chronometer were missing. No one has ever been able to explain what happened to them.

141

The cape of gold

Spectacular **Cape D-Or** at East Advocate is lined by huge cliffs, rising out of the Bay of Fundy. When the sun lights upon its seams of copper from the water, the view is stunning (translated it means "Cape of Gold"). The area is made even more dramatic by the fact that the huge Bay of Fundy splits here. Part of the powerful tidal current heads for Cumberland Basin toward Amherst, and the rest rushes on into Minas Basin. Giant whirlpools and powerful riptides are created. Standing on the high cliff looking down at the maelstrom below can be quite terrifying, sure to cause vertigo. An automated lighthouse sits perched on a ledge at the point. Here you can take in a huge expanse of the Bay of Fundy. To your left you admire the Cobequid Shore. Cape Split points out into the bay. The shores over the ridge of the Annapolis Valley follow in front of you toward Digby Neck. To your right in the bay is Isle Haute, and in the distance, New Brunswick. It is certainly worthwhile to see this place at both low, then high tides, to see its full dramatic effect.

Armouchiquois bands from **Maine** would come to produce copper arrowheads. They were always ready to battle the more peaceful Mic Mac, should they appear. In 1607, **Samuel de Champlain** made the first documented European exploration of this cape and its fabled copper mines. He discovered, however, something he considered more valuable than some ore. He uncovered a very old cross, rotted away and covered with thick moss. Christians had without a doubt, been here long before him. There is no clue however, of who they were. What was the identity of these mysterious people visiting this remote place at least a century before, possibly even predating Columbus?

CAUTION: Use extreme care on these rocks and cliffs! If going on the shore be aware of tide times. This side trip is a memorable spot to spend lunch, or even better, an entire day. Sunsets here are spectacular! This side trip comes highly recommended. The road in is dirt, with a couple of large hills on the way. No doubt you will grumble and possibly even have second thoughts. Keep going- it is well worth your effort! From Advocate there is no sign at the turnoff. Make the first right past the fishing wharf, then right onto the dirt road at house number 1460

The large hills continue. Because of the turns, it is difficult to get runs on them. At Fraserville, blueberry fields reappear. They are among the largest operations in the world. Many harvest areas reach even up to hilltops. Traditional family farms have not fared as well, as you may notice by the numerous abandoned houses and barns.

The hills flatten out at Ward's Brook. **Port Greville** has a general store and an attractive picnic site. Loop Road goes to a quiet section of shore. The tour continues past tiny communities, like Diligent Harbour, with its horseshoe shaped beach.

124.5 (77.4)	**RIGHT** Smith Hollow Rd. (Becomes Western Avenue)
127.2 (79.0)	**LEFT** Lower Main St. (at Irving gas tanks)
127.8 (79.4)	**END Leg One** at War Memorial in Parrsboro.

Parrsboro: rocklover's paradise

After cycling the long, unpopulated stretch from Amherst, Parrsboro might look like a huge city! In town you will find a few stores, restaurants, and even live theatre. This historic town is known as a **rocklovers paradise**. A collector's dream, even along the town's harbour, agates, amethysts, zeolites, jasper and other crystals have been found. Each year a large gathering is held for rock collecting aficionados, the **Rockhound Roundup.**

Close to 30,000,000 tons of goods would pass through Parrsboro on a given year during the *"Age of Sail".* Despite its size, it often led all Nova Scotia in shipping. The busy lumber and shipbuilding harbours along the shore depended on Parrsboro, as did Springhill, to send out its coal. The town hummed, with 5 hotels, and almost 3 dozen shops. 200 vessels called it home, including the mystery ship *Mary Celeste.*

With the end of the wooden ship era, the boom towns of the shore, the ones Parrsboro merhcants depended on, began to fade away. Being their supply centre, a slow decline began. The shift at Springhill to long distance train shipments, then the closing of its mines, hurt the town. Another coffin nail came with the construction of the cross-continental Trans-Canada Highway. Route #2 became a trunk road, losing most pass-through traffic. In addition, the bad luck of Springhill, its closest neighbour seems to have rubbed off on the town, it has sufffered several large fires. Today with 1,700 people,

Parrsboro, surprisingly, is the largest place along the entire shore between Amherst and Truro!

A ferry at one time crossed the Bay of Fundy from here to Wolfville (cyclists would love to have it back, it's over 350 km (210 mi.) to bike around)! The MV **Kipawo** was once the oldest continually operating ferry in Canada (its name comes from its route... Kingsport-Parrsboro-Wolfville). It now spends its retirement as home for the **Kipawo Players** stage company. They hold shows each summer.

It was from Parrsboro that the *"Governor Parr"*, a four-masted schooner was built. It achieved a dubious record- that of drifting the furthest. During a storm in 1923, it broke free, becoming a derelict. It then drifted for an astounding 3,200 km (2,000 mi.)!

Partridge Island, on its west side, is the place of the original townsite. Here in the 1700's, **Loyalists**, refugees after the American Revolution, arrived to start anew. On the way you pass some huge old homes. In 1869, during the ferocious storm known as the **Saxby Gale**, winds drove the beach inland, connecting the island. **Ottawa House** (circa 1840), once the summer home of Prime Minister and Father of Confederation, **Charles Tupper** is filled with period furnishings, and artifacts of the shipbuilding, and lumbering era (small admission). A beach area is nearby, perhaps too muddy to swim in, but offering a good rest spot.

START **Leg Two** begins in Parrsboro. Head out east on route #2. Look for the giant model of **Glooscap** (legendary Mic Mac Indian god). Delouchery Antiques is a short distance along, located on an old farm. You don't have much room on board, but it offers an interesting spot for browsing.

About 5 km (3 mi.) east of town, on the left, is *Hidden Falls.* An easy five minute walk along a trail takes you to the scenic 5 tiered waterfall. You can see the water coming over the mountain in a vertical drop of approximately 37 m (125 ft.) into two pools. A gift shop, with eclectic home made items is worth a visit.

Between Parrsboro and Bass River, you encounter a long wooded stretch. Several dirt roads go up into the hills, a great off-road bike exploration area. Some emerge on the Collingwood -Wentworth road (Tour 28), such as the one from Upper Bass River. Many others trail off at the top of the hill.

As you might guess, **Five Islands** is named from several isles in the basin. Legend

143

has it that **Glooscap** created them when he tossed handfuls of soil into the bay, after his magical powers were mocked. The islands stretch out along the basin in front of you. A sea cave can be viewed on one of them. Five Islands and Economy have unique *backward churches* (you enter facing the pews). Carrs Brook has a beach near what remains of its old dock. Great amounts of driftwood are found here, along this usually deserted section.

You must now deal with **Economy Mountain**. A steep climb, in either direction, it peaks at 215 m (700 ft.) above sea level. One side of the mountain offers a view of the scenic red cliffs while on the other, you may look out on the farms across the valley. At the very top, on the bay side of the road, is a supply of natural spring water. Bentley Branch Road leads into the provincial park, offering camping, picnic spots, trails, and spectacular lookoffs. After cresting, you will have a steep downhill into Economy. Known as "clam country", villagers claim they have both the best, as well as the largest clams in the world. They celebrate each summer with the **Economy Clam Festival.** The village has a cookbook, on how to make fried clams, steamed clams, clam chowder, clam loaf, devilled clams, clam patties, clam gravy...even clam pie!

SIDE TRIP- Economy Falls: North from Economy off River Philip Road, you can take in 20 metre (60 foot) high Economy Falls. It is on a well-worn path to the right 7 km (4.5 mi.). Walk 500 m (1/4 mi.) to an attractive waterfall with lunch area.

A public beach can be reached at the turn off at Cove Road. Along this section of the basin, tide waters recede over 1.6 km (1 mile) at low ebb.

Dutch Farmhouse Gouda Cheese Factory and Tearoom appears on the inland side of the road. **Willem and Maja van den Hoek** offer fresh cheese on site. Pastries such as their specialty- appeltart, are sold in their little teahouse. Small farm animals (sheep, goat, chickens, geese, rabbits, etc.) wander all about. Being Dutch, they naturally love cyclists. (902) 647-2751 Mid-June to mid-Sept., Wed-Sunday).

Along the shore you may notice an old gunnery range tower, used during World War II training. Now threatened by cliff erosion, it was placed here as the basin reminds many of the English Channel.

Small beaches can be accessed along the shore at low tide. **Bass River** (48.2 /29.9) is famous for its **chairs**. The factory has suffered several fires since its start in 1860, each time rebuilding.

SIDE TRIP A pleasant beach is at Saints Rest, an area on Sand Point, accessed by a road near the church (1.5 km/.9 mi. each way).

Between Bass River and Glenholme, remnants of the old Acadian dykes can be seen. **Portapique Beach** is reached from just west of the church. It is a good tide watching area. Next along the shore is an area which is a very good example of the dykes. This one includes sluice gates, over 200 years old, used to drain the marshes.

Great Village - Its large churches and sea captain's mansions, speak of its former glory as a shipbuilding centre. Unlike most of Nova Scotia, which began to decline after the tall ship era, Great Village's prosperity lingered. It was saved by iron and steel from Londonderry, a short distance inland. It loaded from village docks to build an expanding British Empire. **Layton's General Store** which is now a heritage building, operates as a combination store/ museum.

70.0 (43.5)   RIGHT at Glenholme, (Exit #11), at Irving Station. A short stretch of highway #104 is necessary. There will be a wide paved shoulder. This freeway is now the

144

unfortunate setting for Canada's **oldest Presbyterian Church.**

72.9 (50.3)   **RIGHT** Leave #104 back to peace and quiet onto #2, at Exit #12 at Masstown Motel. There is a fruit stand across road. After a distance, **McElmon's Pond** to your left, is a small provincial park with waterfowl and walking trails.

You are now firmly in dairy country, as the low lying tidal basin around Truro widens. This section was settled by homesteaders from **Massachusetts.** Inland, **Camp Debert** served during World War II as the departure point for thousands of Canadian soldiers. Significant finds of implements in this area indicate settlement by distant relatives of the Mic Mac 10,000 years ago!

SHORT-CUT: There are two ways of getting into Truro. The fastest is across the **Salmon River** on #102. There is a paved shoulder, and it is only for a short distance. The official route will enter Truro by keeping on the old road, and turn just before Bible Hill, further up. Cross the Salmon River. This river has several good viewing places for the **world's highest tidal bores.**

94.5 (57.6)   **RIGHT** Park St. Pass through Truro.

96.0 (58.5)   **END** Park and Queen St., Truro (See Tour 23)

Canada's first steel town

When Canada became a nation, steel production meant only one place- **Londonderry**, Nova Scotia. Settlers from Ireland, via **Londonderry**, New Hampshire, felt at home in this lovely piece of country nestled in ,a valley of the Cobequid Mountains. Between 1847 and 1872 the town swelled to 5,000 people. High grade iron ore was mined and converted to steel on the premises. One of the first systems ever of medicare was introduced at Londonderry. A doctor was brought to town in 1860, his wages dedeucted from workers' pay. This was greatly appreciated since it was a most dangerous place to work. Labour disputes were common. One of the biggest involved riots, after hundreds of workers imporetd from Britain were given higher pay.

After a few busy decades ore supplies dwindled. Imported material was brought in from **Nictaux**, in the **Annapolis Valley.** Surprisingly, this ore hardened in the furnaces, rendering them useless. The mills packed it in, and people left in droves. In 1920, an accidental fire caused the destruction of about half of town. With it went the last hopes of any recovery. As the town shrank to a small village, it became known for something totally different... its tough baseball and softball teams.

Today it's hard to find among the woods just where 2,000 workers operated a world reknown complex of blast furnaces, iron ore mines, coke ovens, railways, rolling mills and refining systems.

Londonderry is not a ghost town. It slumbers on, a village of perhaps 150. It has shrunken so much from its former size, however, that it is the only Nova Scotia selection in Ron Brown's book, *"Ghost Towns of Canada"*.

Londonderry Mines Museum depicts photos, artifacts, and other items of Nova Scotia's first boom town. Inquire for directions to hiking trails, caves, waterfalls, old mine sites, slag heaps, and coke ovens.

North to **Westchester** is an attractive road, with the province's highest single-span bridge (Acadia Mines Bridge). The road is accessed from the Anglican church, by the ball field. The bridge is 2 km (1.2 mi.) out. It crosses a deep gorge 30 m (100 ft.) high, the Great Village River charging through a s-shaped chasm below. Your may find the view from this little bridge a bit unsettling.

Accommodation

Blueberry Lane Bed and Breakfast Lloyd and Marilyn Munroe, R.R. #6, Amherst, NS B4H 3Y4 (902) 667-9567. Route #2 south, turn right on Blair Rd. Heated outdoor pool, blueberries in season on property. No smoking

Brown's Guest Home Deane and Nancy Allen, 158 Victoria St. East, Amherst, NS B4H 1Y5. (902) 667-9769.

Chignecto Motel Jude and Gloria Cormier, Gerald & Helen Read. P.O. Box 144, Amherst, NS B4H 3Y6. Located 1.6 (1 mile) north of Amherst. LaPlanche St., Exit 2 off Highway 104.

Fundy Winds Family Motel P.O. Box 1136, Amherst, NS B4H 3Y6, (902) 667-3881. LaPlanche St., from Route #104, Exit 2.

Journey's End Motel 143 South Albion St., Amherst, NS B4H 2X2. (902) 667-0404. Route #104, Exit 4. Open year-round.

Pied Piper Motel Marie Dodge, R.R. #6, Amherst, NS B4H 2Y4 (902) 667-3891. At Upper Nappan.

Victorian Motel Gary and Sharon Goodwin, 150 East Victoria St., Amherst, NS B4H 1Y3. (902) 667-7211.

Reid's Century Farm Mrs. Rae Reid, West Advocate, NS B0M 1S0. (902) 392-2592. 100 year old farm.

Glooscap Motel S. U. Roeslen, P.O. Box 353, Parrsboro, NS B0M 1S0 (902) 254-3135. Route 2, 1.6 km (1 mi.) north of Parrsboro. Hiking, lake swimming, lunches packed to go.

Glooscap Trail Riverview Bed and Breakfast Parrsboro, NS B0M 1S0, (902) 254-2388

Knowlton House Bed and Breakfast Keith and Joyce Knowlton 21 Western Ave., Parrsboro, NS B0M 1S0 (902) 254-2773.

The Maple Inn Bed and Breakfast Bruce Boles P.O. Box 457, Parrsboro, NS B0M 1S0 (902) 254-3735. 17 Western. Large shipbuilding era house. Packed lunches on request.

Riverview Cottages Bernice Byers, P.O. Box 71, Parrsboro, NS B0M 1S0, (902) 254-2388 off-season (902) 254-2416. 1.6 km (1 mile) east of town on highway # 2.

The White House Bed and Breakfast M. McWhinnie, Upper Main St., P.O. Box 96, Parrsboro, NS B0M 1S0, (902) 254-2387.

Rosalind Manor Neil and Louise St. Clair, Lower Economy, NS B0M 1J0, (902) 647-2665. Breakfast included

Thompson's Bed and Breakfast Kathleen Thompson, Lower Economy, NS B0M 1J0. On Route #2, overlooking Minas Basin. (902) 647-2777

Sea Shell and Clover R.R. #1, Great Village, NS B0M 1L0, (902) 668-2800

Maple Lane Bed and Breakfast Sybil Brown, Great Village, B0M 1L0 , (902) 668-2908. 1/2 mile past Great Village corner on right. Large farm house with swimming pool.

Shady Maple Inn Jim and Ellen Eisses, R.R. #1, Masstown, NS B0M 1G0. (902) 662-3565. Dairy farm with trails.

Berry's Motel George and Doris Mallett, 73 Robie St., Truro, NS B2N 1K8. Open year-round. (902) 895-2823.

The Blue House Inn Doug and Enid Jennings, 43 Dominion St., Truro, NS B2N 3P2, (902) 895-4150. Season June 1-Aug. 31; no smoking or alcohol.

Campgrounds

Loch Lomond Tent and Trailer Park Ella and Glen Ripley, R.R. #6, Amherst, NS B4H 3Y4 (902) 667-3890. Open and wooded campground on lake. 0.5 km (0.3 mi.) south on Route #2. Pay showers, washrooms, laundromat.

Fundy Tides Campground Advocate and District Development Association, Advocate Harbour, NS B0M 1A0 (902) 392-2287. Open campground 1 km (0.6 mi.) off Route #209, on Mills Rd. Washrooms, showers.

Glooscap Park Campground Town of Parrsboro, Michael Henderson, P.O. Box 400, Parrsboro, NS B0M 1S0 (902) 254-2529. Open and wooded campground. At Clarke Head, 5.6 km (3.5 mi.) east of Parrsboro.

Atlantic Canada
Cycling Festival

The highest tides in the world

Tour 23   Noel Shore

Tour at a glance

START/ FINISH	Truro
OTHER STARTING POINT	Brooklyn
DISTANCE	214 km (127 mi)
DIRECTION	Counter-Clockwise
TERRAIN	Hilly
CLIMATE	Usually sunny; breezes on hills
NOTES	2 to 3 days suggested to do tour
TRAFFIC	Moderate
REST STOPS	Lawrence House; Anthony Provincial Park
FOOD	Truro (R)(G)(C); South Maitland (C); Maitland (R)(C); Noel (R)(G)(C); Cheverie (C); Burlington(C); Brooklyn (R)(C); Scotch Village (C); Kennetcook (R)(G)(C)
REPAIRS	Truro; Windsor (off-route)
TOURISM	Truro 893-2922
HOSPITAL	Truro 895-5421; Noel (medical centre) 369-2515; Windsor (off-route)
AMBULANCE	Truro 893-3037
POLICE	Truro (R.C.M.P.) 893-6820; Windsor (R.C.M.P.) (off-route)

Easy- that's how you would describe your task of finding the most notable feature of this region. Here flow the largest tides in the world, rising to a height of 14 metres (42 feet)! A land of magic, mystery, and legend, the Noel Shore follows old shipbuilding ports, horse stables, poultry farms, and quiet cliff-lined shores.

The people you will meet along this route have diverse backgrounds, each village has its own story. Called the Glooscap Trail, after the Mic Mac god, there are extremely few Native people today alog the shore. Scots and New Englanders eagerly moved in to take lands vacated by the Expulsion of the Acadians.

The enigmatic "Colonel" McNutt somehow persuaded the British government to allow immigrants from Ireland. The British were normally against such a move, as they did not want the Irish possibly creating future problems for them in their North American colony.

Mostly poor, hundreds of Northern Irish gave all they owned to McNutt to escape famine and come to the New World. They settled along the shores of Minas Basin, thus earning the distinction of being the first Ulster-Scot settlement in Canada. Their villages fanned out on both sides of the bay from Truro. The time of the American Revolution proved difficult, as they refused allegiance to the British, who labelled them American sympathizers. As a result the government turned its back to the needs of their villages.

The Noel Shore side of Minas Basin, is less hilly than the north. Between Truro and Brooklyn, however, still offers you a series of fair sized climbs.

The return is on highway #236. It too has hills, but is easier than the shore. An exception will be in the vicinity of Gore, where the tour will climb for a panorama of much of central Nova Scotia. An abandoned train right-of-way runs along the Kennetcook River. Here you can go on this bed for some off-road explorations.

If you are passing through, and will not be doing a loop, the choice is simple- take the shore section.

START   Corner of Willow and Prince Streets in Truro Tourist Brueau. Go westward, passing shopping malls and fast food outlets. Pass under #102.

Development quickly fades away to prosperous dairy farms, many operated by past arrivals from Holland. A scenic route will take you to South Maitland. **Gosse Bridge** takes you over the Shubenacadie River, giving you a bird's eye view of Nova Scotia's largest tidal river. Along both sides is a primary bald eagle area.

RIGHT #215 (Tidal Bore Farm lies down the road to your left).

Maitland is a gem of a village. Another of the old shipbuilding and lumber towns, the village is a well preserved example of the boom times of the mid to late 1800's. Maitland, in fact, was chosen second after Sherbrooke as the site for a living museum.

Explore the home of **William D. Lawrence**, designer and builder of the largest three-masted ship built in Canada. One of the crowning achievements of Nova Scotia's mastery of the *"Age of Sail"*, his 2,549 ton vessel was launched with much fanfare in 1874. The *"W.D. Lawrence"* immediately set sail on a journey of ports around the world. It returned triumphantly two years and seven months later, its crew very wealthy.

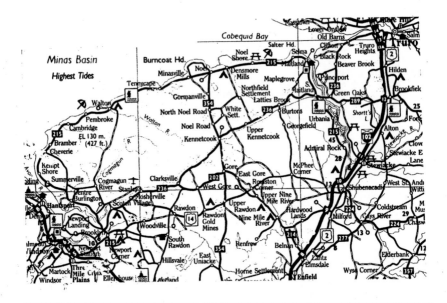

Trains, transporation, and underwear

Ever since the time of the first known habitation, the area now known as Truro has been the *"hub"* of Nova Scotia. Evidence shows settlement as far back as 10,000 years ago. Today the county seat of Colchester County, its area population is just above 18,000.

Stage coaches made Truro their main transfer point, as they travelled the long stretches to populated outposts. Trains and their connections later played an even larger role in development. With the building of the Intercolonial Railway (predecessor of Canadian National) in the 1880's, Truro grew as a major transportation centre. Recently have come the trucks, and they too have found Truro an ideal base.

The town is also known for its underwear factory. It was from here that **Stanfield's** produced knitted rib style garments which kept miners of of the Yukon and Alaska from freezing during the great Klondike Gold Rush.

Victoria Park nestles in a 400 ha (1,000 acre) natural setting, not far from downtown. A steep ravine, walkways, Joe Howe Falls, hiking paths, and a swimming pool await the visitor.

A family-operated bird sanctuary, the **Acres of the Golden Pheasant** is located 8 km (5 mi.) east of town following Queen Street. Over 50 varieties of exotic birds inbclude peacocks, cockatiels, and a bird of paradise. Operated by the Zwanepol family; open daily (893-2734 admission free).

A strange place perhaps, amid the farms of old Anglo-Irish stock, but east of town on route #4 is the location of Canada's oldest Islamic cemetary.

Millbrook First Nation: Just south of Truro is a Mic Mac "Indian Reserve". The unique teepee shape and interior of the church reflects the cultural heritage of this politically active band.

Lawrence House Museum stands today as it did in the heyday of shipbuilding in the 60's and 70's of the 19th century. The museum is located on your way west out of the village (free admission).

The basin here reminds many of the **English Channel**. In fact, the site of what is today the auto speedway was used as a commando training base for the World War II. At **Selma**, you can walk around Salter Head, below the cliffs. One part of it has a hole large enough to walk through. A *"flowerpot"* was formred where the red sandstone has ben eroded from the cliffs.

Anthony Provincial Picnic Park, nestled in an old orchard, has pleasant views over the Minas Basin. A pathway will take you down to the sandy shore, a good place to go swimming in warm water at high tide. A walk brings you to an Acadian dyke. The beach here, is a feeding place for thousands of migratory shorebirds in the spring and fall.

At Stirling Brook, between Selma and Lower Selma, is the huge Cox Brothers Poultry Farm. Here you may view the eggs being graded, weighed and packaged.

55.2 (34.2)   **RIGHT at Noel.** French settlers named their new home on the day they landed, Christmas Day. After the Acadian expulsion, in came the **Northern Irish**. The infamous **Captain Kidd** is said to have brought his pirate ship to Sloop Rock off Noel to be remasted. Here, it his said he threw out bars of silver as payment. Those who had, for fear of their lives, done the work would not touch the pirate money. The bars were left on the beach, and it is said lay in view for years.

Burntcoat Head is the loop taking you on a short diversion off the main road. Its name comes from a simple accident. A farmer was busy at work in his field. He took off his coat and laid it on the newly cut hay, carrying on withb his work. When he returned, he found the area ablaze with fire... he had left his pipe in his coat pocket! When you are ending the peninsula, and are about to rejoin the main road, to your right is **Moose Cove**, the exact point of the **world's highest tides**. As mentioned, due to the sloping nature and lack of distinct reference objects, other sites are more dramatic.

62.0 (38.5)   **RIGHT** Return onto #215. Stay along coast. The village of **Walton** boasts one of the largest single deposits of **barite** in the world. One time it employed a few hundred people. **Gypsum** also kept the town busy. In the 1970's a flood in the mine forced its closure. Population has dwindled to the point where even its school has had to close. Walton Lighthouse (built in 1873), has a scenic view of Minas Basin. Locals (if you can find anyone) can direct you to *"Second Quarry"*, which is now a pleasant *"swimming hole"*.

On the north shore of Rainy Cove at Pembroke, a steeply dipping sandstone bed exposes petrified trees of a buried forest. The outcrop is only a short distance beyond the wharf.

Mutton Cove, at Bramber, got its name from a shipload of sheep were cast into the bay when a vessel was wrecked off the coast.

Soon majestic Blomidon Mountain rising out of the bay will come into your view. Its red cliffs are unmistakable. For not a truly tall peak, it is especially attractive and distinct. It stands as the focal point for your travels through a large part of the Minas Basin and the Annapolis Valley.

At Cambridge, Cheverie, and Kempt Shore are small roads that permit you access to beaches. Here you can collect driftwood, shells and interesting rocks. Cheverie also has a *"swimming hole"* at an old gypsum quarry.

Summerville: Several roads run down to the shore at this old boat-building village. The *"Trojan"* was built here in 1884. Registering 1595 tons, it was planned by its builder to outstrip the largest wooden ship built in Canada, the *"W. D. Lawrence"*, built up the shore at Maitland. However, when the keel was laid, it was found that one end was unsound. Twelve feet had to be cut from its length, thus ruining plans.

Just before Centre Burlington and Lower Burlington, a right turn at Nunns Road leads to a small wharf and beach along the Avon River.

SHORT-CUT: Left at Upper Burlington you can cut through **Scotch Village**, a farming area named after early settlers. Once you have followed the river for a stretch, cross the bridge and onto route #236. When you reach the Kennetcook River look along the shores. Some of the best remnants of the original Acadian dykes are visible on both sides, still keeping out tidal waters.

DETOUR-Newport Landing: To your right the sign directing to Belmont and Avondale leads to Newport Landing (Tour 24).

123.8 (76.9)	**LEFT** #14 at gas station (head toward high school). The tour's turning point- from here you can head inland back to Truro. Westward you can join Tour 24, bringing you to Windsor.
	SIDE TRIP- Brooklyn: Among tall elm trees, the village lies straight ahead down the hill. The village, settled by Rhode Islanders, it has an old general store and coffee shop for a break. **Smiley's Park**, a provincial camping and picnic area a few km away, provides shaded picnic spots along the Meander River.
130.4 (81.0)	**LEFT** Second left at Woodville, just past the church. Roller coaster hills connect this attractive section with #236. Just before the end of the road, the old railway right of way passes through.
135.9 (84.4)	**RIGHT** #236
148.4 (93.2)	**RIGHT** #202 From Gore you can see four counties, perhaps even five. Sections of Hants, Colchester, Cumberland and Kings are in view and as some claim, a few trees in the upper corner of Lunenburg County.
159.2 (98.9)	**LEFT** #354
161.6 (102.3)	**RIGHT** #236
188.9 (117.4)	**LEFT** South Maitland (store). Cross Goss Bridge and return to Truro.
213.7 (127.0)	**END** at Corner of Willow and Prince streets at Tourist Bureau

Accommodation

Berry's Motel George and Doris Mallett, 73 Robie St., Truro, NS B2N 1K8. Open year-round. (902) 895-2823.
The Blue House Inn Doug and Enid Jennings, 43 Dominion St., Truro, NS B2N 3P2, (902) 895-4150. Season June 1-Aug. 31
Elizabeth House Bed and Breakfast Betty Kelly, 401 Robie St., Truro, NS (902) 893-2346. Evening tea and good chance for a cyclist sized breakfast.
Old Farm House Bed and Breakfast George and Betty Henderson, 195 Truro Heights Rd., R.R. 1, Truro, NS B2N 5A9. (902) 895-3671. 1867 farm, near 1.2 km (.7 mi.) from tidal bore.
The Palliser Motel P.O. Box 821, Truro, NS B2N 5G6, (902) 893-8951. West of Exit 14, Route #102, out of town, lighted viewing of tidal bore.
The Stonehouse Motel William Bursey, 165 Willow St., Truro, NS B2N 4Z9. Located in town
The Cobequid Inn Bed and Breakfast Jim & Nancy Cleveland, R.R. #1, Maitland, NS B0N 1T0 (902) 261-2841.
Foley House Inn John and Jean Hicks, P.O. Box 58, Maitland, NS B0N 1T0 (902) 261-2844, (902) 261-2302. In centre of village. Restaurant on site with Italian specialties. "Winner of Innkeeper of the Year Award".
Studio Vista Ted and Karen Casselman, Cheverie, NS B0N 1G0 (902) 633-2837. Operated by retired military oficer, and naturalist.
The Maples Bed and Breakfast Frances and Isabell Wallace, R.R. 1, Kennetcook, NS B0N 1P0 (902) 632-2504. Full breakfast

Campgrounds

Playland Camping Park Kim McCallum, R.R. #1, Brookfield, NS B0N 1C0, (902) 893-3666, (902) 895-4969. Open and wooded campground on Route 2, about 8 km (5 mi.) south of Truro. Season June 1-Oct. 1. Pay showers, laundry, swimming pool, trails.
Whale Creek Campsite Eldridge Burgess and Warren Dill, Walton, NS B0N 2R0 (902)528-2063, (902) 757-3489, (902) 528-2766. Open and wooded campground on ocean inlet.
Smileys Provincial Park Province of Nova Scotia, (902) 757-3131. Open and wooded campground and picnic grounds.

Nova Scotia's amazing tides

Among the most wondrous sights in Nova Scotia is the tidal phenomenon which takes place along its Bay of Fundy shores. Twice a day, 115 billion tons of water pours into this vast funnel, 235 km (145 mi.) long. Residents generally take the tides for granted. Visitors can hardly believe they see a ship resting beside a wharf on flat ground, high and dry, and in a few hours time see the same vessel in deep water.

How does this happen? And why the Bay of Fundy? Tides happen daily in all bodies of water. The sun and moon both have a gravitational effect on the earth. The moon has more than twice the pull, due to its closeness. Another variable at work is the contours of the long funnel-shaped bay, which forces the water into ever narrowing estuaries. It simply has nowhere to go but higher. One interesting facet is their extreme height during a full moon (as high as 53 ft.).

Harnessing such a force would create the greatest source of electrical power on earth. In just one day, the Bay of Fundy could create the equivilent of all the power from Niagara Falls in an entire year! Nova Scotia and New Brunswick would move from being among the least wealthy parts of Canada to "have" areas overnight. With a daily discharge 70 times that of the Mississippi, taming the over 3 1/2 trillion cubic feet of water is said to still be beyond human ability. Ecological difficulties also loom large, such as silting. The pilot project built at Annapolis Royal will tell us of its future.

With the relentless beating by the tides, cliff edges fall along the shore. Gemstones are revealed, and on the upper shore of the bay, fossils. Mud flats exposed at low tide attract animals, which feed on the abundant shellfish.

One of the magnificent wonders of the world- a tidal bore, occurs when the incoming tide forms a wall of water, rushing into the mouth of a river in the opposite direction of the river's flow. Nowhere else can a tidal bore of such size be seen. This wave can be from negligible to a couple of metres. The higher the tide, the bigger the bore, sometimes it is very prominent and other days you can hardly notice it. At times it produces a strange roaring sound.

Tide Watching

To experience Nova Scotia's famous tides go to places with distinct reference points. A few sugestions are the docks at Halls Harbour and Harbourville, or along cliffs, as at Cape d'Or, near Advocate. You have 6 hours and 13 minutes to spend between extreme high and low tide.

The best places in the world to view a "tidal bore" are where the Bay of Fundy narrows at Truro (near tideview Motel is a great spot), Meander River near Windsor, and on the northern branch of the Fundy at Maccan River, off route #242. The days close to a full moon are best, other times are not as impressive. Route #215 crosses the largest tidal river, the Shubenacadie. Nearby Tidal Bore Park offers a rare opportunity- you can go rafting both up, as well as down the rapids on the tide-induced waters (902) 758-2177.

DIAL-A-TIDE 426-5494 provides arrival times. Tides are affected by environmental factors, so get there early. CAUTION: Tides can rise as much as 0.3 metres (1ft.) per minute! Water rising 15 m (45 ft.) against the cliffs is not uncommon. Exploring must be done with an eye on the tide times. Every year several meet with tragedy, unable to get back to their access points. A distant storm will often cause wind-driven tides early and faster than times indicate.

Tides of History

On October 5, 1869, what is now referred to as the Saxby Tide reached a height of over 31.4 metres (103 ft.) above low water mark! Experts, scientists and even psychics around the world foretold of an upcoming extremely high tide. British Navy Lieutenant S.M. Saxby, a student of astronomy, was among the most forceful, publishing in London newspapers his prophecies, claiming that the position of the moon would cause extreme high tides. They were all warnings unheeded, however, as Nova Scotians paid little attention.

The predictions came true! All areas of the world's oceans were subject to the phenpmena. Being the place of highest tides, Nova Scotia was the most affected. The tide is said to have stayed an entire 4 hours, without rising or falling. Hills became islands, surrounded by raging waters. Beaches were moved, some connecting islands with the shore. Thousands of cattle pastured on the marshlands were drowned. People fled their homes from second floor windows by rowboats. Over 120 vessels were driven ashore and many lives were lost. One woman it is said looked out her window to see a three-masted schooner in her yard!

Tales of the tides

Touring along the Bay of Fundy, a group of cyclists I was with were taking a break along the shore. As we were having lunch, watching the bay a large car with two people came through the brush. A man got out and slowly ambled down the bank toward us. He looked out at the bay then back at our group. He asked: "Is the tidal bore expected soon?" Ken, a cycling friend from New England looked up, noticing the car, and its plates from a large neighbouring state. He thought for a second, turned and replied:"Oh... don't you know? Today's a holiday in Nova Scotia... there aren't any tides today!"

The man turned and walked back up the bank. As he got into the car he explained to his wife: "There won't be any tides until tomorow dear", and the car slowly backed out.

We wondered how far they got before they realized the prank, if ever- (it said volumes to this author of just how far from the cycles of nature human kind has strayed).

Leading a club tour a few years ago, I planned a group picnic along the bay. As we ate, a pick-up truck drove onto the mud flats from the shore to get closer to where clams were being dug. After about a half-hour, the tide began to come in. The clammers kept their digging until the water was getting close to them. They then lifted their spades and pails in the back of the truck and casually got in to return. To total surprise, the truck's tires spun in the mud. We could not believe if what we were seeing was actually happening, as the truck began to fill with water, the clammers scurrying to shore. Those in the group with mischievious senses of humour roared with laughter as they watched a power boat speed out to attempt to pull the truck in.

An even grander story, which is now gaining legend status all over the region, involves a tourist, travelling in a small personal airplane. From the cockpit, he saw a large, flat expanse of ground below, and decided to land. You can guess what happened next! The "ground" was actually part of the renown tidal mud flats, and on contact the plane dug in like glue!

Soon, the tide rushed in and the plane was so badly damaged by the force of the muddy water, that it was wreckage within hours!

One more story. To illustrate how tempting the tides are, the final laugh will be on this writer. During lunch break on a tour I organized along the Bay of Fundy, I made sure to advise the group of 30 cyclists, mostly from away, about the importance of respecting the tides. After their departure, my friend Mike and I boarded my Cannondale tandem (two-seater) to go off exploring some back roads. Descending along a long dirt road we arrived at a small village on the Fundy shoreline.

Another village lay nearby across a small creek. There being no bridge between them, we laid the two-seater down on the ground, to look for a easy place to cross over. We found a good spot and returned to bring across the bike. To our horror, water had come in from the bay what must have been a distance of 30 m (100 ft.) and was lapping over the bike's back wheel! We quickly grabbed the bike and moved to a grassy area, which seemed out of range. After our panic had subsided, we laid a rock and a piece of string where the bike had been. Within a minute, the rock was covered. Within 5 minutes it was under 1 metre (3 feet) of muddy salt-water. We could only sit in shock, and for myself, (after my lectruring) great embarrassment. Watching the rush of water, it was all too easy to envision what would have been just minutes later. The water had seemed so far away. It looked like it could never have even come close to where the bike was waiting.

The true horror did not sink in until later. We crossed the creek, bringing the bike to a road on the other side. Going up the short path to the road, we came across a huge field of ripe raspberries. We spent an entire half-hour feasting on them. We then wondered, what would have happened had we spotted them earlier?

These are funny stories, but remember that although peaceful and deserted when you begin to explore, the danger is very real. Get the tide times, and you'll safely enjoy one of Nova Scotia's special gifts.

antic Canada
cling Festival

Mud flats and giant pumpkins

Tour 24 Windsor/Newport Landing

Tour at a glance

START/ FINISH	Windsor
OTHER STARTING POINTS	Brooklyn
DISTANCE	48 km (30 mi.) (Option for longer ride)
DIRECTION	"Figure 8"
TERRAIN	Hilly
CLIMATE	Tail end of Annapolis Valley's warm microclimate
TRAFFIC	Moderate
REST STOPS	Newport Landing
FOOD	Windsor (R)(G)(C); Brooklyn (C)
REPAIRS	Windsor
TOURISM	Windsor 798-2690
HOSPITAL	Windsor
AMBULANCE	Windsor
POLICE	Windsor (R.C.M.P.)

H ome of North America's oldest agricultural fair ...founding place of the country's first college ...in possession of the only blockhouse in Canada ...home of North America's first humourist ...the possible birth place of one of the greatest sports ...and built on ground that sprouts the largest vegetables on earth- there's a lot that makes the town of Windsor special!

A suitable location to base yourself for several attractive rides, Windsor is the starting point for this one to Newport Landing. Tucked away between the Annapolis Valley and the Noel Shore, its small peninsula benefits from the fine weather of the valley, and has the rolling slopes which typify the shore. The total distance of the ride is 48 km (30 mi.), much less if you start at the village of Brooklyn. If you wish for a longer ride, an attractive option runs for a loop inland through Woodville.

This is an area of farming, fruit growing, and sheep raising. Along the way you will visit the Meander River, among the best places to see Nova Scotia's famous tidal bore. It can vary here, from 26 cm (10 in.) to 1 m (39 in.), depending on the moon and other factors.

Acadian by birth, the famous and brutal **Expulsion of the Acadians** in 1755 changed Windsor dramatically. **Fort Edward Blockhouse** was once part of a palisade. Acadian men were ordered to appear at the fort, where the British told them of their fateful decision. Since they would not swear allegiance, they would be deported to Louisiana. Some were sent back to their villages to relay the order, but a few hundred were kept in detention, to prevent mass escapes into the woods. The last such fortification in the country, it stands atop a hill, near the tourist bureau.

Clifford Shand was an avid cyclist. He won a multitude of awards for his bicycle racing. To set the standard for best times of his day, he pushed what we consider antiques over rocky and rutted dirt lanes. He became involved in all facets of cycling. Running a bicycle club in town, it grew to quite a size, and with participation rates to be envied by any group of today. He was not only Windsor's most prized athlete, he also owned its most modern home. Built upon a hill overlooking the Avon River, the house was prepared for services which did not even exist yet. Wired for electric light, its construction went ahead with the expectation of its arrival one day in town. **Shand House** is now a museum. Throughout the home you can note momentos of his cycling. Photos, racing trophies, and bike parts in the attic give evidence that a cyclist was definitely about the house (one can almost still hear the pleas not to conduct repair work in the kitchen or parlours). A small upper attic look-out is reached by a ladder. Most tourists perfunctorily climb up and come right back down, (getting perhaps their only exercise of the day). Bikers, however, will find the tiny space of interest. Around it are old photographs. They are mainly group pictures, taken at large gatherings of cyclists (rallies). Frozen in time, you can almost feel the excitement of the hundreds of bikers assembled in the now obscured locations.

Shand House today looks out over what was once Windsor Harbour. Now a lake, on sunny days it plays host to numbers of windsurfers. Six old churches line King Street. One parish burying ground has tombstones dating back to the 1760's. Ask at the tourist bureau for a walking tour brochure. It will outline the town's attractions and fine old homes.

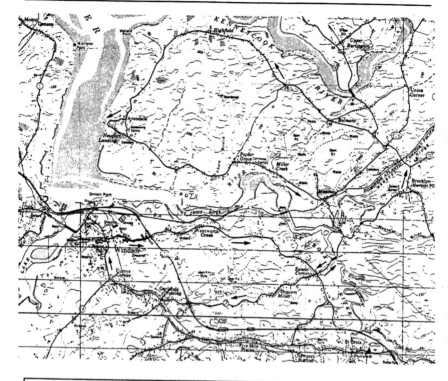

"The early bird gets the worm"
"It''s raining cats and dogs"
"You are barking up the wrong tree"
"Upper-crust"
"Stick-in-the-mud"
"As quick as a wink"
"Six of one and half dozen of the other"
"As large as life and twice as natural!"
"A nod is as good as a wink to a blind horse"
"Give and take, live and let live"

Have you heard any of these quotes? You should make a visit to learn about humourist **Thomas Chandler Haliburton**. His home, **Haliburton House**, stands amid pleasant grounds, worth a visit in itself. From here he penned his witty sayings and stories, now a part of our everyday language. The house tells what it was like to live in his times (at least for the successful). Free of charge- operated by the Nova Scotia Museum system- not far south from the downtown bandstand.

START	Corner of Gerrish and Water streets in downtown Windsor. Head through town on Gerrish St. (highway #1).
0.7 (0.4)	**LEFT** O'Brien Street (at Kentucky Fried Chicken).
1.1 (0.7)	**LEFT** Wentworth Road. The heaviest pumpkins in the world don't have to be carried far to be presented. North America's **oldest agricultural fair** began here in 1765! Since then the **Hants County Exhibition** has been held annually. Prizes have been given for best cattle, sheep, horses, butter, cheese, and produce. When it began there were also competitive events- for the best shooting, running, and wrestling. The contest which attracted the most enthusiasm was one regarding who could consume the most rum and remain standing. After rowdiness at a few fairs, this feature was suspended.
8.5 (5.3)	**LEFT** #14 (sign toward Milford at Gates Canteen). Crossing the St. Croix River, you will notice old **Acadian dykes** along both sides. Muskrats are plentiful in this area, and you may spot them burrowing into our heritage.
13.1 (8.1)	**LEFT** at Country Store and war monument in village of Brooklyn. This area still has many descendants of early homesteaders from Rhode Island. The old store offers a pleasant break spot.
	Go up hill. Stay left at Esso station.

Weird goings-on in the pumpkin patch

Windsor is the "Giant Pumpkin Capitol of the World"! The town is home of **Howard Dill**, a local farmer, whose seeds have been producing almost unsettling large pumpkins. The same day around the world in early October (Canadian Thanksgiving weekend) weigh-offs take place. At the scales in Windsor, thousands turn out to cheer Howard and his friends weigh their pumpkins, squash, zucchini, and other frightening vegetables. Wherever the biggest pumpkin is from, it is always a descendant from Mr. Dill's patch.

They say pumpkins were never designed to weigh 1000 lbs., that they will crush under their own weight before reaching that size. They said that about 400 pound pumpkins. Then 600, then 800. They are now getting very close to that 1000 pound mark, and Mr. Dill says it is only a matter of time. In early October, his farm is covered with the gigantic orange balls, like visitors from another planet. At this time the front lane makes a fantastic photo spot. If October is a bit too late for you to see the gourds at their prime, Mr.

Dill will sell you his *"Dill Atlantic Giant"* seeds, and perhaps you may have one sprout in your yard!

Howard Dill Enterprises: 400 College Road, R.R. #1, Windsor NS B0N 2T0 (902) 798-2728

159

Where it all started

As if having the largest gourds on earth were not enough, it appears that a small pond only a few hundred metres behind Mr. Dill's farm may be the **birthplace of ice hockey!**

When **Kings Edgehill School** was preparing for its 200th anniversary in 1988, researchers made an interesting discovery. They came across a manuscript by **Thomas Haliburton.** In this writing he describes a game of **hurley.** Here, however, he notes it being played, not on a field, but in the forest, **on the ice of a frozen pond!**

Thus so, it is the **earliest record** of ice hockey, pre-dating other claims, such as from Kingston, Ontario. Many have made the assertion as the place where hockey began- the Russians, the Scots, even several North American Indian tribes. The recent discovery in Windsor, however, stands as the oldest record resembling hockey as we know it today.

In Haliburton's time as many as 20 would play per side at one time. Few now visit, let a alone go skating. The pond still exists, though it is slowly shrinking. Many are hoping that it can somehow be saved and be presented with the respect it deserves.

This is where it all started- a trip in solitude, here among the forest and bramble, should be on every hockeyphile's tour list.

SIDE TRIP- Woodville loop To add an attractive extension to the ride, head out on #14, turn left at Woodville, and return on #236. **Smiley's Park** has camping and free picnic facilities a short way in.

Continuing on route, just after crossing bridge you may notice the old train bed, which has its path in good condition for off-road riding.

Stay on #215 through jog, past the turn-off to Mantua

15.4 (9.5) **LEFT** (sign directs to Belmont and Avondale)

26.3 (16.3) **RIGHT** (just before church). Go along shore to dock.

27.0 (17.8) **Newport Landing** This is an excellent spot for your break. A dock has benches to relax and watch the reversing waters. Picnic tables have been set up on shore. The **Meander River** is among the best places anywhere to view the famous **tidal bore.** The remains of older piers of this once thriving shipbuilding port are still visible along the shore. On your way up the hill during your departure from the village, you can't help but notice the huge houses, which no doubt overlooked what were the shipbuilding yards.

Rejoin main road (store st corner)

At **Poplar Grove** is *"the Stone House"*, one of Nova Scotia's oldest residences. Built in the very early 1700's, the house has stone drains, six fireplaces, and two "beehive" ovens.

Tidal Bore Farm welcomes you to visit and take in their good vantage point to see the famous tidal bore (look for house number 1116).

35.0 (21.8) **RIGHT** Mantua *Note*: Distance sign says "Windsor 10". This is an old pre-metric sign, it is actually 16 km (10 mi.).

36.5 (22.7) **RIGHT #14** (Stirling's Farm)

CROSS Intersection at Sweet's Corner (Bates Canteen). You now pass more ground level exposure of gypsum deposits. This older worked district has largely been reclaimed by forest, but even here you can observe from the rambling knolls and hollows, manipulation by human hands.

43.6 (27.1) **RIGHT #1** Garland's Crossing. A motel, restaurants and farm produce stands are found at the intersection. Follow #1 all the way to downtown Windsor. On the way it will follow King, O'Brien, and Gerrish streets.

SIDE TRIP Howard Dill's farm lies to your left entering town. It lies on College Road, to your left (look for sign to Kings Edgehill School, near the cemetery).

48.0 (29.3) **END** Corner of Gerrish and Water streets in downtown Windsor. (Note the "green" Coca Cola billboard).

Accommodation

Avonside Motel Brian and Doris Caunt, R.R. #2, Falmouth N.S., B0P 1L0 (902) 798-8344. The owners are bicycle-friendly. Brian spent many years cycling during his youth in Britain. The motel is close to downtown Windsor, just across the bridge at Falmouth.

Clockmaker's Inn Veronica and Dennis Connelly, 1399 King St., Windsor N.S., B0N 1H0 (902) 798-5265. Very attractive old building, furnished with antiques. Full breakfast. No smoking

Hampshire Court Motel and Cottages P.O. Box 10, 1081 King St., Windsor N.S. (902) 798-2325

Meander Inn Bed and Breakfast Douglas and Joyce Olie, 153 Albert St., Windsor N.S., B0N 2T0 (902) 798-2325

Our House Bed and Breakfast Bob and Lynda Davies 1439 King St., Windsor, N.S., B0N 1H0 (902) 798-2149. Restored late Victorian house. No smoking.

Young's Bed and Breakfast 231 Wentworth Road, Windsor, N.S., B0N 2T0 (902) 798-2516

Camping

Hants County Exhibition and Trailer Park Exhibition Grounds, Wentworth Road, Windsor, N.S., B0N 1H0 (adjacent to Exit 5 of #101). Not an especially pretty location, however, you are almost in town, the price is cheap, and the proceeds go to the Windsor Agricultural Society (who operate the oldest fair in North America). There is also a coffee and donut shop just up the road. No showers

Smileys Provincial Park Province of Nova Scotia, (902) 757-3131. Off-route, east of Broklyn. Open and wooded campground and picnic grounds (no showers).

Windsor to Wolfville

Here is a suggested route between Windsor and Wolfville. A short stretch of #101 is neccessary, unless you have the energy to climb Wolfville Ridge into the Gaspereau Valley. Bluff Road runs a rolling route through apple orchards between Hantsport and Avonport.

Due to its prosperity, **Hantsport** became the smallest place to be incorporated as a town in Canada. To illustrate just how busy it was, in 1895, the town was the 5th largest ship-building centre in the world! What made this competition with the largest of cities possible, was its natural drydock, the tide rising and falling 14 m (42 feet).

The tide can be observed from the dock, where gypsum is shipped after its short train ride from the other side of Windsor. The tug *"Otis Wack"* is on hand to guide ocean-going freighters in and out of port. Things have to move fast- the large vessels must be loaded in only 3 hours or become stranded on the mud .

The town has the usual services needed on tour, and with tall trees, there is welcome shade for mid-day breaks.

Churchill House, the former home of a shipyard owner, has a room dedicated to Hantsport's past glory (open during the summer). Interesting paintings by a Portugese stowaway, **Francis da Silva**, are on the basement walls. Not far away, in front of the Baptist Church at the intersection of Main Street, and Highway #1 is a memorial to incredible courage. **William Hall**, the son of a freed slave, became the first Black, as well as the first Nova Scotian to recieve the British Empire's highest award, the **Victoria Cross**. It was awarded after he fought off an entire batallion at the relief of Lucknow, India in 1857.

Along Avon and Cottage streets, notice the New England influence in the houses. This region was heavily settled from the south, following the American Revolution (War of Independence).

Falmouth bills itself as *"half way between the North Pole and the equator"*. Back roads run in off highway #1. Huge greenhouses line the road, suppling tomatoes and lettuce all year long. One road comes out south of Windsor at Martock, making a good small sized loop.

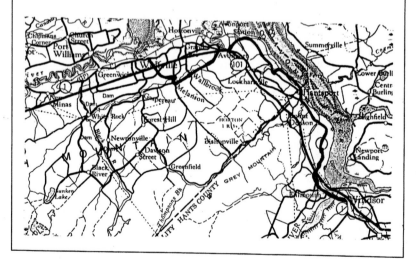

162

Northern

Warmer waters and sunnier skies are just two reasons for including Northern Nova Scotia in your cycling agenda. This area, virtually unknown outside the province, is no less beautiful for that reason. "On the way to somewhere else" is how most people say they discover this region. What they find, is a pleasant area with a relaxed atmosphere and quiet roads, perfect for bicycle touring.

The Northumberland (Northern) Shore is the province's least hilly coastline. This makes it suitable for casual cyclists. Peninsulas extend into the strait at Wallace, Malagash, Cape John, and Caribou. Inland, roads follow rivers and pass through woods, offering first-rate diversions. Several narrow ranges of hills appear as you approach Springhill. The ridges have been partially eroded, exposing underlying gypsum, coal, and salt deposits. There are brackish lakes at Oxford and salt springs between River Philip and Springhill.

Maple sugar camps are spread throughout the hardwood forests. Many of them welcome visitors. In October, the colours of the trees turn brilliant red, orange, and yellow. It is said that this is the area (along with Central Nova Scotia) where the red Maple Leaf was adopted as Canada's national symbol.

The sun graces here more than anywhere in the province! This is a welcome prospect, considering an often wet and overcast marine climate like Nova Scotia's. The Sunrise Trail region has some of the province's best beaches. You will enjoy the warmest salt-water north of Carolina! Thanks to the shallow depths of the strait, the sun heats waters up to an average of 19 degrees Celsius (68.5 Fahrenheit).

The Mic Mac Indians deeply loved these shores. Their place names still identify places as they had for centuries before the arrival of the European.

Few other traces in the area of these original occupants remain. The French-speaking Acadians were the first Europeans to settle the region. After their Expulsion, resettlement was primarily composed of New Englanders. Today, most claim to be descendants of Scottish origin, although Cumberland County was settled by many from Yorkshire. Recent arrivals from Germany have revitalized the Tatamagouche/ Brule area. Small numbers of descendants of the Black Loyalists live in Amherst and New Glasgow.

Northern Nova Scotia played a large part in Canada's westward expansion. Coal mines were dug deep underground at Springhill and Stellarton. Canada's first steel was forged at Trenton, while factories boomed at Amherst. Today, the heavy industry is almost all gone. An ironic victim, the region was displaced by the same Cental Canada it helped build. Some salt mining remains, a rail car works, a pulp mill, and a tire factory, but small scale activity is now the focus of the region. Summer cottages and serving Prince Edward Island bound tourists is important to the economy. Making pewter figurines (in Pugwash), farming, fishing (including lobster and shellfish), harvesting of wild blueberries, and tapping maple syrup provide other major livelihoods.

Deer are plentiful. Seals are sometime spotted basking on rock ledges. Many birds enter Nova Scotia, but venture no further than this section of the province. They are primarily those which do not fly over the sea, arriving by following the coast of New Brunswick. The placid and warm coves along the Northumberland provide havens for many variety of herons. You are guaranteed to see these very tall birds, which stand motionless along the shores. They are joined by thousands of other birds on major migration routes, which converge on the marshlands, particularly near the New Bruswick.

antic Canada
ing Festival

Surf, sand, and Scottish clans

our 25   **Sunrise Trail**

Tour at a glance

START	Pictou
FINISH	Amherst
OTHER STATING POINTS	Caribou (P.E.I. ferry); Tatamagouche; Amherst
DISTANCE	200 km (124 mi.)
DIRECTION	East-West
TERRAIN	Flat to Rolling
CLIMATE	Most days of sunshine in Nova Scotia
NOTES	Warmest waters north of Carolinas
TRAFFIC	Moderate
FOOD	Pictou (R)(G)(C); River John (C); Tatamagouche (R)(G)(C); Wallace (C); Malagash (C); Pugwash (R)(G)(C); Port Philip (R)(C)
REPAIRS	Pictou; Truro (off-route); Amherst
TOURISM	Pictou 485-6213; Caribou (P.E.I. ferry, off-route); Tatamagouche 657-3285; Pugwash 243-2946; Amherst 661-2703; Aulac (N. B. border, off-route) 667-8429
HOSPITAL	New Glasgow (off-route); Tatamagouche 657-2382; Pugwash 243-2521; Amherst 667-3361
AMBULANCE	Tatamagouche 657-3288; Oxford (off-route) 447-2930; Amherst 667-9696
POLICE	Pictou (R.C.M.P.); Tatamagouche (R.C.M.P.) 657-2040; Pugwash/ Wallace (R.C.M.P.) 243-2181; Amherst (R.C.M.P.) 667-3859, (town) 667-8600

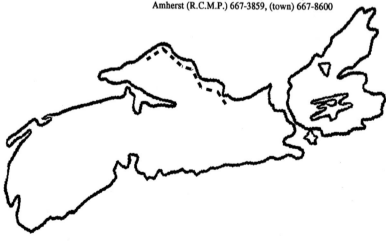

166

B eaches, marshes, estuaries, capes, points, and headlands... there's water everywhere along this meandering shoreline highway. Between Pictou and Tidnish are hundreds of easily accessible stretches of sand, from tiny two-person enclaves to long, wide crescents. Their shallow depths permit wading out to great distances. Many secluded spots can be found at the end of tiny roads or paths- do not be fearful that you will be trespassing- beaches are a public acess right.

The water is warm, in fact, more so than anywhere as far south as Carolina! How can this be? There are shallow depths for long distances into the Northumberland Strait from both Nova Scotia and Prince Edward Island. These low depths allow warming up of the sand. Over the summer it in turn, considerably warms the water. It is, surprisingly, at its peak in early September! Because the water temperature, there are far less days of fog than the other coasts.

This was once a primary area for Mic Mac (native) camps and their annual summer gatherings. Acadians were the first to occupy their land. History, however, shows few conflicts between them. They established a large community around Tatamagouche. Their site was strategic importance in the line of supply for Fortress Louisbourg. Most people think of the Annapolis Valley when the tragic Expulsion of the Acadians comes to mind. In fact, however, Tatamagouche was the first place hit first, and with extreme harshness.

Further immigrants were later to come from Switzerland, and in recent years, Germany. In Cumberland County many settled from Yorkshire. Although arrivals have come from many places, it is strong Scottish heritage, kept alive in places such as Pugwash, that first comes to mind.

Almost every cove once boasted a ship-building yard. Except for one modern slip at Pictou, the art is now almost forgotten. The people earn their living from traditional ways of life, such as lobster fishing and, farming. Others live from servicing the summer cottages and what they can lure away from Prince Edward Island bound traffic.

The area is not nearly as populated, nor as developed as you would expect along such a warm stretch of water. Not one community surpasses the status of a village the entire distance between Pictou and Amherst! Although your route will be slightly rolling, gradients are not too steep. This route is therefore suitable for casual cyclists. Just as easily cycled in either direction, here it will be done east to west, for the "along the shore " factor. This direction however may have a small degree of headwinds. We begin in the old Scottish landing place of Pictou.

Two special islands

Off the coast, in the Northumberland Strait lies **Pictou Island**. Another grand development scheme of the charismatic "Colonel" McNutt, by the late 1820's the Scots had established a moderate sized settlement. Over 400 people kept the 10 km (6 mi.) long, 3.5 km (2 mi.) wide island busy with residences, farms, industry, and even a post office.

There has never been any electricity on the island, and thick pack ice in winter prevents year-round transportation. Incredible stories have been told over the years of people crossing the strait, hopping from one piece of ice to another!

Today, under two dozen people remain. Many of the old houses stand abandoned and crumbling, surrounded by new forest growth. It is hard to imagine the small shipyards and thriving fish plant which were once here. The north side is rocky, an occasional resting spot for seals. There are several arttractive beaches. In addition to old trails, a gravel road crosses the island. With no public facilities, stores, or indoor accommodations- you must provide for yourself. Garbage disposal will also be your responsibility. A passenger ferry service (no cars) usually runs 2 to 3 days a week from May 1 to Nov. 30. For its current status and schdule contact the Pictou Tourist Bureau 485-6213.

Prince Edward Island the land of "*Anne of Green Gables*" lies in view across the strait for most of Tour 25. "P.E.I." is Canada'a smallest province. Magnificent beaches and old Victorian farmhouses are typical of what you will find on its quiet back roads. roads. An entire cycling vacation on its own, you can sample it with a quick visit. Cyclitsts have little difficulty getting on a ferry without a wait. At times cars must wait one boat or even two. The ferry ride is quite cheap, the trip a destination in itself (think of it as a mini-cruise).

To truly enjoy the island, avoid the Trans-Canada Highway. *Note*: P.E.I. 's soil is very pure. It is so much so in fact, that most gravel must be imported. Many roads are therefore built without a stable base. Expect to encounter some rough surfaces.

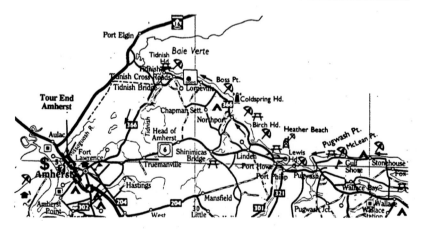

44.5 (27.6)   **River John** was once a large wooden ship-building centre. Producing as many as 16 vessels at any one time, work progressed all year, even while frozen-in. River John's population was then triple what it is today. It was a confident, prosperous place and its ships were christened brazen names, such as *"Alonzo"*, *"Banshee"* and *"Faughaballagh"*. Today, that dynamic era is now over, but the village landscape has not changed much.

SIDE TRIP Cape John: A 7.8 km (5.0 mi.) run follows the shore out to this sandy and scenic point (recommended). Notice the fine old homes of the shipbuilding era along the shore on your way out.

DETOUR: If you find the traffic a bit busy, an attractive back road roams its way from a short distance west of River John, to Tatamagouche.

Brule comes from the French word for *"burnt land"*. It's a summer area, with a golf course, campground and windsurfing. Although this is a primarily a cottage area, dairy farming and lobster fishing can also be found.

In August of 1918, hundreds of whales swam here into the harbour after a school of herring. Over 200 hundred of the creatures became stranded on the shore.

One legend of the area tells of the **phantom ship of the Northumberland**. Many people over the years have reported night-time sightings of a large burning ship in the bay. It is said to be a three-masted square rigger- its sails, spars, and rigging in bright flame outlined against the sky. It then quickly disappears from sight. Some claim this vision to be a result of gasses rising from under the water.

Rushton Beach Provincial Park enclosed by Tatamagouche Bay, features two picnic areas, one close to the road, the other along the beach. The salt marshes here attract a great variety of birds.

63.7 (39.6)   **Junction #311.** Stay on #6. **Tatamagouche** is your only major stop until Pugwash ("major" here means 600 to 800 people). Leaving town you pass the expansive grounds

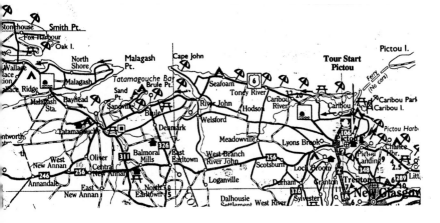

of the Tim Horton Youth camp. The small bridge over the Dewar River brings you across the Colchester/ Cumberland county line.

76.3 (47.4)   **RIGHT Malagash Peninsula** (sign says "Malagash Mines"). This loop will have very little traffic. Road signage is poor, but it is hard to get lost. A flat road follows the peninsula. High-grassed marshes support a healthy heron population. Malagash Co-op a short way in offers produce, ice cream, and a bakery.

SHORT-CUT: Cutting across the peninsula will shave of many kilometres. One of the shore's few climbs (70 m/ 225 ft.) will provide you a look-off from Wallace Ridge over the peninsula and Northumberland Strait.

89.2 (55.4)   **LEFT** (before peninsula's end). After only a few minutes you arrive on the other side.

Stay along the peninsula's shore back to #6. A scenic stretch of old farms brings you along the remainder of the loop. Small beaches are accessible from the roadside along Tatamagouche Bay. A miner's cemetery is evidence of the activity which lasted here from 1918 to 1956. You will pass the remains of an old salt mining village- Canada's first such operation. What were once the miner's houses stand in a cluster. After the excavations were complete, attention was paid to a new operation in Pugwash.

SIDE TRIP- Jost Vineyards A winery is not perhaps what you are expecting you might encounter on your journeys through northern Nova Scotia. That is exactly what you will find on this serene peninsula a short distance down Malagash Mines Road. Grapes are grown, pressed, and processed in the Jost family winery. Arriving in Canada in 1970 from the Rhine Valley of Germany, they planted a few vines for their own use. Growing them here was so successful that they planted them extensively. Today, with a holding capacity of approximately 500,000 litres, Jost Vineyards holds many awards, including from prestigious international competitions. On one of its tours, Jost Vineyards will be able to entertain and educate you on the quality and potential of Nova Scotia wines (257-2636).

106.7 (66.3)   **RIGHT #6.** Just ahead is **Wallace** (pop.322), now a fishing community on the bay of the same name. It was once the centre of a major sandstone operation. Many buildings in Canada and the United States, including the **Parliament Buildings** in Ottawa, **Province House** in Halifax, and important structures such as banks, and courthouses in towns throughout the Maritimes were built from Wallace sandstone.

111.4 (69.2)   **RIGHT** Cross Wallace Harbour Bridge

DETOUR The first road to the right past the bridge offers a dirt road loop around Mullins Point. The low depths of the water offer bountiful feeding for waterfowl. Wallace Bay is an official management area, and you may see herons on the shore. A small picnic park at Fox Harbour offers a sandy beach with warm water.

Gulf Shore Provincial Park is an attractive day-use area on a hill, overlooking Northumberland Strait. It has tables, some with shelters and an excellent sandy beach.

134.1 (83.3)   **RIGHT** Sraid King (Street) into **Pugwash** past Cumberland Hospital (before high school). Pugwash means *"pagweak"* or *"shallow water"* in Mic Mac. The tiny town celebrates its Scottish heritage with a fervour. Note their street signs- they are in both Gaelic and English. Each July 1st, it stages the colourful Gathering of the Clans.

134.8 (83.7)   **LEFT** at Pugwash Harbour. At the turn is **Thinker's Lodge.** This unlikely location was the home of the world-famous **Thinker's Conference.** It was initiated by native son **Cyrus Eaton,** who became one of the United State's leading financiers. His lodge during the height of the **Cold War** in the 1950's was among the first places that began dis-armament and other East/West dialogue.

135.2 (84.0)	**LEFT** on Sraid Durham at the Post Office. **Salt** may be seen being loaded onto freighters. From the evaporation plant, vast caverns of crystals run under the town. There are now over 14,000 recorded uses for salt ...Pugwash is doing a lot more than making your food tasty!
135.4 (84.2)	**RIGHT** onto #6 across Pugwash Harbour Bridge. The major employer of the area is **Seagull Pewter**, which sends its creations world -wide. Further on, **Port Philip** and **Port Howe** share the mouth of River Philip, with a store and seafood restaurant.
145.7 (90.5)	**RIGHT** #366. The following stretch of road has the greatest concentration of beaches in Nova Scotia. The major one is **Heather Beach**, with picnic facilities and lifeguard supervision. **Northport** has a lobster pound near the bridge. Clam digging is popular along its shore.
175.0 (108.7)	**RIGHT** Beecham Road. Near here are crossings of the track bed of the **Chignecto Ship Railway**. Remnants of the ill-fated system's eastern terminus are at **Tidnish Dock Provincial Park**.
178.5 (110.9)	**RIGHT** #366. Shortly after rejoining the #366, a road to your right enters New Brunswick. This is one of only two land entrances which connect Nova Scotia with the world. This route to Port Elgin is by a long margin, recommended as a connection with P. E. I. over the mind-numbing Trans-Canada Highway (New Brunswick #16).
196.8 (122.2)	**RIGHT** Highway #6
200.2 (124.4)	**END** in Amherst, at Canada's oldest drugstore, (Pugsley's)- corner of Church and Victoria Streets.

A truly grand folly

Henry Ketchum had a dream. He wanted to build a railway. His, however, would not just be any railway. His would be a truly special one- it would take ships across Nova Scotia! He vowed to bring to life a long time wish of mariners- to save days of sail and avoid the rough waters of the Atlantic by somehow getting from the end of the Bay of Fundy to the Gulf of St. Lawrence. His scheme was to create special hydrolic lifts, which would raise the ships onto rail cars. They would then be pulled by locomotives to the other side and the process be reversed.

His plans for the **Chignecto Ship canal** got off to an inspirational start. The best engineering minds of the world lent their support. European bankers became involved, and the Canadian government was eager to have such a facility as a showpiece of the new and emerging nation. 4,000 workers were required to build the project, many of the labourers brought from Italy. Due to unforseen problems of deep marshes and underestimation of the Fundy tides, work had to be extended. Funding kept running out and additional investment was obtained. There were also a few examples of fiscal extravagance, such as a church built for the workers neat Tidnish (still standing), and stone masons brought over from Scotland for construction of bridges.

The hydrolic lifts were completed. Only 19 kilometers of track remained to be laid. Then came disaster. Money yet again ran out, and a final rounding up of funds began. This time, however, Europe had just entered a recession, and there was no coming forward with the only 1 million dollars needed. The federal government, which had been supportive all along, refeused to help finish the project. There had just been an election, and the new administration stood by and watched the project come apart. It is said that parties close to the new Prime Minister had much to gain by preventing increased emphasis on shipping, over other transportation.

This episode marked an important signal of Canada's evolution. The Maritimes gained a good glimpse that Confederation would be anything than always kind to the eastern bookend of the nation. The burdgeoning powerbase of what is now central Canada turned its back on Nova Scotia, and one of the most marvellous engineering projects of all time.

It was broken up and sold as scrap by creditiors. Ketchum lived the remainder of his life a bitter and broken man. His last request was to be buried near his railway, and with him his dream of ships crossing the province.

Accommodation

Braeside Inn Thomas Mackay/ J. Claude Ferland, 80 Front St., P.O. Box 1810, Pictou, N.S., B0K 1H0, (902) 485-5046. Recommended in "Where to Eat in Canada".

Consulate Inn Floyd and Claudette Brine, 115 Water St., Pictou, N.S., B0K 1H0, (902) 485-4554. 1810 Scottish town house and former American Consulate.

Johnston Motel and Cabins Jean Morrison, P.O. Box 209, Pictou, N.S., B0K 1H0, (902) 485-4157. On West River Road.

Munro's Bed and Breakfast Laurie Munro, 66 High St., P.O. Box 1613, Pictou, N.S., B0K 1H0 (902) 485-8382.

The Walker Inn Bed and Breakfast Felix and Theresa Walker, 34 Coleraine St., Pictou, NS B0K 1H0 (902) 485-1433. Registered Heritage Property.

Willow House Inn Karin MacDonald, 3 Willow St., Pictou, NS B0K 1H0, (902) 485-5740. Registered Historic Property.

Mountain Farm R.R. #2, Mountain Road, River John, N.S., B0K 1N0 (902) 351-2821 No smoking.

Balfron Bed and Breakfast Anita Mingo, R.R. #5, Tatamagouche, NS B0K 1V0, (902) 657-3559.

Balmoral Motel Adolf and Gerda Hoetten, P.O. Box 178, Tatamagouche, NS B0K 1V0 (902) 657-2000, restaurant on site.

Barrachois Harbour Bed and Breakfast Helen Cockburn, R.R. #1, Tatamagouche, NS B0K 1V0, (902) 657-3009, overlooking wharf.

Train Station Inn James and Shelley and James LeFresne, Station Rd., P.O. Box 67, Tatamagouche, NS B0K 1V0. (902) 657-3222. Inn at restored train station.

Bollard Bed and Breakfast Alan Booth and Joyce Gillard, P.O. Box 209, R.R. #3, Wallace Bridge, N.S. B0K 1Y0 (902) 257-2878

The Crumpety Tree Joyce Langille, R.R. #3, Wallace, N.S., B0K 1Y0, ((02) 257-2610

Dutch Mill Motel Ken Marriott, E.R. #1, Wallace, N.S., B0K 1Y0, (902) 257-2598

Blue Heron Inn John Caraberis/ Bonnie Bond, P.O. Box 405, Pugwash, N.S., B0K 1L0 (902) 243-2900 (June 10- Labour Day)

The Apple Inn Edward and Linda Benoit, P.O. Box 28, Route #6, Port Howe, N.S., B0K 1K0 (902) 243-2814

Blueberry Lane Bed and Breakfast Lloyd and Marilyn Munroe, R.R. #6, Amherst, NS B4H 3Y4 (902) 667-9567. Route #2 south, turn right on Blair Rd. Heated outdoor pool, blueberries in season on property. No smoking

Brown's Guest Home Deane and Nancy Allen, 158 Victoria St. East, Amherst, NS B4H 1Y5. (902) 667-9769.

Chignecto Motel Jude and Gloria Cormier, Gerald and Helen Read. P.O. Box 144, Amherst, NS B4H 3Y6. Located 1.6 (1 mile) north of Amherst. LaPlanche St., Exit 2 off Highway 104.

Fundy Winds Family Motel P.O. Box 1136, Amherst, NS B4H 3Y6, (902) 667-3881. LaPlanche Street

Journey's End Motel 143 South Albion St., Amherst, NS B4H 2X2. (902) 667-0404. Route #104, Exit 4. Open year-round.

Pied Piper Motel Marie Dodge, R.R. #6, Amherst, NS B4H 2Y4 (902) 667-3891. At Upper Nappan.

Victorian Motel Gary and Sharon Goodwin, 150 East Victoria St., Amherst, NS B4H 1Y3. (902) 667-7211.

Campgrounds

Harbour Light Trailer Court and Family Campground J.R.C. MacDonald, Pictou, NS B0K 1H0, (902) 485-5733; (902) 485-4206. Open and wooded campground on ocean inlet. 4.8 km (3 mi.) east of town. Pay showers, washrooms, laundromat.

Caribou Provincial Park Province of Nova Scotia, (902) 485-6134. No reservations 10 km (7 mi.) north of junction of Routes #6, #106 and #376 through Pictou, 4 km (2.5 mi.) east of Caribou ferry wharf.

Fraser's Camp and Picnic Grounds (902) 657-2707, 6.4 km (3.8 mi.) east of Tatamagouche off Route #6 on Brule Point Road. Open campground on ocean. Play area, swimming, fishing, boating. Windsurfing, sailing and canoe rentals.

Nelson Memorial Park and Campground (902) 657-2730, 1.6 km (1 mi.) west of Tatamagouche off route #6. Open and wooded campground, canteen, swimming pool. Community owned.

Braemar Trailer Park (902) 257-2417. Located near Wallace on highway #6. Open campground on harbour. Boating, beach, swimming, fishing.

Gulf Shore Camping Park Gulf Shore, N.S. (902) 243-2489. Open campground along shore. Swimming, putting green.

Amherst Shore Provincial Park Province of Nova Scotia (902) 667-6002. No reservations. Forested sites with trail to beach on Northumberland Strait. 6km (4 mi.) east or Lorneville. May 15-Labour Day.

Loch Lomond Tent and Trailer Park Ella and Glen Ripley, R.R. #6, Amherst, NS B4H 3Y4 (902) 667-3890. Open and wooded campground on lake. 0.5 km (0.3 mi.) south on Route #2. Pay showers, washrooms, laundromat.

172

The land they called New Scotland

Tour 26

Greenhill

Tour at a glance

START/ FINISH	Pictou
DISTANCE	43 km (27 mi.)
DIRECTION	Counter-Clockwise
TERRAIN	One big hill
CLIMATE	Some winds on Greenhill
TRAFFIC	Moderate
REST SPOTS	Greenhill
FOOD	Pictou (R)(G)(C)
REPAIRS	Pictou
TOURISM	Pictou 485-6213
POLICE	Pictou
HOSPITAL	New Glasgow
AMBULANCE	New Glasgow

I t was a weary band of Scottish immigrants who waded ashore at Pictou Harbour on September 15, 1773. Following their 77 day voyage, the immigrants on board the ship *"Hector"* were most pleased to see land. Their home in the New World was purchased from a group of Americans, known as the **Philadelphia Company** (which included one **Benjamin Franklin**). The Scots arrived to find "their" land inhabited by **Mic Mac** Indians), along the shore. The natives, understandably, were less than pleased to see the kilted arrivals.

Violent altercations, however, were avoided. It seems the natives were so terrified by the sound of the Scots' bagpipes that they let the settlers be! A time of reasonable harmony prevailed here in the wilds. And what an eclectic group it was. Picture among the small isolated outpost... the Gaelic -speaking Scots; Americans- both loyal and revolutionary; the Mic Mac speaking Indians; Blacks, who had been brought as slaves, and a few stray Acadians!

With the **Highland Clearances** of Scotland in full effect, those who sailed on the Hector were followed by thousands more. They settled throughout the nearby hills. Others moved outward, to Antigonish, Cape Breton, other parts of Nova Scotia, Prince Edward Island and beyond, giving the town the rightful claim of being the *Birthplace of New Scotland.*

Ignoring a few modern intrusions, **Pictou** still resembles a small, Scottish town. Many buildings date to the early 1800's, with a style unique in Canada. A statue of a bonneted and kilted Scot stands in town as a monument to settlers who arrived to a new life in a hostile land. The docks of Pictou have seen a great deal of activity in their time. It was from here in 1833, that the *Prince William*, owned by Halifax merchant **Samuel Cunard** made history. It became the first ship to cross the Atlantic with steam as its main power source. Ironically, its success began the end of *"The Age of Sail"*, with it an era of great prosperity. **Lobstering** is important to the local economy.

This tour is focused on a challenging climb to Green Hill. Two spectacular look-off points will allow you to see five counties, as well as Prince Edward Island.

To reach Green Hill, the route will skirt Pictou Harbour. As for the hill itself, for the effort required, your reward here will be a bargain! For only a large hill, you will feel you are on a mountain. On the return the route passes **Loch Broom Church**, a replica of that of the first arrivals.

Northumberland Fisheries Museum On Front Street, in the former Pictou railway station is a display of fishing gear and photos relating to the fisheries of Northumberland Strait. Season July-Aug. Daily 9:30 am - 5:30 pm. (Admission is free).

Grohmann Knives manufacturer of the world-famous Russell Belt knife is located downtown. Visitors are welcome to tour the factory, which produces knives of many purposes. 88 Water Street (485-4224; 485-6775).
Hector Heritage Quay At the quay, the Pictou Waterfront Development Corporation has undertaken the building of a

replica of the ship Hector. The reconstruction is in harmony with the design and construction method used in the original vessel. Originally built in Holland, the Hector belonged to a class of vessel known as a "Flute", ships with a flat bottom, pear-shaped, and rounded right up to the main deck. Additional details on the Hector, its voyage, the reconstruction, and the people it carried is available by guides on the site (small admission 485-8028).

McCulloch House Part of the Nova Scotia Museum system, built in 1806. Thhe home of Thomas McCulloch, one of early Pictou's most illustrious residents. (Free admission 485-4563).

Cormorant Colony: Its a strange place for a bird colony- next to a major highway, and in the shadow of a pulp mill, but here is a site chosen by cormorants for their yearly summer residence! This is a rarity, no boat trips, or difficult hikes are required to reach it. They are directly along the causeway, on pilings along the east lane, almost to the New Glasgow side. They return here every year, and your chances of seeing them are very good.

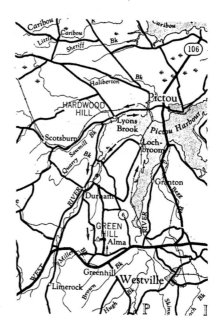

175

START	**Hector Heritage Quay** on the waterfront. Head west along the harbour on Dawson Street (named for Yukon explorer **George Dawson**). Start off toward the harbour cuaseway.
0.5 (0.3)	**LEFT** Water St.
0.6 (0.4)	**LEFT** Haliburton Road (toward hospital). Watch for **McCulloch House**. Go under causeway
2.3 (1.4)	**LEFT #376.** Stay along the shore at intersection of #256
12.3 (7.6)	**LEFT** Cross bridge at Durham (ice cream stand near turn).
12.4 (7.7)	**RIGHT** along river. You now begin your climb up Greenhill. Below you is the path of the Trans-Canada Highway and further on the valley of the East River (Tour 30). The forests from here go unhampered most of the way to the Atlantic Ocean.
18.0 (11.1)	**LEFT** Crunch up the last little bit. Watch for the park to your left.
19.1 (11.9)	**LEFT** Green Hill Park entrance
19.3 (12.0)	**Green Hill look-off**-- The reward for this climb is a spectacular backdrop for a well deserved break. From this point 700 ft. up, you can see the patchwork valley below, and the Cobequid Hills in the background. The view from the fire tower looks out for an incredible view over 5 counties. After your break is another panorama, that of Pictou Harbour and its forested hills. Prince Edward Island sits off in the distance.
21.7 (13.5)	**RIGHT** towards Sylvester
23.1 (14.4)	**LEFT**
24.2 (15.0)	**RIGHT** Follow around small peninsula. **Loch Broom Church** is a replica of that originally built by Gaelic speaking Presbyterian Scots. Built of hand-hewn logs, all furnishings are appropriate to its pioneer period. It is named after Loch Broom, Scotland, where most of the passengers of the Hector came from. Without the benefit of roads, on the Sabbath, parishoners would arrive on paths through the woods, or by boat. The original church was constructed under the direction of a most devout minister. A great amount of compromise apparently was arrived at. A blind eye was apparently turned to the volunteers, arriving each day equipped with huge quantities of rum, which they drank as they erected the house of worship.
33.3 (20.7)	**RIGHT**
34.4 (21.4)	**RIGHT #376**
40.9 (25.4)	**RIGHT** Haliburton St. (toward hospital). Follow shore back to Hector Quay.
43.0 (26.7)	**END** at the Hector Heritage Quay on the waterfront.

Accommodation

Braeside Inn Thomas Mackay/ J. Claude Ferland, 80 Front St., P.O. Box 1810, Pictou, N.S., B0K 1H0, (902) 485-5046. Recommended in "Where to Eat in Canada".
Consulate Inn Floyd and Claudette Brine, 115 Water St., Pictou, N.S., B0K 1H0, (902) 485-4554. 1810 Scottish town house and former American Consulate.
Johnston Motel and Cabins Jean Morrison, P.O. Box 209, Pictou, N.S., B0K 1H0, (902) 485-4157. On West River Road.
Munro's Bed and Breakfast Lauire Munro, 66 High St., P.O. Box 1613, Pictou, N.S., B0K 1H0, (902) 485-8382.
The Walker Inn Bed and Breakfast Felix/ Theresa Walker, 34 Coleraine St., Pictou, NS B0K 1H0 (902) 485-1433. Registered Heritage Property.
Willow House Inn Karin MacDonald, 3 Willow St., Pictou, NS B0K 1H0, (902) 485-5740. Registered Historic Property.
Shady Lane Bed and Breakfast Hilda and Don MacKenzie, R.R. #2, Pictou (Lyons Brook), NS, B0K 1H0, (902) 485-4512. Route #376, 2 km (1.2 mi.) south of Pictou Rotary; or Route #104, Exit 20 at West River, 14.7 km (8.8 mi.) to Lyons Brook.
Stoneycombe Lodge Bed and Breakfast Keith and Edith Selwyn-Smith, R.R. #3, Westville (Alma), NS B0K 2A0, Pictou County, (902) 396-3954. Near Green Hill by Trans-Canada Highway #104) They are bicycle-friendly, Keith having spent many years cycling in Britain.

Campgrounds

Birchwood Campground Eric Coffin and Cathy Wiens, P.O. Box 433, Pictou, NS B0K 1H0, (902) 485-8565. Open and wooded campground. Route #376, 4 km (2.5 mi.) from Pictou Rotary at Lyons Brook.
Caribou Provincial Park Province of Nova Scotia, (902) 485-6134. No reservations 10 km (7 mi.) north of junction of Routes #6, #106 and #376 through Pictou, 4 km (2.5 mi.) east of Caribou ferry wharf.
Harbour Light Trailer Court and Family Campground J.R.C. MacDonald, Pictou, NS B0K 1H0, (902) 485-5733; (902) 485-4206. Open and wooded campground on ocean inlet. 4.8 km (3 mi.) east of town. Pay showers, washrooms, laundromat.

Atlantic Canada Cycling Festival

Mills and maple syrup

Tour 27   Balmoral

Tour at a glance

START/ FINISH	Tatamagouche
OTHER STARTING POINT	Earltown
DISTANCE	59 km (37 mi.) (short-cut 42 km/ 26 mi.)
DIRECTION	Counter-Clockwise
TERRAIN	Rolling
CLIMATE	Moderate
TRAFFIC	Moderate
REST SPOTS	Balmoral Mills; Sutherlands Steam Mill; Denmark Pork Shop
FOOD	Tatamagouche (R)(G)(C); Earltown (C); Denmark (R)
REPAIRS	Truro (off-route); Pictou (off-route)
TOURISM	Tatamagouche 657-3285
POLICE	Tatamagouche (R.C.M.P.) 657-2040
HOSPITAL	Tatamagouche 657-2382
AMBULANCE	Tatamagouche 657-3288

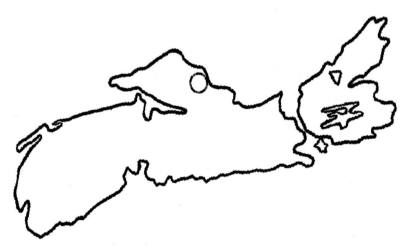

Of all pioneer buildings, few are as romantic and yet as practical as the mill. Cast aside by the march of progress- grist mills, saw mills, woollen mills - have been reborn with a new purpose- to instruct and entertain about the enterprising ways of our past. At one point, Nova Scotia had 414 water, steam, and wind driven mills. Today, only a handful survive. You will find two of these, tucked away on this tour among the hardwood hills and old farms just in from the shore of **Northumberland Strait**.

Tatamagouche is a Mic Mac (Indian) name meaning *"meeting place of the waters"*. Acadians settled here and established a large community, of strategic importance in the line of supply for **Fortress Louisbourg**. Burned to the ground during the tragic Expulsion of the Acadians, it was later filled with Scots, New Englanders and Swiss. The supply "town" for the region, the area has recently been attracting many Germans, who have developed successful enterprises.

Sunrise Trail Museum has exhibits on the North Shore, Mic Mac Indians; the Tatamagouche Acadians, 19th and early 20th century agriculture, the shipbuilding era, and the giantess Anna Swan.

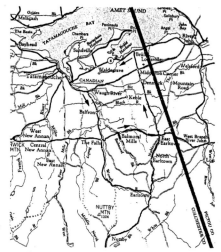

Anna Swan, Nova Scotia's Giantess

From the moment she was brought into this world, Anna Swan was destined not to have a normal life. Born at **New Annan**, south-west of Tatamagouche on August 6, 1846, she at birth weighed 8.1 kg (18 pounds)!

She immediately attracted the curious. Stories of the huge baby spread throughout the countryside. People arrived from all around to see the infant. The third in a family of 12 and the only one to grow tall, by the age of four, Anna was already **1.4 m (4 ft., 6 in.)** high.

When Anna was five years old, her father took her to Halifax to place her on exhibition. She was billed as *"The Infant Giantess"*. At 17 years of age she reached her full height of **2.3 m (7 ft., 6 in.)**. After very increasingly attractive offers from **Phineas T. Barnum**, the great American showman, the family let him exhibit their daughter in his New York museum. They felt his offer of an education and $1000 a month (a lot of money for 1880), could not be provided by parents of such a large family. Barnum billed her as a bit taller-eight feet one inch, and exhibited her with **Commodore Nutt**, the shortest of all men, who became her constant companion. Two years later, **Captain Martin Van Buren Bates** of Brightsburg, Kentucky, one inch shorter than herself came to the circus. Their troop went for a 3 year visit of Europe. On the sea voyage over, Anna and the captain became engaged, making plans to marry upon reaching port.

Upon arrival, they were received most enthusiastically by **Queen Victoria**. Her Majesty was so impressed by their charm and grace that she ordered special gifts prepared for them. She presented both the giants watches, with 2 m (6 ft.) of gold chain, and for Anna a specially- made wedding gown.

They returned to the captain's home at Seville, Ohio, where they built a house suited to their height. After travelling for several years in the United States and Canada with the circus, they semi-retired.

Her height remained that of her teenage years, although she filled out to 231 kg (509 pounds). Anna gave birth to a son. He was 76 cm (30 inches) long and weighed 10.8 kg (23 3/4 pounds), considered possible the largest live birth inhistory. Unfortunately, this child only lived 12 hours (there is a wax mummy of this baby in a museum in Cleveland, Ohio). Information, pictures and clothing of both giants are at the museum in Tatamagouche.

179

START	**Tatamagouche-** intersection of #6 and #246. Head east on #6.
1.5 (0.9)	**RIGHT #311**
11.3 (7.0)	**LEFT** Balmoral Mills Road
13.6 (8.5)	**RIGHT** Peter MacDonald Road. Look to your left. Along the fence of the area known as Archie's Well, is a wooded picnic site, with a functioning grist mill.

A Glimpse of Early Nova Scotia: A red building, visible through the trees is **Balmoral Mills**. Since 1830, this little mill along Matheson Brook has never ceased operation. In its heyday, it was but one of five operating on the same stream. It is said to be perhaps the only grist mill in North America still capable of milling any type of grain growing. Demonstrations of the milling process - from drying to bagging - take place every day. See wheat, oats and buckwheat being ground into flour. A series of wheels, pulleys, belts, and rope elevators allow the miller to control the flow of grain step by step, making the milling process a one-person operation. Except the few iron pieces and the drive belts, everything is made of wood, covered with the fine milling dust from generations. Free tours are conducted of the mill and you can pick up some of the freshest oatmeal possible. Part of the Nova Scotia Museum complex, (free Admission 657-3016)

13.8 (8.6)	Return to road.
14.0 (8.7)	**LEFT** Back to highway

SHORT-CUT: An option heads east of here. Turn right and head towards East Earltown.

16.1 (10.0)	**LEFT #311** Farms give way to roadside stands of wild blueberries. You are now on the eastern edge of the world's largest producing regions.
27.9 (17.3)	**LEFT** Earltown sits at the edge of the Cobequid Hills. Nuttby Mountain, an alomost 300 m (1000 foot) barier lies between here and the tidal basin of the Bay of Fundy at Truro. Among the hillsides are stands of sugar (rock) maple, the best known source of maple syrup. Each August the **Piper's Picnic**, a tribute to the area's Scottish heritage is held. The village was settled by families from Sutherlandshire, Scotland.

Sutherland Steam Mill: When **Alexander Sutherland** built his sawmill in **Denmark, N. S.** in 1894, steam was replacing water as the most efficient way to cut logs. A steam mill could turn out 10 to 20 times the footage of the older mills. Lumber, cut in the mill, was loaded onto railway cars and shipped to Pictou or Pugwash to be loaded onto ships for England. It is still fired up several days per year. Part of the Nova Scotia Museum complex (657-3365). The rail bed can now cycled by mountain bikes.

Of the things you expect to see at the next country crossroads, you most likely are not including a **Bavarian restaurant!** Over 40 different kinds of home made sausages, a European delicatessen and coffee shop is open at the **Pork Shop and Bavarian Garden.** As you walk in its yard, it may look and at times sound as if you were at an Oktoberfest (9 am-5 pm every day except Monday).

47.5 (29.5)	**LEFT #6.** Brule comes from the French word for "burnt land". It is a summer place, with a golf course, campground and windsurfing. Ask residents about the *phantom ship of Northumberland Strait*. **Rushton Beach Provincial Park** features two picnic areas, one close to the road, the other on a sheltered knoll behind the beach. The salt marshes here attract a great variety of birds.
57.0 (35.4)	**END** Tatamagouche

*Wild blueberries and
a hard luck town*

Tour 28   Springhill/Wentworth

Tour at a glance

START	Springhill
FINISH	Wentworth
OTHER STATING POINTS	Wentworth
DISTANCE	53 km (33 mi.)
DIRECTION	West- East
TERRAIN	Hilly, then rolling
CLIMATE	Temperate; one of few rides not influenced by the ocean
TRAFFIC	Low
FOOD	Springhill (R)(G)(C), Collingwood (C)
REPAIRS	Amherst (off-route); Truro (off-route)
TOURISM	Springhill 597-3141
HOSPITAL	Springhill 597-3773
AMBULANCE	Springhill 597- 2361
POLICE	Springhill (R.C.M.P.) 597-3779

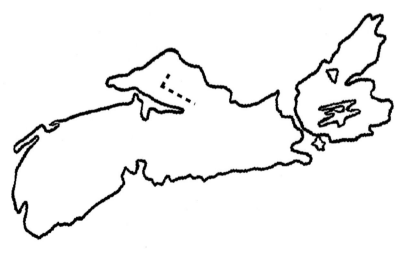

I n this marine oriented province, inland areas go ignored, and that is a shame. Magnificent coastal rides follow both the Bay of Fundy and the Northumberland Strait. Vying with these shores for your attention is a pleasant route along the base of the Cobequid Hills.

This is most certainly a "hidden corner" of Nova Scotia. Once the primary cross-province trail for the Mic Mac (Indians), and later, pioneer settlers, today it it is a back road. The Trans-Canada Highway (#104) thunders through this region. It siphons off all traffic for miles, leaving the back areas free for car-less biking.

If there was room in this province for any more official "scenic trails", this would no doubt be called "The Blueberry Trail". The route follows the heart of Nova Scotia's reknown blueberry barrens. Field

after field thrive with bushes of the wild berries. If you are fortunate to be touring in August, you will find the berry plains a mass of blueish-purple. During autumn, the bushes turn a brilliant crimson, blending with the coloured leaves of the area's hardwood trees.

The tour begins in one of the world's best known mining communities - Springhill. Standing as the name suggests, on a hill 215 m (700 ft. above sea level, the site overlooks the isthmus connecting Nova Scotia with New Brunswick.

Along the route is one of the province's best mountain-biking areas. Trails lead up into the Cobequid Hills. Many go all the way through, descending to Bay of Fundy. At Wentworth, two areas have cross-country ski trails, providing kilometers of groomed routes.

A town of courage

T he story of **Springhill** is not a happy one. Mine collapses; explosions; hundreds of deaths in dark coal mines; entombment for others for as long as a week; and town- engulfing fires have left deep scars on the small town. The community's continual strength and courage in the face of such repeated tragedy has earned it the awarding of the world respected **Carnegie Medal**. The population is now down to pre-mining levels and the town has accepted having a penitentiary to provide jobs. Though silent, the mines still may be of use, as the town is utilizing geo-thermal energy from the warm water in the mine shafts to heat many town buildings. Tailings and mine remnants lie about the area's periphery as reminders. Now beaten down by trail bikes, they make for some "post-industrial" mountain biking.

Memoirs of a hard-luck town

1872	First coal mining begun
1879	The first legalized trade union in Canada is formed
1891	A collapse kills 125 coal miners
1895	A major fire destroys commercial area
1909	A strike hits Springhill- two years follow of extreme poverty and bitterness
1912	World War I - over 500 Springhill men serve their country... 76 fail to return
1942	World War II- Springhill has the largest percentage of men to enlist of any place in Canada
1956	Town at its peak: a total population of 8,000, with over 1,500 employed mining coal
1956	A mine explosion kills 39
1957	Half of Springhill's downtown is again destroyed by fire (the day following Christmas).
1958	A mine collapse takes 75 lives. A historic drama is played out as survivors remain crushed or trapped 1220 m (4,000 ft.) underground. A chilling new use of radio technology enables the men to speak to the surface from a mile underground in the world's deepest mine. Springhill holds the world's attention as millions around the world listen helplessly. A week later, after extreme efforts, 19 miners are carried alive to the surface.
1959	Coal operation ceases. A one-industry town, Springhill endures hard times.
1975	Disaster, still not through, another fire devastates a large part of what had been rebuilt of their downtown.

The whines and snarls of the immense hoisting machinery that lifted men out of the world's deepest mines are gone. The streets encrusted black with coal dust; the company stores; the early morning lights from smoky union halls; and the long lines of coal miners, their lamps dancing in the dark, heading from the mines are gone too. Its death-trap mines have fallen silent, and with them has gone the prosperity of Springhill.

A recommended visit to make is to the **Springhill Miner's Museum**. This fine tribute to the men and boys who went underground. Included are implements, displays on the tragedies and notes written by entombed miners. You can root around memorabilia of time past, and learn what was like to survive disaster underground (902) 597-2873.

Your tour guides include men who were actually in the tragedies. They will take you down a short way to a safe part of the mine. A dramatic moment occurs if your guide momentarily turns off the lights. The eerie sensation of absolute darkness is as many a coal miners faced for extended periods.

START   Corner of #2 and #321 (Junction Rd. and Main St.). Buy your supplies before leaving, there will be only one or two small stores the entire way. If beginning from Wentworth, head out on Valley Road, by the provincial park.

Go downhill on **Main Street** through Springhill. Its name changes to McDougall St., then to McGee St.

1.8 (1.1)   **LEFT** Herrett Street at convenience store and "*the liar's bench*".

Continue past penitentiary

Road turns and becomes **Athol Road**

Follow directions to Rodney/ Windham Hill. After a climb up to a barren hill top, a fast downhill will take you to the turn along River Philip.

Full Steam Ahead

In an ironic twist, a much dreaded threat to livelyhood, could now be a salvation. Springhill, decimated by its mine closures, may just return from the dead, as its abandoned mine shafts may offer as much energy as came from the coal!.

The mines of Springhill were among the depest in the world. At 1.4 km deep, water which would find its way into the shafts could be expected to be warm. How the warmth circulates to the top, however, is a bit mystifying. Like a scene from a miracle, warm spring water pours from the old mines, at one place turning winter's snow covered fields to green.

Now truly a "spring hill", it is all the result of Ralph Ross, a local resident was tinkering with "heat pumps", devices which draw warmth from other objects. He wondered about the mines, and if there was a reservoir of warm water built up beneath the town. Once the battle of permission was finally won to open the mine shafts, Mr. Ross went ahead. Despite the still vivid memories of tragedy, there was no shortage of assistance to unseal the shafts. Retired miners offered assistance, no doubt compelled to relive the bittersweet times of life underground.

The miners were insistant that any water Mr. Ross found in the shafts would quickly drain off. They were wrong. When pumped out, the water kept coming ...and coming. It was so warm, there was steam upon meeting the outside air. With an estimated 1,600 kilometers (one thousand miles) of tunnels dug over a

century, and with areas opened up or sealed by the fateful explosions, no one can determine just what the resevoir size, its origins, or limits of the supply are.

The project is the first geothermal project of its kind in Canada. Enquiries and visiting delegations have come from old mining towns around the world, all hoping to save their own economically depressed communities. Companies are being attracted to the area, interested in the significant savings from the cheap energy.

Applications would also be perfect for aquaculture and greenhouses. Some mine shafts run directly under the main street. What is most impressive, is that there is zero pollution (so vivid in a comparison to the previous dirty, and life-taking struggles). Everyone hopes that Springhill will becoming a centre of alternative energy. Plans are underway to use this clean form of erergy, and transform Springhill into a "giant radiator".

From Springhill to the world

The town's most famous citizen is singer **Anne Murray**. A place knowing only hardship and disaster, Springhill is perhaps a strange place to have emerge a singer of such soft and contented music. The town is very proud to see one of its own go so far beyond knowing only hard times. Anne decided to build this centre here in her home town, instead of the usual Nashville style theme-park. The Anne Murray Centre has three-dimensional displays exhibiing the awards and memorabilia of her illustrious career (admission charge 597-8614).

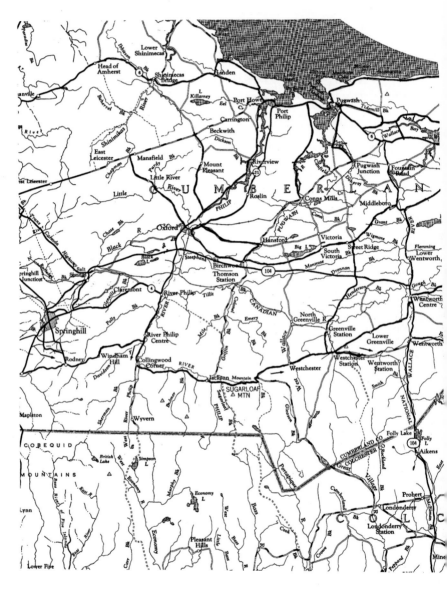

17.2 (10.7)   **RIGHT** toward Collingwood at River Philip. Just before the village ia a pioneer cemetery. This area was settled by groups from Yorkshire. County Court was held here for years, before being moved to Amherst.

19.7 (12.2)   **LEFT** at **Collingwood**- before post office. A store lies just past the turn. Collingwood is the heart of **blueberry** country. A rough but attractive ride at harvest time is the loop around **Wyvern** and **Farmington**, taking you through the berry fields.

        Just outside Collingwood, is the **Beattie Hatfield Hiking Trail.** About 9.6 km (5.8 mi.) long, it takes hikers around **Simpson's Lake**.

        Williamsdale Winery: The Spacek family have put blueberries to a unique use. At their farm they have come up with several varieties of wine, produced here from wild Nova Scotia blueberries. Surprisingly, the wine is clear, and not blue as you might expect. Season mid-May until mid- October- wine-tasting room, gift shop and wine salesroom (admission free 686-3830).

Where blue is gold

I n Germany they are called *"heidelbeeren"*. In England their name is *"huckleberry"*, in Wales, *"whimberry"*. The French refer to them as *"myrtille"*. In Finland you will hear people ask for *"mustika"*. Smooth, pefectly round, and a rich dark blue, in the fields of Northern Nova Scotia grows the world's largest blueberry crop.

Between 6 and 9 million kg (14- 19 million lb.) of the tiny berries are harvested annually. They grow in their natural state and are collected semi-manuallly, by hand rake. They are now favoured around the world as the finest available. Wild blueberries, with their pure image, have reached an almost revered status with the overcrowded Japanese.

The grow in a low, dense carpet, called a "barrens". In late spring the fields are burned, to speed up the growing season. At this time the ground turns black. From August to the first frost in September, the fields are vibrant purple-blue. After harvest, in the fall, the plants turn a beautiful crimson.

The Mic Mac Indians quickly learned that the newly arriving Europeans had a strong weakness for the little fruit. They would pick large quantities and save them, selling them to the colonists to liven up their sparse meals through the long winter.

Annual blueberry festivals are held, such as in Oxford, which proclaims itself to be the "Blueberry Capitol". Extremely diverse foods are created with the small fruit, including a good-tasting blueberry wine.

Medium sized rolling hills continue, with side roads running off to more blueberry barrens. Along your right, are dozens of roads heading into the Cobequid Highlands. Most sooner or later come out along the Bay of Fundy (a few just dead-end in logging areas or old farms). One scenic dirt back road runs from Westchester to Londonderry.

44.5 (27.6)

A fish hatchery is along the roadside at **Jackson**. A small store may be open.

RIGHT (Valley Road) at **Westchester**, just past railway tracks, is a 5.8 km (3.6 mi.) gravel section. If you have a strong aversion to dirt roads, you may continue straight ahead, and turn right on the #104. A paved shoulder follows the road until the end point at the park.

53.1 (33.0)

END Wentworth Provincial Park. Highways #246 and #307 are fine connecting roads to other regions, such as through Earltown toward Pictou and Prince Edward Island.

Accommodation

J. Noiles House Bed and Breakfast Betty and David Delaney, 18 MacFarlane St., Springhill, NS B0M 1X0, (902) 597-8530. Home built in 1900. In centre of town.

Rollways Motel Bert Farnell, 9 Church St., P.O. Box 404, Springhill, N.S. B0M 1S0 Open May 1- Oct.1 (902) 254-2388

Valley Inn Dorothy Weatherbee, R.R. #1, Wentworth, N.S., B0M 1Z0, Highway #104 (902) 548-2202

Hostel

Wentworth Hostel R.R. #1, Wentworth, NS B0M 1Z0, (902) 548-2379, open year-round, capacity: 22 male, 20 female bunks, turn off about 1 km (.6 mi) before #104, dining room, kitchen, common room.

Camping

Wentworth Provincial Park Province of Nova Scotia, (902) 548-2782. Wooded and open sites. No reservations.

Eastern

Y ou can not cycle any further east on the North American mainland. The Eastern Shore (Tour 29) is one of the few quiet places remaining along the entire Atlantic coast. Far removed from the same shore lined with large cities further south, it is rare to get so close to the ocean with so few hassles. Here you can enjoy a meandering seaside road, which weaves you around endless protected inlets, many without a house insight. Occasional small, charming communities offer an almost frontier-like atmosphere. Canso marks the furthest point east on the continent that you can reach by bicycle (there is an isolated piece of road in Labrador which requires first flying or sailing in).

The area is less populated now than it was a century ago. Only 3 locations on the 350 km (217 miles) of the tour have in excess of 500 people! There is very little development. Secluded beaches run along the coast, while deep forests proliferate inland. Peninsulas take you out to the "real" Nova Scotia- fishing villages where visitors are uncommon. You will, without doubt, cherish the peace and quiet you will find on your days along the Eastern Shore.

The northern part of the Eastern region is more populated. The area, however, is by no means urban. With currently just over 5,000 people, Antigonish is considered to be "town" for the entire eastern mainland. Decidedly Scottish, these people argue their celtic roots are even stronger than Cape Bretoners'. The Highland Games at Antigonish draws competitors from across North America as well as Scotland, and is the oldest continuing highland spectacle on this continent.

Near Antigonish is Cape George (Tour 31). A very large and dramatic hill, it is part of the chain of highlands which continues across St. George's

Bay. From there it runs up the Cape Breton coast to form the Cabot Trail. Views from the hill look out over the Northumberland Strait to Prince Edward Island.

The New Glasgow region is a transition zone, separating the lowland farms and beaches of the Northumberland Shore (Sunrise Trail), from the forests, fishing villages, and Scottish highlands of the eastern mainland.

The East River Valley flows to the strait from Sunny Brae (Tour 32). A "gateway to the interior", the tour covers both sides of the river. Little is changed in the valley since it was first settled by the Scots. Farm houses lie settled along its banks. Once at Sunny Brae, you are already well inland into Nova Scotia. From here across to the Atlantic, it is even more unspoiled than this area's shorelines.

The provincial highway map shows many inland communities. Map makers, it is said, dislike blank space. Places marked have sometimes only a handful of people, and next to no services. Some are even abandoned, such as the old mining village of Forest Hill. If going inland bring back-up food.

The Mic Mac Indians were well acquainted with this area's swift rivers, teeming with fish, including the Atlantic Salmon, and the forests abundant with game. Today hunters and fishing enthusiasts travel long distances to stalk these rivers and woods. Liscomb Game Sanctuary is a 250 sq. km (200 sq. mi.) refuge for moose, deer, mink, muskrat, and other animals.

Mountain biking opportunities abound. Through the forests is a maze of woods roads and trails. This area is not suggested for casual off-road cyclists.

189

Nova Scotia's quiet coast

Tour 29   Eastern Shore

Tour at a glance

START	Musquodoboit Harbour
FINISH	Cape Breton Causeway
OTHER STATING POINTS	Halifax/ Dartmouth, Sheet Harbour, Cape Breton Causeway
DISTANCE	350 km (218 mi.)
DIRECTION	West- East
TERRAIN	Occasional hills; closely follows shore
CLIMATE	Occasional Fog; changing wind directions around coves
NOTES	Low population- services limited
TRAFFIC	Low to Moderate
FOOD	Musquodoboit Harbour (R)(C); Lake Charlotte (R)(C); Tangier (R)(C); Sheet Harbour (R)(G)(C); Sherbrooke (R)(G)(C); Port Bickerton (G)(C); Larry's River (C); Guysborough (R)(G)(C); Mulgrave (R)(C)
REPAIRS	Dartmouth (off-route)
TOURISM	Musquodoboit Harbour (at railway museum); Sherbrooke
HOSPITAL	Dartmouth (off-route); Port Hawkesbury (off-route)
AMBULANCE	Dartmouth (off-route)
POLICE	Musquodoboit Harbour (R.C.M.P.); Sherbrooke (R.C.M.P.); Guysborough (R.C.M.P.); Port Hawkesbury (R.C.M.P.)(off-route)

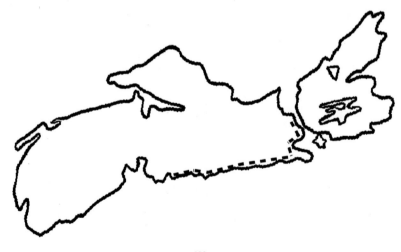

192

W hat can you say about a tour that takes you to Musquodoboit Harbour, Necum Teuch, and Ecum Secum? The Eastern Shore (Marine Drive) is a place of peace and quiet. There is little commercial development to detract from the natural beauty of the landscape. The light traffic you will encounter here is what one might expect to find on a minor inland road. It is, however, along the Atlantic Ocean, the same body of water which "private property" signs and crowded developments run along most of. Here, it is yours to enjoy.

The Eastern Shore provides very pleasant cycling. However, the story of the coast is a sad one. For years, people, especially the young, have been drifting away to the city. This is in itself not a story that is unique, but here, it's impact has been felt acutely. With a small population spread along such a long coast, the draining away of several generations has created a melancholy stagnation. People have lived here for centuries, and they will for many to come, but one experiences an unsettling feeling to see abandoned houses, schools closed from consolidation, and most of what remains part of the past. In fact, there are fewer people than 100 years ago. Sheet Harbour, with only 800 residents, is the largest locality on this trip between Musquodoboit Harbour and Cape Breton! Only a few thousand people live along the entire 350 km (217 mi.) of your route!

The waters of the Eastern Shore are a bit calmer than its "South Shore" cousin, thanks to the many long narrow harbours. The deep coves offer rustic beauty, on sunny days reflecting the forests, on others dense with atmospheric fog. The spruce and maple trees are gnarled and stunted from lifetime exposure to the wind, mist and salt spray. Inland, where the forests stand much taller, salmon and trout pools await intrepid anglers. Deer and moose are plentiful. Along the bays and inlets are rows of cultivated mussels and oysters.

Hundreds of years ago Portuguese and other Europeans camped for short times, but quickly left from fear of Mic Mac (Indian) attacks. Only a few dozen native people can still be found. Their tonque-tying original place names live on. Local residents take delight in watching visitors tackling the names of their villages.

Acadians, evading both the famous expulsion, and the fall of Louisbourg, settled in small groups along the shore to avoid future harassment. They have now been mostly assimilated. In this unlikely area, Black Loyalists from the southern United States also founded a handful of their own settlements.

The Eastern Shore was a booming place in the mid to late 1800's. Lumbering, fishing, and a small gold rush were part of what drew fortune seekers to the area. Sherbrooke Village has been tastefully restored, and depicts these glory days of yesteryear.

Few large hills follow the shore, though frequent shifting will be required while you cross between coves. Remember, the shoreline's villages are small, planning of food is necessary. Stores appear every 15 km (9 mi.) or so along the coast, and hardly ever inland.

START   **Musquodoiboit Harbour**- corner of highways #7 and #357. The story of Nova Scotia's railways is contained within the adjacent Canadian National station (c.1918) and three rail cars. No admission is charged. A small grocery and cafe are adjacent. The name Musquodoboit is from the Mic Mac word meaning *"rolling out in foam"*. The largest community along the western portion of the Eastern Shore, it is divided by the Musquodoboit River, a noted trout and salmon stream.

SIDE TRIP- Martinique: On the first peninsula is a road to one of the best beaches on the shore. Acadians, deported to France during the Expulsion, they attempted to settle on Martinique, in the French West Indies before returning to Nova Scotia.

Jeddore means *"a place of sea duck"* in Mic Mac. An extension of Jeddore West's road leads to beach and marsh. **Jeddore Oyster Pond** offers **Fisherman's Life Museum**. It will show you what is was like to live in an inshore fishing family. In this tiny house, picture what a busy place it was, with 13 daughters! Free of charge, part of the Nova Scotia Museum complex (889-2053).

DETOUR- Clam Harbour Turn right at the large general store at Lake Charlotte. A supervised beach is at Clam Harbour, where an annual sand-castle competition is held. A hiking trail follows the beach and a picnic area is on top of a bluff. The road returns a bit further ahead on route.

Continuing on tour, thousands of white buoys in the water indicate North America's largest cultivated mussel farm at **Ship Harbour**. The **Department of Fisheries Aquaculture Demonstration Centre** allows visitors at its spawning and research facilities.

Tangier marks the start of old **gold rush** country. Here, as well as inland at Mooseland and Moose River, several thousand were attracted for mostly futile searches for gold. Old shafts are still visible beside the road. Near the village a small sign announces **Krauch's Danish Smoked Fish Shop**, down a lane to your left. Their modest operation is famous for smoked salmon, mackerel, and eels. It has a world-wide reputation, as their scrapbook will show you (902) 772-2188.

Soon you pass **Pope's Harbour**, at last count, with only 15 souls.

70.9 (43.2) A huge oil tank, now "Flipper's Beverage Room", announces you have arrived in **Sheet Harbour**. Hunters know this area well, it lies in the heart of a good moose and deer district. It may be hard to believe, but you are now in the largest community (800 people) on the entire 350 km (218 mi.) tour! If you thought the road was quiet up to this point, east of Sheet Harbour, it *really* calms down.

Place names recall early native fishing areas. **Quoddy**, for example was the Mic Mac name for the "seal hunting place." **Necum Teuch** (pop. 45) (pronounced Nee-kum-taw) is a another, today with a breakwater to protect its boats. There are many local versions of how **Ecum Secum** got its name. One is how an early settler sent his son to find their strayed cows. "Ecum," he said, "go seek'um." Another story tells of an Indian who conversed with the settlers: "He come, she come," meaning that his female partner was also in the area. Still others say that it simply means "red sand".

Many salmon are taken from the Ecum Secum River, which serves as the dividing line between Guysborough and Halifax Counties. In these sheltered coves, mussels, European oysters, trout and salmon are cultivated. At **Marie Joseph**, the next coastal village, notice the fish weather vane on the church. Just before reaching it, a picturesque roadside site overlooks the rocky shoreline. There are a couple of eagle nests here. Between Liscomb Mills (pop. 42) and Liscomb is **Spanish Ship Bay** (pop. 98). It is so named from a ship, whose crew had mutinied.

152.9 (93.1) Sherbrooke is the largest village on this section of the tour. Restaurants and services are available. Stock up for the next leg. **Sherbrooke Village Historical Recreation** is a must visit. Sherbrooke Provincial Park lies just north on the bank of the St. Mary's River, a top salmon stream.

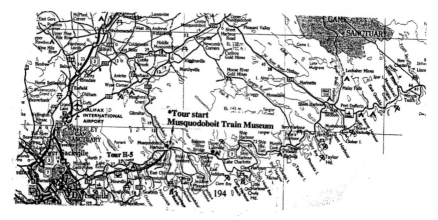

DETOUR: A secondary road provides an attractive alternative route along St. Mary's River to Sonora. Unpaved, it passes through softwood forests to join route #211. Along the way is Wine Harbour, named from cargo spilled on the shore.

.9 (102.5) **RIGHT #211** Following is **Port Hillford** with its sandy beach. Here is the birthplace of country music legend, **Wilf Carter**. **Port Bickerton** (pop. 430) is a fishing community. The "lighthouse road" leads to a seafood-processing plant and public wharf.

LEFT at fire station and small grocery. A short run through barrens will lead you to the **Country Harbour Ferry** to Isaac's Harbour North. Stock up for your time at the dock and the hill on the other side (boats each hour; 7 minute crossing; 7am to 11 pm).

.9 (119.9) **RIGHT** Follow toward the next narrow cove. **Isaac's Harbour** lies down the western side. Goldboro, as its name implies, is the site of yet another find of gold. At **New Harbour** you will notice a good sandy beach. Barren lands along the highway produce an excellent crop of cranberries, blueberries, and fox berries.

SIDE TRIP A tiny boat canal joins White Haven and Tor Bay. **Atlantic Provincial Park** is a covered picnic area on a rocky point looking out to the open ocean.

Larry's River was settled by Acadians on the run from deportation. Once French speaking, it has for some time been assimilated by English. Its name is obviously far from French. How "Larry" came to join forces with these people is not really known. Some postulate it was named for a man who came here moose hunting. Notice the foot-bridge to your right as you pass the Parish Centre. This span connects the two parts of the village.

SHORT- CUT Lundy: This road comes out on the #16. The isolated village of Lundy sits near large Donahue Lake. After passing by, notice the road to the Lundy Fire Tower. It can be mountain-biked to the summit, (2.5 km/ 1.5 mi.) each way, or of course you could walk. On a clear day, there is a 360 degree panoramic view of the region, and its long "finger" lakes.

Continuing on route, you soon pass an old pioneer graveyard at Port Felix.

SIDE TRIP Whitehead is a pleasant village with a charming setting.

.9 (162.1) **LEFT #16**

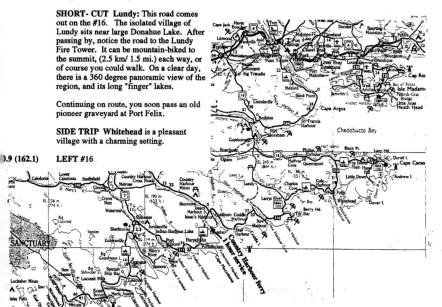

195

Along the forested shore...
villages of yesterday

Once it was called *"The Little Klondike"*.
Goldenville at one time had several thousand
people, almost as many as today live along the
entire shore. They came rushing when gold was
discovered during the 1860's. After a few years of
prosperity, dwindling finds started people drifting away
as fast as they had arrived. Many buildings erected
during this era have been moved. Others, from their
hasty "boom town" construction, have fallen down.
Only a handful of families now live here. Mining
companies with modern extraction methods are
showing renewed interest both here and at the Cochrane
Hill mine, on the other side of Sherbrooke. Perhaps
some day Goldenville will shine again.

The Village of **Sherbrooke** was a bustling place from
the middle to late 1800's. Fishing and lumbering were
in full swing. Then the cry of **"Gold"** was heard and it
soon became a bawdy mining town. Merchants,
harness makers, blacksmiths, and carpenters were
working full tilt. Taverns overflowed into the streets
with either recently wealthy, or despondent miners.
The town's character changed so much, that citizens at
one point were moved to entreat the province: "Enough
has occurred within a few weeks to alarm those who
have the best interests of the community at heart".

Nova Scotia was searched village by village, for a place
as preserved as possible from its important boom era to
construct a living museum. Sherbrooke was selected, it
being so little changed from that time (Maitland on
Tour C-2, was second choice).

The **Sherbrooke Village Restoration Project** is a
"must" to visit. It carefully depicts the glory days of
the early settlers, and brings to life some of the rich
history and heritage of the community. An important
characteristic that sets it apart is the fact that it was
decided that a living museum should be the end result.
People still reside within the historic compound.
Regular sittings are held in the courthouse and services
are conducted in St. James Presbyterian Church.

Tastefully restored and operated, it is seldom crowded,
and seems free of the tackiness and hype of other such
productions. Its many historic buildings and people in
period costume make it an enjoyable location for

shuterbugs. Plan at least half a day to explore the
entire range of buildings and shops needed to run an
1860's village. Admission charge (522-2400)

On Christmas Day, 1784 the ship *"Nymph"* arrived
from Carolina into the long wooded inlet now known as
Stormont. Others followed, on a transport of 900 men,
women, and children, including many elite citizens and
Blacks who had been their servants. They were
Loyalists, those who supported England during the
American Revolution. With the United States now an
independant nation, there seemed little future for them.

They disembarked onto a heavy blanket of snow unlike
they had ever seen in Carolina. Unused to such bitter
cold, they were unprepared. In addition, much of their
supplies had been washed overboard. They
endeavoured to make do with what was at hand. Crude
log cabins were built and roofed with boughs from the
trees. Having been acquainted with a more gracious
background, it was a shock for most to accept their
harsh new lives. Money had little value here in the
snow and woods, and their servants were their equals.

It became even colder and more dismal. The weaker
settlers became ill. It was a hopeless struggle. Soon
300 graves lined the hill they named *"Mount Misery."*
When spring finally arrived, most moved further up the
inlet to found a new "Country Harbour". Many Blacks
moved to Guysborough, and to found villages off what
is now route #16, at Lincolnville, and Upper Tracadie.

Isaac Webb, a Black Loyalist was a survivor of the
horrific winter at Country Harbour. Considering the
landing place bad luck, he moved down the harbour to
the ocean shore. While most settlers feared possible
death from Indian attack, he became very good friends
with them, and looked forward to their visits. A very
charismatic and friendly man, it is reported that
everyone: red, white, and black, were welcomed at his
lonely crossroads. Eventually, others joined him,
proclaiming the site Isaac's Harbour. It became a
shipbuilding community, trading brisk until around
1873. Like nearby Goldboro, the village is now only a
fraction of what it was at its peak. The last Black
resident, and descendant of Isaac Webb died in 1935,
leaving a unique legacy for the villagers of today.

SIDE TRIP Canso- " A Collector's Item " You can go all the way down Highway #16 to Canso, where without a doubt you will be able to claim that you have bicycled as far east as possible on the North American mainland! Founded in 1504, Canso is the oldest fishing port in North America. During the American Revolution much damage was done by privateers. Whitman House Museum has a finely crafted interior, and a "widow's walk" on the roof. Getting to Canso can often be a battle, with nasty winds- you are exploring a point jutting into the Atlantic, with many barren sections. On the way, **Fox Island** has an attractive beach. **Queensport**, formerly called Crow Harbour, was changed in 1898 to honour Queen Victoria in the year of her Diamond Jubilee. At Half Island Cove, arrangements can be made with local fishermen to guide you to the gull colony. **Little Dover**, down a side road is a paradise for artists, photographers and lovers of marine beauty. Brightly painted fishing boats rest in the protected cove's calm waters.

SIDE TRIP Erinville/ Goshen: On your left, just before Guysborough, a wooded, almost deserted road goes inland to Ogden, Erinville, and Goshen. Settled by Irish immigrants, the interior was later mostly abandoned for fishing areas.

294.4 (182.9)   **Guysborough:** You can tell from looking at the Guysborough Post Office, and streetscape, that this was once a prominent place. In fact, this was once one of the major spots in all Nova Scotia. Now with under 500 people, this, the county seat is far smaller than it was over 100 years ago. The town was a prosperous centre for the lumber industry until the demand fell. The harbour has since deteriorated, and now ships could not enter even if they had reason to. The village is home of the **Mulgrave Road** theatre group. Unlike most small town stage playhouses, they do not shy from controversial and political material.

SIDE TRIP- Roman Valley: A pleasant inland diversion follows the Milford Haven River. Starting along Guysborough harbour, it goes through Guysborough Intervale (pop. 54) and Roman Valley (pop. 11), to St. Andrews, 38.6 km (24 mi.) away, on route #316. This is a beautiful ride, most of it following the waterway, bordered by hills. In the fall, the coloured leaves of the hardwoods are quite attractive. A good loop is to go 7.2 km (4.5 mi.) in and cross at North Riverside. Cross three tiny bridges and return on the other side to come out near Boylston.

301.7 (187.4)   **RIGHT** Highway #344 will provide you with some spectacular Atlantic Ocean scenery, on a dead-quiet section or road. Here are abandoned properties, blissfully ignorant of their busy past.

DETOUR Highway #16 Named after U.S. President Abraham Lincoln, the community of Lincolnville, as other small settlements off the highway, were settled by Blacks, who sailed to Nova Scotia with the Loyalists in 1784. At route #4, you can pass through a small Acadian region, to bring you to Auld's Cove at the causeway.

At **Sand Point** you turn and follow the **Strait of Canso.** A communication centre controls shipping in the waterway. Because of the great depth, the largest ships on earth can enter, thus making it one of the world's finest "*superports*". You, will remain in rural solitude. Except for a couple of token gestures, the entirety of this modern "progress" is on the Cape Breton side. Mega-projects, both operational and abandoned lie across the strait, belching from tall smoke-stacks, or rusting away. Amid the long tangle of pipes and towers are an oil refinery, a generating station, an old nuclear energy "heavy water" plant, a gypsum facility, and a pulp mill.

Mulgrave, at one time, was a busy place. Before the Canso Causeway was built, it served as the gateway to Cape Breton, its ferries busy providing the only public transport across the strait. Today, it faces stagnation, even losing its bank. As one town official explained: "These days our town's major income is from old age pensions and baby bonuses". If you want to get a conversation going, ask someone why all the industries seem to be on the other side!

The last stretch of the tour has the longest hill (Porcupine Mountain).

350.0 (218.0)   **END Aulds Cove.** To your right is the **Canso Causeway** and **Cape Breton.**

Accommodation

Camelot Inn Ms P. M. "Charlie" Holgate. P.O. Box 31, Musquodoboit Harbour, NS B0J 2L0, (902) 889-2198. On Route #7, 1.9 ha (5 acres) of woodland, overlooks river rapids and salmon pool.

Murphy's Bed and Breakfast Ralph and Judith Murphy. P.O. Box 29, Musquodoboit Harbour, NS B0J 2L0, (902) 889-2779. On Ostrea Lake Rd., 215 m (700 ft.) off Route #7, no smoking.

Seaview Fisherman's Home Bed and Breakfast Mildred and Ivan Kent. Pleasant Point, R.R. #1, Musquodoboit Harbour, NS B0J 2L0 (902) 889-2561. Ostrea Lake (Pleasant Point Road) to Kent Road, 12.8 km (8 mi.). Nature walk to lighthouse.

Wayward Goose Inn Bed and Breakfast Judy and Randy Skaling. R.R. #2, West Petpeswick, Musquodoboit Harbour, NS B0J 2L0, (902) 889-3654. On road to West Petpeswick, 1.7 km (1 mi.). Walking trail

Lake Charlotte Motel Ford Webber. Lake Charlotte, NS B0J 1Y0 (902) 845-2080, Fax (902) 845-2477. Junction #7 and Clam Hbr. Rd.

Black Duck Inn Bed and Breakfast Gloria V. Walsh-Horne. P.O. Box 26, Sheet Harbour, NS B0J 3B0, (902) 885-2813

Cousins Motel and Marina Ralph and Vera LeBlanc. Box 144, Sheet Harbour, NS B0J 3B0 (902) 885-2502 off-season (902) 885-3219. Salmon Lake Lodge Bryan Lowe. R.R. #1, Sheet Harbour, NS B0J 3B0, (902) 885-2058 off-season (902) 462-2550.

Sheet Harbour Motel Al and Linda Cousins. P.O. Box 59, Sheet Harbour, NS B0J 3B0, (902) 885-2502

Liscomb Lodge Liscomb Mills, NS B0J 2A0, (902) 779-2307, Fax (902) 779-2700. Cottages and chalets, hiking trails.

Kelly's Housekeeping Cottages Robert and Lois Kelly. Box 127, Sherbrooke, NS B0J 3C0, (902) 522-2314.

Marine Motel and Cabins Aubrey and Carol Beaver. P.O. Box 40, Sherbrooke, NS B0J 3C0, (902) 522-2235.

St. Mary's River Lodge Pat and Marg McGinn. P.O. Box 39, Sherbrooke, NS B0J 3C0, (902) 522-2177.

Harbour Bed and Breakfast Doug A. Uloth. Cole Harbour, Guysborough County, NS B0H 1T0, (902) 358-2889. A picturesque setting with view of the harbour.

By the Sea Bed and Breakfast Bruce and Dolores Kaiser. P.O. Box 136, Port Bickerton West, NS B0J 1A0, (902) 364-2575. No smoking

Sea Breeze Cottages Doreen and Henrik Hoglund. P.O. Box 142, Canso, NS B0H 1H0, (902) 366-2352. In Fox Island, grocery store.

The Dorian Motel Dorian and Patricia Harnish. R.R. #1, Canso, NS B0H 1H0, (902) 366-2400.

Belmont Resort Faukland Lane, P.O. Box 229, Guysborough, NS. B0H 1N0, (902) 533-3904

Grants Hotel Bed and Breakfast Mary K. Connolly. P.O. Box 136, Guysborough, NS, B0H 1N0. Corner of Main and Broad St. 533-3395

Campgrounds

E. F. Webber Lakeside Park The Webbers. R.R. #2, Oyster Pond, Jeddore, NS B0J 1W0, (902) 845-2340. Wooded campground on lake. At Upper Lakeville, 4 km (2.5 mi.) left off Route #7. Groceries; laundromat; swimming.

Murphy's Camping-on-the-Ocean William Murphy. Murphy Cove, NS, B0J 3H0, (902) 772-2208. Open campground on ocean, showers.

East River Lodge Campground and Trailer Park Jack MacDonald. West East River Rd., Sheet Harbour, NS B0J 3B0, (902) 885-2864, (902) 885-2057. Showers; laundromat.

Ocean View Tent and Trailer Park Frank and Kay Whitman. Beaver Harbour, NS B0J 2R0, (902) 654-2910. Open and wooded campground on ocean; pay showers.

Dolphin Tent and Trailer Park Eva Cameron. Port Dufferin, NS B0J 2R0, (902) 654-2739. Along campground on ocean; swimming.

Riverside Campground Pearl Cook. P.O.Box 41, Sherbrooke, NS B0J 3C0, (902) 522-2913, (902) 522-2173. Open and wooded campground on river, showers, groceries.

Nimrod's Rest St. Mary's Fish and Game Association P.O. Box 86, Sherbrooke, NS B0J 3C0, (902) 522-2441, (902) 522-2964. Open and wooded campground on lake at Stillwater, on Route #211. Pay showers.

Salsman Provincial Park Province of Nova Scotia, (902) 387-2877. Open and wooded campground on west side of Country Harbour, north of Isaac's Harbour on Route #316; no reservations

Sea Breeze Camp and Trailer Park Doreen and Henrik Hoglund. P.O. Box 142, Canso, NS B0H 1H0, (902) 366-2352. Open and wooded sites on ocean; pay showers; laundromat; groceries; lobster pound.

Boylston Provincial Park Province of Nova Scotia. (902) 533-3326. Open and wooded campground; no reservations.

Atlantic Canada
Cycling Festival

A hidden corner of Nova Scotia

Tour 30   Sunny Brae

Tour at a glance

START/ FINISH	Stellarton
OTHER STARTING POINTS	New Glasgow, Sunny Brae
DISTANCE	53 km (33 mi.)
DIRECTION	Clockwise
TERRAIN	Rolling; along sides of a narrow valley
CLIMATE	Protected by valley; usually sunny
TRAFFIC	Low
FOOD	Stellarton (R)(G)(C); Sunny Brae (C)
REPAIRS	Pictou (off-route)
TOURISM	New Glasgow
HOSPITAL	New Glasgow
AMBULANCE	New Glasgow
POLICE	Stellarton

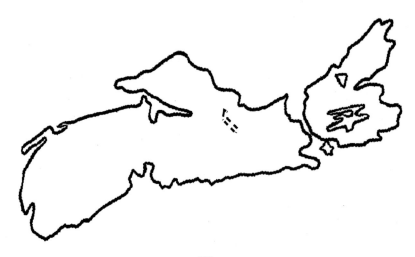

"A Gleann Boidheach"

This Gaelic phrase meaning "beautiful valley", can still be used to describe the land along the winding East River. Unknown and unpromoted, this is a "hidden corner" of Nova Scotia. The province refers to it as Sunnybray. The people of the valley, however, would prefer it referred to as *Sunny Brae*, and so shall we.

The Gaelic tongue is now gone, but not much else has changed since the Scots built their first homesteads years ago. Once past Stellarton, there are few gaudy modern intrusions.

The route is fairly simple. Once on the east side of the river you follow it inland. You cross over where it becomes much narrower, at Sunny Brae. The turn-around lies deep in Nova Scotia's interior. From here it is dense woods all the way to historic Sherbrooke, near the Atlantic Ocean.

Your ride back on the other side views the river valley in the foreground and Stellarton and New Glasgow in the distance.

You might consider starting from New Glasgow or Pictou for flexibility of tour distance and accommodation.

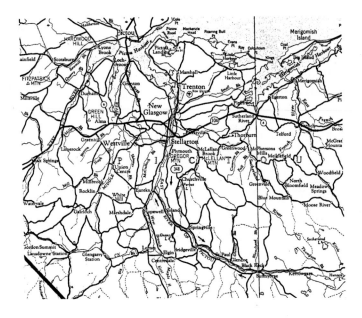

201

START   Corner of Foord and Acadia Streets in **Stellarton**. To begin the tour you will first head north a short distance toward New Glasgow, to cross the river.

Stellarton is a small coal mining town. It's name derives from the star-shaped sparks the area's high quality rock creates when burned. Underneath the town runs the **Foord Seam**, considered to be the world's **thickest and richest layer of coal**. It is so pure, it is almost porous, bringing with it the risk of methane gas. In the gamble for this valued coal, the town has paid a high price. Like at Springhill, Cape Breton, and River Hebert, there have been many disasters underground. The town's **Miner's Museum** preserves many items from the past, including memorials of its tragedies. An attractive monument on Foord Street commemorates those lost. The latest was in May 1992. At a time when mine tragedies seemed to be a thing of the past, the huge modern **Westray Mine**, "one so big you could drive a truck into", suffered an explosion from a pocket of methane, claiming 26 lives.

A source of pride is the town's **Balmoral Girls Pipe and Drum Band**. Also here is headquarters of Sobeys, the giant grocery chain, operated by one of the wealthiest families in the country.

0.5 (0.3)   **RIGHT**   Bridge Avenue. Go across the East River to #348

1.5 (0.9)   **RIGHT #348**

2.7 (1.7)   **RIGHT** River Road. This is **Plymouth**, site of the tragic coal mining disaster of May, 1992.

Spring water can be found on left hand side 10.4 km (6.3 mi.) along.

14.9 (9.2)   **RIGHT** #348 Stay on east side of river until Sunny Brae.

26.9 (16.7)   **RIGHT** Cross bridge into **Sunny Brae** (store in village). The turn-around point of the ride, from here, roads head into the interior. A dirt stretch continues on past the point of origin of the East River to the curiously named Garden of Eden. Highway #348 crosses atop an old pioneer route to historic Sherbrooke.

27.0 (16.8)   **RIGHT** Return, following west side of the river

46.3 (28.7)   **RIGHT** at Eureka. Go towards Stellarton, road becomes South Foord Street.

52.8 (32.8)   **END** Corner of South Foord and Acadia St.

Accommodation

MacDonald's Bed and Breakfast James/ Rena MacDonald P.O. Box 831, 292 South Foord St., Stellarton, NS B0K 1S0, (902) 752- 7751
Heather Motor Hotel Matt Vohs. Foord Street P.O Box 2090, Stellarton, NS B0K 1S0, (902) 752-8401
Country Inn and Suites 700 Westville Road, New Glasgow, NS B2H 2J8 (902) 928-1333.
Journey's End Motel 740 Westville Rd., New Glasgow, NS B2H 2J8 (902) 755-6450.
Lord Provost Inn 222 Provost St., New Glasgow, NS B2H 2R3 (902) 752-1515. Route #104, Exit 25.
MacKay's Bed and Breakfast Mrs. Evelyn MacKay. 44 High St., New Glasgow, NS B2H 2W6 (902) 752-5889.
Morgan's Bed and Breakfast Bill and Shirley Moran. 151 Hillcrest St., New Glasgow, NS B2H 3T7. (902) 752-0966. From Route #104, Exit 25, North on East River Rd., right on Temperance St., right on Mountain Rd., left on Hillcrest.
Peter Pan Motel Bill Crandell, 390 Marsh St., New Glasgow, NS B2H 4S6. (902) 752-8327
Stoneycombe Lodge Bed and Breakfast Keith and Edith Selwyn-Smith, R.R. #3, Westville (Alma), NS B0K 2A0, Pictou County, (902) 396-3954. Situated near Green Hill (just off the Trans-Canada Highway- #104). They are bicycle-friendly, Keith having spent many years cycling in Britain. No smoking.
Sundowner Motel Isabel and Garnet Cook, 601 Westville Rd., New Glasgow, NS B2H 2J6 (902)752-8496.
Tara Motel Robert MacKean. 917 East River Rd., New Glasgow, NS B2H 3S5 (902) 752-8458.
Wynward Inn Bed and Breakfast Dorothy Leahy Walsh, 71 Stellarton Rd., New Glasgow, NS B2H 1L7 (902) 752-4527.

Camping

Elm Glen Campground Walter Johnson, R.R. #1, Eureka, NS B0K 1B0, (902) 923-2915. On route, half-way to Sunny Brae. Showers
Trenton Steeltown Park c/o Martin Bates, Trenton, N.S.; B0K 1X0. Large wooded campground in Trenton, just north of New Glasgow. Trails for walking or mountain biking. (902) 752-1019

antic Canada
cling Festival

A highland trail by the sea

Tour 31   Cape George

Tour at a glance

START	Antigonish
FINISH	Antigonish, New Glasgow
OTHER STARTING POINT	New Glasgow
DISTANCE	Loop- 77 km (48 mi.)
	Sunrise Trail-to New Glasgow 108 km (67 mi.)
DIRECTION	Counter-Clockwise
TERRAIN	Hilly
CLIMATE	Sea breezes; windy on Cape George
TRAFFIC	Moderate; Busy during Highland Games
REST SPOTS	Ballantyne Cove wharf; Cape George lighthouse;
	Malignant Cove
FOOD	Antigonish (R)(G)(C)
REPAIRS	Pictou (off-route)
TOURISM	Antigonish (near exit 32 of #104)
HOSPITAL	Antigonish 863-2830
AMBULANCE	Antigonish 863-2312
POLICE	Antigonish (R.C.M.P.) 863-6500

Situated 304 m (1,000 ft.) above sea level, the look-off at Cape George provides an overview of St. George's Bay. Tiny fishing boats can be seen working the waters below. Obscured by mist and cloud, looming across the water you can see Cape Breton Island's hills along the skyline.

Cape George is part of the same chain of hills that form the Cabot Trail. After running down Cape Breton's west coast as the Creignish Hills, it pops up again here, on the other side of St. George's Bay. Like the shore along Advocate, Cape George is referred to as the *"Mini Cabot Trail"*. This has however, scenery all its own and deserves not to be treated as any kind of warm-up or substitute. The route follows closely to the coast. It passes beaches, and old farm sites, some prosperous with dairy cows, others being reclaimed by forest. The highlands of Antigonish County are densely wooded, a favoured region for many of Nova Scotia's moose.

This tour requires reasonably fit cyclists, but not athletes. The hills can be walked in a short period if desired. A good spot for lunch is at the lighthouse on top of the cape, or at the dock at Ballantynes Cove.

The tour begins in **Antigonish**, university town, county seat, and stronghold of Scottish heritage. Although having only 5,000 people, Antigonish is the largest place and "town" to the entire eastern mainland. Its name is a Mic Mac word. It is thought to mean *"place where the branches are torn off by bears gathering beechnuts"*.

In the mid-1600's the **Acadians** arrived, but unlike most parts of Nova Scotia, here the Mic Mac drove them away. A century later they tried again, settling at nearby Tracadie, and Havre Boucher. **Irish Loyalists** are given credit for actually starting the current town, arriving in 1784. Looking at it today however, its background is strongly **Scottish**. They arrived in large numbers, direct from landings at Pictou.

Being almost entirely Catholic, Antigonish's status of diocese centre was enhanced by the powerful

influence of its university. Even today, some journalists good naturedly refer to it as the "little Vatican". First established at Arichat, Cape Breton, St. **Francis Xavier University** moved to Antigonish in 1855. It is here that both the **Credit Union** and **Cooperative Movements** have been developed. Principles of self-help expounded by the leaders of the *"Antigonish Movement"* are taught to students from 80 countries worldwide, particuarily developing nations. Recreation facilities are open to visitors. There is an indoor pool, gym, tennis and racquetball courts, saunas, and tracks (867-2181).

St. **Ninian's Cathedral**, dating from 1868, is constructed of blue limestons and granite. It took nine years to build.

Stamp collectors often have dealings with Antigonish. well. It is here that **Canada Post** has located its philatelic division. The town is home to several reknown pipe bands and highland dance groups. They figure prominently at a very popular annual Nova Scotian tradition. The **Antigonish Highland Games** since 1861has been a celebration of Scottish music, dance, and sports. *Note:* During the games expect increased tourist traffic around Cape George.

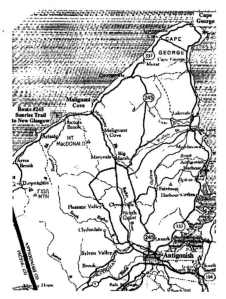

START	Antigonish Tourist Bureau Exit 32 of #104. Begin by heading into town on highway #7. Main Street becomes route #337.
32.2 (20.2)	**Ballantyne's Cove** has a large dock, with several fishing boats. An ice cream stand is occasionally open. **Cape George** stands at 304 m (1000 feet) directly up from the cove. Strange as it may sound, a lighthouse stands near the top! Built in 1895, from this vantage point on a clear day you can see in the distance Cape Breton and Prince Edward Island. Below you, the fishing fleet of St. George's Bay can be seen working its waters, mainly harvesting lobster. In the bay are also tuna. The largest one ever caught was in 1979. After the battle of the sportsman's life, it was reeled in... weighing an incredible 679 kg (1496 lb.)!
	Past Cape George, you face only small hills. Turning west, P.E.I. follows on the horizon.
55.8 (34.7)	**LEFT** Perhaps the least appealing place name in Nova Scotia belongs to **Malignant Cove**. Its population though has resisted several attempts to have it changed. The name comes from the British Man-of-War *HMS Malignant*, wrecked here on its way to Quebec during the American Revolution.
	To complete a circle, you can head in on #245, passing through forested countryside and a few farms. The coast is a far superior route, so if you have the time, go back the same way as you came out.
76.3 (44.5)	**RIGHT** #4 (West St.) in Antigonish
76.7 (46.7)	**LEFT** Stay on West St.
77.3 (46.9)	**END** Antigonish Tourist Bureau

Option: Sunrise Trail- Malignant Cove to New Glasgow

Many cyclists carry on to New Glasgow following the Sunrise Trail. There connections can be made with Tours 25, 26, and 30. It is about 31km (19 mi.) from Malignant Cove. **Arisaig** was settled in 1791 by Catholic Highlanders. Its attractive church was once the centre of the regional diocese, before being moved to Antigonish. Locals may be able to direct you to fossils, near the dock. **Merigomish** was a summer gathering place for the Mic Mac (Indians). Here they would convene and play games. You must join #104 for a short section- use extreme caution! Just past the high school, turn back off it at Exit 27A.

Accommodation

Auberge Wandlyn Inn Ron Chisholm, 158 Main St., Antigonish, NS B2G 2B7 (902) 863-4001
Best Western Claymore Ernie Curry, Church St., Box 1720, Antigonish, NS B2G 2M5 (902) 863-1050
Chateau Motel Anne Cusack. 112 Post Rd., Antigonish, NS B2G 2K5 (902) 863-4842; (902) 863-4871. Route #104, 0.4 km (0.2 mi.) west of Antigonish (near bus terminal)
MacIsaac's Bed and Breakfast Hugh and Bev MacIsaac, 18 Hillcrest St., Antigonish, NS B2G 1Z3 (902) 863-2947.
Oasis Motel Leonard/ Josephine Rhynold, P.O. Box 1448, Antigonish, NS B2G 1M7 (902) 863-3557.
Old Manse Inn Leonard and Barbara Pluta, 5 Tigo Park, Antigonish, NS B2G 1M7 (902) 863-5696; (902) 863-5259. 1874 Victorian manse. Cyclist's breakfasts. Near downtown off Hawthorne Street.
Valley View Motel The O'Hallorans, 295 Hawthorne St., Antigonish, NS B2G 1B9 (902) 863-0990. Route #245 1.6 km (1 mi.) west of town.
Whidden's Motel Apartments Karen Jackman, 11 Hawthorne St., Box 1744, Antigonish, NS B2G 2M5 (902) 863-3736. Downtown, (near the post office).
Cribbon's Cottages Paul and Loreen Boyd, Cribbon's Point, NS B2G 2L2 (902) 863-6320; (902) 863-2936. 20 km (12.4 mi.) north on Route #337.

Camping

Whidden's Campground John H. Whidden, P. O. Box 1744, Antigonish, NS B2G 2M5 (902) 863-3736. Open and wooded campground on Brierly Brook in downtown Antigonish (near post office). Pay showers, washroom, laundromat.
Farm View Camping and Trailer Park Valmar and Donald Beaton, Brierly Brook, NS B2G 2K9 (902) 863-6252; Off-season (902) 863-4141. Route #104, Exit 31A, 3 km (2 mi.) west of Antigonish at Brierly Brook. Pay showers, washrooms, laundromat.

Cape Breton Island

Nova Scotia's major cycling destination is a place of dramatic seacoasts, beautiful lakes, and rugged small mountains. This is Cape Breton Island, one of the most highly rated places for bicycle touring in the world!

Being an island, this final region has the most defined boundaries. In Cape Breton, the scenery is more spectacular, the cycling is more challenging. Comprising roughly one-seventh of Nova Scotia, the island is about 160 km (100 mi.) long, and 130 km (80 mi.) wide. It is actually a group of islands. It includes Boularderie Island and Isle Madame, which in turn has islands of its own. Many smaller islands. such as Port Hood Island, the Bird Islands, Scaterie, St. Paul's and others, enhance Cape Breton's atmospheric marine environment.

In the north lies one of the finest cycling regions of the world. The Cabot Trail is overwhelmingly the favourite bicycle tour in Atlantic Canada. Winding along the coast, with challenging climbs, ocean cliff descents, forests, and protected wildlife, it can not be compared with any other single route. The most hilly part of Nova Scotia, many agree that it is also, perhaps, the most rewarding. Off the trail are side trips, leading to spectacular coves and ridges. One such diversion is a trip in itself. If you want a ride through some wild country, you could take the road to St. Lawrence Bay and, if your nerve doesn't fail, you an go all the way out to Meat Cove, which, as you will discover for yourself, is definitely the end of the road.

Cape Breton deserves to be looked at as much more than simply to route to the Cabot Trail! Anywhere else the other Cape Breton routes would stand out, drawing much attention. Here, they get lost in the trail's shadow.

The heart of the island is undoubtedly Lake Bras D'Or. Regarded as a lake, it is in reality an inland sea! On a map, it may be at first difficult to locate its ocean connection- a narrow gap at its eastern end. In fact, it has a mild level of salt water and even a minor tide.

This vast basin of many coves provides a water paradise for sailing enthusiasts. You can take several days to circle its 960 km (600 mi.) coastline, or sample just a section of its pleasant shore. This sea of remarkably clean water is ringed by wooded hills, cottages, and forgotten farms. The majority of Nova Scotia's Mic Mac aboriginal people live on reserves in Cape Breton, most of which rest on the Bras D'or.

To the east, the region around Sydney and Glace Bay is known as *Industrial Cape Breton*. For many years, it lead all Atlantic Canada with its dynamic productivity. Cape Breton steel laid down the rails that pushed the new nation of Canada to the Pacific. Coal mines were busy all over the region, their shafts digging deep under the sea. All over the island, people gave up their subsistance farms for the promise of a new life.

This region has an interesting heritage. Many diverse groups of people, attracted by the mills and mines built scattered small towns between the mines. Dominion was settled by Italians; Ukranians and Greeks built homes in sections of Sydney; Blacks arrived from communities across Nova Scotia and the Caribbean to work and live under the red smoke at Sydney's steel mill. These enclaves were colourful and optimistic, each taking on the atmosphere of the countries of their origin.

Increasing use of oil closed many coal markets. Mine disasters, labour unrest and aging factories ushered in an era of decay. A total of 900 million tons of coal lie waiting below the ground and ocean. Industrial history, and the romance of its melancholy remains, is an acquired taste. Between the towns lie rough grassy fields and overgrown slag pits. Worn pathways have been already worked in, for those who like off-road biking with a post-industrial flavour. The region is far from blighted. Several good beaches line the Atlantic shore. Being off the usual tourist routes, they are known only by the locals. There are historic houses, museums, and other points of interest. The people here are another reason to visit. They are extremely forthright, with strong accents and biting wit. Bicycle tourists here are are looked at like birds far off their flight path. In fact, the people may joke with you as being a stray off the Cabot Trail!

The south of Cape Breton is a quiet region, centred by the pleasant Mira River, one of the longest in the province. Not far away lies the magnificent Fortress of Louisbourg, once North America's fourth busiest port. Here, at the former centre of France's empire in the New World, you enter the town gates to homes, gardens, hotels, and taverns of colonial times. Louisbourg is truly a world-class attraction, worth a visit. Many cyclists inquire about the coastal road, along the far south from Gabarus to Route #247. Unfortunately, this road has almost no water access, and is not exactly dramatic.

The south-west section of the island is reasonably flat. Isle Madame is an attractive, atmospheric place. Its villages, such as Sampson's Cove and Little Anse are among the prettiest villages in Nova Scotia. Isle Madame is one of the oldest Europeanized places on the continent. Many of the people here are French-speaking Acadians. They have lived here for centuries. Cape Breton, in fact, got its name from homesick fishermen from France's Brittany. Acadian French is an oral language. It has evolved less than has the mother tongue back in France. Some words used have long been disused on the other side of the ocean. Satellite dishes, however, are causing more damage than English bullets ever could. The electronic age continues to strip away the culture that has been guarded for 400 years. Many people now speak French, but "think" in English.

To the left off the causeway onto the island from the mainland is Cape Breton's rugged west coast. This rolling region follows St.George's Bay and the Gulf of St. Lawrence. It starts off level, becoming more hilly as you approach the Cabot Trail.

A rugged climate for a rugged land

Host to Nova Scotia's coolest weather, spring and summer are slow to arrive, and quick to leave. Snowfalls in early May, as well as October are quite possible. While not being mountainous enough to trap clouds, the Cape Breton Highlands react with incoming patterns off the Gulf of St. Lawrence, to cause the highest precipitation in the province. Along the Atlantic Coast, there is often dense fog, While this is often pleasantly moody, the dampness can seep bone deep. Bring warm clothing. Along the west coast and into the Cabot Trail, the wind can be vicious. It has been known to stop cyclists in their tracks!

From a visitors perspective, one might gain the impression that the population lives entirely from crafts and tourism. Cape Breton, however, is a working island, a place of farmers, fishermen, loggers, steel workers, and coal miners. They are known across Canada and far beyond for their friendliness and wit. They pride themselves on their independent and at times rebellious nature. Also, the people are, on the whole, happy to meet tourists! You may also notice that people are direct, having little difficulty expressing what their opinions are.

Individuality seems to be admired, and there is a strong tolerance to those who want to live a little differently. There are, it has been observed, more characters per kilometer of Cape Breton hills than perhaps anywhere in the country. People will tell you they live here by choice. Few are envious in any way of big city life and the 9 to 5 rat race. After a visit to this island you will see why Cape Bretoners are so tenaciously attached to this rugged island.

Atlantic Canada
Cycling Festival

Through a quiet valley,
along an inland sea

Tour 32 Marble Mtn./Skye Valley

Tour at a glance

START	Cape Breton Causeway (Port Hastings)
FINISH	Mabou
OTHER STATING POINTS	Mabou, Whycocomagh
DISTANCE	110 km (67 mi.)
DIRECTION	West- East
TERRAIN	Hilly
CLIMATE	Moderate; varying winds directions
NOTES	Dirt section from Malagawatch to near Orangedale
TRAFFIC	Low to Moderate
FOOD	Port Hawkesbury (R)(G)(C); Orangedale (C); Whycocomagh (R)(G)(C); Brook Village (C); Mabou (R)(C)
REPAIRS	Sydney (off-route)
TOURISM	Port Hastings 625-1717
HOSPITAL	Port Hawkesbury ; Baddeck (off-route); Inverness (off-route)
POLICE	Port Hawkesbury (R.C.M.P.); Mabou (R.C.M.P.)

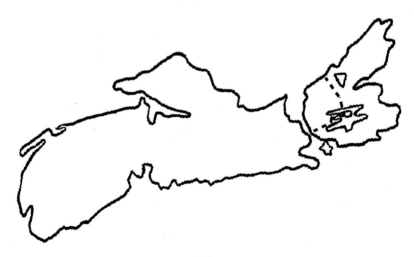

Meandering through the heart of Cape Breton, this is much more than a pleasant route across the island. A "strategic" ride, this is well suited as a way to reach the major "destination" tours. The Cabot Trail, Creignish Hills (Ceilidh Trail), Mira/ Louisbourg areas, connect with the mainland by way of this route. It is quite probable that the Marble Mountain/ Skye Valley tour will be explored in sections, as you follow your island itinerary. The village of Whycocomagh makes a good spot to either interrupt or join the route.

The tour uncovers two distinctive regions. After leaving the Canso Stait, you approach the first focal area, **Lake Bras d' Or**. You pass along a side of the lake known as the **Marble Mountain** area. There are no actual mountains, but a continuous ridge of about 215 m (700 ft.) runs along not far in from the lake. **Bald Eagles** build their huge nests in rock faces atop the hills. You will stay mostly along the shore, but will have some climbing. Dirt roads going off-route up the escarpment offer panoramic views of the lake. Some go all the way through to the other side, many just taper off.

The **Skye River Valley** is the second distinct region of the tour. Well off the beaten track, it passes through an area of old Scottish homesteads. It is a worthwhile cycling route to or from Cape Breton's west coast.

START	At the Nova Scotia Information Centre at Port Hastings (directly off the causeway at traffic circle). Head along the **Strait of Canso** on #4 into Port Hawkesbury. Mainlanders moved mountains to reach Cape Breton. From where you begin at the entry point trrafic circle, you have a good view of the strait. Crosing it, the **Canso Causeway**, completed in 1955 is the **world's deepest**. The scarred face of **Porcupine Mountain** reveals where 10 million tons of rock and fill were taken. The stone from the **largest pyramid of Egypt** would not be enough to fill the channel. It carries both rail and highway traffic, and locks on the Cape Breton Island side allow for the passage of small vessels. Cape Bretoners demanded that "*not one spoonful of island soil*" be used to join the mainland.
4.1 (2.6)	Highway #4 becomes Reeves St. If traffic is unpleasant (lumber trucks), you can go along the lower road through town. **Port Hawkesbury** is home to the **Nova Scotia Nautical Institute**, where mariners learn the art of sea navigation. Known as a"super-port" the deep waters of the strait has encouraged industry such as oil refineries, "heavy-water" plants, and wood processing. The town is the only service area until you reach Whycocomagh. Pick up your suplies here. There is not too much else to keep you in town (unless you have an interest in the pulp and paper industry).
6.0 (3.7)	**LEFT #4**
7.9 (4.9)	Route #104 branches off. Peace and quiet begins.
17.9 (11.1)	**LEFT** at bridge at **Cleveland**. Once named River Inhabitants Bridge, the village was renamed in honour of United States President **Grover Cleveland**.
18.0 (11.2)	**RIGHT** Immediately after last turn, just before church. A rolling, twisting road now takes you up and over a plateau for your first glimpse of magnificent

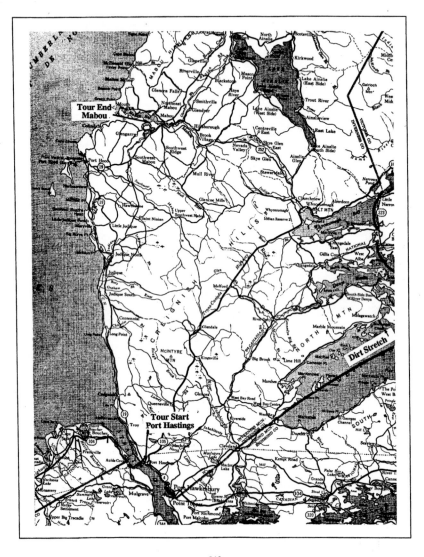

Lake Bras d'Or. This land-locked sea was formed when the ocean flooded into valleys carved out by moving glaciers. Surrounded by forested hills, its shoreline hills are home of perhaps the largest **Bald Eagle** colony in the world! They build their huge nests amid rock faces in the large hills. The pristine waters offer trout and other fish for their sizable appetites.

25.0 (15.5)   **LEFT** at West Bay

> **SIDE TRIP- St. George's Channel/ St. Peter's:** This rolling road takes you around the south edge of Lake Bras d'Or to the historic canal at **St. Peter's.** Expect rolling hills around the edge of the lake. Kayak Cape Breton offers tours and introductory courses on the lake (902) 535-3060.

Continuing on tour, a ridge of about 215 m (700 ft.) runs along inland close to the lake. You will stay mostly along the shore, but there will be occasional hills. Dirt roads going off-route up the escarpment offer panoramic views. Some go all the way through to the other side, many just taper off.

33.9 (21.1)   Marble Mountain: Here on the shore of Lake Bras d'Or is a **marble deposit,** recognized as being among the finest in the world. Similar to the marble fields of western Ireland, it is exposed in a face over 30 m (100 ft.) in height.

Marble Mountain

Not always as silent as you will find it today, at the turn of the century, **Marble Mountain** was a boom town. As many as 1,000 were employed quarrying dolomite and limestone for the Dominion Steel Company of Sydney, as well as running businesses in the village. One of these was in a five level building along the shore. A store, as impressive as any found on the streets of Victorian Halifax, boasted marble topped counters, shining brass railings and glass showcases. It was said to sell *"everything from a needle to an anchor"*.

The mines eventually closed and the village grewsilent. Occasional schemes came and went to quarry its marble deposit. Of an extremely high quality, you will find examples of it at the village's marble-chip beach. These operations were short lived. The problem was transportation. Marble Mounatin lay isolated,

separated by a ridge from Orangedale. The road over it, and along the lake were in too poor condition to even bring in the proper equipment, let alone ship out marble stone to Orangedale's train yards. despite constant campaigning, good roads were not forthcoming, due to a differeent alliegence of the area's voters than that in power at the time.

In the early 1930's it became known by a few visitors from the United States. They were entranced with Lake Bras d'Or's sparkling waters and many islands. abandoned farms were snapped up and new summer homes were built. It is not difficult to understand why. A trail leads up to an overview of the scenic lake and nearby islands.

Located in an old schoolhouse, **Marble Mountain Museum and Library** tells the story ofthe activities here years ago. The museum is open in the summer (free admission).

Malagawatch (a name of Mic Mac origin), announces your turn around the end of the peninsula. An 8 km (5 mi.) dirt section begins.

63.0 (39.1)   **RIGHT** Cross River Denys

Pavement resumes

70.2 (43.6)   **LEFT Orangedale.** Originally Called Mull's Cove, and then Blue's Cove, this was an important railway junction for central Cape Breton, including the resort of Baddeck. Today that former activity is remembered at the **Orangedale Train Station Museum.** Dating back to 1887, it is one of the few remaining relics from the days of the **Intercolonial Railway.** It houses railway artifacts, station master quarters, scale model railway and original furniture (free- open by appointment-upkeep donations appreciated 756-2028, 756-2026, 756-2874).

76.6 (47.6)   **RIGHT #105** Trans-Canada Highway. You must now follow a short distance on this primary throughfare. From here you can continue on to Baddeck and the Cabot Trail. It is a busy highway, but much quiter than the same highway on the mainland. A wide shoulder protects you all the way along. There is noise, however, and far too many billboards.

81.6 (50.7)   **LEFT #252** at Vi's Restaurant. Connect with Tour 35. **Whycocomagh** is two villages in one. A **Mic Mac** (Indian) "reserve" and an area descended by **Higland Scots**, lie separated by the Skye River. For a small place, there does not seem to be much mingling.

Both sides of the village offer resaurants and sevices. Whycocomagh Provincial Park to the east, has picnic sites overlooking the lake. **Salt Mountain** hiking trial from the park has three different loook-offs over Lake Bras D'or.

On the way to the Gulf of St, Lawrence, you wind your way through the **Skye River Valley**, settled by the Gaelic Scots.

99.4 (61.8)   **Brook Village** (store)

108.5 (67.0)   **LEFT** Trunk #19 (connection point with Tour 36).

109.5 (67.4)   **END Mabou** Gaelic culture is making its last stand among these highlands. In Mabou, and other villages, people are doing all possible to maintain the traditions they brought with them from Scotland. Gaelic is still taught in the village school, and the people hold a Ceilidh (kay-lee) or Scottish concert with dance and picnic every Canada Day (July 1).

"The Bridge" Once a general store, the Mabou Gaelic and Historic Society now uses it as a local centre for crafts, geneology and research on Scottish culture. The museum is open in the summer during the week (Admissision free). The **Mother of Sorrows Pioneer Church** is another point of interest, a small chapel near the village.

Accommodation

(Port Hastings and Port Hawkesbury included together)

Auberge Wandlyn Inn David Rutherford, 689 Reeves St., P.O. Box 759, Port Hawkesbury, NS B0E 2V0, (902) 625-0320.

Keddy's Inn Joyce O'Brien, P.O. Box 50, Port Hastings, NS B0E 2T0 (902) 625-0460; Fax (902) 625-1275. Junction of Routes #19, 104, and 105.

MacPuffin Motel MacKenzie Jones, P.O. Box 558, Port Hawkesbury, NS B0E 2V0, (902)625-0621. On Route #4 at Port Hastings.

Skye Motel Bernice Richard, P.O. Box 190, Port Hastings, NS B0E 2T0 (902) 625-1300. Junction of Routes #19, 104, and 105.

Troy Lodge Cottages Mrs. Anna Guzdziol, P.O. Box 399, Port Hawkesbury, NS B0E 2V0 (902) 625-1684 (902) 625-2680. Route #19, 4 km (2.5 mi) before causeway.

Dundee Resort Dundee, Cape Breton, R.R. #2, West Bay, N.S., B0E 3K0 (902) 345-2649, fax (902) 345-2697. At the western end of the shores of Lake Bras d'Or. 2 lit tennis courts, pool.

Joseph Doucette Bed and Breakfast Joseph Doucette, R.R. #1, West Bay, N.S., B0E 3K0 One double and one single room

Mary Maclean Bed and Breakfast Mary Maclean Mary MacLean, R.R. #1, West Bay, N.S., B0E 3K0 (902) 345-2630. One double and one single room

The Points Danny Ellis, R.R. #2, West Bay Rd., The Points (West Bay), N.S., B0E 3K0 (902) 345-2485. Off Route #4, 37 km (22.9 mi.) from Port Hawkesbury, or 26 km (16.1 mi.) from St. Peter's.

Fair Isle Motel Miriam J. Munro, P.O. Box 53, Whycocomagh, NS B0E 3M0, (902) 756-2291.

Island View Bed and Breakfast Anna and Bill MacKinnon, P.O. Box 96, Whycocomagh, NS B0E 3M0, (902) 756-2951. At entrance to Whycocomagh Provincial Park. No smoking.

Mary Smith Bed and Breakfast Mary J. Smith, Main St. Whycocomagh, NS B0E 3M0, (902) 756-2157. Right of Royal Bank, garage available for bikes.

Trout River Cottages Jean and Arnold Tobey, R.R.1, Whycocomagh, NS B0E 3M0 (902) 258-2391. East Lake Ainslie on route #395, 19.3 km (12 mi.) north of Whycocomagh.

Clayton Farm Bed and Breakfast Isaac W. Smith, P.O. Box 33, Mabou, NS B0E 1X0, (902) 945-2719. Working beef farm on an 185 acre peninsula with paths leading through fields and woods to Mabou Harbour's shore. Bald Eagles in area. No smoking.

Doiremaple Mills Bed and Breakfast Kenneth and Harriet Murphy, R.R. #4, Mabou, NS B0E 1X0, (902) 945-2455. Working dairy farm, in the same family for 200 years. Beavers, bald eagles, and blue herons frequent the ponds and river.

Ceilidh Cottages Alex Doyle, P.O. Box 94, Mabou, NS B0E 1X0 (902) 945-2486, (902) 945-2624. On West Mabou Rd., 4 km (2.5 mi.) from Route #19 at Mabou.

Glendyer Mills Bed and Breakfast Kathy McIntyre, Glendyer Smithville Rd., R.R. #4, Mabou, NS B0E 1X0, (902) 945-2455. Off route on road toward Glendyer. 1850 Heritage property. A brook runs through the property and in the playground for the resident ducks and geese. Other pets include two donkeys.

215

Glenora Inn Pamela Widmeyer, R. R. 4, Mabou (Glenville), NS BOE 1X0 (902) 258-2662; fax (902) 258-3133. On Route #19, 9 km (5.6 mi.) north of Mabou. Distillery on premises.

Rankin's Bed and Breakfast Donald and Mary Rankin, R.R. #3, Mabou Harbour, NS BOE 1X0, (902) 945-2375. 100 acres with waterfront. Sunsets can be seen from the house.

Anne Beaton Bed and Breakfast Anne Beaton, P.O. Box 78, Mabou, N.S., BOE 7X0, (902) 945-2806

Camping

Triple "C" Campground Catherine Hughes, P.O. Box 523, Port Hawkesbury, NS BOE 2V0, (902) 625-1472. Open and wooded campground. 3.2 km (2 mi.) from Causeway. Route #105 to Long Stretch Rd., 2.4 km (1.5 mi.) to campground. Pay showers, pool.

Glenview Campground Robert A. Jardine, Whycocomagh, NS BOE 3M0, (902) 756-3198; (902) 756-2258. Open and wooded campground on Skye River. Route #252. Washrooms, laundromat, groceries.

Whycocomagh Provincial Park Province of Nova Scotia, Whycocomagh, NS (902) 756-2448. Open and wooded campground. Route #105, 0.4 km (0.2 mi.) east of Whycocomagh. No reservations.

Ceilidh Trailer Park A. Doyle, P.O. Box 94, Mabou, NS BOE 1X0, (902) 945-2486. Open campground. On paved West Mabou Rd., adjacent to Ceilidh Cottages. Pool, free shower, tennis, canteen, laundromat.

216

Atlantic Canada
Cycling Festival

*Some of the oldest fishing
ports in North America*

Tour 33   Isle Madame

Tour at a glance

START/ FINISH	Louisdale
DISTANCE	58 km (36 mi.) (further with options)
DIRECTION	Counter-Clockwise
TERRAIN	Flat to gently rolling
CLIMATE	Be prepared for dampness and fog
NOTES	Good route for casual cyclists
TRAFFIC	Moderate
REST SPOTS	Pondville; Petit-de-Grat Island
FOOD	Louisdale (R)(C), Arichat (R)(G)(C),
	Petit-de-Grat (C)
REPAIRS	Sydney (off-route)
TOURISM	Port Hastings (off-route) 625-1717; Martinique (seasonal);
	Arichat (seasonal)
HOSPITAL	St.Peter's (off-route)
POLICE	Arichat
	Arichat (R.C.M.P.)

River Bourgeois, D'Escousse, Petit-de-Grat... this area is pure Acadia. French since 1650, **Isle Madame** is named for **Madame de Maintenon**, second wife of **King Louis XIV**. This is a land of barren coasts, with small spruce trees, bushes and wild berries. The mist, more likely present than not, enshrouds brightly painted *"salt-box"* houses. This is as perhaps as close as Nova Scotia gets to the allure of Newfoundland. Separated from Cape Breton Island by **Lennox Passage**, the island has in turn, islands of its own. **Janvrin and Petit-de-Grat** islands are connected by bridges to Isle Madame. They are worth exploring. Being dead-ends, they are at times a little testing, but the scenery will no doubt be found to be worth the effort.

An Enduring Seafaring Life

For over four hundred years, these misty ports have seen generations dependant upon the sea. Rocky, open, and mist shrouded, farming is virtually impossible on this barren island. Other than fishing there is little else. The region was originally settled by **Channel Islanders**, from the small islands of **Jersey and Guernsey**, near France. Many people of Isle Madame are descendants of the citizens of the old French fortress city of **Louisbourg**. At one time, **Arichat**, its largest village was an major port. Almost 300 ships once called the harbour home. It was also an important educational and religious site.

With time, its influence slipped away, **Antigonish** becoming the dominant regional centre. With the building of the Trans-Canada Highway (#105), commercial traffic was diverted from the area. Hampering any non-fishing aspirations, its fateful path has been inferred to have had more to do with political science than engineering (that poor Acadian fishing families had less power of persuasion, compared to that found on the yachts, golf courses and summer homes of Baddeck).

Over the past three and a half centuries Isle Madame has endured. Its people have prevailed expulsion and oppression following British takeover of the province, and survived repeated attacks from American privateers. Today, the islanders face a different threat- uncertainty from a declining harvest from the sea.

The **Acadian** influence predominates. Their language is spoken with a 17th century accent, long gone from France itself. Most people speak in French but "think" in English. Many young people are being lost to English completely.

The villages are among the prettiest in Nova Scotia. A visit to **Little Anse**, and **Sampson Cove** near Petit-de-Grat, are recommended. Narrow roads run seemingly all over the place, hard to tell apart from driveways. The rocky Atlantic takes breaks at frequent beaches lining its shores. Although the road travels through undulating countryside, the gradients are not steep. This area is therefore great for casual cyclists.

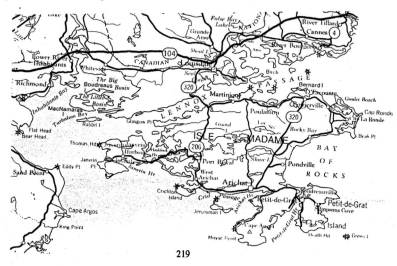

219

START	At the school parking lot in **Louisdale** (at store and restaurant). Head west on #4 towards #320
0.9 (0.6)	**LEFT #320**
5.5 (3.4)	**RIGHT #206 Lennox Passage Bridge** connects Cape Breton with Isle Madame.

Janvrin Island connects with Isle Madame by the road to your right, including harbours, coves, and passages. Further along route, **Brodie's Point** is reached from the church at West Arichat. From the point you can see **four** lighthouses at one time.

18.5 (11.5)	**RIGHT** Short distance to shore. **Babins Cove** is a good rest spot, overlooking **Chedabucto Bay**.
18.7 (11.6)	**LEFT** Shore Road. A small picnic park overlooks Arichat Harbour and the offshore islands, which are used as nesting grounds by seabirds. **Arichat** is Isle Madame's main village. Once it was located off-shore on an nearby island. There privateer **John Paul Jones** burned it had to the ground during the American Revolution. **Lenoir Forge**, a stone building on the waterfront was an 18th-century blacksmith shop, with working forge. Inquire locally for hours. (Admission charged).

SIDE TRIP: A dirt road past **Arichat Goulet** (harbour) runs to your right. It goes out along the barren shore to the light at **Cape Auguet**. Along the way are trails, leading to coves across the point.

CROSS bridge at church onto **Petit-de-Grat Island**. Exploration of the island's little coves and winding lanes is recommended. Characteristic multi-coloured houses brighten up an often bleak landscape. Short roads weave about, in a very random order, tailing off into short paths. To the right is the first of two runs on the island. At 4 km (2.4 mi.) each way, this winding road passes through an old fishing port on the western side of Petit-de-Grat. **Sampsons Cove**, an attractive village is on your way to **Petite (Little) Anse**. **Petit-Nez Beach** has an excellent hiking trail along the shore out to **Gros Nez**. Along the road to its end point are several good shore rest areas.

24.9 (15.5)	**RIGHT** at church
26.6 (16.5)	**RIGHT** onto #206
29.1 (18.1)	**RIGHT #320**
32.4 (20.2)	**SIDE TRIP Pondville Beach** This 1km (0.6 mi.) long beach is backed by sand dunes, behind which is a large lagoon and salt marsh, providing a home for many different species of shorebirds. A short-cut heads out of the park back to the route.
32.5 (20.2)	**RIGHT** Just past Pondville
40.5 (25.2)	Continue along shore, join #320 after passing the small bridge. You can take a lane along the harbour for 1.5 km (1 mi.) before returning to the #320. **Lennox Passage Park** is located on the way, offering a saltwater beach, lighthouse, and walking trail.
52.5 (32.6)	**RIGHT** Lennox Passage #206
57.1 (25.5)	**RIGHT #4**
58.0 (35.1)	**END**

Accommodation
Sampson's Bed and Breakfast Vivian Sampson, R.R. #1, Lousidale, NS B0E 1V0, (902) 345-2155
Vollmer's Island Paradise Arthur Vollmer, P.O. Box 51, West Arichat, NS B0E 1J0 (902) 225-9853 (on Janvrin Island)
L'Auberge Acadienne Leo and Beverly Boudreau, High Rd., P.O.Box 59, Arichat, NS B0E 1A0, (902) 226-2200. 19th Century style Acadian inn. Bike rentals; regional Acadian cusine

Camping

Acadian Campsite Charles and Connie Davenport, P.O. Box 24, Arichat, NS B0E 1A0 (902) 226-2447

*A landlocked sea below,
bald eagles above*

Tour 34   Washabuck

Tour at a glance

START/ FINISH	Little Narrows
OTHER STARTING POINT	Iona
DISTANCE	58 km (35 mi.)
DIRECTION	Counter- Clockwise
TERRAIN	1st half, rolling; 2nd half, very hilly
CLIMATE	Sea-coast like conditions
NOTES	When completed a new bridge replacing the ferry at Iona may change traffic patterns
	Bring food/ supplies with you
TRAFFIC	Low to moderate
LUNCH SPOTS	Iona; MacCormack Park
FOOD	Little Narrows (C), McKinnons Harbour (C), Iona (C)
REPAIRS	Sydney (off-route)
TOURISM	Whycocomaugh
HOSPITAL	Baddeck (off-route)

A tiny connection of land is all that saves **Washabuck Peninsula** from being an "island within an island". For this tour directions and cue sheets are almost unnecessary. Simply edge along the peninsula's shores, along **Lake Bras D'Or**, Cape Breton's inland sea.

This is a truly remarkable route. Surrounded by water, in the heart of Cape Breton, it is a wonder how an area this attractive has remained so unspoiled. **Iona**, with only a couple of hundred people is the largest place along the entire route. An area of original Scottish settlement, along the roads, many old homesteads stand abandoned, instilling a melancholy, introspective mood.

"Lake" Bras D'or is actually a land-locked sea. It joins the ocean at a small, but very deep opening along Boularderie Island. It has an amount of salt water, and even a detectable tide. It was formed when the ocean flooded into valleys carved out by moving glaciers. Surrounded by forested hills, and largely undeveloped, many say that this is probably the cleanest inland sea on earth.

Nova Scotia's magnificent **Bald Eagles** claim this as their major nesting area. Thriving on the highland ridges, this is condidered perhaps the most healthy population in the world. Rainbow Trout and other of their favourite fish still populate the clear waters. The huge birds can often be seen overhead, scanning the waters, their wings spreading as much as 1.8 m (6 ft.) wide.

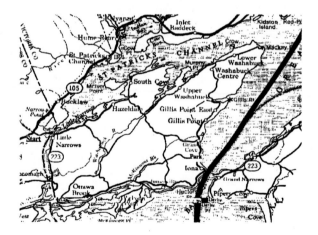

START Ferry dock at Little Narrows. The village is 1.7 km (1.2 mi). from Route #105. Begin tour by heading west (to the right as coming off the ferry) along "water side". Small beach and picnic tables are a short way along.

Follow the shore. You will pass through the little settlements of Estmere, Ottawa Brook, Red Point, and MacKinnon Harbour. These nestle among the woods, bordered by the famous Lake Bras d'Or. Suddenly, shoreline hills begin just past Ottawa Brook.

While speeding down the hill into Iona (pop. 120), look to your right for the old post office (now closed). You can see where this was operated in both of Canada's official languages- English and French, plus one more...Gaelic!

23.4 (14.5) LEFT at Iona. There is a small grocery here (if it is closed, you can get snacks from the friendly folks at the gas station). **Nova Scotia Highland Village** is located on the hillside overlooking Lake Bras d'Or. Buildings illustrate the way of life of the early Scottish settlers (Admission charge). If you are "museumed out" you can leave others in your party to their discussion on tartans and walk the trail to the top of the hill, where you can see parts of all four counties of Cape Breton.

Your turn takes you to the quiet side of this "almost island". Judging the white cliffs, you can tell that this is an area of major gypsum deposits.

23.8 (14.4) **MacCormack Park** is a small picnic area overlooking **Barra Strait** with nearby beach.

From here on, few houses line the road. Wooded hills protect small coves and beaches, including **Maskell's Harbour**, where there is a large shipwreck. While on the tallest climb, as you crest you will take in a view across **St. Patrick's Channel**, to Baddeck.

36.1 (22.4) LEFT at St. Patrick's Channel. To the right a run follows to the point along the channel's shore where there is a small swimming area.

The rich bed of gypsum beneath the peninsula's top soil becomes quite apparent as you can not ignore the conveyor belt above your head. It transports the dusty white powder to waiting ships and train cars.

54.4 (33.8) END Little Narrows ferry

Accommodation

Highland Heights Inn J. Bruce and Sheila MacNeil, P.O Box 19, Iona, NS B0A 1L0, (902) 725-2800, (902) 725-2360

(Whycocomagh area)

Fair Isle Motel Miriam J. Munro, P.O. Box 53, Whycocomagh, NS B0E 3M0, (902) 756-2291.

Island View Bed and Breakfast Anna and Bill MacKinnon, P.O. Box 96, Whycocomagh, NS B0E 3M0, (902) 756-2951. At entrance to Whycocomagh Provincial Park. No smoking.

Mary Smith Bed and Breakfast Mary J. Smith, Main St. Whycocomagh, NS B0E 3M0, (902) 756-2157. Right of Royal Bank, garage available for bikes.

Camping

(Whycocomagh area)

Glenview Campground Robert A. Jardine, Whycocomagh, NS B0E 3M0, (902) 756-3198; (902) 756-2258. Open and wooded campground on Skye River. Route #252. Washrooms, laundromat, groceries.

Whycocomagh Provincial Park Province of Nova Scotia, Whycocomagh, NS (902) 756-2448. Open & wooded campground. Route #105, 0.4 km (0.2 mi.) east of Whycocomagh. No reservations.

Atlantic Canada
Cycling Festival

Around a romantic lake- echoes of a Gaelic past

Tour 35   Lake Ainslie

Tour at a glance

START/ FINISH	Whycocomagh
OTHER STARTING POINT	Inverness
DISTANCE	70 km (44 mi.) (shorter from Inverness)
DIRECTION	Clockwise
TERRAIN	Rolling
CLIMATE	Ocean winds, despite inland setting
TRAFFIC	Moderate
REST STOPS	MacDonald House Museum, Trout Brook Park
FOOD	Scotsville (C)
REPAIRS	Sydney (off-route)
TOURISM	Inverness (off-route); Baddeck (off-route)
HOSPITAL	Inverness (off-route); Baddeck (off-route)

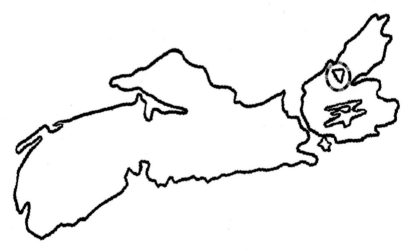

Triangle shaped **Lake Ainslie** is the largest body of fresh water in Cape Breton. Overshadowed by the dramatic inland sea, the **Bras D'Or**, Lake Ainslie is circled by tall hills of dense fir trees. A narrow band of old farmsteads follows the shore.

The **Highland Clearances of Scotland** forced thousands off their land. It was brutal and humiliating. The English wanted them out- not to be replaced by themselves, or perhaps another group, but by livestock! The *Industrial Revolution* was off and running and the factories of central England demanded wool to clothe a growing empire. Forced to leave, Cape Breton was the destination of choice. Its hills and lakes were reminiscent of home, and they would once again have the freedom of language, dress, and music, being denied them. Many settled here around Lake Ainslie (Catholics on the west side, Protestants on the east).

Their Gaelic language is still alive, but no longer one of everyday use. Ties with their heritage are strong here, the tiny area even has its own tartan, on display at **MacDonald House Museum**.
This pleasant route is easy to follow- once at the lake, simply follow it around. It is just as good starting from Inverness as from Whycocomagh.

This run will count distance from Whycocomagh, deduct a few kilometres if you start from Inverness.

There are no other dissertations required- this picturesque lake will speak for itself!

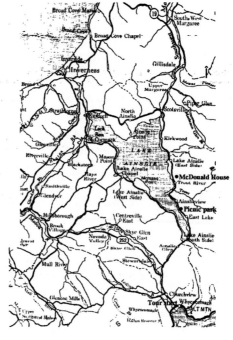

START   At **Whycocomagh** (corner #105 and #252- Vi's Restaurant). Whycocomagh is actually two villages, a **Mic Mac Indian** reserve (or "first nation") on one side of the **Skye River** and an area descended from **Highland Scots** are on the other. They connect, but seem to be of two solitudes. **Whycocomagh Provincial Park** offers a picnic ground overlooking the lake. An excellent hiking trail leads you up to **Salt Mountain**. When you reach the top, you must remember that there are three different look-offs. It's a great spot for sunrises and sunsets.

5.5 (3.4)   **RIGHT** #395 branches from #252

9.3 (5.8)   **LEFT** West Lake Ainslie Road. Once by the lake, simply follow its shores, around the "triangle".

32.3 (20.1)   **RIGHT** At church at Kenloch (Strathlorne). The province's largest tree nursery raises 17 million seedlings annually. Continue along lake, skirting a 300 m (1000 ft.) small mountain. From the roads going up you can look down at the lake's distinct shape.

42.3 (26.3)   **RIGHT** Scottsville (store at corner)

SIDE TRIP: To your left from Scotsville is a pretty connecting road along a renown salmon river to Margaree.

Coming up on a hill, situated with a panoramic view of the lake is **MacDonald House**. Once a post office and gathering point, it has been united with a renovated 1920's one-room school. A barn, displaying period tools and fishing equipment adds to this pleasant diversion. You may arrive on a day planned for square dances (Cape Breton style), concerts, or milling frolics (parties where freshly woven wool is softened). This is a great place for a rest, and to take in the flavour of rural Cape Breton life years ago. Open July to September (admission is free).

Trout Brook Park, further along the shore has a white sandy beach and picnic facilities.

70.3 (43.7)   **END** Whycocomagh

Accommodation

Fair Isle Motel Miriam J. Munro, P.O. Box 53, Whycocomagh, NS B0E 3M0, (902) 756-2291.

Island View Bed and Breakfast Anna and Bill MacKinnon, P.O. Box 96, Whycocomagh, NS B0E 3M0, (902) 756-2951. At entrance to Whycocomagh Provincial Park. No smoking.

Mary Smith Bed and Breakfast Mary J. Smith, Main St. Whycocomagh, NS B0E 3M0, (902) 756-2157. Right of Royal Bank, garage available for bikes.

Trout River Cottages Jean and Arnold Tobey, R.R.1, Whycocomagh, NS B0E 3M0 (902)258-2391. East Lake Ainslie on route #395, 19.3 km (12 mi.) north of Whycocomagh.

The Gables Motel Mr. and Mrs. James Walker, P.O. Box 454, Inverness, NS B0E 1N0 (902) 258-2314, (902) 258-2412.

Inverness Beach Village Ivan MacLeod, P.O. Box 617, Inverness, NS B01 1N0 (902) 258-2653. On route #19, 0.4 km (0.2 mi.) north of town.

Inverness Lodge Hotel and Motel Hugh Wallace, P.O. Box 69, Inverness, NS B0E 1N0 (902) 258-2193

Glendyer Mills Bed and Breakfast Glendyer Smithville Rd. Mabou, NS B0E 1X0 (902) 945-2455. Off route on road toward Glendyer. 1850 Heritage property.

West Lake Ainslie Cottages Ray and Gwen MacFarlane, R.R. 3, W. Lake Ainslie, NS B0E 1N0 (902) 258-2654, (902) 258-2949. At Strathlorne

Camping

Glenview Campground Robert A. Jardine, Whycocomagh, NS B0E 3M0, (902) 756-3198; (902) 756-2258. Open and wooded campground on Skye River. Route #252. Washrooms, laundromat, groceries.

Whycocomagh Provincial Park Province of Nova Scotia, Whycocomagh, NS (902) 756-2448. Open and wooded campground. Route #105, 0.4 km (0.2 mi.) east of Whycocomagh. No reservations.

Ainslie Village Tent and Trailer Park Kenneth Pyne, South Lake Ainslie, NS B0E 3M0, (902) 756-2333. Open and wooded campground on Lake Ainslie. Route #395, 9.6 km (6 mi.) from Whycocomagh. Pay showers, washrooms

MacKinnon's Campground Michael and Karen Gillis, R.R. #1, Whycocomagh, E. Lake Ainslie, NS B0E 3M0. On Lake Ainslie. 3.2 km (2 mi.) on #395, 12.8 km (8 mi.) from Whycocomaugh. Pay showers, washrooms, laundromat, groceries.

Atlantic Canada
Cycling Festival

A land of song along a craggy coast

Tour 36
Creignish Hills (Ceilidh Trail)

Tour at a glance

START	Margaree Harbour
FINISH	Cape Breton Causeway
OTHER STATING POINTS	Cape Breton Causeway, Mabou
DISTANCE	113 km (70 mi.)
DIRECTION	Counter-Clockwise
TERRAIN	Rolling
CLIMATE	Possible headwinds
	At least 2 days recommended
TRAFFIC	Moderate
FOOD	Margaree (C), Inverness (R)(G)(C), Mabou (R)(G)(C), Port Hood (R)(C), Campbell (C), Creignish (C)
REPAIRS	Sydney (off-route)
TOURISM	Margaree Forks 248-2803, Port Hastings 625-1717
HOSPITAL	Inverness; Port Hawkesbury (off-route)
POLICE	Inverness; Port Hawkesbury

C ape Bretoners are looked upon by the rest of Canada as among its most warm, hospitable and happy people. Perhaps you will gain insights into their pleasant dispositions after you experience the beauty and spirit of this rugged coast.

The "*Ceilidh Trail*" and it's highlands echo with the sounds of bagpipes, fiddles, and song. **Gaelic** culture is making its last stand among these hills. Traditions brought from **Scotland**, such as step dancing, fiddle music and milling frolics (softening freshly woven wool) are still very much alive. To "ceilidh" means "to party", and cultural events abound, in the form of community festivals and dances. Music is a strong force in the everyday lives of the people. The last Sunday in July features the island's **largest Scottish concert,** at Broad Cove, near Inverness.

What is reassuring is that all this is real- from the hearts of the people themselves, not an artificial scheme to attract tourists.

The coast is fairly quiet these days. Once it rang with the sound of hammers of ship- building yards. Coal mines bustled, scattered among the hills and along the coast, from Margaree to Mabou. What activity there is today involves forestry and fishing. Large sheep farms are found on the hillsides. You will also come across scattered dairy farms, some in the Mabou area operated by Dutch families who came to the area after World War II.
The area has not, in commercial terms, regained the commotion of its past. It has learned to make do without big smokestacks and megaprojects. The traffic is low, the scenery is magnficicent. There is not one mall or fast food strip along the entire coast! While this many make development agencies cringe, for the true visitor, it is a boon. It has given the area a chance to have seen the ruination of other places, and perhaps (perhaps) not repeat the blunders here.

The terrain is rolling, but only hilly in a few sections. Between Margaree Harbour and Port Hastings, highway #19 has several areas with access to the **Gulf of St. Lawrence.** This craggy shore shares some of the warm waters of Prince Edward Island and northern Nova Scotia mainland. The water is warm, due to the shallow depths of the Northumberland Strait.

The entire shore along the **Creignish Hills** is famous for its sunsets. The tour begins in Margaree Harbour.

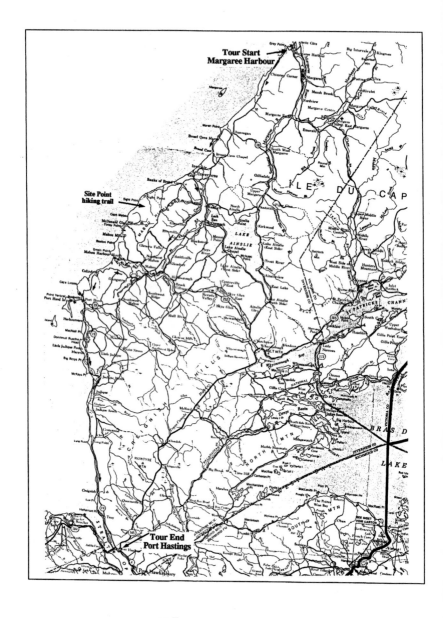

START   Corner of Cabot Trail and #219, at the **Schooner Restaurant** (junction of Tour 38). Head south-west along #219.

At the starting point is a rambling white "mock-Tudor" building. Its owner conceived of the complex as a way to help preserve Cape Breton's connections with Scotland. Blessed with a touch of folly, as the structure ages, each year it becomes a little more eclectic. Tartans, clothing, weaving, clan regalia, and music recordings are for sale. The schooner "*Marion Elizabeth*" alongside had a long career, including a time smuggling during Prohibition. The complex stands as the unofficial centre of the community. The people inside are friendly and known for being involved in social issues, such as the environment (and have been, long before it becoming vogue).

Just after your start, to the right is **Margaree Harbour** wharf. Below twin lighthouses lies a good sized beach, with changehouses. The Acadian Trail, built a few years ago by the Canadian Youth Hostel Association, can be found along the shore. Ask directions at the Schooner Restaurant or store.

Once out of Margaree, heading off the route on the inland side are very steep climbs, as much as 270 m (900 ft.) in a few hundred metres. They lead up to look-offs over the **Gulf of St. Lawrence**.

Whale Cove is a small secluded beach, 3 km (2 mi.) south of Margaree Harbour. Chimney Corner is next, 7km (4.2 mi.) further. **St. Rose** has a small coal mine, one of the last ones operating in the region a short distance in off the road. Before **Dunvegan** a popular beach offers such facilities as change rooms, washrooms and camping.

20.1 (12.5)   **RIGHT** Route #19 at Dunvegan

20.3 (12.6)   **RIGHT** Broad Marsh Rd., turn just after small bridge. This gravel road takes you down to a very appealing section of coastline (if you do not want to ride on the dirt, you may go straight and rejoin where it comes out). A large crescent offers excellent camping, beaches and hiking. A bit further on, an interesting rock formation may be seen. The popular **Broad Cove Concert**, Cape Breton's largest Scottish music celebration, is held on the grounds of St. Margaret's Church, the last Sunday in July.

29.2 (18.2)   **RIGHT** #19 Return to highway

34.2 (21.3)   **Inverness** *(Alternate starting point for Tour 35)*. Serving as the regional supply centre, Inverness is a former coal mining and railway town. Notice the pockets of identical "*company*" houses as you cycle its streets. **Inverness Beach**, (in back of the Highland Restaurant) has both lifeguard service, as well as an unsupervised area (1.6 km/ 1 mi. outside town).

Miner's Museum: The old **Canadian National Railway** station by the beach has been converted into a museum. The depot (circa 1901), features exhibits and films explaining how coal was extracted from the mines. Arts and crafts from the area are also on display (admission free).

The beautiful area between Inverness and Mabou is known as the **Mabou Highlands**. A highly recommended hiking trail to **Site Point** follows the shore between Inverness and Mabou. Spectacular cliff look-offs peer over the gulf and down on the collapsed ground of old mines near **Mabou Harbour**. The trail is not reccommended for biking, due to tree roots and a section eroded along the cliff.

"Uisge Beatha" - "The Water of Life" The Glenora Inn and Distillery complex, situated on a 80 h (200 acre) site maintains the highland Scot's tradition of distilling whisky. North America's only single malt whisky plant also blends and bottles white and dark rum. An inn, pub, dining room and gift shop surround a courtyard with a pleasant brook. 258-2662

Glenora Falls: About 3/4 of the way to Mabou from Inverness, to the right is a road to Glenora Falls. Go in about 600 m (.3 mi) and cross the river. As you approach the bridge you should hear it. Walk in a very short distance southward just after crossing.

Just before Mabou, you connect with Tour CB-1, heading down the **Skye River Valley** to Whycocomagh.

52.6 (32.7) **Mabou** Here, as well as in other villages, people are doing all possible to maintain the traditions they brought with them from Scotland. **Gaelic** is still taught in its school, and the village holds a **Gaelic Ceilidh** (kay-lee), a Scottish concert with dance and picnic every Canada Day (July 1).

"The Bridge (An Drochaid)" Once a general store, the Mabou Gaelic and Historic Society now uses it as a local centre for crafts, genealogy and research on Scottish culture. The museum is open in the summer (free Admission). **The Mother of Sorrows Shrine** is an interesting chapel in the village open daily.

55.0 (34.2) **RIGHT** Colindale Rd. Spectacular views overlook Mabou Harbour, and the highlands lead you along old farms with occasional beach access. A dirt road, a paved short-cut goes straight ahead on #19.

67.2 (41.8) **RIGHT** onto #19 at **Port Hood.** Besides being the county seat, it offers some of the best beaches in Atlantic Canada. One stretch of sand is directly behind the court house in the village (changehouse provided). Just south of the village is another. Port Hood was another thriving coal-mining centre, at one point with three times its present population. Lack of markets and flooding in the mines forced the collieries to shut down. The region's best known resident is **Al MacInnis**, of **National Hockey League** fame.

Port Hood Island was the source of much of the stone which was used to build the town-sized **Fortress of Louisbourg** in the early 1700's. The quarry walls still show blurred inscriptions written in early French.

Chestico Museum Housed in an old schoolhouse, exhibits detailing the local Scottish culture are on display. (Admission is free- hours vary).

70.6 (43.9)   **RIGHT** toward **Judique** off #19 onto Shore Road. Here several more beaches line the shore, with marshes and good birdwatching, including possible sightings of eagles. The Judique area was founded by families from the **Hebridean Islands** of Scotland. The village became known for its rugged form of **square dancing**. On a stranger note, the area is said to have a curious tendency for the birth of twins!

81.2 (50.5)   **RIGHT #19**

Cape George on the mainland may now be visible. The Creignish Mountain Road leads to a breathtaking view of the bay and surrounding countryside.

Craigmore offers **Long Point Park**, a small picnic area amid softwood trees (Aggressive squirrels here are known to eat through bike bags to get at sweets).

Watch for the old Scottish style stone house on the hillside, one of the oldest on the island.

Follow the shore to the **Strait of Canso**. The tour ends at Port Hastings by the **Canso Causeway**. Mainlanders moved mountains to reach Cape Breton. From where you end (or begin) at the traffic circle, you have a good view of the causeway. Completed in 1955, it is the **world's deepest**. Filled from masses of rock from **Porcupine Mountain**, its scarred face reveals where 10 million tons of rock and fill were taken. The stone from the **largest pyramid of Egypt** would not be enough to fill the channel. It carries both rail and highway traffic, and locks on the Cape Breton Island side allow for the passage of small vessels. Cape Bretoners demanded that *"not one spoonful of island soil"* be used to join the mainland.

112.5 (69.9)   **END** Cape Breton Information Centre, Port Hastings (at traffic circle).

Accommodation

Duck Cove Inn Gordon Laurence, Margaree Harbour, NS B0E 2B0, (902) 235-2658, fax (902) 235-2592. Junction of Cabot and Ceilidh Trails.

Harbour View Inn Connie Jennex, P.O. Box 52, Margaree Harbour, NS B0E 2B0, (902) 235-2314.

The Gables Motel Mr. and Mrs. James Walker, P.O. Box 454, Inverness, NS B0E 1N0, (902) 258-2314, (902) 258-2412. On route #19.

Inverness Beach Village Ivan MacLeod, P.O. Box 617, Inverness, NS B0l 1N0 (902) 258-2653. On route #19, 0.4 km (0.2 mi.) north of Inverness.

Inverness Lodge Hotel and Motel Hugh Wallace, P.O. Box 69, Inverness, NS B0E 1N0 (902) 258-2193. On Central Avenue.

Ceilidh Cottages Alex Doyle, P.O. Box 94, Mabou, NS B0E 1X0 (902) 945-2486, (902) 945-2624. On West Mabou Rd., 4 km (2.5 mi.) from Route #19 at Mabou.

Glenora Inn Pamela Widmeyer, R. R. 4, Mabou (Glenville), NS B0E 1X0 (902) 258-2662; fax (902) 258-3133. On Route #19, 9 km (5.6 mi.) north of Mabou. Distillery on premises.

Haus Treuburg Guest House and Cottages Georg Kargoll, P.O. Box 92, Port Hood, NS B0E 2W0 (902) 787-2116. Central Ave.

Hebridean Motel Mary Claire MacDonald, P.O Box 149, Port Hood, NS B0E 2W0 (902) 787-3214. Off Route #19 on Company Rd.

Lighthouse Cottages Colin and Rachel MacDonald, P.O. Box 53, Judique, NS B0E 1P0 (902) 787-3345, off-season (902) 787-2787. Route #19, 1.6 km (1 mi.) south of Port Hood. Laundromat.

(Port Hastings and Port Hawkesbury included together)

Capeway Motel Gill MacIsaac and Pat Sangster, General Delivery, Port Hastings, NS B0E 2T0 (902) 625-2524. On Route #19, 1 km (0.6 mi.) north of Canso Causeway.

Keddy's Inn Joyce O'Brien, P.O. Box 50, Port Hastings, NS B0E 2T0 (902) 625-0460; Fax (902) 625-1275. Junction of Routes #19, 104, and 105.

MacPuffin Motel MacKenzie Jones, P.O. Box 558, Port Hawkesbury, NS B0E 2V0, (902)625-0621. On Route #4 at Port Hastings.

Skye Motel Bernice Richard, P.O. Box 190, Port Hastings, NS B0E 2T0 (902) 625-1300. Junction of Routes #19, 104, and 105.

Troy Lodge Cottages Mrs. Anna Guzdziol, P.O. Box 399, Port Hawkesbury, NS B0E 2V0 (902) 625-1684 (902) 625-2680. Route #19, 4 km (2.5 mi) before causeway.

Camping

Buckles Trailer Court and Campsite Gerald and Martha Buckles, Margaree Forks, NS B0E 2A0, (902) 248-2053. Pay showers, washrooms, laundromat.

Ceilidh Trailer Park A. Doyle, P.O. Box 94, Mabou, NS B0E 1X0, (902) 945-2486. Open campground. On paved West Mabou Rd., adjacent to Ceilidh Cottages. Pool, free shower, tennis, canteen, laundromat.

Triple "C" Campground Catherine Hughes, P.O. Box 523, Port Hawkesbury, NS B0E 2V0, (902) 625-1472. Open and wooded campground. 3.2 km (2 mi.) from Causeway. Route #105 to Long Stretch Rd., 2.4 km (1.5 mi.) to campground. Pay showers, pool.

Atlantic Canada
Cycling Festival

Out on the Mira- solitude along a tranquil, tree-lined river

Tour 37 Mira/Louisbourg

Tour at a glance

START/ FINISH	Mira Provincial Park
OTHER STARTING POINTS	Mira Gut
DISTANCE	103 km (64 mi.) (Short option available)
DIRECTION	Clockwise
TERRAIN	Flat to gently rolling
CLIMATE	Temperate
NOTES	One of few rides not influenced by the ocean
	Prepare majority of food before arrival in area
	Services available in Lousibourg
TRAFFIC	Low
REST STOPS	Two Rivers Park; Mira Gut
FOOD	Albert Bridge (C)
REPAIRS	Sydney (off-route)
TOURISM	Sydney River (off-route), Louisbourg (off-route)
HOSPITAL	Sydney (off-route)
POLICE	Louisbourg (off-route) 564-1323

A myriad of islands, numerous peninsulas and sheltered coves follow along one of the longest and most attractive rivers in Nova Scotia. The slow and tranquil **Mira** provides easy shoreline cycling within an atmosphere of solitude.

Occupying a elongated, narrow valley, the Mira is thought to follow an old fault line. Long been considered an easy canoe route, for cycling, it still lies largely undiscovered. Despite its proximity to the **Fortress of Louisbourg**, it remains almost unknown by outsiders. This suits Cape Bretoners fine, who know it well.

You move first toward the southern end of the Mira. Here the river is docile. Several thousand years ago, glacial deposits interrupted its flow, forming a chain of small lakes. After crossing where it narrows into a stream, you travel along the upper side all the way to the river's mouth. Here the river cuts a narrow gap through bedrock, with steep banks. Reaching the Atlantic at Mira, after a rest by the ocean you then return on the other side.

The Mira's first inhabitants were the **Mic Mac Indians**, who established seasonal camps. In the early 1700's, **French** settlers arrived and began exporting timber back home. They also established a brickyard, within what is now the boundary of the provincial park. Old farm fields, orchards and traces of an old convent can still be found. Along the route are occasional homesteads, echoing the days when **Scottish** immigrants settled along its banks.

The starting point is situated on a peninsula in the midst of the beautiful Mira River. **Mira River Provincial Park** offers an attractive setting. Activities include camping, swimming, picnicking, canoeing, or simply relaxing.

A short option is available, by starting, or short-cutting at Marion Bridge. Stock up before you come to the tour area, rather completely than relying on the availability at the few stores in the area.

START	**Mira River Provincial Park (parking area)** Begin by heading out of the park to the highway.
0.2 (0.1)	**RIGHT** Brickyard Road. Continue along river. Highway #22 joins for short section. Between Marion Bridge and Albert Bridge, fossils are engraved in the rock cuts along the edge of the road.
	Cross Highway #327, continue along shore.
	Short gravel section
	SIDE TRIP: A short dirt stretch from Victoria Bridge, at the turning point of the tour, will take you to toward Gabarus, and the shore route to **Point Michaud.**
36.8 (22.9)	**RIGHT** toward Victoria Bridge. You cross where the Mira expands from a stream into the wide section of the Mira.
	Pavement resumes
38.3 (23.8)	**RIGHT** Victoria Bridge. Follow northern side of river.

239

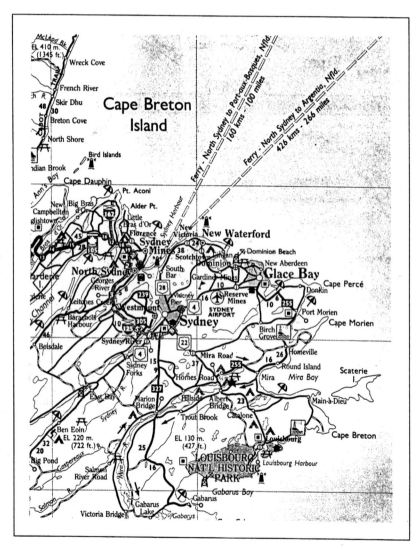

Near the turn-off for Salmon River Road is **Two Rivers Wildlife Park**. It features a variety of native Nova Scotian animals. This is the suggested lunch stop. The park also offers swimming and hiking. If you are cycle-touring while travelling by a car, and have also brought along a canoe, the Mira is a relaxing, easy body of water. There is an access area available.

62.3 (38.7)   CROSS #327 at Marion Bridge, (the road here is known as Hillside Rd).

76.9 (47.8)   LEFT Highway #22

SHORT-CUT: By turning right on #22, you can head back early to the park.

86.5 (53.8)   RIGHT #255 (Catalone Road)

Song for the Mira

1. Out on the Mira on warm afternoons,
    Old men go fishing with black line and spoon.
    And if they catch nothing they never complain,
    And I wish I was with them again.

2. Boys in the boats call to girls on the shore
    Teasing the ones that they dearly adore.
    Then into the evening the courting begins.
    And I wish I was with them again.

CHORUS:
    Can you imagine a piece of the universe
    More fit for Princes and Kings.
    I'll trade you 10 of your cities
    For Marion Bridge and the pleasure it brings.

3. Out on the Mira on soft summer nights,
    Bonfires blaze to the children's delight.
    They dance round the flames singing songs with their friends,
    And I wish I were with them again

4. Out on the Mira the people are kind,
    They'll treat you to home brew and help you unwind.
    And if you come broken, they'll see that you mend,
    And I wish I was with them again.

5. Now I'll conclude with a wish you go well;
    Sweet be your dreams and your happiness swell.
    I'll leave you now for my journey begins
    And I'm going to be with them again.

Yes I'm going to be with them again.

Allister MacGillivray

241

96.2 (59.8)	**RIGHT** Mira. To the left is the village, and its beach on the Atlantic. Years ago, when coal mining was at its peak, this was the site of an annual miners picnic. Coal crews and their families would board a train from Glace Bay, leaving behind the danger and the dust for a day together by the sea.
	Cross Mira Gut
96.8 (60.2)	**RIGHT** Brickyard Road
102.7 (63.9)	**RIGHT** into Mira Provincial Park
102.9 (64.0)	**END** Mira Provincial Park

Accommodation

Sunlit Valley Farms Bed and Breakfast Don and Hazel Ferguson, 821 Brickyard Rd., R.R. #2, Marion Bridge, NS B0A 1P0 (902) 562-7663, (902) 562-2222; (902) 562-7663. Close to provincial park on Mira River. Homesite settled by the Ferguson family in the 1830's.

Victoria Bridge Housekeeping Cottages Donald Gillis, Victoria Bridge, P.O. Box 176, Glace Bay, NS B1A 5V2 (902) 727-2920.

Keating's Bed and Breakfast Phyllis and Frank Keating, R.R. 2, 1828 Hillside Rd., Marion Bridge, NS B0A 1P0, (902) 727-2800. Off Route #22, 10 km (6 mi.) from Louisbourg, overlooking the Mira River, large deck in front and a private beach in back.

MacLeod's Bed and Breakfast and Cottage Ramona MacLeod, R.R. #1, Louisbourg, N.S. B0A 1M0 (902) 733-2456. 10 km (6 mi.) north of Louisbourg on #22 at Catalone.

Peck Tourist Home Bed Bed and Breakfast Mrs. Camilla Peck. R.R. #1 Louisbourg, N.S., B0A 1M0 (902) 733-2649. Farm animals, small trail.

Camping

Mira Water Park and Campground Wendell Greer, P.O. Box 63, Hillside Rd., Marion Bridge, NS B0A 1P0. (902) 562-3164, (902) 564-1674. Open and wooded campground on Mira River. Washrooms, free showers, laundromat, canteen.

MacKeigan's Bay Beach Park Beverly MacKeigan, Sandfield Rd., Marion Bridge, NS B0A 1P0, (902) 727-2369. Open and wooded campground on Mira River.

Burke's Campsite Walter Burke, R.R. #2, Albert Bridge, NS B0A 1P0, (902) 564-9239. Open campground on Mira River. Swimming, fishing.

Mira River Provincial Park Province of Nova Scotia, (902) 563-3373. Open and wooded campground. No reservations.

Stonewall Trailer Park and Campground Len and Shiril Ogilvie. R.R. #1, Louisbourg, N.S., B0A 1M0 (902) 733-2058; (902) 733-2612. Open and wooded campground on lake. At Catalone 10 km (6 mi.) from Louisbourg on Route #22. Showers, pool, canteen.

Louisbourg Motorhome Park Louisbourg Merchants Association, P.O. Box 10, Louisbourg, N.S., B0A 1M0, (902) 733-3631. Open campground by ocean.

"For most Canadians, Louisbourg stands as a proud symbol, not only of the two great cultures who made our nation possible, but of the traditions that both have bequeathed us. Without these traditions and the dialogue stimiulated by them, Canada would have few claims to nationhoood." Louisbourg sentry guard

One of the most intense recreations anywhere in history. Such is described the site where battles decided the mastery of North America. A major attraction of Nova Scotia is the **Fortress of Louisbourg National Historic Park.**

Incredible efforts have been made to restore the fortress to exact detail. Almost 800,000 pages of documents, photos, and sketches were gathered to tackle the project. Even the harbour was dredged, in an attempt to locate every possible artifact. Homes, barracks, taverns, government buildings, and guardhouses appear as in 1744. This huge project has been a major help in allieviating the unemployment resulting from the closure of many of Cape Breton's coal mines. Local residents, who dress in period costume, go about the duties required to operate a fortress-town.

The recovery of the fortress recalls Louisbourg's era as one of the busiest seaports in the New World. Built near rich fishing banks. The fortress-town also became an important centre of commerce. It traded goods from Europe, with that of Quebec, and from the West Indies (for much desired rum and molasses). New England was also a trading partner, even though dealing with the enemy was illegal.

In 1758 Louisbourg was attacked by British **General James Wolfe.** His victorious seven week seige required 150 ships and 16,000 troops. To prevent the French from regaining control, the British scuttled the entire town.

Painstakingly recreated, the **King's Barracks** was once the largest structure in the New World. Splendid decor in the **Governor's Building** is graced in the style of the **French Court.** Cobblestone streets connect with the simpler homes of officers and merchants.

There are 3 themes: seaport, fortress, and community. Plan on an entire day, part of it to explore the reconstructed fortress and buildings, and the rest for the remaining 50 sq. km (20 sq. mi.) of the park and the current town. If possible wear comfortable shoes, you will be walking cobblestone streets and through stone buildings. Bring warm clothes, Louisbourg is often damp and foggy.

There have been no sell-outs to corporate sponsors or concessions (you won't see Coke machines hidden in corners, or find hamburgers at the canteen- they apparently were not available in the 1700's)!

A shuttle bus runs from the reception parking lot. It is used to minimize traffic, to make an atmosphere "as authentic as possible" (bicycles not being able to approach the fort in the name of authenticity while a motorcoach putters about is hard for some cyclists to swallow). Fortress of Louisbourg (902) 733-2280

There is also a town of Louisbourg. Built on the fishing trade, it has several points of interest. Standing at its entrance is the **Sydney and Louisbourg Railway Museum.** It is located in an old train station, opened to supervise coal which was at one time shipped through here from Glace Bay. Today the depot records its history. Two passenger sedans still remain, from their days of service among the coal cars. A marine room and paintings round off its displays.

The first fireproof building in North America was **Louisbourg Lighthouse**, begun in 1731 and completed two years later.

A memorial has been built in an unused train underpass in the town. It serves as a chapel in memory to those lost to the sea.

Of perhaps a more specialized interest are the 1,900 residents of the **House of Dolls** (small admission fee)

243

Riding to the Fortress

There are two routes you can take from the Sydney area to Lousibourg. Both on the way connect with the the Mira Tour. The most straightforward is directly out on route #22. It has only moderate traffic, but is an unremarkable stretch of road. An alternative is via #255, through Port Morien and Main-a-Dieu. Refer to the Cape Breton Introduction for information on reaching route #255 at Glace Bay.

At Glace Bay in 1902, **Guglielmo Marconi**, established three transatlantic wireless stations, sending the first such cross-ocean messages. Visitors also can explore one of the world's largest mining museums. The Glace Bay Miner's Museum and Village fills a 15 acre site along the atlantic, telling the story of the industry and way of life, starting in the early 1700's (small admission charge). An old mine can be explored, which runs directly underneath the exhibit hall.

Hornes Road around **Cape Perce** to Donkin is preferable to cuttting inland through the scrub on #255. On the way is a migratory bird sanctuary.

Donkin, as most places here along the coast, is an old coal town. Its gargantuan generating station can be seen as far as Cape Smoky on the Cabot Trail! For the next few kilometres, outcroppings of coal are visible along the ocean shore cliffs. This accesibility of the mineral made it possible for the **first coal mine** on the continent to be dug at **Port Morien** in the 1720's! This is also the location of the **first Boy Scout troop in North America,** 11 boys being organized in 1908. A monument celebtates this event at the #255 intersection. Port Morien also has a long sandbar nearby.

From **Homeville**, a left turn leads travellers over the False Bay Bridge. Waddens Cove has a small beach near the end of the peninsula. A trail follows the coast the rest of the way out. At **Mira** route #255 turns inland. Continue along the shore on an nonnumbered road. **Main-a-Dieu** is a small fishing port, with an ocean beach. **Scaterie Island**, offshore, was once a fishing colony. The island is known as one of the most difficult anywhere to navigate. Mariners keep a wide berth, its dangerous waters have taken down countless ships. Several hundred men would be sent here each year from **France** to fish cod. They lived in unheated huts, and earned very little money. Many perished in the bitter cold, or among the rocky shoals. After the fall of France in the New World, several **Newfoundland** families were allowed to move onto the island. They found it to be haunted by ghosts of the previous residents who died from its harsh conditions. They gradually abandoned the island. Today, among decaying houses, roads, and wharves the island is only populated by deer and fox.

Cape Breton, Cape Breton
The island is named after its most easterly point of land. Fishermen from Breton, France named it for their home. **You are now virtually at the easternmost point of land in continental North America.** If you sailed directly southward from here, you would keep going... all the way to **Guyana,** South America!

On your way to Louisbourg, watch for short, unserviced dirt roads on the left that lead to beaches and coves. Two of these are Gooseberry Cove and Wild Cove, both rockstrewn shelters with pounding surf in remote, natural settings.

Atlantic Canada
Cycling Festival

Misty cliffs and ocean lookoffs-
Atlantic Canada's No. 1 tour

Tour 38   Cabot Trail

Tour at a glance

START/ FINISH	Baddeck
OTHER STARTING POINTS	Nyanza, Margaree, Englishtown
DISTANCE	305 km (190 mi.)
DIRECTION	Clockwise
TERRAIN	Challenging
CLIMATE	Coolest area in province
	Above average precipitation
	Snow possible in early May/ late September
	Periods of very strong winds
NOTES	3 or more days suggested for tour
TRAFFIC	Moderate; (higher in July/ August)
	No shoulder; Tour busses and tourist traffic
	Quiet early morning; Heaviest at early-afternoon
FOOD	Baddeck (R)(G)(C), Margaree Harbour (R),
	Cheticamp (R)(G)(C), Pleasant Bay (R)(C),
	Cape North (R)(G)(C), Ingonish (R)(G)(C),
	Numerous other stores and restaurants along route
REPAIRS	Sydney (off-route)
TOURISM	Baddeck; Margaree Forks 248-2803; Cheticamp;
	Ingonish
HOSPITAL	Baddeck 295-2112, Cheticamp 224-2450,
	Neil's Harbour
AMBULANCE	Baddeck 295-2200; Cheticamp 224-2316
POLICE	R.C.M.P. Island-wide 1-564-1323

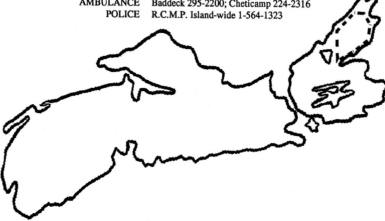

246

"I have travelled around the globe. I have seen the Canadian and American Rockies, the Andes, the Alps and the Highlands of Scotland, but for simple beauty Cape Breton outrivals them all" Alexander Graham Bell

Described as having some of the most spectacular scenery in North America, this is overwhelmingly Atlantic Canada's most popular bicycle ride. Here, you wind your way into Cape Breton's forested highlands, the tundra-like barrens on top resembling the Canadian north. Coming down the steep mountain cliffs you scan across valleys, or directly down at the ocean.

This is not a trip to be taken lightly! With several large climbs, it requires a moderate level of fitness. Elevations may not seem that lofty to many, especially to those who have cycled in mountainous regions. Remember however, that along the Cabot Trail you rise and fall from sea level, not already at high points of elevation. Edged by the ocean, there is also often no room for grading, you must go straight up.

 Trail Trivia: The Cabot Trail is named after explorer John Cabot, who landed on the northern shores of Cape Breton in 1497.

Just because a road is marked "The Cabot Trail" does not mean that it is the best road to take! Remember that this title went to the first road that was put through. Since then, other roads have been connected, some offering more scenic and peaceful options. This tour offers you the best of the Cabot Trail, plus scenic alternate sections.

Almost all of this tour is quite enjoyable. One section stands above the rest, and is what most people come to see. This is the top part, between Margaree Harbour and Englishtown. The remainder is pleasant, but you will not miss out if you do not do the the trail's full circle! An example is taking the western shore (Tour 36) to Margaree, then

going around the top part of the trail, exiting at Englishtown for Sydney.

When is the Best Time: There is no clear cut answer. Many factors must be considered -there are both good and bad points to each season on the trail. Tolerances to the following factors will determine the optimum time for you personally.

Terrain: There is no way around it- you must go up hills on the Cabot Trail! You face a few challenging climbs, some in fact, quite steep. To walk them, you are looking at fair periods of time, from 1/2 to 1 hour for the big ones. This of course is not the worst thing you could do on a summer's day, there are spectacular views and lay-by areas to enjoy, which are less appreciated while sweating your way up on your bike. If you have much gear on board, however, pushing your bike can be as hard on your arms as biking would be on your legs!

Traffic: Only a few communities lie around the trail. There is therefore negligible local traffic and very few trucks. Tourist travel here is your primary concern. An estimated 500,000 people circle the trail each year. In mid-summer, it is hectic, the road has too many busses, motorhomes and automobiles. Before July and after August are the best times traffic-wise. While it can at times be busy, it is positively deserted compared to some U.S. National Parks. Being of a recreational nature, traffic does not pick up until mid-morning- early birds will have much to gain.

After Labour Day in early September, the trail becomes quiet. It is strange that numbers go down, since this is when the scenery, with the coloured leaves, is perhaps at its most appealing.

247

Climate: The highlands have an additional climate influence, that of the cold Labrador Current. Warmer weather makes an even shorter stay than in the rest of Nova Scotia. Frequent precipitation encourages the abundant greenery that you find surrounding you. The rain water is often cold. Be prepared, as shelter is hard to find in the national park.

Beginning with the far ends of the shoulder seasons, April and November are far too brutal to even consider (those who cycle the trail at these times, and enjoy the experience, may require counselling beyond the scope of this volume).

Short lasting snowfalls are possible in the highlands during May and October. There is a **big** difference between the first and second halves of these months, when definite changes of season are experienced.

July and August are the warmest months. Despite the sea breezes, you still sweat going up the hills (on some days you can feel like you are going to melt)! Mid-summer is however, the period of the least precipitation, and kindest winds.

In late summer/ early fall, the days become shorter. If you over-plan your itinerary, you could find yourself cycling small mountains in the dark. In late afternoon, in the shadows it can be cool, especially when coming down hills along the ocean.

Wind: Along the Gulf of St. Lawrence (Margaree / Cheticamp side), the wind is strong. In fact, you may notice in some spots trees grow on a slant. They are telling you something- that winds here come mostly from the west (pushing clockwise). Gusts along the shore on occasion can be so strong as to prevent cycling altogether. On the Atlantic side the wind is less predictable than the Gulf. It is generally much tamer, and you will be protected by more stretches of inland forest .

CAUTION: Up in the highlands, the wind seems to be all over the place- whipping around curves and funnelling up valleys. Alternating between protected spots and sudden gusts, on some days wind can threaten your stability. In fact, cyclists have been known to be knocked off their bikes! If these conditions are prevalent, riders of slight build should be accompanied in closer proximity than usual.

July and August have the tamest winds. The earlier or later from summer months you visit, the stronger the wind you will face.

Insects: Mid to late May sees the beginning of blackfly season. There is a time in June before they fade away which sees overlapping with the start of mosquito time, which can be unbearable. As late summer approaches, the pests subside.

248

Miscellaneous: During off-season (May, June, September, October) prices go down. The carnival atmosphere subsides and people begin to look at you as more than part of the day's receipts.

If considering off-road exploring, on woods trails, you will still find snow, or perhaps mud until later in June.

The first cool nights in mid-autumn, have a spectacular effect on the trail's hardwood trees Leaves change into brilliant hues of red, yellow, and orange. Eastern Canada is world reknown for this display of nature and there are no better viewing places than from atop Mackenzie or North Mountain.

Authors's Preference: Thoroughly confused? Here is at least your author's preference: Camping tour -between Labour Day (1st weekend of September) and mid-September. Indoor Accommodation-between Labour Day and late September.

 Trail Trivia: If you're looking to meet other cyclists, the Cabot Trail is the place to head. An estimated **4,000** bicyclists, tour this route each year!

Be Prepared: Before you head for the Cabot Trail, be as ready as possible. Bike repair is nil. Banking, services, and things such as drug stores and camera supplies are limited to basics.

Safety: Remember- motorists, like yourself, have come to look at the scenery. The spellbinding views, the distractions, the long hours of driving, the restless children and pets... don't expect the motorist alertness of a city freeway. In addition, their vehicles frequently are pulling trailers, often wider than their cars, a fact of which they may be totally oblivious! It is up to you to protect yourself, using defensive cycling. If possible keep in eye contact and make use of a rear view mirror. Rememer, there is little

commuter traffic around the trail, so get out there early in the day, before the busses hit the road and the animals hide in the woods.

Caution on the hills: Extreme force will be put onto your braking system. Aging brake cables and worn pads must be attended to before your trip. Check your brakes before descents, inspect racks for loose bolts and items such as clothing and loose straps that could come free and go into your wheels.

Don't forget that the going will be slower, so plan not to get caught riding at night. Bicycle lights simply can not provide enough light to securely negotiate these hills at night- Don't be like a friend of this author, who coming down the curves of North Mountain in the dark, "zigged", when he should have "zagged"!

Home port of Lake Bras D'Or, **Baddeck** will act as the starting point. Especially popular with **Americans**, it has long had a reputation as a resort community. Villagers are used to quick visits by the rich and famous. **Lake Bras D'Or** is on the wish list for lovers of sailboats and yachts. You should see some fancy craft afloat in its coves. The villages has full services here to prepare you for the following few days, including luxury resorts and first-class restaurants.

The name Baddeck is derived from an Indian word, *Abadek*, which means "an island near by". This no doubt refers to **Kidston Island**, where the Baddeck Lions Club offers boat transportation daily to its supervised beach and walking trails.

You know him as the man who invented the telephone. He preferred to be known as the man who helped deaf people to speak. **Alexander Graham Bell** was among those who adopted the resort of Baddeck (back when the Cabot Trail was no more than a hiking path). **Alexander Graham Bell National Park Museum** is the most comprehensive display of his achievements and experiments (1,860 square metres/

20,000 sq. ft.) of exhibit space). They include his work on the telephone, fresh-water from salt-water, artificial respiration, x-rays, toys, sound recording, hydrofoil, kites, flight, and teaching the deaf to speak. (Small admission-no flash cameras 295-2069). *Beinn Bhreagh*, ("beautiful mountain") his immense summer home, can be seen across the cove from the museum. It is still occupied by the Bell family. It was here that Alexander conducted his experiments. His wife, Mabel locally organized the first Home and School association in Canada. Dr. and Mrs. Bell lie at rest at the top of the mountain.

 Trail Trivia: Highwheeler Cafe Deli and Bakery on Chebucto Street in Baddeck has a bicycling theme.

An oasis of nature

The last remaining tracts of protected wilderness in Nova Scotia... so is described the highlands of Cape Breton. A variety of species can be visited in their natural environment. Wildlife in the park include white-tailed deer, red fox, and snowshoe hares. Smaller species are deer mice, voles, red squirrels and shrews. Beaver and muskrats are found busy at work near rivers and ponds.

Moose can be spotted in boggy areas. The best bet to see them while biking is on top of French Mountain. Walking trails there are even better prospects of meeting one face to face. The raccoon, coyote, and bobcat are new residents, arriving since the completion of a fixed link with the mainland. Few skunks or porcupines have yet to find their way across the causeway. Several threatened species have found protection within the park. The Canada lynx is quite rare, as is the pine martin. Rumours persist of sightings of the almost extinct eastern panther.

Black bears also roam the highlands. Remember, although residents of a busy national park, they are still wild animals. Like most of the park's wildlife (except the deer and rabbits) bears tend to keep well off the highway. However, cyclists, being more silent, are more likely than autos to encounter a bear crossing the road. Take pictures only from a distance. When camping in a small site, keep your area clean and food out of your tent.

Along the coast are whales of many varieties. Porpoises, harbour seals, and sea birds can also be spotted. Boat tours take visitors up close. The trips are enjoyable, irregardless of sightings. They allow access to the solitude of the ocean, and follow inaccessible shorelines, without roads or habitation, impossible to see by bike.

Bird Tours

Bird Island Boat Tours Van Schaik Family, Big Bras d'Or, NS8 (902) 674-2384. Trips to the famous Bird Islands, Hertford and Ciboux. Seafowl include cormorants, razorbills, Atlantic puffins, petrels, and terns. Navigation requires good visibility- tours at times postponed. Dress warm, if possible bring binoculars.

Whale Watching

Whale Watch Bay St. Lawrence Dennis Cox, (902) 383-2981 Sailing is aboard the 10m (32 ft.) Bonnie Susan. Minke whales, pilot whales, dolphins, fin whales, eagles and sea birds. Trips 2 1/2 gours long. Spotted whales on 40 consecutive trips in 1991

Whale Cruisers Bill Crawford, Grand Etang, NS B0E 1L0 (902) 224-3376. Two 13m (42 ft.) ships; coast of Cape Breton Highlands National Park

Pleasant Bay Boat Tours Ariland Fitzgerald; three tours daily; 2 1/2 hour tours (902) 224-2547

Aspy Bay Boat Tours Nelson Morris; shipwrecks, whales, and occasional sea turtles. Tour each Sunday to St. Paul's Island (902) 383-2847

A Cyclist's Debate

The Scene: An Indian encampment in the Cape Breton highlands
The Time: An ancient era before the arrival of the European
The Topic of the Day: Which way through the highlands is better...
Clockwise or Counter-Clockwise?

U ntil 1932, Cape North, Pleasant Bay and other area communities had no road, reachable only from the sea. After many years of work, a route was finally pushed through to these outports. Cyclists riding one-speeds were among the first to eagerly navigate around what would one day become known as the Cabot Trail. At some point a debate began- one which may never be settled: *Which is the best way around?*

There is no "*right*" way to do the trail. **Clockwise** seems preferred by the majority of cyclists (as well as many with the national park). The predominant westerly wind is their overwhelming reason, over terrain, the "water side of the road", and other arguments.

Clockwise

* Margaree to Cheticamp- Strong tailwinds or "beneficial" crosswinds.

* Full use of Cheticamp Information Centre services at western park entrance.

* Surprisingly fast speeds possible on foothills just north of Cheticamp

* Famous view of trail up French Mountain

* Difficult, but not extreme climb up French Mountain. After plateau, slow downhill speed but spectacular views on switchbacks into Pleasant Bay on MacKenzie Mtn. side.

* Challenging climb up North Mountain, one of the hardest in province, its downhill perhaps the fastest.

* Scenic views through Sunrise Valley towards Meat Cove and Cape North.

* Smoky Mountain: An "easy" climb, broken into two sections. Descent presents phenomenal views out over the Atlantic. Its steep decline and sharp bottom turn prevent any high speeds and demands care.

Note: Strange from looking on a map perhaps, but you will not be without cliffside views going clockwise as the trail descends into occasional valleys.

Counter-Clockwise

* Smoky Mountain: A real work-out - possibly the hardest climb in Nova Scotia! Descent into Ingonish is in two sections, in terms of energy expended, "a net loss".

* Scenic Atlantic shoreline past Ingonish.

* Challenging climb up North Mountain, one of the hardest in N.S. Extremely fast downhill.

* Switchbacks and lay-bys provide "easy" climb up MacKenzie Mtn. After plateau, fast ocean-side downhill and spectacular views descending French Mountain side.

* Surprisingly high speeds possible on foothills before Cheticamp.

* Cheticamp to Margaree: Strong headwinds or difficult crosswinds can make rough going along barren coast.

251

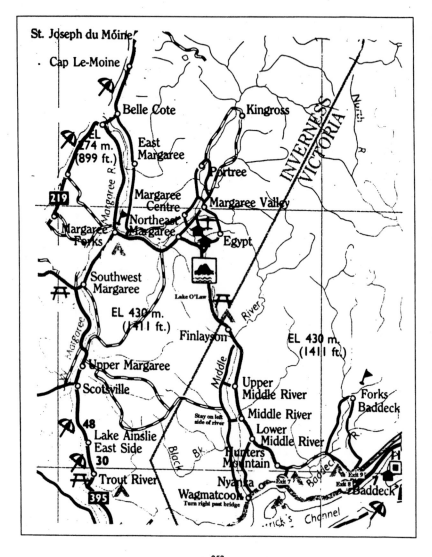

START	**Town Hall/ Library in Baddeck** (park cars by the marina or at the Bell Museum). Head west along Lake Bras D'or on #205
	SIDE TRIP Forks Baddeck: In back of Baddeck, a pleasant ride takes you through a river valley to Forks Baddeck. Here, a well-trodden trail takes you on an easy 30 minute round-trip to spectacular Uisge Ban Falls. Pronounced "Ishga-Ban", the water drops 15-m (50-ft.) in two sweeps into a granite gorge.
2.8 (1.7)	**MERGE** with #105 Exit #8 Trans-Canada Highway. You must now follow a short distance on this primary thoroughfare. There are a couple of hills. Safe, with a wide shoulder, it is noisy however and coated with billboards.
10.9 (6.8)	*SHORT-CUT*: Hunter's Mountain/ Cabot Trail (Exit 7). The official Cabot Trail turns here, as do the travel trailers and tour busses. However, this tour turns off a bit further ahead (onto an alternate stretch of peace and quiet).
	Herring Choker Deli - Indian Bay Bakery: This natural food store is coming up, 2.2 km (1.3 mi.) west of the official Cabot Trail turn-off. Run by Albert Rodriquez, a very avid cyclist, this is a suitable place to load up before your run to the other side of the island.
	Pass Yankee Line Road and cross Middle River to Wagmatcook Reserve.
14.8 (9.2)	**RIGHT** Nyanza. West Middle River road follows the Nyanza Indian Reserve ("first nation") inland. You will now cycle a long quiet road, before rejoining the Cabot Trail, just where it becomes scenic. A gentle climb, watch for raspberries growing along road to your right.
24.4 (15.2)	**LEFT** Stay on west side of river (paved road- no signs- turning right will take you across bridge and onto the official route of the Cabot Trail). Watch for **Parson Stone House**, one of only a few non-wood houses on Cape Breton.
28.9 (17.9)	**LEFT** MacLennans Road
33.6 (20.9)	**LEFT** Cabot Trail. Lake O'Law approaches shortly, with a picnic park and nearby restaurant.

 Trail Trivia: The only highway in Nova Scotia referred to by name, not by number, few know that for official purposes, the Cabot Trail actually does has a number- Route #30.

Pleasant roads follow the Margaree inland. Villages such as Portree, and "Egypt" offer care-free exploring. Kingross is surounded by big hills and plenty of off-road trails. The area was settled by arrivals from the Isle of Skye, led by Angus Ross. The newcomers were so happy they called him "King Ross". Margaree Forks was the home of Dr. Moses Coady and Dr. J. Tompkins, founders of the **Co-operative Movement**. "The forks" is the location of a tourist information bureau.

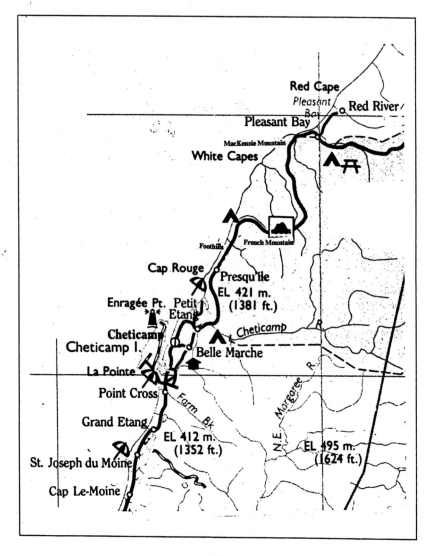

Edging the Margaree River, you now go in a gentle downward direction to the **Gulf of St. Lawrence**. Acknowledged widely as perhaps the most beautiful salmon stream in North America, it is renown for its spring and fall run. Hatched in eastern Nova Scotia rivers, salmon head out to sea. Following a year in salt water, they return to the same rivers they were hatched. Unlike the Pacific species, the Atlantic Salmon does not die after spawning, but returns to the sea again, as a "kelt." In a former schoolhouse is the **Margaree Salmon Museum**. This specialty museum in Northeast Margaree explains the life cycle of the Atlantic Salmon. Exhibits include techniques used to catch these fish, Indian and old time fishing tackle, and poaching equipment. Look for the photo of the 24 kg (53 pound) salmon. (Admission is $ .50)

DETOUR: While the Cabot Trail follows the west bank of the Margaree, another winding road hugs the east. It is more hilly than the west "Cabot Trail" side, but quieter. This is known as the "French" side of the river.

SIDE TRIP- Route #19 The Margaree Valley continues westward along this famous salmon stream to Lake Ainslie and Tour 35.

68.5 (42.6) **RIGHT** Margaree Harbour- Junction of Tour 36. At the bend to cross the Margaree, stands a rambling white "mock-Tudor" building. Its owner conceived of the complex as a way to help preserve Cape Breton's connections with Scotland. Blessed with a touch of folly, as the structure ages, each year it becomes a little more eclectic. Tartans, clothing, weaving, clan regalia, and music recordings are for sale. The schooner "*Marion Elizabeth*" alongside had a long career, including a time smuggling during Prohibition. The complex stands as the unofficial centre of the community. The people inside are friendly and are known for being involved in social issues, such as the environment (long before it became vogue).

Around the bend on the #219 is the harbour, with a beach. As with the entire west coast, Margaree Harbour is famous for its sunsets. The Acadian Trail, built a few years ago by the Canadian Youth Hostel Association, can be found along the shore. Ask directions at the restaurant or store.

The trail crosses the Margaree over the longest wooden bridge east of Montreal. Crossing over brings you into another culture, settled by French speaking Acadians several hundred years ago. Visitors from France and even Quebec arrive astonished to hear the locals speaking with a 17th century accent! The lyrical Acadian dialect is still spoken (intermingled with bits of English). Separated across the island from fellow Acadians near Isle Madame, this small enclave hangs on. Swamped by English, and on a highway bringing thousands of tourists, it is a wonder how the culture survives.

This coast is barren, the few trees rooted on the shore grow on a slant, conceding to the strong winds. The shore's commercial fishing fleet catches lobsters, salmon, cod, hake and crab.

Just before Cheticamp, on your right is a huge scarecrow patch. Joe, their owner, welcomes you to drop by to meet and perhaps even have your picture taken with them. Joe refuses to charge admission, but you can leave a donation in his box. (224-2834)

255

Magnificently situated, Cheticamp lies at the foothills of Cape Breton Highlands National Park. With a population of 3,500, the town can prepare you for your memorable journey through the highlands. Watch for Acadian cuisine, such as chicken fricot, meat pie and poutine.

St. Peter's Church, the towering structure dominating the town, is visible for long distances along the coast and far at sea. The interior must be considered to be to be the most highly ornamented of any church in Nova Scotia. Everywhere you look is adorned with lavish gilt-trim. The Baroque style ornamentation covers its arches, galleries, and even the ceiling, creating a fanciful yet at the same time structured pattern.

 Trail Trivia: Cheticamp is the *hooked rug capital of the world*. Villagers have turned stitchery - knitting, crocheting, rug hooking - into an elegant form of art. Watch for its famous needlework and rugs displayed in village shops.

Whales frequent off shore. The pilot whale, known locally as the "pot head" and the minke, a smaller cousin of the great humpback whale can be seen on whale-watching tours. The tours often also pass eagle's nests in the cliffs along the coast.

Cheticamp Acadian Museum: Demonstrations are offered of wool carding, spinning, weaving, rug hooking and other facets of traditional life. Acadian cuisine is prepared and served on the premises. 744 Main St. (Admission free, donations welcome)

SIDE TRIP- Cheticamp Island A good short ride includes wharves, farms and a stone church. There is also a beach, with changehouses, washrooms and canteen facilities. A lighthouse stands at Enragée Point at the north end. Excellent views look over at Cheticamp, and the Cabot Trail winding into the highlands. On the west side, the island is a good spot to watch sunsets.

Once past Cheticamp, the Cabot Trail escorts you into the province's most dramatic cycling, through **Cape Breton Highlands National Park**. Pass the park entrance and drop into the **Cheticamp Visitor's Centre**. Staff will show you exhibits on the park, including a 3-D map. A colour album here will show you what the hiking trails are like. Here you may inquire which are currently open to mountain bikes. A booklet, listing 28 trails is available. **Acadian Trail**, from the visitor's centre, can not be biked but offers a spectacular climb overlooking the entire region.

Immediately, the first hills begin. While not nearly as tall as what is shortly ahead, these foothills have no turns and thus they allow fast speeds, surprisingly, often exceeding that of higher points of the trail!

Brief pauses at lookouts over the gulf are rewarding before beginning your first long climb, up **French Mountain**. This ride along the coast, is one of the most dramatic and photographed vistas in North America, with the highway disappearing among the coast's hills. Although you do not in any way want to do the trail in the dark, the sunsets from French Mountain are spectacular.

Trail Trivia: At **459 m (1506 ft.)**, **French Mountain** stands as the highest point of pavement in Nova Scotia. (Remember, before you compare with other spots, here you start your climb from **zero** elevation).

The plateaus of the highlands have conditions which you would expect to encounter in Canada's north. Extreme wind conditions prevail over bogs, barrens, and dwarf spruce trees. It has the environment in many ways of the "tiaga" of the sub-arctic. You may think the trees are young, perhaps 5 to 20 years old. These however have been stunted due to the harsh environment. Passed over by wood cutters for generations, some are upwards of 200 years old! This setting makes for prime moose territory, in fact, perhaps the best roadside location in all Nova Scotia! *Bog Trail* is a wooded boardwalk, giving a taste of the interior marshlands. Wheelchair accessible, and with frequent walkers, this is a suitable place to explore without your bike. You may see moose, frogs, orchids, and insect "eating" **Pitcher Plants**, more common to Newfoundland.

After a small rise to the top of **Mackenzie Mountain**, you begin a 4 km (2.5 mi.) descent. A series of fun hairpin switchbacks take you into Pleasant Bay (expect to do lots of braking). The views from here are incredible! On a clear day it is possible to see all the way to the **Iles de la Madeleine**.

Pleasant Bay until 1927 could only be reached by boat or hiking trail. Enclosed by large hills, it must have been a most peaceful place before the roads were put over the peaks. This setting almost was the village's undoing. In 1948, a huge forest fire came close to engulfing the entire community. Fragile hillsides are still recovering.

 Trail Trivia: Before the building of a road to Pleasant Bay, the village had a unique winter mail service...through the mountain snow by husky dogs. In its early years, the Cabot Trail was so narrow that in mountain sections it was barely one lane wide, piles of rocks all that separated travellers from tall cliffs. Drivers would have to call ahead to determine if any traffic was coming the other way. Often cars would have to back down the mountain before continuing.

SIDE TRIP- Red River: A pleasant short ride along the shore to this dead-end along the edge of steep hills. A great early evening or rest-day run. A curious addition to the village, is its small community of Buddhists.

Ascend **North Mountain (449 m/ 1473 ft.).** Beginning your approach, to your right is the *Lone Sheiling*. The hut, built as a tribute to Scottish heritage, is as used by sheep crofters on the **Isle of Skye**. There is a short 800 m (.5 mi.) trail here through an area of 300 year old sugar maple trees! This is a delightful place to have your lunch under the shade and by a small brook.

In either direction, North Mountain is one of the hardest climbs in Nova Scotia. After a few turns, the entire second half of your way down is a long straight run into the **Sunrise Valley**. A small rest area is at the bottom by the

257

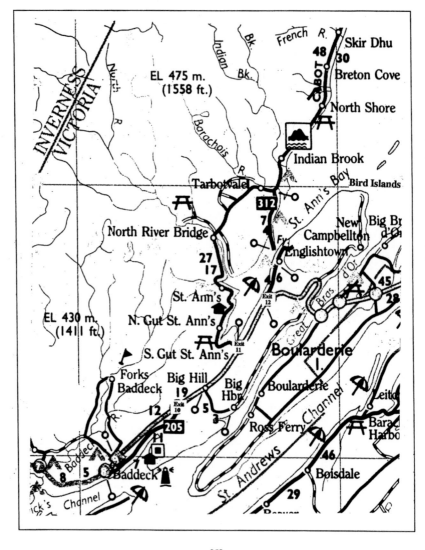

Aspy River, where you can get your nerves back after what is considered Nova Scotia's fastest downhill! **CAUTION:** Wind gusts on the upper sections of North Mtn. can be fierce!

Following a gradual climb out of the valley, you ascend above Cape North. On the way you can see a strongly defined escarpment, extending along the west side of the river. This ridge goes along the shore, some 32 km (20 mi.) to Meat Cove (Tour CB-8).

Cape North :Bay St. Lawrence Rd. Out of the park limits, stores and restaurants can be found. Behind the stadium on the way downhill toward Dingwall, a trail designed for skiers offers a demanding route for experienced off-road bikers (two national cross-country ski championships have been held here. 6 km (3 mi.)

SIDE TRIP- Dingwall: You may notice this area's white cliffs, exposing gypsum deposits. Here, until 1933 a large operation produced some of the best quality gypsum in North America. Few tourists are seen going down into the village. Two lighthouses operate on either end of a long sandbar (Aspy Bay Beach), where you may enjoy swimming and clam digging away from the crowds. Mountain bikers may like the abandoned gypsum workings, perhaps finding their curious landforms fun to explore.

169.7 (105.4)   **LEFT** Turn at bottom of hill, just past bridge. This road to Neil's Harbour is far superior to the Cabot Trail route over South Mountain. Here you ride along on the white cliffs overlooking rocky coves. About 5 km (3 mi.) further than the long, steady climb over South Mountain, the shore has a series of incessant rolling hills. Settled by Newfoundlanders, the fishing village of Neil's Harbour stands just before rejoining the trail.

188.9 (117.3)   **LEFT** Cabot Trail. You now pass a long stretch of rugged Atlantic coastline. There are many pleasant rest spots just off the road by the ocean surf. **Black Brook Beach** lies just down the hill. A pleasant 10 minute hike takes you to the edge of the bluff.

Centuries ago a Portuguese fishing camp, **Ingonish** is the eastern service region for the highlands, offering restaurants, groceries and accommodations. **NOTE:** Due to the one-street layout, and "party" attitude of visitors staying in the area, bicyclists might find the traffic here at times a bit unpleasant.

Whales have been known to come right up to the beach. Overlooking the Atlantic Ocean, is Nova Scotia's first resort hotel, **Keltic Lodge.** An easy 3 km (2 mi.) trail to **Middle Head,** from nearby views steep cliffs, meadows, dense thickets and a seabird colony (please respect trail closure during nesting season). *Highlands Links Golf Course*: Designed by **Stanley Thompson,** this par 71, 18-hole course located within the National Park is rated among the best in the world, meandering for 11km, with sea and mountain views. It is common for deer or even moose to stroll onto the greens.

Clyburn River Trail follows the golf links. Mostly level, except for a few sections, it offers 9.2 km (5.7 mi.) of good off-road riding. An abandoned gold mine from 1910 can be found, as well as old beaver ponds.

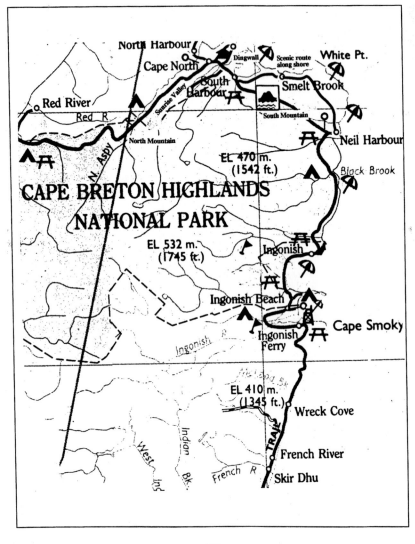

Not long out of Ingonish you commence the climb of **Cape Smoky**. Your ascent from sea level to the summit is **365 m (1200 ft.)**. Fairly easy for such a peak, it is in broken into a couple of sections. On top of old Smoky sits a look-off park. Extraordinary ocean views are afforded at its picnic tables and hiking trail. Descending Smoky Mountain is steep, a real brake-burner! Stop to enjoy the view on the way down (while moving you will be too busy controlling your bike). Look out from here out over Atlantic Ocean. If you are curious what the lone structure is on the horizon, it is the energy generating station in far off Lingan.

CAUTION: You drop 365 m (1200 ft.) in only 3.2 km (2 mi.). An extremely sharp turn awaits at the bottom, so use extreme care- if you are the type to go full-throttle on hills you will be in for a horrific surprise!

You now pass a fairly unpopulated inland stretch of woods. The name of the tiny village of **Skir Dhu** (pop. 10) means "*black rock*" in Gaelic. Soon you are faced with a choice-through Tarbotvale, or via the ferry shortcut to Englishtown on #312.

Now That's Charisma!

The tale of one of history's most remarkable migrations give's tiny St. Ann's ties with several nations. A number of emmigrants from Scotland, under the authority of one **Reverend Norman MacLeod**, set sail for the New World. Not long after their arrival at Pictou, he accepted a call to preach in Ohio, in the United States. They agreed to go with him. A storm however, sent them scurrying for shelter into St. Ann's Harbour. It so entranced them they decided to stay. Here, far from any other settlement, Reverend MacLeod became not only minister, but school teacher, postmaster and justice of the peace, (so he oversaw their lives both here and hereafter).

Thirty years on, settlement well established, Reverend MacLeod one day made an announcement. He was convinced the promised land lay on the other side of the world. The people did not doubt him for a moment, agreeing to give up everything.

After a long voyage they sailed into the harbour of **Adelaide, Australia.** A few years later they would follow this magnetic personality yet again, this time to **Waipu, New Zealand.** There they were astonished to find the it very similar to St. Ann's! In total, 876 people crossed the earth to share his visions. To this day, **New Zealanders** frequently travel to this part of Cape Breton in search of their roots.

The Cape Breton Giant

Angus MacAskill was born on the **Hebrides Islands**, off Scotland in 1825. He arrived in Canada a normal boy, his parents of average size as were his nine brothers and three sisters. At the age of 16, however, he grew to become known as the *Cape Breton Giant*, 2 m (7 ft. 9 inches) tall and 193 kg (493 lb.)!

He joined **Barnum and Bailey's Circus**, where he teamed up with the 0.7 m (2 1/2 ft.) high **Tom Thumb** (at their exhibitions, he used to hold Colonel Thumb in the palm of his hand). In London, he accepted an invitation to Windsor Castle, where, like Nova Scotia giantess Anna Swan, he was received enthusiastically by **Queen Victoria.**

Few people realize that MacAskill was also thought to be the **strongest man in the world**, perhaps in history! He often performed spellbinding feats of strength. In New York a crowd on a pier goaded him that he would be unable to lift up a large anchor. Weighing (1225 kg) (2700 pounds), unbelievably, he did manage to lift it. However, upon trying to walk around with it, the weight slipped, trapping him underneath. He lived for the rest of his life in pain.

Returning to St. Ann's he operated a popular store and grist mill. It is said at times his pain would subside, and he would have energy for practical feats, such as turning his own mill wheel when there was low water. In 1863, he passed away after a short illness. Across the road from the ferry dock is a small cemetery, where he is buried. **Giant MacAskill Museum** has many of Angus's personal belongings, including a vest, jacket, boot, walking stick, chair and bed. (Small admission charge- check locally for times)

261.7 (162.5)　　*SHORT-CUT-* #312 Englishtown: It is not easy to recommend a stretch of the Trans-Canada Highway, however, this short-cut has a ferry ride, a run up on side of Kelly's Mountain with pleasant views of Gut St. Ann's and is considerably shorter. There is a paved shoulder. A cable ferry takes you across St. Ann's Gut (24 hrs.).

 Trail Trivia: Englishtown was the site of an early Jesuit mission. Later it was the site of the first permanent settlement of Europeans in Cape Breton. As it grew along the shore of Gut St. Ann's additional sevices were required. One enterprising merchant came up with the notion of a second location, down the bay. Little did he realize that he was opening....the first chain store in Canada!

Continuing along the Cabot Trail, here, in the hardwoods, the coloured leaves of Autumn are especially stunning. North River Provincial Park offers an attractive 30 m (100 ft.) waterfall. Enter in a short distance on Oregon Road. The trail to the falls is then 9.5 km (5.5 mi.) each way. It follows a river, with trout and salmon pools. **St. Ann's Park**, (1.5 km .9 mi.) before reaching the Trans-Canada Highway (#105) offers a picnic site and a short hiking trail.

The **Gaelic College of Celtic Arts** is one of the world's last remaining centres of **Scottish Gaelic** culture. The **Great Hall of the Clans** depicts the history of the Scots and their migration from the highlands. If you are of Scottish descent, you have the opportunity to trace your roots! Visit classes in bagpipes and drums, clan lore, highland and country dancing, fiddling, handweaving, traditional dress and Gaelic language writing and singing. Open from to mid-June to October (Nominal Admission) 295-2877

289.0 (179.5)　　**RIGHT** #105 Exit 11

All its hand played, the Cabot Trail ends on an uneventful note. Your final stretch into Baddeck allows you time to think over the last few days, the memories of which will last your lifetime. Start planning a celebration in Baddeck for your completion of this challenging route. Treat yourself to a big meal, or a night in a cosy inn- its yours, you've earned it!

298.5 (185.3).　　**LEFT** #205 Exit 10

307.3 (190.8)　　**END**

Further Information

Cape Breton Highlands National Park
Ingonish Beach, Nova Scotia, B0C 1L0 (902) 285-2691

Les Amis Du Plein Air Nature Bookstore
Located at Cheticamp and Ingonish National Park Entrances. Open mid-May to mid-October. Mail Order Service available. Nature books (over 1,000 selections), cookbooks, nature videos and cassettes, souvenirs and hiking supplies. Included are sales of 50,000 scale maps of the Cape Breton Highlands National Park, and their own guide to hiking the park trails. Contact them for current prices. P.O. Box 472, Cheticamp, NS B0E 1H0 (902) 224-3814.

Accommodation

Cabot Trail Motel Gary and Ann Ross, P.O. Box 309, Baddeck, NS B0E 1B0, (902) 295-2580. 1.6 km (1 mi.) west of Baddeck.

Inverary Inn P.O. Box 190, Baddeck, NS B0E 1B0, (902) 295-2674, Fax (902) 295-2427. Shore Rd.

Restawyle Tourist Home Russell and Ada Manzuk, P.O. Box 112, Baddeck, NS B0E 1B0, (902) 295-3428.

Silver Dart Lodge Warren Janes, P.O. Box 399, Baddeck, NS B0E 1B0, (902) 295-2340, Fax (902) 295-2484. On Shore Rd.

Telegraph House Buddy and Mary Dunlop, P.O. Box 8, Baddeck, NS B0E 1B0, (902) 295-9988. Off Route #205 on Chebucto St., in the heart of Baddeck.

Middle River Inn Bed and Breakfast Marion Hancock, P.O. Box 571, Baddeck, NS B0E 1B0, (902) 295-2321 At Nyanza.

Normaway Inn David MacDonald, P.O. Box 101, Margaree Valley, NS B0E 2C0, (902) 248-2897. On Egypt Rd., 3.2 km (2 miles) off Cabot Trail. Tranquil 1920's inn. Tennis, walking trails, horseback riding.

The Lakes Cottages The Taylors, North East Margaree, NS B0E 2H0, (902) 248-2360. At Lake O'Law.

Buckles Cabins and Motel Gerald and Martha Buckles, Margaree Forks, NS B0E 2A0. 248-2053.

Duck Cove Inn Gordon Laurence, Margaree Harbour, NS B0E 2B0. Junction of Cabot & Ceilidh Trails. 235-2658. Fax 235-2592.

Harbour View Inn Connie Jennex, Box 52, Margaree Harbour, NS B0E 2B0. 235-2314.

Acadian Motel Ron Aucoin, P.O. Box 11, Cheticamp, NS B0E 1H0, (902) 224-2640, (902) 224-2089

Cheticamp Motel Ethel Merry, P.O. Box 698, Cheticamp, NS B0E 1H0, (902) 224-2711, (902) 469-3380

Laurie's Motel Laurie McKeown, P.O. Box 1, Cheticamp, NS B0E 1H0, (902) 224-2400.

Ocean View Motel G. R. "Bill" LeBlanc, P.O. Box 419, Cheticamp, NS B0E 1H0, (902) 224-2313.

Beachside Motel Joan and Michael Meers, Pleasant Bay, NS B0E 2P0, (902) 224-2467

Mountain View Motel Lorna and Bernie, Pleasant Bay, NS B0E 2P0, (902) 224-3100

MacDonald's Motel and Cabins Mrs. A. J. Morrison, Cape North, R.R. #1, Dingwall, NS B0C 1G0, (902) 383-2054.

Keltic Lodge Alexander MacClure, P.O. Box 70, Ingonish Beach, NS B0C 1L0, (902) 285-2880, (902) 285-2859. Prestigious resort on shore.

Knotty Pine Cottages and Tourist Home Roland and Patricia MacKinnon, R.R. #1, Ingonish Ferry, NS B0C 1L0, (902) 285-2058.

Skyline Cabins Joyce Marra, P.O. Box 26, Ingonish Beach, NS B0C 1L0, (902) 285-2055. 0.4 km (1/4 mile) from entrance to Cape Breton Highlands Park.

Piper's Guest House James and Lucy Piche, R.R. #1, Englishtown, NS B0C 1H0, (902) 929-2067, (902) 929-2233

Greer's Bed and Breakfast Ann and Bob Greer, Tarbotvale, R.R. #4, Baddeck, NS B0E 1B0, (902) 929-2115. Close to the Gaelic College and a lovely swimming hole.

Camping

Baddeck Cabot Trail KOA Campground Bruce and Peggy Anderson, Baddeck, NS B0E 1B0, (902) 295-2288; (902) 295-2279. Large open and wooded campground on river. Route #105, 8 km (5 mi.) west of Baddeck. Washrooms, free showers, laundromat.

Bras d'Or Lakes Campground Sandy and Janice Hudson, Baddeck, NS B0E 1B0, (902) 295-2329, (902) 295-3467. Open campground on Bras d'Or Lake. Route #105, 4.8 km (3 mi.) west of Baddeck. Free showers, washrooms, laundromat, groceries.

Silver Spruce Resort Earl Timmons, P.O. Box 373, Baddeck, NS B0E 1B0. Open and wooded sites. #105, 8 km (5 mi.) west of Baddeck. Free showers, supplies. (902) 295-2417, (902) 295-3036.

The Lakes Campsite The Taylors, Lake O'Law, N.E. Margaree, NS B0E 2H0, (902) 248-2360. Open & wooded campground on lake along Cabot Trail. Pay showers, washrooms, laundromat, restaurant.

Buckles Trailer Court and Campsite Gerald and Martha Buckles, Margaree Forks, NS B0E 2A0, (902) 248-2053. Pay showers, washrooms, laundromat.

Plage Saint Pierre Campground Gilles Deveau, P.O. Box 430, Cheticamp, NS B0E 1H0, (902) 224-2112. Open and wooded campground on ocean inlet, off Cabot Trail on Cheticamp Island.

Cape Breton Highlands National Park Ingonish Beach, NS, B0C 1L0, (902) 285-2691, six campsites are available in the park: Inquire regarding current reservation policy. Smaller locations require reservation at park entrances.

* *Cheticamp*: huge campsite at park entrance. washrooms, showers

* *Corney Brook*: 10 km into park. 20 unserviced sites, fills early in the day, tenting park along ocean, washrooms, good sunsets

* *MacIntosh Brook*: 5km before North Mountain. 10 sites washroom, trails

* *Big Intervale*: Small 10 site camping area by river at bottom of descent of North Mountain

* *Broad Cove*: 11 km (7 mi.) north of Ingonish entrance. Busy- fills early, showers, beach, hiking, fishing

* *Ingonish Beach*: Late June-Labour Day 1.5 km (.9 mi.) north of Ingonish entrance. Park is busy- fills early in day, showers, beach, hiking, golf

Piper's Trailer Court James Piche, Indian Brook, NS B0C 1H0, (902) 929-2233, (902) 929-2067. Open campground on ocean. Between Baddeck and Ingonish. Pay showers, laundromat, licensed restaurant.

St. Ann's Bay Campark Frank and Ann Gentile, Englishtown, NS B0C 1H0, (902) 929-2582. Open campground on ocean. Route #312, 2.4 km (1.5 mi.) north of Englishtown ferry. Free showers, laundromat, canteen, small beach.

A breathtaking ride to the top of Nova Scotia

Tour 39   Meat Cove

Tour at a glance

START/ FINISH	Cape North
DISTANCE	58 km (36 mi.)
	Option of going part way/ side trips available
DIRECTION	South-North-South
TERRAIN	Challenging
CLIMATE	Coolest area in province
	Above average precipitation
	Snow possible in early May/ late September
	Periods of very strong winds
NOTES	Very few services- you must be self-sufficient. Store hours and supplies vary; leave prepared
	Section of dirt road
	Wild off-road side -trip to Money Point
	Whale watching trips available in Bay St. Lawrence
	(See section on wildlife in tour CB-7-Cabot Trail)
	Occasional wildlife sightings including moose and bear
TRAFFIC	Low
REST SPOTS	Sugarloaf Beach/ Mtn.; Bay St. Lawrence; Meat Cove
FOOD	Cape North (R)(G)(C); Bay St. Lawrence (C); Capstick (C)
REPAIRS	Sydney (off-route)
TOURISM	Cheticamp (off-route); Ingonish (off-route)
POLICE	R.C.M.P. (Cheticamp- off-route) 1-564-1323
HOSPITAL	Neil's Harbour (off-route)

"Meat Cove is a magical place, a cluster of humanity dug into a cleft in the dark bones of the world" T. W. Burger

Meat Cove is the end of the line. You don't go there on your way to somewhere else. This special place off the beaten track must be your destination, because there is nowhere else beyond it.

American columnist Burger perfectly describes this wild and beautiful country. A strongly defined escarpment extends along the shore. Stretching from the Cabot trail to the tip of the province, it is, in fact, the tail end of the Appalachian chain, making one last appearance before dipping into the Atlantic. This challenging terrain will stalk you as you make your way along the lonely coast. While not mountainous, you should expect rolling hills, with several climbs in the (500 ft.) range.

You can go out just part way, it makes a great spot for a part-day or evening run. Go as far as the landing site of explorer **John Cabot**, and return, making a good mini-ride from Cape North. You could go even further, to the gorgeous cove of Bay St. Lawrence.

If your nerve doesn't fail, you can go all the way to Meat Cove, where without a doubt you will be able to claim you have gone to the top of Nova Scotia!

The Last Outport: The thread of what we call civilization came late to the northern reaches of the province. Until only recent memory, Meat Cove was reachable only from the sea. Forced kicking and screaming into the world of the automobile, a road was pushed through and many residents of the once isolated cove "enticed" to leave.

Meat Cove has a reputation - a bad one. Stories, stories, and more stories pour forth about this little place. Words can not, and will not here put into print the tales, told of this tiny harbour. Embellished by the Cape Breton art of storytelling, the fact is- most islanders have never even been here. Remembering this should place the myths you may hear into perspective!

The pavement ends before Meat Cove. You have to navigate the same gravel both over the ridge into the village and then back out. Bald Eagles nest in the area, and whales are often visible off the coast. Coming out of the dense woods of the ridge, deer, moose, and on occasion, bears can be sighted.

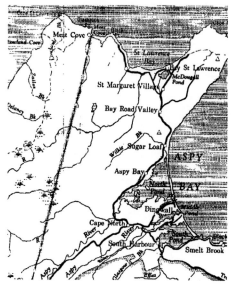

START	Corner of Cabot Trail and Bay St. Lawrence Rd. in Cape North (by Morrison's Pioneer Restaurant). Start off with a big downhill to the Aspy River.

Our first stop is indeed a historic one. **Sugar Loaf Beach** is 10.3 km (6.2 mi.) along route. On 24 June, 1497, from Bristol, England, **John Cabot** made the first European landing in North America. In 1857 the first Atlantic cable was landed at this unassuming edge of the continent. The message was transmitted from **Queen Victoria to President Buchanan** of the United States. The park provides picnic tables and toilet facilities at its sand beach.

Just ahead to the left, signs point to a steep path, which takes you to the top of **Sugar Loaf Mountain**. The view is breathtaking, with Aspy Bay, the harbours of three small fishing villages and Cape Smoky. After a long coastal stretch, the road heads inland ("Buck's Turn"). To your right a short way in a dirt road leads to a side-trip described below. Stay left for Meat Cove.

SIDE TRIP- Bay St. Lawrence: Isolated from the homogenizing effects of the Cabot Trail, Bay St. Lawrence was one of the last places to give up the Gaelic language. St. Lawrence Bay is a magnificent place for a stop on a day trip from Cape North, or on the way to Meat Cove.

SIDE TRIP- Money Point: Have you had enough of this wild country, or could you take something even wilder? Something adventurous? Perhaps a hike to Money Point is in order. There are two ways to reach the starting point at the top of the mountain. Both are brutal. The first is the road you passed after turning inland. This road heads up onto a plateau, with views of both St. Lawrence Bay, and the Atlantic Ocean. The other way is to take the trail at the end of the road at Bay St. Lawrence and then somehow grind up the extremely steep road to the top. If you thought the view on the hill up gave you vertigo, on top, it is dizzying. Extremely powerful winds can make you feel like you'll be blown down into Bay St. Lawrence. The roads meet at the Canadian National Microwave Station. On a very clear day, it is actrually possible to see Prince Edward Island , and the horizon of Newfoundland! A steep path goes down the other side to the Atlantic, to Money Point lighthouse.

The last few kilometres of the tour are over a series of large climbs. While not of Cabot Trail magnitude, they still are a fair work-out. Along the way, rarely will you lose sight of the ocean. The road turns to dirt just past Capstick, making your final segment into Meat Cove even more demanding.

28.7 (17.8)	**Meat Cove- A Name You Can't Ignore:** Even Meat Cove's name brings a multitude of stories, all extreme. Locals say the name comes from the trading of deer meat with passing ships. Another is a more grisly tale. It is said bands of rebel hunters roamed this part of Cape Breton to hunt caribou. The beasts were driven off the high cliffs and skinned, leaving their bodies on the shore (this behaviour is perhaps why the caribou is now extinct in Nova Scotia).

In 1968, the government decided the people of Meat Cove would be better off relocated in Baddeck (one rumour why was to clear away rudimentary homes for good impressions for tourists, another a bit more insinuating). About 50 people resisted and continue to enjoy living at "the top of Nova Scotia". If you wanted a few minutes of peace and quiet this summer, here is a place to find it.

A walking trail starts from Meat Cove and follows a fairly good path westward. You can actually come out all the way at the Gulf of St. Lawrence side (Lowland Cove). To find it simply continue from the end of the road.

RETURN the same route back

58.0 (36.1)	END Cape North

Accommodation

MacDonald's Motel and Cabins Mrs. A. J. Morrison, Cape North, R.R. #1, Dingwall, NS B0C 1G0, (902) 383-2054.
Markland Inn Charles MacLean Dingwall, NS B0C 1G0, (902) 383-2246. Log suites, outdoor pool.
Oakwood Manor Bed and Breakfast Sharon McEvoy, P.O. Box 19, Dingwall, NS B0C 1G0, (902) 383-2317 Short distance from Cape North, near Aspy River

Camping

Meat Cove Campground Kenneth A. McLellan, Meat Cove, NS B0C 1E0, (902) 383-2379. Rustic campground overlooking ocean. The McLellan family has lived in the cove for six generations, and know just about all there is to know about the trails and history of the area.

The Nova Scotia Bicycle Book

Appendix

Oversights Most Often Made on Atlantic Canada Bicycle Vacations

1) Plans that are not realistic: The provinces of Atlantic Canada seem small compared with the rest of Canada. In terms of bicycling, however, they are large indeed and surpass in size many European countries. A common sight is that of bicycle tourists rushing along on major highways, bypassing great cycling routes to "catch up" with their plans. They can also be spotted in bus terminals, making hasty arrangements for transportation to their intended destinations.

Acquaint yourself with the scale of the region. It is 648 km (403 miles) from Yarmouth, Nova Scotia to the Cabot Trail. That's the most direct route, A to B. Nova Scotia's shoreline weaves along for many times that! Plan on your routes here being "twisty" and longer than expected. Maps can not show the many inlets that roads must weave in and out of, extending the distance. Count on at least one day per week with heavy rain and one in three with some period of precipitation.

Roads are not well signposted in many areas. Expect occasional wrong turns if using backroads. Plan for a relaxed itinerary- do not worry about 'wasting time" - in accordance with Parkinson's Law, any alloted spare time will be matched with encountered delays.

2) Not Seeing the Real Nova Scotia: The best places are often those off the main roads. You at times find them at dead-ends, at the end of peninsulas, or up and over small ridges. Too many visiting cyclists stay on the well-travelled trunk roads, returning with memories of a place not too much different from what they left at home. Save some time to explore, even "backtracking", if need be and see the real Nova Scotia!

3) Unprepared Bikes: Human nature suggests for us to do what is easiest- with maintenance of our bicycles it means fixing them "later" or "when we get there." Few towns in Atlantic Canada are blessed with bicycle shops. Many of the stores that do exist have only the basics. Those shops which can do serious repairs are booked solid during summer months. Priority is usually given to tourists with breakdowns at most shops, however, even then there may be backups since the province is a popular bicycle touring destination. Do your repairs, check-ups and purchasing of new parts before you leave home.

It is also common to meet cyclists with breakdowns and hear: "My bike just had a check-up", or "I don't understand, that's a brand new wheel." Do your repairs in time to find out if the job was done right. Don't wait until you get to Nova Scotia to find out your mechanic had a bad day!

4) Lack of Clothing: Pleasant cycling temperatures and ocean breezes provide Nova Scotia its perfect biking environment. Evenings here, unlike more southern or inland areas, cool down. In addition, when it rains the air can be quite chilly. Extra clothes are recommended.

5) Atlantic Canada is NOT Flat: For some reason, perhaps because of its closeness to the shore, visitors arrive with the impression there will be few hills. Prepare yourself to encounter rolling terrain, mostly anywhere in the province.

Cycling in Nova Scotia

Scenic Trails

Nova Scotia was among the first places to begin naming highways as "Trails" for tourism purposes. The Cabot Trail, Evangeline Trail and Sunrise Trail were among the first. They proved so successful, that places not covered have seen tourism pass them by. The province is now saturated with "scenic trails", with no doubt more on the way. To the visitor it is now impossible to detect which are the result of outstanding natural beauty or interest from what is the result of an agressive chamber of commerce.

• Many of the trails were designated when they were the only paved road in the area. Since that time, other roads have been paved, many a lot more scenic and conducive to cycling.

• Much like laying track of railroads a long time ago, every community with as much as a hot dog stand demands a trail to pass through their town. Some trails seem therefore to "connect the dots" to every possible place, to encourage spending as much time (money) in that area as posible. They often bypass incredible cycling country. For example, the Evangeline Trail moves non-stop through the Annapolis Valley on highway #1. Now that the scenic road along the shore of the Bay of Fundy is paved, it will be next to impossible to wrest away the trail from towns on route, which have become dependant on tourism.

Operating Hours

Before you head into the countryside, inquire regarding opening times of points of interest you plan to visit. Many museums are volunteer operated, or dependant on periodic grants. Hours of operation vary.

Food

In Nova Scotia, when going anywhere off the main roads, be prepared to find villages without food supplies. In small communities, stores find it hard to survive, opening and going out of business at a quick rate. If you plan to camp, or stay in what could be a small place a small community, buy your food before arrival. The worst that will happen is that you will carry the weight of your food a bit further than necessary.

Resting Places

The province of Nova Scotia operates close to 30,000 acres worth of forested parks, beaches, seascapes and heritage sites. Close to 120 sites welcome cyclists to rest, hike, swim, or learn of their surroundings. The cost is free! They range from a single picnic table by the roadside, to full-sized wildlife parks and hiking trials. For an overnight fee, 21 of them offer camping facilities.

Many service groups maintain facilities for residents and tourists. they are often found at old schoolhouses, churhgrounds and community halls. Remember- they are operated by volunteers, so keep their work to a minimum.

Nova Scotia Traffic

* Halifax and Dartmouth:
The area surrounding the twin cities of Halifax and Dartmouth and to a much lesser extent
our other urban centres are a world apart from the peaceful roads of rural Nova Scotia.
During week-day commuting hours, heavy traffic heads into Halifax and Dartmouth from
outlying areas from 7:00 a.m. until about 9:00 a.m. You are better off heading in before or
after the rush.

Conversely, the outbound rush leaving the cities is from 4:00 until about 6:00 pm. After 8
hours of work (and no doubt countless cups of coffee), motorists are both tired and irritable.
This is the period of most impatience and disrespect in traffic.

Split by a huge harbour, special logistics must be taken into consideration when moving
about the "metro" region. Two bridges span the gap, each with "cyclist unfriendly" attitudes
and restrictions. There are also two ferries plying the gap, much more accomodating to
cyclists.

* Weekend pleasure driving:
"The Complete Guide To Bicycling in Canada" suggests "the road from Halifax to Chester is
great for a hot summer weekend". I must suggest an opinion exactly the opposite. Try not
to cycle coastal areas near *any* large cities on hot weekends! Peggy's Cove, and beach areas
such as Lawrencetown and Hubbards have a fair amount of "cruising" by motorists during
warm months. Just as anywhere else in North America, a small minority of passengers on
these "pleasure drives" feel cyclists are part of the entertainment. If you must enter Halifax/
Dartmouth on a weekend, try to head in early (before 9 am) or hope for an overcast day.

* Sydney/ Industrial Cape Breton:
Most of Cape Breton's population live amid a cluster of towns along its south-east coast
known as Industrial Cape Breton. With close to 30% unemployment, rush hour in the area
isn't what it used to be. With several nodes of population rather than one however, it means
cars are going in no particular pattern. There is a fair amount of shift work, which brings
brief, but long lines of cars. Expect "industrial strength" highway manners. There are only
a few serious cyclists among the region's 100,000 population. The area is in some ways
seems a decade (or two) behind, motorists have had less experience sharing roads with
cyclists. A rowdy atmosphere prevails at night, with a "muscle car" circuit, "burning rubber"
between Sydney Mines and Glace Bay.

* Annapolis Valley:
The area between Wolfville and Berwick on highway #1, is cramped enough at the best of
times. At commuting hours, it is best to take alternate side roads, such as through Port
Williams.

Bicycle Legal Requirements

In condensed form, edited for readability, the following is a review of laws pertaining to bicycles in Nova Scotia. Classified as a vehicle in Nova Scotia, as the operator of a bicycle, you have the same rights and restrictions as that of a motor vehicle, with these additions:

Section   **Chapter 293 of the Revised Statutes, 1989 Amended 1990.**

2 (c)   "Bicycle" means a device propelled by human power upon which or in which a person may ride and which has two tandem wheels either of which is 350 millimetres or more in diameter or which has four wheels any two of which are 350 millimetres or more in diameter but does not include a wheelchair.

50   No person shall deface or alter bicycle serial or identification numbers.

169 (1)   It is an offence to carry any other person on handle-bar or frame.

169 (2)   It is an offence for any person to attach person or bicycle to any other moving vehicle.

171 (1)   Bicyclists must not proceed by inertia momentum, with feet removed from the pedals. They must not remove both hands from the handle-bars while riding the bicycle nor practice any trick or fancy riding.

171 (2)   No person shall ride a bicycle, tricycle, or similar machine on a sidewalk. (Except children in a public square, park, city, or town).

171 (3)   Bicycles must be ridden as near as practicable to the extreme right of the main travelled portion of the highway and no person shall ride a bicycle abreast of or generally parallel to another bicycle in motion on the highway except for the purpose of passing another bicycle.

172 (6)   Every bicycle shall be equipped with a front light visible under normal conditions from a distance of at least 100 meters in front of the bicycle.

183 (5)   Every bicycle shall be equipped with a reflex mirror or light on the rear exhibiting a red light visible under normal conditions from a distance of at least 60 meters to the rear of the bicycle.

305 (1A)   Every bicycle shall be equipped with a bell or horn in good working order. It shall be an offence for any person to use any siren or whistle.

The council of a municipality may make regulations or by-laws regulating and licensing bicycles owned by residents of the city, town, or municipality.

In case of an accident:

1. Call the police IMMEDIATELY
2. Do not move any vehicle
3. Do not attempt to move any injured persons
4. Obtain the following:
   --Name and address of all involved vehicle operators
   --License plate numbers/ registration numbers
   --Name and address of all involved insurance companies
   --Name and address of all witnesses
5. Request police follow up
6. Request a copy of the accident report

Additional Rules:

* Bicycles are restricted from some controlled access highways
* Some bridge crossings are also restricted
* All traffic signs, signals and traffic control devices must be obeyed
* Bicycles must stop at all railroad crossings
* Cyclists must stop for a police officer desiring to inspect the bicycle
* Standard arm signals are used to alert motorists or pedestrians of your direction (Extended right arm is not officially accepted as legal for a right turn. People will know what you mean however!),
* Yield for pedestrians
* Move to the right and stop for emergency vehicles
* Stop for school busses when warning lights are flashing
* Pass vehicles only on the left
* You must stop and assist if first upon the scene of an accident
* In rare cases you must assist if on the scene of other emergency

Restricted roads

All Nova Scotia's roads which are restricted to cyclists are in the Halifax area. They are few in number, and although a hindrance for local residents are not ones bicycle tourists would want to normally use anyway.

Bedford By-Pass; from Exit 1 on highway #101 toward Dartmouth to highway #7
#101 Bedford to Middle Sackville; from Exit 1 to 2
#102 Halifax to Sackville; from Exit 1 to 4
#111 Circumferential Highway: Ring road circling Dartmouth; bicycles banned on rush hours only

Major Bridges, Causeways

From- To	Name	Conditions
Halifax-Dartmouth	MacDonald Bridge	Bicycles restricted to sidewalk and must be walked
Halifax-Dartmouth	MacKay Bridge	No bicycles allowed
Port Hastings- Auld Cove	Canso Causeway	Proceed with extreme caution! At times moderately quiet, at others busy, with high truck traffic. Road has no shoulder. Make yourself visible to lumber trucks- they may have logs sticking out further than the driver realizes! Leave space between yourself and the guardrail, In the event you are squeezed too close you will then have breathing room to move over into.
Pictou- Trenton	Pictou (Veniot) Causeway	Stay single file. Exercise caution when pausing on causeway to view Cormorant nesting area.
Boulardrie Island	Seal Island Bridge	Trans-Canada Highway (#105); truck traffic.

Traffic Circles

There are 3 traffic circles (rotaries) in Nova Scotia; Halifax, Pictou and at the Cape Breton side of the causeway to Nova Scotia (Dartmouth has a "Parclo"). Entering vehicles must yield to those already in the circle. It is a good idea for cyclists to work out which exit they need before entering.

Bicycle Paths

Nova Scotia has no official bicycle paths. There is one small 10 km (6 mi.) system of "multi-use" paths" at Forest Hills, a Dartmouth suburb. Due to deterioration and glass build-up however, this can not be recommended. A recreation trail on an abandoned railway bed is being developed near Liverpool.

Off- Road Cycling

Old logging roads, deer paths, and trails blazed before European arrival make cycling off-road a pleasant experience. A map, compass, extra pair of socks and some food are all you'll need to discover the interior of Nova Scotia. Wander through forest paths. Come across an old settler's farm, logging camp, or old gold mines. Hilltop clearings give incredible views of the ocean. You will come across many streams and lakes, many briming with fish. Shorelines offer entirely different experiences. Peninsulas reaching into the ocean skirt cliffs. Salt marshes and tidal flats, revealing driftwood and mysterious remnants of a longtime fishing industry.

Some consider "rough-stuff" anything other than smooth pavement. Others don't mind trails with tree roots, streams, and occasional walking. "Mountain" biking is an activity of growing interest. Outside urban areas, however, it is far more likely you will encounter users of all-terrain motor vehicles. Bicycle/ hiker conflicts are relatively unknown here. Concerns have arisen only over areas of heavy usage, meaning our two National Parks, and occasionally Cape Split, near Blomidon. To this point, far more confrontation occurs over the coffee tables of sport bureaucrats than ever does on a trail.

* Few signposted trails exist, so 50,000 scale topographical maps are recommended. Telling someone where you're going won't hurt.

* There are few well marked, and maintained routes. Paths and cart-tracks, however, seem to be everywhere.

* Land Ownership You are permitted to go on any property, unless it is signposted "No Trespassing" or told to leave. Note: some persons have been known to put signs up on land not theirs.

* Insect repellant may be needed from May to the end of August. Bugs can be especially bad if there has been a mild winter. Coastal routes can have less insects than inland.

* Off-road motorized vehicles (A.T.V's) are registered and operators must act in a responsible manner.

* Where work is put into maintaining trails, or providing maps, it is suggested to offer a small donation to show you appreciate the use of their services and land.

* Don't forget not to cycle in any sand dunes. They are actually quite delicate and can be easily destroyed. In addition, colonies of birds, some endangered species, nest in them.

Selected Off-Road Routes

Annapolis Valley

*Upper Clements Wildlife Park
Provincial Map Code: K3
Location: Highway 1 between Annapolis Royal and Digby
Distance: 7 km (4.3 mi.)
Trails: 2 loop trails through woods from the parking lot

*Old Orchard Inn
Provincial Map Code: H5,6
Topographical: 21 H 11 (Trails not shown on map)
Location: Near exit 11 of the #101 at Wolfville (Tours A-5 to A-10)
Distance: 20 km (12 mi.)
Trails: A series of 5 trails, groomed for cross-country skiing through woods and fields. Owned by Old Orchard Inn.

South Shore

*Kejimkujik National Park
Provincial Map Code: L3, 4
Location: Near Maitland Bridge, half way between Liverpool and Annapolis Royal on Highway #8
Distance and Trails: Long trails run deep into the interior from the park boundaries (no trails for cyclists in park itself).
Reception Centre (902) 682-2772

*Municipal Activity and Recreation Complex
Provincial Map Code: L5
Location: Off #3 (LeHave Tour) Turn left at Leary Fraser Rd. by Snyder Shipyard.
Distance: 7 km (4.2 mi.)
Trails: Well used ski trails on varying terrain. Area is quite close to Bridgewater.
A map is available. 543-1354

Metro Halifax

*Bowaters Trails
Provincial Map Code: K6
Location: Off #3 at Head of St. Margaret's Bay, cross #103 to the entrance. The parking lot and trail are a further 3 km (2mi.).
Trails: Countless loops and roads throughout interior of province.
Note: This is an active forest management area, so only weekend use is permitted.

*Kearney Lake
Provincial Map Code: K7
Topographical: 11D/ 12
Location: Off Kearney Lake Road, (near exit 2 on highway #102) Turn onto road along lake near exit. Trails begin by Maskwa
Rowing Club.
Distance: 15 km (9 mi.)
Trails: Well- used system of trails and dirt roads. Varied terrain; some routes colour coded. Used by city area mountain bikers.

*Lake Echo Trails
Provincial Map Code: K8
Topographical: 11D/ 11
Location: 11 and 25 km (7 and 16 mi.) east of Dartmouth
Between Preston and Porter's Lake is a network of hiking trails in various conditions. Another trail, reached from the very north end
of Porter's Lake, at the end of the road north along Porter's Lake is possible to cycle all the way to highway #212.
Distance: 30 km (18 mi.)
Trails: Series of fire roads

*McNab's Island
Provincial Map Code: K7
Topographical:11D/ 12
Location: In Halifax Harbour
Distance: 30 km (18 mi.)
Trails: Tracks and paths throughout island. Within forest, yet at times in sight of downtown Halifax.

Northern

*Wentworth Hostel
Provincial Map Code: F7
Topographical: 11 E 12
Location: At Wentworth Station, close to exit #9 on Highway #104 and off road from Collingwood/ Springhill (Tour N-4)
Distance: 60 km (36 mi.)
Trails: An extensive system of 16 trails in the Cobequid Hills. Maintained for cross-country skiing, this is perhaps the best off-road
biking area in the Nova Scotia. Connected to the Wentworth Hostel. An additional 15 trails are nearby, off highway #104, owned by
Ski Wentworth. Groomed for cross-country skiing, they are found at the top of the ski lift. Both systems are located in a hilly region.

*Spiddle Hill
Provincial Map Code: F8 G8
Topographical: 11E/ 11
Location: Off Highway #311 at Earltown, or #256 at Balmoral Mills (Tour N-3)
Distance: 11 km (6.6 mi.)
Trails: 2 trails groomed for cross-country skiing. Very hilly area.

Eastern

*Taylors Head Provincial Park
Provincial Map Code: K10
Topographical: 11 A 15
Location: Off Highway #7 on dirt road past Spry Bay, west of Sheet Harbour
Distance: About 10 km (6.1 mi.)
Trails: Various looped and one-way trails from beach.

*Beaver Mountain Park
Provincial Map Code: G11
Location: Exit 30, 16 km (10 mi.) west of Antigonish; 3.2 km (2mi.) south of #104. Dirt road into park
Distance: 6 or 3 km (3.6 or 1.8 mi.)
Trails: Groomed for cross-country skiing, one large loop passes an active beaver colony, while a short-cut passes fields being
reclaimed by forests.

Cape Breton

*Cape Breton Highlands National Park
Provincial Map Code: B14, 15
Location: Along Cabot Trail (Tour CB-7) at far north end of province.
Distance Over 100 km (60 miles)
Trails: Most of the system is reserved for the enjoyment of hikers. Some trails are open, ask at centre which are currently open to
cycling. It makes sense to check in, since it an a large park of extremely dense woods. Expect wet ground. Good chances of seeing
wildlife! Visitor Centre (902) 224-3403

Preparation

Your Bike

Any bike that moves will bring you pleasure. The simplicity of one and 3 speed bikes should not to be swept aside for the sake of new technology. Remember- cycle touring has existed for over a hundred years. Roads in much worse condition were pedalled (including the Cabot Trail) before gears were even invented!

For most, efficiency is desired at the cost of complication. Bicycles with 15 and more speeds will provide you with efficient gears for Nova Scotia's rolling hills. The choice between a road bike or a "mountain bike" is a personal one. Mountain or "off-road" bikes cover less distance in a day. Many people consider them comfortable, despite fewer hand posistions. Others find them good for riding with physical ailments such as back or bottom soreness. They generally have fewer flat tires. Perhaps most important, you can explore places road bikes dare to tread. You can feel free to putter about on fishing wharfs, seacoast trails, or forest tracks. Road bikes however, will take you over a lot more ground per day. There appears to be an even split between both types among cycle-tourists in Nova Scotia.

If you are planning a long trip, it is always worth having your bike overhauled before you leave home. If at all possible- do so before late spring, when bike shops are swamped with work. The best time is in the winter when your bike will receive a great deal more time and attention to detail. This will also allow you to test run your bike to be sure everything has been put back where it should.

Horror Story

A Californian couple for years had wished for a bicycle trip around Nova Scotia. Finally their long wait was over, and they eagerly prepared for their journey. They made sure to have their two-seater bike (tandem) given a check-up. They even had their back wheel re-spoked as it was getting old. Into their second day's ride, in an isolated forested area, their new back wheel collapsed! The mechanic had made what seemed a routine procedure of replacing the spokes. However- their bike was a mid-seventies model that required larger than normal spokes. The hub's holes were therefore also larger and the new replacement spokes pulled through, while under stress on a major hill. With the nearest bicycle shop 250 kilometres (150 miles) away, and no spares available there which would work anyway, they were faced with at least a one-week wait for a repair job.

Don't go far afield with a new bike without first test- touring it. Take it for a run or two, packed if possible. Get it tuned up after the initial "settling" of threads and stretching of cables.

Rubbed Raw! - Saddle Considerations

Use a padded saddle (not a plastic one). Most bikes sold come with men's seats. Anatomically designed saddles for women are available. Some shops will tell their customers they are "generic", (perhaps meaning they have none available to sell). Be sure to well use any new saddle before you begin your vacation. Once soreness has developed on a tour little can be done except end it, or ride in discomfort (unless you like riding "rubbed raw"). Baby powder and in an emergency, vaseline, will reduce saddle sores and perhaps save your trip.

Padding your saddle until it becomes a sofa will give you a comfortable ride. Don't however expect to cover much ground. Mountain bike saddles have a fair amount of protection while still having some claim of efficiency. "Spring" saddles do not have such claims, but have been known to extend daily distances dramatically, or make the same distance you do more comfortable.

Toe Clips

Toe Clips are pedal "covers" which fasten onto your pedals to increase efficiency (you pedal up -as well as down). Use these well before you face the distractions of touring. Leave them loose, almost non- functional, and over time tighten them until they seem comfortable.

Tires

You can manage the province's roads if you prefer narrow tires. With are only a few urban areas, there are not many grates and other tire catchers. Having beefier tires, however, will take you down country lanes, through unexpected road construction and all the elements which make up bicycle touring. 32 or 35mm (1 1/4 to 13/8 are still traditional sized touring tires. Mountain bikes come set up for the roughest of conditions. Under 2" will be a good balance to tour Nova Scotia with an off-road bike.

European cyclists are advised to bring a spare tire and tube as North American sizes are often different, and you could waste valuable cycling time looking for a bicycle shop with what you want. The new mountain bikes are fairly standardized.

Sample Tool Kit

* air pump   * spare inner tubes
* patch kit   * tire irons
* 8, 9, and 10 mm wrenches   * 4, 5 and 6 mm allen keys
* spare derailleur cable   * spare brake cable
* lubricant   * spare derailleur cable
* small 10-15 mm (4-6 inch) adjustable wrench
* assorted nuts, bolts, washers, and twist-ties
* few spare spokes (4 -6)- freewheel (gear) side are different length than other, so bring both.
* small amount of duct tape- perfect temporary solution for almost unimaginable numbers of breakdowns- from loose racks to even some tube and tire emergencies.
* Wire/ twist ties. (Another temporary aid) Note: remember to not treat quick fixes as solutions- get breakdowns fixed properly.

Mid-tour is perhaps not the time to start learning bicycle maintenance. If you expect to be taking your bike for repair if you have a breakdown, then realize that these further items may only be taking up space and weight at the bottom of your bags.

* spoke wrench
* cone wrenches (for looseness in hubs)
* freewheel remover

Your Gear

*"The most beautiful things in the world are those from which all excess weight has been eliminated" --
Henry Ford I, 1893*

Remember once again, cycle touring has existed for a long time. You can survive without specialized gear, but at the cost of saddle and hand sores, and less efficiency. Cycling in Nova Scotia requires not much different gear than for other places. You must have some insect repellent, if you plan to camp before mid-August.

Another urge would be to bring warm clothing. Visitors are pleasantly surprised how evenings cool down here. Be prepared as well for cool evenings and days with damp fog. Rain gear is also recommended.

Helmet Head injuries account for over 75% of all bicycling related fatalities. Head protection could save your life.

Yourself

Identification: U.S.A.: Passports or visas are not required for entry. You must have however some type of official identification, such as a driver's license. Those who are young or tend to draw attention from unconservative appearance may escape some border interrogation if they can show a recent work pay cheque stub.

Insurance: If you are not a Nova Scotian, make sure your coverage includes the provinces you will be cycling in.

Planning Resources

Books

Bicycle Tours in Nova Scotia

This 48 page booklet covers 19 cycling tours throughout Nova Scotia. Close to twenty years have passed since its production. Time has not fared well for a few of its listed tours, although at being a booklet its small price makes it a "can't lose" gamble. $7.00 incluing postage **A**, **B**

Maps

Provincial Highway Map

Nova Scotia's highway map shows just about all of the province's paved roads. Unlike most provincial and state maps, the Nova Scotian road map is a functional guide to use for cycle-touring. There are 2 primary reasons. First, the population is relatively low and therefore, so is the road density. Secondly, the province is mostly settled around the coast, leaving the interior mostly undeveloped. The only exception is the Annapolis Valley, where the number of small lanes can not be accurately depicted, or at times folowed.

Note: Map makers cannot stand blank spaces. Every piece of the map appears to contain communities. province seems to be represented on the map. Inland, spots with as little as a handful of people are represented, in a few cases, abandoned mill sites, pioneer homesteads, or mines. When you are planning to take runs through the interior, remember that many names on the map are just that, and the ice cold cola you are waiting for, or shelter from the elements may not be there up the road. Source: Free of charge **C**

National Topographic System of Maps

1 -50,000 scale: These are the ultimate for exploring. A series of maps, which covers all of Canada, they show every road, river, orchard, power line, dirt track, church, cemetery and other prominent roadmark. Contours are also shown. On the down side, they take you 40 kilometres (25miles) before you find yourself off the map area. At over $8.00 CDN each, the cost goes up quickly, and for a long route, they can take up valuable pannier space. They are highly recommended if you plan for a several day stay in one area. **D**

1-250,000 scale: These are the same type of map, except they cover a larger area with of course less detail. The stretch across is about 160 Kilometres (100 miles). They give a good overall view of the elevation, land use and road density. They fail as a compromise between the provincial road map and 50,000 scale topographics. While useful as an overall planner, navagation is not practical. **D**

Tourism Information

Nova Scotia Travel Guide

The thick and informative Nova Scotia Travel Guide is considered one of the finest government tourism publications anywhere. It is jam-packed with information and best of all is free. It contains most general information needed to give a good overview of the province. Comprehensive listings are included of accomodations. keep in mind that directions and suggestions are primarily based on automobile travel and like any such promotional publication, will only mention the positive. Free of charge **C**

Check-Ins

Check-ins is a free reservation system for accomodations incliuding campgrounds. Information is also available on festivals and events, exchange rates and up to date ferry schedules. Suite 515, 21800 Argyle St. Halifax, N.S. B3J 3N8

Canada 1-800-565-0000   Continental USA 1-800-341-6096
Maine 1-800-492-0643 Halifax Dartmouth 425-5781

Nature/ Environment

The Flora of Nova Scotia
A listing of all outr native plants.748 pages

In Forest and Field
Essays on plant life 52 pages

Natural History of Nova Scotia
Huge, complete volume covering everything natural; on the land or in the water. 736 pages

Natural History Map of Nova Scotia
Colourful map covering wildlife, geology and landscapes, including facts on our climate and vegetation.

Summer Key to Woody Plants in Nova Scotia
A listing source with illustrations of the trees and shrubs of Nova Scotia

Source (all of above) D

Miscellaneous

Hiking Trails of Nova Scotia
Hiking Trails in Cape Breton Highlands
Nova Scotia's Nordic Ski Trails
These guides intended for are hiling and skiing the province's trails offer suggestions for off-road riding. Trails are of varying conditions.

Houses of Nova Scotia
A field guide to help identify and date Nova Scotia houses. Includes chronological guide, illustrations and glossary- 148 pages

Nova Scotia Resource Atlas
For those who have to know everything about an area. Chart lovers will be in heaven as information is displayed in easy to read diagrams. Included are layouts of population, land use ,forest cover, minerals, wildlife habitat, fisheries, manufacturing and geological zones.

Silent Steeds
Heather Watt's history of the bicycle in Nova Scotia, from introduction to the Great Bicycle Boom

Tracing your Ancestors
Introduction to the archives, procedures and materials involved with geneology in Nova Scotia. 15 pages.

Source (all of above) D

Sources: *Demand for materials in spring and summer and mailing time to the U.S.A.and other foreign countries requires mail orders be made several weeks ahead. Prices not listed due to periodic increases*

A Atlantic Canada Cycling Festival P.O. Box 1555 Station M Halifax, Nova Scotia B3J 2Y3

B Bicycle Nova Scotia P.O. Box 3010 S. Halifax, Nova Scotia B3J 3G6

C Nova Scotia Tourism P.O. Box 4563010 S. Halifax, Nova Scotia B3J 2R5

D Nova Scotia Government Bookstore P.O. Box 637 1700 Granville St.Halifax, Nova Scotia B3J 2T3 (902) 424-7580. Catalogue with other selections available.

When To Go

Almost an island, Nova Scotia is influenced by the sea. Within this land you experience several micro-environments. The Annapolis Valley is the warmest part, the Sunrise Trail (Northern) region the sunniest, Cape Breton, particularly around Cabot Trail, the wettest and coolest.

The coast is on average 4- 6 degrees Celcius cooler than inland. The last frost ranges on average from May 2 in Yarmouth, to May 23 in Sydney. In Fall, the first frost arrives on October 16 in Sydney to the 24th in Yarmouth.

Spring is not gentle. Cold winter winds linger. Blossoms are beaten to the ground before they can finish bloom. What is considered the rainy season ends in June, but it seems everybody who spends a week or so on the road gets wet. Mid-Summer overnight lows average about 12 C (54 F) and daytime highs usually don't exceed 28 C (80 F) degrees. While riding in the rain, wool garments probably won't be enough to keep you comfortable, so a rain-repellent shell will be welcome.

Nova Scotia is the stormiest place in Canada! Several batterings hit the region annually. Although less prevalent in summer, when storms do occur the winds are ferocious, the air thick with salt water, whipped up off the sea. Every year both visitors, and locals who should know better are lost forever as they "storm watch" at lighthouses or beaches. Waves can be as high as 14 metres (45 feet). When you hear a storm warning, believe it!

The wettest part of the province is in the highlands of Cape Breton. It is belted with 1600 mm (630 inches) of annual precipitation. The South Shore is runner-up, experiencing 1500 mm (590 inches). In contrast, Northern Nova Scotia (aptly named the Sunrise Trail) encounters less than 1000 mm (390 inches). Most years see plenty of rain. Occasionally however, every 7 to 10 years brings a drought, to which Nova Scotia's delicate water table is rapidly affected. While having no rain offers perfect cycling conditions, it may create havoc with your plans, as many campgrounds and parks must close due to fire hazards.

After Newfoundland, Nova Scotia is perhaps the foggiest place in North America. In the Spring and early Summer, cool air above the current from Labrador meets moisture-laden air from the Gulf Stream. The result is sea fog, which drifts in off the Atlantic. Yarmouth, and Canso are among the foggiest places on earth, each with around 110- 120 days per year with some period of mist.

	April		May
Climate:	Wet	Climate:	Spring: Cool days/ cold nights
Precipitation:	Snowfalls/ cold rain	Precipitation:	Rainy season, surprise snowfalls early in month
Wind:	Raw gales with strong gusts. Cape Breton and Northern N.S. encounter winds off ice in the Gulf of St. Lawrence	Wind:	Brisk winds: cool air
Traffic:	Normal- no tourists	Traffic	Normal, except for Victoria Day weekend (3r week)
Accommodation:	Most campgrounds, some B+B's and motels not open; off-season rates	Accommodation:	Campgrounds and some B+B's/ motels not open until 3rd week; shoulder-season prices
Off-road:	Expect deep snow or mud	Off-road:	Lingering snow in woods, muddy conditions; good time to spot young animals such as baby deer
Insects:	None, unless mild Winter	Insects:	Quite bad; Black Fly season begins mid-mont
Comments:	Some nice days for cycling, however- too great a chance of snowfalls or cold days. Frost at night (especially in Cape Breton Highlands); gets dark quite early; before tourist season- peace and quiet at attractions/ museums etc (some not open); cheaper ferry prices; dirt roads are in poor shape; no foilage; too early to recommend- but if here for other reasons bring your bike	Comments:	Unpredictable- Rapid change from winter to summer. Beautiful days interspersed with late snowfalls or cold rains. Autumn recommended over spring. Before tourist season-peace and quiet at attractions/ museums etc. (some may not be open); cheaper ferry prices; no foilage month. Water for swimming is cold; apple blossom season late in month.

June

Climate: "Spring"; Pleasant days/ cool nights
Precipitation: Dry at end of month
Wind: Moderate
Traffic: Less than July or August
Accommodation Busy
Off-road: Mud early in month
Insects: Overlapping of Blackfly and Mosquito seasons
Comments: Before heavy part of tourist season, evenings stay light until very late (almost 10 PM!) nights are chilly; water for swimming is cool. Lanscape still barren-until mid-month

July

Climate: Warm
Precipitation: Moderate
Wind: Moderate
Traffic Tourist season-- schools out-- families with camper trailers on road- higher traffic levels. Horrendous on Canada Day (July 1st) weekend.
Accommodation Very busy--full price/ limited space
Off-road: Pleasant- dry trails; occasional bans on entering woods due to danger of forest fires
Insects: Mosquito season
Comments: Summer finally arrives. Evenings stays light until late in evening; Other cyclists about. Late in month you can discover treasure troves of raspberries.

August

Climate: The warmest month- hot, but seldom overbearing,
Precipitation: Slightly wetter than July
Wind: Moderate, stronger toward end of month
Traffic: Tourist season-- schools out-families with camper trailers on road- higher traffic levels.
Accommodation Very busy- full price/ limited space
Off-road: Pleasant, dry trails; occasional bans on entering woods due to danger of forest fires
Insects: Mosquito season tapers off mid-month
Comments: Other cyclists about. Blueberry season; raspberries early in month; water is warm for swimming.

September

Climate: Cool to warm, but seldom hot
Precipitation: Moderate
Wind: Strong, cool winds
Traffic: "Normal" after Labour Day (1st weekend)
Accommodation Shoulder season- some campgrounds not open (cold nights for camping from mid-month) prices better than summer
Off-road: Pleasant- dry trails
Insects: Fewer than summer or spring.
Comments: Highly recommended time to visit Nova Scotia! Shoulder season... people are more relaxed and welcoming. You have the roads to yourself and people take an interest in who you are and what you are up to. Water is warm for swimming; cheaper ferry prices, shoulder season rates; peace and quiet at attractions/ museums etc.

October

Climate: Wide range, pleasant days to occasional storms (rain is cold water)
Precipitation: Wet- short-lived snowfalls late in month
Wind: Strong, on a few days nasty
Traffic: Normal-few tourists
Accommodation Most campgrounds closed, some B+B's; shoulder season rates
Off-road: Very pleasant, couloured leaves
Insects: None
Comments: Unpredictable; first 10 days or so can offer very pleasant cycling. Leaves change colour into spectacular hues of red, orange and yellow, and the air is fresh and clear. Off-season prices. Can be uncomfortable after mid-month, especially in Cape Breton. Annapolis Valley recommended-- plenty of spots to get warm if needed; protected from winds; harvest activity.

November

Climate: Cold (frost at night)
Precipitation: Cold rain, snow possible
Wind: Vicious
Traffic: Normal
Accommodation Campgrounds not open; some B+B's closed; winter rates
Off-road: Hunting season: the woods are filled with the magical mixture of liquor, pickup trucks and guns. Expect anything- from friendly offers of a drink, to physical confrontation.
Insects: None:
Comments: Occasional good late fall days- overall uncomfortable and too unpredictable to recommend- If visiting for other reasons bring your bike- you should get in a few short day trips. It gets dark very early (5:00 PM!); cheaper ferry prices, peace and quiet at attractions/ museums etc.

Average High and Low Temperatures

		April	May	June	July	August	Sept.	Oct.
1. South-West	C	9.3 / 0.6	15.5 / 5.5	20.2 / 10.1	23.2 / 13.4	22.4 / 12.9	18.9 / 9.2	13.6 / 5.3
	F	49 / 33	61 / 41	70 / 50	76 / 57	75 / 56	68 / 48	57 / 41
2. Annapolis Valley	C	9.1 / -0.3	16.2 / 4.7	21.8 / 9.9	25.0 / 13.0	24.3 / 12.7	19.7 / 8.6	13.8 / 4.1
	F	48 / 31	62 / 39	74 / 50	80 / 56	79 / 55	69 / 47	58 / 38
3. South Shore	C	8.6 / 0.6	14.3 / 4.8	19.3 / 9.5	22.8 / 12.9	22.6 / 13.0	19.2 / 9.3	14.0 / 4.8
	F	47 / 33	59 / 40	69 / 49	76 / 56	75 / 56	68 / 49	58 / 45
4. Metro Halifax	C	8.6 / 1.0	13.9 / 5.1	19.2 / 10	22.7 / 13.8	22.7 / 14.4	19.6 / 11.5	14.3 / 6.9
	F	47 / 32	58 / 40	68 / 50	75 / 58	76 / 59	69 / 53	59 / 44
5. Central	C	7.8 / -2.2	14.8 / 2.7	20.5 / 7.9	23.7 / 11.8	23.2 / 11.0	19.2 / 8.0	13.2 / 4.1
	F	16 / 28	60 / 36	71 / 17	77 / 54	76 / 53	68 / 46	56 / 38
6. Northern	C	7.8 / -1.7	14.8 / 3.8	21.4 / 9.7	24.8 / 13.5	24.0 / 13.0	20.0 / 8.8	14.0 / 4.0
	F	46 / 30	60 / 38	73 / 49	80 / 57	78 / 56	70 / 48	58 / 38
7. Eastern	C	7.3 / -1.5	14.2 / 3.3	20.1 / 9.5	23.4 / 14.1	23.0 / 13.7	19.1 / 9.4	13.2 / 5.1
	F	45 / 31	58 / 37	70 / 49	77 / 58	76 / 57	68 / 49	56 / 40
8. Cape Breton	C	5.7 / -2.3	12.2 / 2.6	18.8 / 7.9	22.3 / 12.0	21.8 / 11.9	17.5 / 7.6	12.3 / 3.0
	F	41 / 27	54 / 35	68 / 46	75 / 54	74 / 54	65 / 45	55 / 36

C = Celcius F= Farenheit

Humidity   Sunrise/ Sunset

	6 a.m. Average	3 p.m. Average	Morning	Evening
April	87	64	5:32	6:57
May	82	62	4:47	7:34
June	88	64	4:28	8:00
July	92	65	4:42	7:58
August	92	64	5:15	7:22
September	92	65	5:52	6:27
October	90	67	6:28	5:35

Information based on long-term averages, derived from data from Environment Canada
station at Halifax Airport 44° 53 N 63 °31W
Sunrise/ Sunset based on the 15th of the month

Precipitation

		April	May	June	July	August	Sept.	Oct.
1. South-West	Rain	85.1	101.2	88.7	93.6	102.1	102.8	114.5
	Snow	2.3	1.0	0.0	0.0	0.0	0.0	1.1
2. Annapolis Valley	Rain	59.8	82.1	75.6	70.0	102.1	86.7	101.0
	Snow	8.5	0.8	0.0	0.0	0.0	0.0	1.7
3. South Shore	Rain	85.5	94.8	84.7	78.0	93.8	89.0	102.1
	Snow	7.0	1.7	0.0	0.0	0.0	0.0	5.2
4. Metro Halifax	Rain	79.3	99.1	81.0	90.6	103.8	81.6	110.6
	Snow	13.5	2.3	0.0	0.0	0.0	0.0	1.0
5. Central	Rain	62.4	69.6	76.9	82.2	70.8	74.9	98.1
	Snow	17.6	1.8	0.0	0.0	0.0	0.0	1.5
6. Eastern	Rain	78.6	93.5	85.8	85.5	107.7	87.7	124.4
	Snow	23.2	3.0	0.0	0.0	0.0	0.0	3.3
7. Cape Breton	Rain	49.9	73.9	86.0	76.9	108.9	99.2	130.6
	Snow	44.7	6.7	0.0	0.0	0.0	0.0	2.5

In Millimetres
1 mm = .03937 inch

Wind Direction

"*May the roads rise with you and the wind be always at your back*" --Translated from a Gaelic blessing.

Being a coastal region, Nova Scotia is often frequented by strong gales. Shorelines can be barren, leaving you at the mercy of the winds. Summer is generally more gentle than spring or autumn.

Note that wind does not pick up until mid-morning. Influenced by ocean patterns, wind can change in late afternoon.

The following charts indicate the percentage of time you will find wind coming **from** each direction. Information is listed from readings taken at an Environment Canada station in a focal point of each region, such as Greenwood in the heart of the Annapolis Valley, or Cheticamp, on the temperamental Cabot Trail.

Wind Direction   April

	N	NE	E	SE	S	SW	W	NW	Calm
South-West	12.3	17.7	3.4	5.8	5.7	27.5	10.2	17.1	0.3
Annapolis Valley	10.0	14.8	8.1	3.7	6.4	13.1	12.5	9.3	9.3
South Shore	7.3	19.1	4.7	6.7	9.5	20.2	10.8	21.6	0.1
Metro Halifax	16.3	7.5	6.9	9.6	8.9	15.4	12.6	18.1	5.2
Central	14.5	11.0	12.5	9.6	7.9	8.5	21.4	9.7	4.9
Northern	12.0	12.0	4.1	9.6	11.5	17.9	10.5	22.2	0.2
Eastern	11.4	9.0	4.6	21.8	5.8	11.3	10.3	22.3	3.5
Cape Breton	17.8	8.0	7.1	6.7	13.4	16.2	15.6	13.1	2.1

Wind Direction   May

	N	NE	E	SE	S	SW	W	NW	Calm
South-West	9.9	18.8	4.2	6.6	4.6	39.8	4.9	10.9	0.3
Annapolis Valley	5.9	11.1	3.2	23.6	9.4	24.9	8.8	12.1	1.0
South Shore	6.1	18.9	5.2	5.2	13.0	30.3	7.8	13.4	0.1
Metro Halifax	14.8	4.1	4.4	12.4	15.2	20.1	10.4	12.2	6.4
Central	11.1	8.9	12.3	10.6	13.0	11.0	20.9	7.1	5.1
Northern	7.1	16.1	5.2	8.7	10.8	26.1	6.0	19.8	0.2
Eastern	10.7	10.2	5.7	28.1	7.4	12.2	6.2	17.9	1.6
Cape Breton	16.8	7.8	7.4	6.8	17.6	19.1	11.4	11.1	2.0

Wind Direction   June

	N	NE	E	SE	S	SW	W	NW	Calm
South-West	7.4	13.7	3.0	7.3	6.3	48.6	9.1	4.7	0.9
Annapolis Valley	3.5	6.9	2.5	21.8	11.4	32.9	9.1	10.6	1.3
South Shore	4.2	16.4	2.9	3.9	12.5	41.6	7.9	10.5	0.1
Metro Halifax	11.7	4.2	4.9	13.4	13.0	24.9	12.1	10.1	6.5
Central	8.9	6.7	8.6	8.8	13.5	15.7	26.4	5.3	6.1
Northern	7.4	12.5	4.9	13.0	22.1	29.3	3.8	6.9	0.1
Eastern	8.2	4.7	4.2	25.9	14.7	18.0	6.2	15.4	2.7
Cape Breton	12.2	6.6	6.2	6.7	22.0	27.2	10.3	6.2	2.6

Wind Direction July

	N	NE	E	SE	S	SW	W	NW	Calm
South-West	4.5	10.3	1.9	3.9	6.0	61.2	5.4	5.9	0.9
Annapolis Valley	2.1	3.9	3.1	16.7	14.0	40.3	10.4	7.9	1.6
South Shore	3.3	9.9	2.1	4.1	10.2	53.7	7.1	9.4	0.2
Metro Halifax	7.0	3.0	2.8	10.1	15.6	26.8	12.0	9.0	7.7
Central	5.0	4.8	8.1	9.9	16.4	17.0	26.8	4.4	7.6
Northern	11.6	6.2	2.8	5.0	14.2	36.3	16.4	13.2	0.3
Eastern	4.5	3.1	2.5	30.1	13.4	22.3	7.8	11.8	4.5
Cape Breton	7.3	4.6	5.3	6.3	24.7	30.9	12.6	5.3	3.0

Wind Direction August

	N	NE	E	SE	S	SW	W	NW	Calm
South-West	6.5	13.0	2.0	4.3	4.5	55.1	5.4	8.3	0.9
Annapolis Valley	2.8	3.9	3.3	17.3	11.1	41.0	9.7	8.6	2.3
South Shore	4.4	10.2	1.7	3.9	9.6	46.5	9.6	13.7	0.4
Metro Halifax	10.7	3.3	4.3	8.4	12.2	24.9	13.7	14.9	7.7
Central	5.3	4.8	9.3	8.4	14.0	17.8	27.6	5.3	7.5
Northern	6.8	9.6	2.9	6.0	19.8	25.4	17.4	11.5	0.6
Eastern	7.8	4.7	2.5	21.2	12.8	21.9	10.4	11.6	7.1
Cape Breton	7.5	5.0	4.9	5.5	20.6	31.3	15.6	6.9	2.7

Wind Direction   September

	N	NE	E	SE	S	SW	W	NW	Calm
South-West	7.9	14.2	1.6	5.9	5.6	43.7	5.7	14.3	1.1
Annapolis Valley	2.1	5.6	4.0	19.1	10.0	34.1	13.5	9.3	2.3
South Shore	6.7	14.8	3.5	6.5	9.4	28.2	10.2	20.5	0.2
Metro Halifax	10.2	6.1	4.9	7.6	8.2	24.8	13.9	16.8	7.5
Central	8.4	6.6	10.8	10.5	14.2	14.1	22.8	6.2	6.4
Northern	9.3	6.4	2.6	4.7	20.8	21.9	21.2	13.1	0.0
Eastern	9.0	2.3	2.1	18.9	8.5	18.3	12.4	21.1	7.4
Cape Breton	10.1	5.5	5.8	5.8	12.9	28.3	17.7	10.4	2.5

Wind Direction   October

	N	NE	E	SE	S	SW	W	NW	Calm
South-West	7.6	16.0	2.8	6.7	6.9	33.9	7.1	18.4	0.6
Annapolis Valley	4.3	6.1	2.8	19.0	10.6	32.6	12.6	10.8	1.2
South Shore	8.6	11.8	2.5	5.6	19.5	21.7	15.1	22.0	0.2
Metro Halifax	13.0	7.3	6.0	6.8	8.2	18.1	17.4	17.7	6.7
Central	8.7	6.6	10.5	8.7	10.8	14.5	24.2	8.5	7.5
Northern	9.6	4.4	3.1	8.5	19.1	20.2	21.0	13.9	0.2
Eastern	6.6	3.5	2.8	15.6	7.9	19.5	13.2	26.2	4.7
Cape Breton	10.4	6.2	4.4	6.5	16.7	23.9	17.9	12.1	1.6

Where To Stay

Bed and Breakfasts

The Cheshire Cat... the Gingham Dog... Bread & Roses- inviting names call you in off the road to cosy old homes and farms (who could resist a place called Waken n'Eggs)? Unlike predictable chain motels, no two bed and breakfasts are alike. All offer warm hospitality and reflect the character of the communities you will visit along the way. Expect a shared bathroom, and policies preferred by the hosts (bicycle storage, smoking, alcohol, etc.). In addition to the selection, included in this book, below are further listings..

Nova Scotia Travel Guide, c/o Nova Scotia Tourism; P.O. Box 456, Halifax, NS B3J 2R5
Cape Breton Bed and Breakfasts; P.O. Box 1750, Sydney, NS B1P 6T7
Nova Scotia Farm and Country Bed and Breakfast Association; Site 5, Box 16, R.R. 31, Elmsdale, NS B0N 1M0
Pictou County Tourist Assc.; 980 East River Rd., P.O. Box 782, New Glasgow, NS B2H 5G2 (902) 755-5180
South Shore Bed and Breakfast Assc.; 96 Cornwall Rd., P.O. Box 136, Blockhouse, NS B0J 1E0 (902) 624-8192
Unique Country Inns; 26 Dufferin St., P.O. Box 1407, Lunenburg, NS B0J 2C0; (902) 634-3963.

Hostels

Hostels have two special advantages: low cost and friendliness. They appeal to people of all ages, alone, and in groups. Standards and operating times vary greatly. To reduce costs, they are closed for part of the day and have a night curfew. They usually have a 3 night maximum and hostellers should bring sleeping bags. Some hostels have separate dorms for men and women. Some provide "family rooms" with advance reservation. Camping is allowed on some grounds. They operate on a self-help basis; hostellers may be asked to pitch in on light housekeeping duties. Short-term introductory memberships are available or you can pay a slight non-member surcharge each day. To make a reservation, send the hostel manager a deposit equal to the first night for each person. Check-in times are usually about 5 pm. Prices may be a bit higher than indicated- Note: Seasonal hostels tend to start-up or close operations frequently.

Canadian Hostelling Assc., 5516 Spring Garden Rd., P.O. Box 3010 South, Halifax, NS B3J 3G6, (902) 425-5450

1) Sandy Bottom Lake Hostel, Granville and Maggie Nickerson, R.R. #4, Annapolis Royal, NS B0S 1A0, (902) 532-2497; Year Round; Capacity: 10; Fees $8.00 members/ $10 non-members; Provincial Map Location: K3; Near South Milford, 1 1/2 to 2 hours biking from Annapolis Royal. Turn off Route #8 onto Virginia/ Bear River Road. Driveway is 3 km (2 mi.) on the right. Located on shore of lake. Has kitchen, shower, common room, basic groceries. Swimming, canoeing, wilderness exploring. Sleeping bags required.

2) Liverpool Hostel, P.O. Box 219, Liverpool, NS B0T 1K0, (902) 345-3533; Seasonal: Mid June- late August; Capacity: 15; Fees $5.00 members/ $8 non-members; Provincial Map Location: N5; In town of Liverpool. Located on Main St., showers, common room, and small kitchenette.

3) LaHave Marine Hostel, P.O. Box 92, LaHave, NS B0R 1C0, (902) 688-2908; Seasonal: Early June- October; Capacity: 8; Fees $8.00 members/ $10 non-members; Provincial Map Location: M5; In village of West LaHave, one hour cycling from Bridgewater, a bit longer from Lunenburg on Route 331, not far from the ferry from East LaHave. Kitchen, laundry facilities, common room, bakery.

4) Halifax International Hostel, 1253 Barrington St., Halifax, NS B3K 2Z4, (902) 422-3863; Year-round; Capacity: 50; Fees $11.45 members/ $13.75 non-members; Provincial Map Location: K7; Close to downtown Halifax, Downtown. Kitchen facilities, large common room, laundry. Bicycles may be locked in a special area. Reservations recommended as city hostels are busier than rural ones.

5) Wentworth Hostel, R.R. #1, Wentworth, NS B0M 1Z0, (902) 548-2379 Year-round; Capacity: 22 male, 20 female bunks; Fees $8.50 members/ $10.50 non-members; Provincial Map Location: F7; Near route #104 at Wentworth. Dining room, kitchen, common room. Great mountain biking area.

6) Glenmore International Hostel, R.R. #1, Whycocomagh, Twin Rock Valley, Cape Breton, NS B0E 3M0, (902) 258-3622; Year-round; Fees $7 members/ $9 non-members; Location: On Lake Ainslie, near route #104 at Wentworth. Dining room, kitchen, common room.

University Dorms

College campuses offer a good place to eat, rest and explore from. Funding raised from the renting of rooms in the off-season goes toward a good cause- keeping the cost of education accessible. Some of their cafeterias remain open during summer months, providing plenty of food at a good price. Most also offer some form of bicycle security. Inquire before confirming your stay. For discounts, ID must be shown.

* Acadia University, Wolfville, NS, B0P 1X0, (902) 542-2201. Rates +$22 per night plus tax.

* Technical University of Nova Scotia, O'Brien Hall Residence, 5217 Morris St., Halifax, NS, B3J 1B7. (902) 420-7780, (920) 422-2495- until mid-night; fax: (902) 420-7551. Rates $17 -$38 per night plus tax. Open May 1- August 31, 24 hour check-in, bicycle storage in residence. Downtown Halifax.

* Dalhousie University, 6136 University Ave., Halifax, NS B3H 4J2. (902) 494-8876; Rates: Campus $28 - $41.50 per night plus tax; includes breakfast, students $17.25- $29.25 plus tax , does not include breakfast. Fenwick Place: (Halifax's tallest building) minimum 3 night stay. 2 bedroom apt. $40; 3 bedroom apt. $60; Sharing apt. $21, students $18 Pleasant area of city.

* Saint Mary's University, 923 Robie St., Halifax, NS, B3H 3G2 (902) 420-5486, (920) 420-5591 (after 4); Rates $21 -$31 (twin) per night plus tax. May 15 to August 15. $21 ($31 twin) Weekly rates and discounts to students, seniors and groups. food services on-site; near Point Pleasant Park in attractive south end of Halifax peninsula.

* Mount Saint Vincent University, Halifax, NS, B3M 2J6; 443-4450 Ext. 364/ 351; fax: (902) 445-3960. Rates $24 -$35 per night plus tax. Special rates for students and seniors. Wooded campus off Route #2 (Bedford Highway). Away from downtown. One of the leading female oriented learning institutions in Canada.

Camping

Federal: Nova Scotia is graced with two of Canada's National Parks. One is of course Cape Breton Highlands National Park, with the Cabot Trail running along its coastal edge. The other is Kejimkujik (Ked-gee-mah-coo-jik) National Park at the western end of the province. Both have plenty of camping sites available.

Provincial: The Nova Scotia government runs 21 parks with camping facilities. They are usually located in scenic and important natural locations. Some have showers. Like federal sites, they are well cared for and protecting the environment is a major objective. Camping is not permitted in provincial day parks.

Private: Private campgrounds are more personal. You find considerations and favours extended to you. Seasonal campers are happy to keep an eye on your things, owners who open the canteen if you arrive late and other touches you often can not find at a government site. With federal and provincial grounds, you come to expect a uniform level of quality. Each private campground is different from the next. Standards such as cleanliness, ground quality for tents, showers, control over rowdy campers and pricing. They vary from almost carnival-like operations holding hundreds of people, with recreation halls, restaurants and amusements, to someone's backyard. There is a chance to find that special place you will instantly take a liking to and return to again and again (such as your author's choice- the eclectic Colonial Camping in Upper Sackville, near Halifax). It is unfortunate many campgrounds charge the same for a tent as for full hook-ups for a family in a motor-home. Expect $8.00 - $12.00 CDN for a site.

Bicycle Shops

1. **Manser's Bicycle Repair**, 165 Pleasant St., Yarmouth, NS Close to ferry terminal. Small part time garage-type shop. (902) 742-0494.

2. **Goodwin's Bicycle Shop**, R.R. #1, Glenwood, Yarmouth Co., NS B0W 1W0 (902) 643-2279. Well stocked shop, just west of Pubnico on highway 3. Run by Gayland Goodwin, an experienced bicycle racer. Shop opened by appointment. Phone calls welcomed.

3. **Phil's Bicycle Repair**, Digby, NS, B0V 1A0, 245-4564.

4. **Andy's Bicycle Repair**, 663 Main St. Kingston, NS B0P 1R0, 765-4347.

5. **Valley Stove and Cycle**, 232 Main St., Wolfville, NS, B0P 1X0, 542-7280. The shop often has mountain bike tours- visitors welcomed.

6. **Lunenburg Bike Barn**, R.R. #1, Blue Rocks Rd., Lunenburg, NS, 634-3426. On route to scenic Blue Rocks. Run by Alan Heubach, an experienced mechanic. Bed and Breakfast on premises.

7. **The Bicycle Doctor**, David Marder, Halifax, NS, (902) 455-1677. David makes house calls. He will travel with his mobile shop to anywhere in the metro Halifax area.

8. **Cyclepath**, 5240 Blowers St., Halifax, NS, (902) 423-0473.

9. **Cycledelics**, 1678 Barrington St., Halifax, NS, 425-7433. Downtown Halifax. Rentals available.

10. **Cyclesmith**, 6112 Quinpool Rd., Halifax, NS, 425-1756. Large shop in central Halifax.

11. **Jack Nauss**, 2571 Robie St., Halifax, N.S., 429-0024. Halifax's oldest bicycle shop.

12. **Trail Shop**, 6210 Quinpool Rd., Halifax, NS 423-8736. Camping gear available.

13. **Bicycles Plus**, 950 Bedford Highway, Bedford, NS B4A 1A8. (902) 832-1700.

14. **Edgecombe Sports**, 1595 Bedford Highway, Bedford, NS B4A 3Y3

15. **Sportwheels**, 209 Sackville Dr., Lower Sackville, NS, 865-9033 BMX specialists.

16. **Ace Bicycle Repair**, 102 Arklow Drive, Dartmouth, N.S., In Cole Harbour area. General and family-oriented bike repair and sales. Varied hours.

17. **Ron's Bicycle Shop**, 166-B Main St., Dartmouth, NS, 435-0513.

18. **Slickrock Cycle**, 114 Woodlawn Rd., Dartmouth, NS B2W 2S7, 434-6266. Shop offers rides and clinics.

19. **Edgecombe Sports**, 21 Gerrish St., Windsor, NS 798-9595

20. **Hartley Weatherby Cycles**, 590 Prince St. Truro, NS, B2M 1G2, 893-2087

21. **Sports Experts**, Fundy Trail Mall , Truro, NS,

22. **Bicycle Expert**, 49 Albion Street, Amherst, NS B4H 2V7, 667-3949

23. **Kranack's Bike 'N Sports**, Cumberland Mall, Amherst, NS, 667-7346

24. **Pictou Bicycle Shop**, 27 Water St., Pictou, NS, B0K 1H0, 485-8797

25. **Bill's Bikes**, 653 George St, Sydney, NS B1P 1L2

26. **Carl's Sales and Service**, 249 Charlotte St, Sydney, NS B1P 2C4

27. **Dave's Paints and Bicycle**, 3523 Plummer Ave., NewWaterford, NS

Cycling Specialties

Frame Building/ Repair

28. Tamarack Cycles Mark Beaver, P.O. Box 9588, Station A. Halifax, NS B0P 1R0 (902) 455-2878
Tamarack can build any type of bike. Their specialty is touring bicycles. They not only have a great
deal of technical knowledge, but actually do a great deal of cycling. Frame repair: If you have
recieved serious frame damage- all is not lost! Tamarack may be able to perform realignments.
Note: they do frame work only, no regular bike repairs.

Restoration

28. Tamarack Cycles Mark Beaver, P.O. Box 9588, Station A. Halifax, NS B0P 1R0 (902) 455-2878

29. William Rudolph 3 Dale Avenue, Halifax, N.S., B3R 1A1 (902) 477-9734 Specializes in antiques.

Frame Painting

28. Tamarack Cycles Mark Beaver, P.O. Box 9588, Station A. Halifax, NS B0P 1R0 (902) 455-2878

Antiques

29. William Rudolph 3 Dale Avenue, Halifax, N.S., B3R 1A1 (902) 477-9734

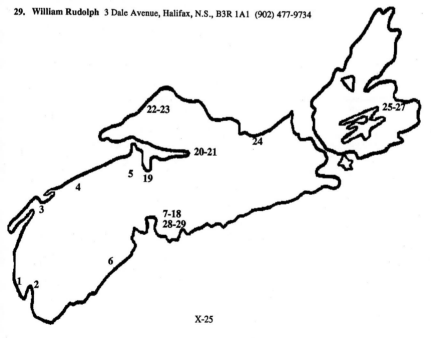

X-25

Commercial Tours

For a fee, some private businesses offer special tour packages. Generally the package will include a guide, overnight accommodations, meals and in some cases rental of a bicycle. Companies listed are for your planning information. They are not by endorsed by their inclusion. Nova Scotia is one of the most highly serviced areas by professional touring companies. The last entry covers which Maritime provinces are covered. Listings should be used as a rough guide only, since companies change their itineraries.

Classic Bicycle Tours and Treks, P.O. Box 668, Clarkson, NY 14430, U.S.A. (716) 637-5970, (800-777-8090 toll free- U.S.A. only); fax (716) 637-9075: hotels, inns, B+B's; sag wagon; equipment rental; optional vegetarian meals; 1 or 2 week trips; Average 60 kilometers (35 miles) per day; minimum age 18; Nova Scotia and Prince Edward Island

Covered Bridge Bicycle Tours, Ward Campbell; P.O. Box 693, Main Post Office, Saint John, New Brunswick, Canada E2L 4B3 (506) 849-9028, inns, B+B's; sag wagon, equipment rental; optional vegetarian meals; easy to moderate; under age 19 with parent; New Brunswick

Easy Rider Tours P.O. Box 1384, Arlington, MA 02174 U.S.A. (800) 488-8332 hotels, inns, B+B's, sag wagon, equipment rental, optional vegetarian meals; easy to moderate; Nova Scotia and Prince Edward Island

Freewheel Experience R.D. #1, Box 397, Mohawk, NY 13407 U.S.A. (315) 866-7842; camping, motels, hotels, sag wagon; equipment rental; easy to advanced; Youth tours - minimum age 12; Nova Scotia and Prince Edward Island

Freewheeling, R.R. 1, Boutilier's Point, Nova Scotia, Canada B0J 1G0 (902) 826-2437; inns, B+B's, sag wagon; equipment rental; easy to moderate; Nova Scotia and Prince Edward Island. Tours planned and escorted by Nova Scotians.

MacQueen's Bicycle Tours, 430 Queen St., Charlottetown, Prince Edward Island, Canada C1A 4E8 (902) 368-2453; camping, motels, inns, B+B's; sag wagon, equipment rental; 1/2 to 6 day trips; all ages; Prince Edward Island

Maine Coast Cyclers, P. O. Box 1234, Camden, Maine, U.S.A. 04892 (802) 496-4603. Before June 1 (207) 236-8608. Inns, 5 day tours, longer days. Independent cyclists select own routes and meet each evening.

Open Horizons Cycle Touring, P. O. Box 390 Margaree Valley, Nova Scotia B0E 2C0, Canada (902) 248-2987 (June-Oct.), (902) 425-0770 (Nov.-May) 1-800-565-9463 from U.S.A. Fax (in season) (902) 248-2600. Camping, motels, cabins, B&B's sag wagon, equipment rental, optional vegetarian meals. 1 to 7 days; 25-40 km (15-25 miles) per day. Minimum age 12: Nova Scotia.

Outward Bound, Hurricane Island, P. O. Box 429, Rockland, Maine 04841 U.S.A. (800) 341-1744 toll free U.S.A. only. Camping, sag wagon, optional vegetarian meals. Easy to moderate: Nova Scotia

Schole, Box 10, R.R. #1, Margaree Valley, Nova Scotia, Canada B0E 2C0 (902) 248-2601. Camping, sag wagon, equipment rental, optional vegetarian meals. 3-4 weeks, 10-25 km (6-15 miles) per day. Summer camp with mountain biking in addition to other activities for young people 12-16: Nova Scotia.

Sea Spray Cycle Centre, R.R. 2, Dingwall, NS B0C 1G0. Guided tours in Cape Breton Highlands (902) 383-2732. Tours planned and escorted by Nova Scotians.

Spinning Spokes, 8244 SW 184th Terrace, Miami, Florida 33157 U.S.A. (305) 233-2135. Camping, cabins, sag wagon, equipment provided. Easy to moderate, minimum age 14: Nova Scotia.

Spinning Wheels Bicycle Tours, Box 51, Jordan Station, Ontario. L0R 1S0 Canada (416) 562-7169. Motels, inns, B&B's, sag wagon, equipment rental. Easy to advanced, minimum age 16: Nova Scotia and Prince Edward Island.

Sunset Bicycle Tours, 455 University Avenue, Charlottetown, Prince Edward Island, Canada (902) 892-0606. Inns, B&B's, sag wagon, equipment rental, optional vegetarian meals. Easy to moderate, minimum age 18: Nova Scotia and Prince Edward Island.

VCC Four Seasons Cycling, P. O. Box 145, Waterbury Center, VT 05677 U.S.A. (802) 244-5135 Fax (802) 244-6126. Hotels, inns, sag wagon, equipment rental, optional vegetarian meals. 5 day tours, 2-3 options per day ranging from 25-78 km (15-50 miles). Minimum age 18 (8 with parents): Nova Scotia and Prince Edward Island.

Vermont Bicycle Touring, Box 711, Bristol, VT 05443 U.S.A. (802) 453-4806. Hotels, inns, B&B's, sag wagon, equipment rental, optional vegetarian meals; 9 day tours, average 63 km (38 miles) per day (longer and shorter options offered). Minimum age 16: Nova Scotia.

Womantrek 1411 East Olive Way, Seattle, WA 98102 U.S.A. (206) 325-4772 (1-800-477-TREK from U.S.A.). Motels, hotels, hostels, inns, camping, cabins, sag wagon, equipment provided. 14 day tours 70-100 km (40-60 miles) per day. Women only. Minimum age 18: Nova Scotia.

Rental Bikes

Want to leave your bike and rent one here? A growing number of businesses are leasing quality bicycles to visitors. Please be aware that there is a large demand by summertime and early reservation is strongly reccomended. Do not rule out renting a bike in New Brunswick or Prince Edward Island. Outlets When renting, check if there are racks for bike bags. Inquire if racks or bags are available. Also ask what they will require for identification or deposit. Companies listed are for your planning information. They are not endorsed by their inclusion.

Crescent Beach Centre Lockeport, NS 656-3123

Cycledelics 1678 Barrington St. Halifax, NS (902) 425-7433

DalPlex Dalhousie University, South Street, Halifax, NS B3H 3J5 (902) 494-6818.

Freewheeling R.R. 1, Boutilier's Point, Nova Scotia, Canada B0J 1G0 (902) 826-2437. Good selection, both road and mountain bikes.

Island Eco-Adventures Brian Doncaster, RR2, Baddeck, NS B0E 1B0. Mountain and hybrid bikes. Camping gear. At the start of the Cabot Trail.

Kayak Cape Breton R.R. 2,, West Bay, Nova Scotia B0E 3K0 (902)535-3060 Near St. Peter's

Lunenburg Bike Barn R.R. 1, Blue Rocks Rd., Lunenburg, NS, 634-3426

Margaree Valley Bike Rentals Jeff Ross. Box 400, Margaree Valley, NS, B0E 2C0 (902) 248-2987; fax (902) 248-2600. Mountain and touring bikes

Open Horizons Cycling P. O. Box 390 Margaree Valley, Nova Scotia B0E 2C0, (902) 295-2849; fax (902) 295-2033. hybrid bikes

Pedal and Sea Bicycle Rentals Sheraton Hotel Boardwalk, Halifax, NS., c/o (902) 471-1616. Operated by experienced bicycle mechanic

Sea Spray Cycle Centre R.R. 2, Dingwall, NS B0C 1G0. Mountain bikes (902) 383-2732

Trail Shop 6210 Quinpool Rd., Halifax, NS 423-8736. hybrid bikes.

He had acquired a rust-eaten bicycle and increasingly took to pedalling into the countryside to dull his pain with the monotonous grind at the worn out pedals and the peacefully bitter silence of the fields and woods. Heedless of route or destination he would turn his handlebars at random; when night fell he lit his lamps and mournfully pushed on. It was a powerful drug, and he turned to it whenever his daily toil allowed.

-- John Wain

Hurry on Down, 1953

For all your cycling NOTES...